1

3495 1597
not in pb

First 2 chapters

read through
quickly

Controlled by Heredity 106
Educators measure where
you are
Traditional American View

2 chapters → Piaget
2 → Neo-Piaget

Info Processing

last 2 (contextual
Chapters)

No ≠ learning

Read ⇒ Cognitive   How Cog. Psych
say adults learn

Piget
Neo Piaget
Info Proc.
Contextual

8 chapter

Summarize
Explain
Cognitive
View of
Adult
Learning

Mon. 26th
9:45 a.m.

LEARNING
IN ADULTHOOD

Sharan B. Merriam
Rosemary S. Caffarella

LEARNING IN ADULTHOOD

A Comprehensive Guide

Jossey-Bass Publishers · San Francisco

Copyright © 1991 by: Jossey-Bass Inc., Publishers
350 Sansome Street
San Francisco, California 94104
&
Jossey-Bass Limited
Headington Hill Hall
Oxford OX3 0BW

Library of Congress Cataloging-in-Publication Data

Merriam, Sharan B.
    Learning in adulthood : a comprehensive guide / Sharan B. Merriam,
Rosemary S. Caffarella.
        p.   cm. — (The Jossey-Bass higher and adult education series)
    Includes bibliographical references and index.
    ISBN 1-55542-312-4
    1. Adult learning.   I. Caffarella, Rosemary S. (Rosemary Shelly),
date.   II. Title.   III. Series.
LC5225.L42M47   1991
374 — dc20   90-47292
                                                                    CIP

Manufactured in the United States of America

The paper used in this book is acid-free and meets the
State of California requirements for recycled paper
(50 percent recycled waste, including 10 percent
post-consumer waste), which are the strictest guidelines
for recycled paper currently in use in the United States.

Figure 9.1 is reprinted, with the publisher's permission, from Rumelhart, D. E.,
& Norman, D. A. (1978). Accretion, tuning, and restructuring: Three modes
of learning. In J. W. Cotton & R. L. Klatzky (Eds.), *Semantic factors in cognition* (p. 51). Hillsdale, NJ: L. Erlbaum Assocs.

FIRST EDITION
HB Printing   10 9 8 7 6 5 4 3 2
Code 9114

The Jossey-Bass
Higher and Adult Education Series

Consulting Editor
Adult and Continuing Education

Alan B. Knox
University of Wisconsin, Madison

Contents

Preface

Learning in adulthood is an intensely personal activity. Yet at the same time, a multibillion-dollar enterprise has arisen in response to adult learning interests — an enterprise that spends more dollars than elementary schools, high schools, and postsecondary schools combined. Indeed, the field of adult and continuing education is characterized by a bewildering array of programs, agencies, and personnel working to assist adults in their learning. It is precisely the focus on adults as learners, however, that unites an otherwise extraordinarily diverse field. It is also the nature of *adults* as learners and the distinguishing characteristics of the adult learning process that differentiate adult education from other kinds of education.

Preparation for work with adult learners ranges from on-the-job training to formal graduate course work, but a key component of all the different modes of preparation is understanding adult learners and how they learn best. To facilitate the process of learning, it is especially important to know who the adult learner is, why adults are involved in learning activities, how adults learn, and how aging affects learning ability. *Learning in Adulthood* addresses these topics among others.

There is a voluminous literature on adult learning — ranging from technical articles on various aspects of adult learning to handbooks, guides, and pamphlets summarizing material for the new instructor of adult students. The Educational Resources Information Center (ERIC) data base, which catalogues journal articles, monographs, conference proceedings, papers, and so on, has well over a thousand citations under the topic "adult learning." More than a dozen books have been written on specific topics in adult learning, quite a few of them within the past five years.

Despite the number of books and other resources on adult learning, there is no single text that synthesizes current thinking and research on the topic. The most popular overview of adult learning is K. Patricia Cross's *Adults as Learners,* published in 1981. The focus of this very readable book, which summarizes some of the literature on adult learning, is on participation—who participates and why, and how and what adults learn. The participation chapters in our book expand on Cross's contributions. Another popular text is J. Roby Kidd's *How Adults Learn* (1973). In contrast to Cross's book, Kidd's emphasizes the learning process and traditional learning theory, with little coverage of participation or adult learning needs. Neither book, of course, examines the important contributions of the last decade or more to our understanding of adult learning.

Learning in Adulthood brings together significant research and theory, including material covered by both Cross and Kidd. The book is more than an update of these two authors' work, however, and also more than a restatement of positions on adult learning by current authors such as Daloz (1986), Brookfield (1986), and Jarvis (1987a). *Learning in Adulthood* is a comprehensive overview of what we know about adult learning—including the context in which it takes place, who the participants are, what they learn and why, the nature of the learning process itself, the development of theory in adult learning, and other issues relevant to the practice of adult learning.

The book furthermore takes into account recent work in sociology and philosophy, as well as psychology. In most writing on adult learning, the sociocultural perspective has been widely neglected in favor of the predominant psychological orientation. We attend to the *context* in which learning takes place and to learners' interactive relationship with it and with the learning activity. Another unique feature of our book is the inclusion of an entire section on *theory development* in adult learning, for enough has now been written to warrant chapters on theory development in the areas of participation, self-direction, and adult learning. A third unusual feature of *Learning in Adulthood* is its coverage of the *social issues* involved in the provision of learning opportunities for adults and the *ethical issues* inherent in the teaching/learning transaction. Only within the last few years have these important matters received attention in the literature and at gatherings of adult educators.

This book is intended primarily for educators of adults. We have organized the material so that it will make sense to readers who are new to adult education and will at the same time challenge those who are already familiar with the knowledge base of the field. The organization and presentation of this material reflect our struggle over the years to find the best way to organize courses, workshops, and seminars in adult learning and development for audiences with varying levels of expertise. We have striven to put together a text that is at once readable, thorough, and up-to-date in its coverage. In particular, the book is designed for use in courses in adult learning. In addition to those associated with the field of adult education itself, however, those in counseling, health, social work, administration, and instructional technology and in such institutions as libraries, churches, business and industry, and higher education often deal on a daily basis with adult learners. We also intend this to be a resource for practitioners in these fields who would like to know more about adult learners and the learning process.

Overview of the Contents

Learning in Adulthood is divided into five sections: Part One contains three chapters about the context of adult learning; Part Two focuses on adult learners themselves—who they are, why they participate, and their developmental characteristics; the four chapters in Part Three explore various components of the learning process; Part Four reviews theory-building efforts in adult learning; and Part Five deals with issues that affect the provision of learning opportunities for adults.

Part One describes various adult learning environments. Chapter One sets the sociocultural context for adult learning in North America. In it, we discuss three forces — demographics, economics, and technology — that have shaped adult learning today. It is equally important to understand how the interaction of those three factors has led to changes both in what adults want to learn and in the learning opportunities provided for them. Adults learn in formal settings that range from public schools to workplaces. The variety of institutional settings and the ways in which they influence learners and the learning process are the subject of Chapter Two. Chapter Three posits that learning on one's own is itself a learning context. We review the literature on self-direction in learning and explain how this type of learning differs from learning that takes place in formal institutional settings.

Central to the practice of adult education is the adult learner. Part Two focuses on who participates, why people participate, and what they choose to learn. The more we understand about these factors, the better we can design and implement programs for adults. Chapters Four and Five stress that studies of participation in formal adult education are a means of knowing all we can about the participants. We review reports from major national studies of participation in Chapter Four with an eye to the salient social and personal characteristics of adult learners. Chapter Five focuses on the reasons adults do or do not participate in learning activities. Again, we take a look at national studies, along with recent work on barriers and deterrents to participation, and present some of the sociological explanations for the participation patterns that characterize adult education. This part of the book concludes with Chapter Six, on adults' developmental characteristics. Educators who want to understand adults as learners will profit from this summary of research on physical aging, psychological development, and sociocultural determinants of growth.

Part Three, "The Learning Process," consists of four chapters. In Chapter Seven we examine four traditional theories about learning — behaviorism, cognitivism, humanism, and social learning theory — along with their implications for adult learning. Chapter Eight focuses on the nature of adult intelligence and how it may or may not be affected by the aging process. Several different theories of intelligence and its components are discussed. Chapter Nine deals with memory and cognition in adulthood. Drawing on several disciplines and summarizing recent work on memory and aging, schema theory, cognitive styles, and contextual influences on cognition, this chapter is the first compilation of its kind in an adult learning textbook. Chapter Ten, which covers cognitive development in adulthood, presents a synopsis of Piagetian theory, postformal operations, dialectic thought, and several concepts of wisdom.

The amount of research and writing that has been done in the last decade indicates the maturing of the field of adult learning. Accompanying this growth has been the development of models and theories to help explain and guide practice as well as to direct future research efforts. Three areas in particular have been the focus of theory building — self-direction, participation, and adult learning overall. The three chapters of Part Four review these theory-building efforts. Chapter Eleven presents recent thinking on self-directed learning as a form of study as well as self-direction as a characteristic of individual learners. No longer are we satisfied with just documenting the existence of self-directed learning. More sophisticated questions about the phenomenon and the learners are now being asked. So too with participation. The field has moved from a preoccupation with describing the phenomenon to building models that attempt to explain participation in formal adult learning activities. These models, discussed in Chapter Twelve, draw on what is known about participation (as covered in Chapters Four and Five) but also attempt to predict who will participate. Each model is analyzed here for its utility in explaining and predicting participation. The last chapter in this section, Chapter Thirteen, chronicles efforts to formulate overarching theories that explain learning in adulthood. The best known of these is Knowles's concept of andragogy, which we describe here, along with numerous other theories, models, and frameworks that have been proposed to explain what is unique about *adult* learning.

In Part Five, the last section of *Learning in Adulthood,* we step back from the accumulated knowledge base and examine how values and beliefs affect the practice of adult learning. Chapter

Fourteen explores societal values that shape the provision of learning opportunities for adults. In particular, we address the key questions of access and opportunity and examine the gaps between the rhetoric and the reality in the provision of formal learning activities in our society. In contrast to Chapter Fourteen, which approaches adult learning from the perspective of social structure, Chapter Fifteen focuses on the ethical issues in the teaching/learning transaction. We explore the questions of responsibility and control one encounters in planning, implementing, and evaluating a learning activity, as well as the ethical issues involved in the outcomes of a learning experience — some of which may be unanticipated. Chapter Sixteen, the final chapter, summarizes and integrates the material on adult learning presented in earlier chapters. It also reflects how we ourselves have come to think about learning in adulthood.

Acknowledgments

Learning in Adulthood is a direct response to our need for a single, comprehensive, up-to-date text to use in our adult learning classes. In a very real sense, then, it was the students in our programs and the participants in our workshops and seminars who inspired us to write *Learning in Adulthood.* Others, of course, have been of invaluable assistance at various stages of the project. Lynn Luckow, executive vice-president at Jossey-Bass, was instrumental in helping us conceptualize the book and in assisting us through the process. Brian Bouldrey, Gale Erlandson, and Alan Knox worked as a team with us to facilitate the book's publication. Colleagues Ralph Brockett, Katherine Cauley, Ronald Cervero, Carolyn Clark, Phyllis Cunningham, Laurent Daloz, Barbara LeGrand, Linda Lewis, Judith O'Donnell, Margaret Overton, and George Spear unselfishly took time out from their own work to read and critique draft chapters. Their comments, insights, and suggestions considerably strengthened the final product. Special thanks also go to Camille Carr and Cassandra Drennon, graduate research assistants, for tracking down references and to Susan Goins and Leslie Lamb for their help in text entry and editing. To all of you, and to the reviewers of the entire manuscript, we offer our heartfelt thanks. Finally, we wish to thank our family members and friends for their support and patience over the last two years.

February 1991

Sharan B. Merriam
Athens, Georgia

Rosemary S. Caffarella
Greeley, Colorado

*This book is lovingly dedicated
to Rosemary's husband, Ed,
and daughter, Christy,
and to Sharan's husband, Bob,
for their care, support,
and patience in this endeavor*

The Authors

Sharan B. Merriam is professor of adult education at the University of Georgia. She received her B.A. degree (1965) in English from Drew University, her M.Ed. degree (1971) in English education from Ohio University, and her Ed.D. degree (1978) in adult education from Rutgers University. Before coming to the University of Georgia, she served on the faculties of Northern Illinois University and Virginia Polytechnic Institute and State University.

Merriam's research and writing activities have focused on adult development and learning and on qualitative research methods. She has served on steering committees for the annual North American Adult Education Research Conference and the Commission of Professors of Adult Education. Currently she is coeditor of *Adult Education Quarterly,* the major journal of research and theory in adult education. She is also coeditor of the *Handbook of Adult and Continuing Education* (1989, with P. Cunningham). A book reporting the findings of a large-scale study on work, love, and learning in adult life (coauthored with M. C. Clark) is forthcoming. Her other books include *Adult Education: Foundations of Practice* (1982, with G. Darkenwald), winner of the 1985 Cyril O. Houle World Award for Literature in Adult Education, *Themes of Adulthood Through Literature* (1983), *A Guide to Research for Educators and Trainers of Adults* (1984, with E. L. Simpson), and *Case Study Research in Education* (1988).

Rosemary S. Caffarella is associate professor in the Division of Educational Leadership at the University of Northern Colorado.

She received her B.A. degree (1968) in community leadership and development from Springfield College, her M.A. degree (1973) in rehabilitation counseling from Michigan State University, and her Ed.S. (1973) and Ph.D. (1978) degrees also from Michigan State University. Before coming to the University of Northern Colorado, she served on the faculties and in administrative positions at the University of Maine and Virginia Commonwealth University.

Caffarella's research and writing activities have focused on adult development and learning and on program planning and evaluation. Among her most recent works are a monograph on self-directed learning (1989, with J. O'Donnell), a book, *Program Planning and Evaluation Resource Book for Trainers* (1988), and several chapters in edited collections.

Caffarella has served on the steering committees for the annual North American Adult Education Research Conference and the Commission of Professors of Adult Education; on the board of directors for the American Association for Adult and Continuing Education, the Virginia Adult Education Association, and the Maine Association for Public School Adult Education; and on the Academic Relations Committee of the American Society for Training and Development. In addition, she is currently a consulting editor for *Adult Education Quarterly.*

LEARNING
IN ADULTHOOD

The Context and
Environment of
Adult Learning

It is very much the perspective of this book that learning is a personal process. It is also the perspective of this book that the context of adult life and the societal context shape what an adult needs and wants to learn and, to a somewhat lesser extent, when and where learning takes place. As Jarvis observes, learning "is intimately related to [the] world and affected by it" (1987a, p. 11). The three chapters in Part One explore different dimensions of the context of adult learning — the sociocultural context, the institutional context, and the learner's life context.

Chapter One describes three factors characteristic of present-day American society that affect what adults want to learn. First, dramatic changes are occurring in the demographic base of our society. Adults outnumber those under eighteen years old for the first time ever. Moreover, the percentage of the population over sixty-five continues to grow, commanding the attention of policymakers, business people, and educators alike. Our population as a whole is also better educated than ever before, and, finally, there is more cultural and ethnic diversity. Thus there are simply more adults seeking learning opportunities, as well as more groups of adults with special learning needs.

The second and third factors shaping the learning enterprise are economics and technology. These are very much interrelated, of course, as technology has had an enormous impact on the economy. Robotics and automation displace production workers but create other jobs; technology in the home frees women to enter the work force; and so on. The effect of the global economy and technological advances on the nature of adult learning is staggering. Adults find that they must continue their learning past formal schooling in order to function at work, at home, and in their communities. The need for new knowledge, for updating old information, for retraining, has resulted in a multibillion-dollar educational enterprise.

Some of this learning, of course, takes place in formal settings sponsored by a myriad of institutions and agencies. As might be expected, business and industry and educational institutions offer a large number of adult learning opportunities, but so do the military, cooperative extension, churches, hospitals, and other institutions. Chapter Two, "Learning in Formal Settings," explores how the context of institutions influences the learner and the learning process. In particular, three major factors — people, structure, and culture — are discussed in terms of how they shape the adult learning that does take place. The chapter demonstrates how these factors, especially the structural components such as time, standard operating procedures, and facilities, depending on their configuration, can either enhance or impede learning.

The third chapter in this part of the book is about learning on one's own outside of formal institutions. Commonly known as self-directed learning, this type of learning too is affected by context. Rather than focusing on society or institutions, though, the context for learning on one's own is more easily understood in terms of the adult's life situation. Although learning on one's own is the way most adults go about acquiring new ideas, skills, and attitudes, we have often regarded this context as less important than learning that takes place in more formal settings. Chapter Three describes how the process of learning, when primarily designed and managed by the learners themselves, may be different from that which takes place in institutional settings. Rather than progressing along a linear path from assessing needs to evaluating the learning, adults who learn on their own do not necessarily plan what, how, or when they want to learn. In essence, self-directed learning may occur by design, by chance, or by a combination of the two, depending on the interests, experiences, and actions of learners and their life circumstances. The adult educator's role in this process is also explored in this chapter.

One

Social and
Cultural Influences

This book is about learning in adulthood. But learning, even self-directed learning, rarely occurs "in splendid isolation from the world in which the learner lives; . . . it is intimately related to that world and affected by it" (Jarvis, 1987a, p. 11). What one wants to learn, what is offered, and the ways in which one learns are determined to a large extent by the nature of the society at any particular point in time. Contrast the young male apprentice of colonial times learning to be a blacksmith with today's middle-aged woman learning data processing, for example, or the preparation needed to become a medical doctor at the turn of the century, less than a high school diploma, with today's long and specialized training.

It can also be argued that the nature of society at any particular point in time determines the relative emphasis placed on *adult* learning. In preindustrial societies, the rate of change was such that what a person needed to know to function as an adult could be learned in childhood (Jarvis, 1983). In societies hurrying to catch up, however, and in our own society with its accelerated rate of change, the urgency of dealing with today's social realities lies with adults. Society no longer has the luxury of waiting for its youth. As Marien (1983, p. 21) observes: "The most important learning needs are not among children, but among adults — especially our political, intellectual, scientific, corporate, and religious leaders — the decision-makers who will be shaping the Information Society over the next two decades.

Their decisions, for better or worse, will largely determine whether the Information Society is humane, just, productive, free, participatory, and safe, or whether it is a society characterized by greater inequalities, more centralization, accelerating dangers, and further alienation."

Hence the learning that goes on in adulthood can to some extent be understood through an examination of the social context in which it occurs. How is learning in adulthood shaped by the society in which it takes place? How does the sociocultural context determine what is learned and by whom? What is it about the American context in particular that promotes learning in adulthood? This chapter explores several dimensions of the current sociocultural context that contribute to shaping the nature of adult learning in today's world. Although demographics, economics, and technology are treated separately at first, they are very much interrelated and thus their convergence and subsequent impact on learning in adulthood are discussed in the final section of this chapter.

Demographics

ıg demographics is a social reality shaping the provi-
learning in contemporary American society. Demo-
g....... is about people, groups of people, and their respective characteristics. For the first time in our society adults outnumber youth, there are more *older* adults, the population is better educated than ever before, and there is more cultural and ethnic diversity. For various reasons, individuals and groups of people seek out learning experiences; for other reasons, society targets learning activities for certain segments of the population. Thus certain learning activities are learner-initiated and others are society-initiated in response to the changing demographics. Gardening and medicine are two metaphors commonly used in our field to reflect demographic realities. We are concerned with the growth and development of adult learners whom we nurture in a climate conducive to learning. At the same time, there are emerging groups of learners with special needs whom

we diagnose, prescribe for, and treat; we offer remedial programs to cure perceived problems or deficiencies.

There are simply more adults in our society than ever before. Indeed, notes Cross (1981), "With the exception of the World War II years, children under the age of 15 have always been the largest single age group in the nation. . . . By the year 2000, the largest age group will be 30 to 44 year olds, with a rising curve for 45 to 64 year olds" (p. 3). The median age of the American population continues to rise—from 30.6 in 1982 to 36.3 in the year 2000 (Cetron, Soriano, and Gayle, 1985). The so-called baby boomers—the seventy million people born between 1946 and 1964—are a contributing factor to this change in the population. Cross notes that such a large cohort, "because of its political and economic strength, manages to gain the attention of the society throughout the life span of the cohort. Because of its sheer size, it has commanded the attention of education, industry, and government for some three decades now." She speculates that "there is no reason to think that the influence of America's largest generation will subside in the future. Should we expect an 'adult revolution' within the next two decades comparable to the youth revolution in the 1960s? If so, how will it affect education? Whether a possible 'adult revolution' will erupt into newsworthy events or quietly seep into all aspects of American life is not known, but we may expect that the impact of an aging population on education will be profound" (1981, pp. 6–7).

The shift from a youth-oriented to an adult-oriented society is solidified by the increasing numbers of *older* adults in the population. In 1987, for the first time ever, Americans over the age of sixty-five outnumbered those under twenty-five (Spear and Mocker, 1989). Furthermore, the oldest old, those over eighty-five years old, are the fastest-growing segment of the older population. "The 'old old' will increase a staggering 131% in developing countries between the year 2000 and 2025" (Mercer and Garner, 1989, p. 16). Older adults are also increasingly better educated, in better health, and economically better off than previous cohorts. Society is already heeding their learning needs with such policies as tuition waivers for higher and continuing education programs and especially designed programs such as the popular elderhostel program. There has also been a subtle change in the philosophical rationale — at least among those working in the fields of gerontology and educational gerontology — underlying the provision of education for this group. Along with an economic rationale (the better educated need fewer social services) and social stability rationale (millions of healthy retired people need to be kept busy) is an awareness that older adults as well as younger ones have an unending potential for development. Marcus and Havighurst (1980) explain what it means to ignore this need: "The belief that the development of the individual is a lifelong process, never fully completed until terminated by death, implies that denying the privilege of continuing education actually constitutes a form of deprivation for many, which closes off opportunities to continue growing" (p. 27).

Thus more adults and older adults are two demographic factors influencing the provision of learning activities in our society. So, too, is the rising level of education characteristic of our population. This is dramatically illustrated by the fact that over 80 percent of today's twenty-year-olds have completed four years of high school compared with less than half (49 percent) of those in their grandparents' generation (Mercer and Garner, 1989). Since previous education is the single best predictor of participation in adult education, the rising educational level of the adult population is a contextual factor of considerable import. Participation data from the Center for Education Statistics show, for example, that only 4 percent of adults with less than four years of high school participate in organized adult education, while 10.6 percent of high school graduates and 29.2 percent of college graduates participate (Center for Education Statistics, 1987). But while the educational attainment level of the population as a whole continues to rise, an alarming number of high school students drop out before graduating. And "as a high school education becomes the minimum educational standard, those who drop out are more likely to become members of an educational underclass, from which adult education (especially in the form of adult basic and secondary education) may be the only hope of escape" (Rachal, 1989, pp. 10–11).

Enter the medical metaphor whereby adult education seeks to treat this problem with remedial education.

Another demographic characteristic of the social context is the gowing cultural and ethnic diversity of America's population. Briscoe and Ross point out that "not only is America graying, the skin color of America is also changing" (1989, p. 584). In contrast to the influx of European immigrants at the end of the nineteenth century, today's immigrants are more likely to come from Asia and Latin America. "If current trends in immigration and birth rates persist, the Hispanic population will have further increased an estimated 21%, the Asian presence about 22%, blacks almost 12%, and whites a little more than 2% when the 20th century ends" (Henry, 1990, p. 28). By the year 2000 Hispanics will be the largest minority group in America, with blacks the second largest (Briscoe and Ross, 1989). Furthermore, "the average age of the minority population is decreasing, while the majority population is growing older. Minorities also tend to be clustered in metropolitan areas, and, in the future, fifty-three major U.S. cities will have minority populations that outnumber the present majority population" (Briscoe and Ross, 1989, p. 584). Not only is the composition of the minority population changing, but so too are the overall numbers. By the year 2000, "minorities are expected to compose 29 percent of the population" (Fay, McCune, and Begin, 1987, p. 17).

The implications of this demographic trend for society in general and adult education in particular are staggering. While the "browning of America" offers tremendous opportunity for capitalizing anew on the merits of many peoples from many lands, there are also risks involved (Henry, 1990, p. 29). Minority adults, for example, are disproportionately represented among the unemployed, the low-income stratum, and the less educated. These characteristics are correlated with low rates of participation in organized adult education. A quarter of the nation's population constitutes a sizable resource. Briscoe and Ross (1989) stress the urgency of the problem: "The consequences to North American society of leaving this resource undeveloped are great. It is likely that young people who leave school early will never participate fully in society or in the decision-making processes of government, and that they will neither enjoy the benefits of good health, nor experience the upward mobility needed as adults to make them full contributors and partners in shaping and participating in the larger society. One cause of the problem is educational institutions not responding quickly enough to change, even though educators are aware of the impact they can have on societal systems" (p. 586).

The growing ethnic and cultural diversity of our population has been identified by Naisbitt and Aburdene (1990) as one of the megatrends for the twenty-first century. They have observed that "even as our lifestyles grow more similar, there are unmistakable signs of a powerful countertrend: a backlash against uniformity, a desire to assert the uniqueness of one's culture and language. . . . Outbreaks of cultural nationalism are happening in every corner of the globe" (p. 119). Adult educators are slowly becoming aware of the instructional implications of the fact that "as our outer worlds grow more similar, we will increasingly treasure the traditions that spring from within" (Naisbitt and Aburdene, 1990, p. 120).

In summary, the composition of one's society is an important factor in the provision of learning opportunities for citizens of all ages. In the United States, there are more adults than youth, there is a growing number of older adults, the population as a whole is better educated than ever before, and there is a large minority population. The field of adult education with its orientation to the learners themselves is especially sensitive to these demographic trends — whether by focusing on individual growth or by diagnosing and addressing the needs of special groups.

Economics

A second dimension of the social context that has a direct bearing on learning in adulthood is the economic structure. Two metaphors that reflect this reality are sports and banking. To compete or keep pace in the world market, we emphasize training the work force. In reference to both the economy and individual learners we want to be in the running, one jump ahead, and score well. From the banking metaphor comes an emphasis on investing time and effort, accumulating wealth and knowledge, engaging in learning transactions, being held accountable, and respecting the bottom line. Clearly the American economy is changing and with it the learning needs of adults. In particular there is a recognition of global interdependence, a shift to a service economy, and a change in composition of the labor force.

Within the last few decades Americans have become conscious of the interrelatedness of their lives with the rest of the world. Naisbitt and Aburdene identify the global economy as one of the megatrends for the twenty-first century: "We are in an unprecedented period of accelerated change, perhaps the most breathtaking of which is the swiftness of our rush to all the world's becoming a single economy. Already it may be said that there is no such thing as a U.S. economy, so enmeshed is it in all the other economies of the world" (1990, p. 19). Our economic position in the world has changed dramatically within the last several decades. Moebius summarizes some of these changes:

> According to U.S. Department of Commerce figures, since 1960 our share of world trade has dropped from 18 percent to 15 percent. Today, 70 percent of all U.S. goods compete at home and abroad with foreign-made goods. In 1985, the value of manufactured goods exported by the U.S. trailed West German and Japanese exports by sizable margins. As a percentage of gross national product, U.S. exports declined 20 percent from 1979 to 1983. This rate far exceeded that of any other major industrialized nation. Only 10 percent, or 30,000 out of 300,000, U.S. firms export. Less than 1 percent of those firms do 80 percent of the exporting. . . .
>
> Compounding these problems is the fact that the U.S. imports far more than it exports. The last time a trade surplus was registered was in 1981. Alarming increases in the trade deficit, from $9 bil-

lion in 1982 to $148.5 billion in 1985, alerted the
nation that something needed to be done [1987,
p. 68].

What does all this mean for adult learning? For one thing,
learning opportunities are being structured to allow Americans
to be more competitive in the world market. Moebius, for example, reviews programs designed to teach staff in small busi-
nesses the skills needed to export their products abroad. And
to help combat upheavals linked with foreign competition, "economic literacy" programs are being developed to help workers
chart their own and their industry's economic future (Derber,
1987). Apps (1988) sees the global community having a "profound" effect on learning: "We are beginning to see Asian languages taught in our public schools. We see short courses for
American business people who must learn something of the cultural characteristics of their Japanese counterparts. Increasing
numbers of citizens want to learn about people and events beyond the borders of their cities and states. And more subtly
perhaps, we may see the beginnings of changes in fundamental
assumptions Americans hold about other peoples and cultures"
(p. 22).

A second economic shift has been from a society employed
in producing goods to one employed in providing services. The
decline in industrial labor is due to automation and to competition from other countries with low labor costs. Dislocated workers from both the industrial and agricultural sectors with few
if any transferable skills find themselves in low-skill, low-paying
service jobs. Ironically, "the ready supply of displaced workers
with limited employable skills will lead to low wages in parts
of the service sector and thus will promote the general growth
of service-related business" (Charner and Rolzinski, 1987, p.
8.). This sector is "by far the dominant sector of employment
with about two-thirds of the work force employed in service jobs
in 1984" (pp. 7–8).

Concurrent with the shift to a service economy is the shift
to what has been called the information society. Our economy
is based increasingly on information rather than heavy industry: "Already more workers are engaged in generating, process-

ing, analyzing, and distributing information than are engaged in agriculture, mining, and manufacturing combined" (Hart, 1983, p. 10). Fay, McCune, and Begin (1987) estimate that by the year 2000, "80 percent of all workers in the United States will be employed in the information industry. . . . This will have a major impact on workers as economic units. In an industrial age, workers are expendable cogs in the machine; in an information age (and to a lesser extent, in a service age), human capital is the most valuable capital an organization has" (p. 20). The implications for learning — and in particular for work-related training — are enormous. Indeed, the majority of adults in organized learning activities cite job-related reasons for their participation (see Chapter Five). Furthermore the amount spent annually by business, industry, and government agencies on job-related training is in the billions of dollars ($60 billion by some estimates) and exceeds that which is spent on public higher education (Nowlen, 1988; Watkins, 1989).

Closely related to shifts to a service and information economy are changes in America's labor force. The largest job-growth categories are jobs related to service — cashiers, orderlies, fast-food workers — and to information and technology — computer programmers and operators, engineers, teachers, and so on (Rachal, 1989). Not surprisingly, women, minorities, and the elderly are overrepresented in the lower-paying service jobs. Since the middle of this century, however, the labor force has changed from one dominated by blue-collar occupations to one where the majority of jobs are considered white collar. But perhaps the greatest change of all has been the entry of women into the work force. In 1940 only 29 percent of women worked outside the home; today 66 percent are wage earners (Axinn, 1989). Economic necessity and the freeing of occupations traditionally assigned to men have contributed to this change. Cross observes that "the revolution in women's roles is the result of two complementary forces. On the one hand, social and technological changes push women out of the home; on the other hand, new opportunities in education and the labor market pull women into the new worlds of work and education. 'Displaced homemakers' and 'reentry women' are a social phenomenon of considerable importance to the learning society" (1981, p. 26).

In summary, economic factors are shaping the nature of our society and, by extension, the nature of learning that adults are most likely to undertake. A global economy, the shift to a service and information society, and consequent changes in the configuration of the labor force are determining, to a large extent, what learning takes place, what is offered, and who participates.

Technology

If the language of gardening and medicine can be associated with demographics, and the terms of sports and banking with economics, then there is no more apt metaphor for reflecting the rate of technological change than the computer. Itself a major component of our highly technological age, computer language has invaded the ways in which we talk of adult learning: We process students and information; we plan learning activities with an eye to inputs, flow, and outputs; we provide feedback to individual learners and to programs. Indeed, we program learning experiences and ourselves. Technology has had an enormous impact on society and adult learning. It has been instrumental in bringing about the so-called information society, which in turn has created new jobs and eliminated others. The technology-driven information society has also affected the field of adult education.

The move to an information society has been a function of technological developments associated with an information "explosion." The speed of technologically related change in our society can be illustrated by "the fact that there are some 2.7 million living Americans who conceivably could have witnessed the Wright brothers' lift-off at Kitty Hawk" (Rachal, 1989, p. 3). Within a short span of time, electronic, communication, and information technologies have changed society as a whole and affected how people go about their daily lives. From shopping by computer to making telephone calls from one's car to faxing a request to the local radio station, everyday life has been irrevocably influenced by technology.

Concurrent with these technological advances has been an information explosion. It has been estimated that the amount of information in the world doubles every seven years (Apps, 1988, p. 23) and that half of what most professionals know when they finish their formal training will be outdated in less than five years. Thus the need for continuing education has dramatically increased with the increase in knowledge production. Not only is there considerably more information than ever before but links with technology have made its storage, transmission, and access more feasible than ever before. Laser technology in particular is revolutionizing the dissemination of information as well as its storage and retrieval (Naisbitt, 1985, p. 94). A compact disk using laser technology makes it possible to store huge amounts of information in a very small space, for example, and Grolier's twenty-four-volume encyclopedia takes up just 10 percent of one CD-ROM digital data disk (Lewis, 1989).

Boucouvalas (1987) and others make the case that a major societal shift, such as moving from an industrial to an information society, results in profound changes in the society's structure. In an industrial society, machine technology extends physical ability; in an information society, computer technology extends mental ability. Material wealth has major value in an industrial society; knowledge and information are key assets in an information society. The social structure changes from hierarchies and bureaucracies to multicentered and horizontal networks; labor movements versus citizen movements are the locus for social change (Boucouvalas, 1987). These changes in society's underlying structure can be seen most dramatically in changes in the work force. The shift is eliminating certain classifications of work while at the same time creating others not yet dreamed of. Charner and Rolzinski (1987) estimate that "the total loss of jobs is projected to be between 15 and 20 million by the year 2000. At the same time, the production of these new technologies will create 2 to 3 million new jobs, while positions related to the maintenance and repair of these new technologies will generate an additional 4 to 5 million high-technology service positions. In addition, these new technologies will affect the production of finished information products (books, magazines, disks, cassettes, and video media) in their 'publishing' industry. Between 1.5 and 2.5 million jobs are expected to be generated in this area. The new result is a loss of between 5 and 13 million jobs due to the new technologies" (p. 9).

In addition to the creation and elimination of jobs, technological changes are giving rise to entrepreneurial forms of self-employment. Currently there is a host of self-employed consultants specializing in computers, videodiscs, laser technologies, and so on. Another development that technology has made possible is the expansion of home work into new areas. Some companies allow employees to work at home computer terminals. "This home work," some predict, "will increase because of the new technologies, and it is desirable because it fits in with new family patterns (such as more single-parent families), worker concerns for independence and autonomy, and organizational efforts to trim budgets and remain flexible by subcontracting rather than hiring human capital" (Fay, McCune, and Begin, 1987, p. 22).

Clearly, technology and the information age that it spawned are changing the nature of adult learning. Professionals whose knowledge becomes outdated in a few short years, auto mechanics who must now master sophisticated electronic diagnostic systems, homemakers who must learn new ways to shop and prepare meals — all must be able to function in a fast-changing society and this necessitates continued learning. Technology is not only making learning mandatory, it is providing many of the mechanisms for it to occur. Computer-assisted instruction (CAI), teleconferencing, interactive videodisc, and so on are expanding the possibilities of meeting the growing learning needs of adults.

Simultaneous with the development of technologically sophisticated delivery systems is the development of new roles for educators and trainers. Hiemstra (1987) has delineated several possible roles. One of these is information counseling — helping adults access information — since "the increasing availability of immense amounts of information via electronic data banks means that learners will need assistance in sorting through the possible knowledge bases and search mechanisms" (p. 11). Facilitation of individualized learning is another role — since "obtaining information for desired individualized or self-directed learning will become quicker and easier," adult students will need help in using this information effectively (p. 11). Yet another role is instruction specialist — there is a growing need for educators who know how to use technology in the delivery of instruction. And, finally, there will be a need for international facilitators of development and information exchange — in this role, educators must be able to assist learners worldwide to deal with the transition to an information society. In addition to these roles, Hiemstra points out that educators must be able to cope with change itself and that research must be conducted on the effects of technology on adult learning.

Technological advances also raise difficult questions with regard to access and equity. The more affluent and better-educated adults with home computers have access to information and instructional packages that make them even more informed. While "the prospects for increased interaction among peoples of the world, for access to almost unlimited information, and for the crumbling of parochial barriers give a bright hue to the future . . . greater awareness of alternatives has led to greater dissatisfactions with things as they are" (Spear and Mocker, 1989, p. 647). On a global level, the "have" nations can communicate and exchange information in ways that will never be a reality to the majority of the world's people. Even job training necessitated by technological change tends to favor the "haves." In a review of current research on job training, Mincer (1989) found that the likelihood of workers receiving training " (a) increases with education; (b) declines with age and with length of seniority; (c) is greater for married than for single men; (d) is smaller for women, especially married women, than for men" (p. 28).

On the other hand, technology's *potential* for increasing access to learning for people of all ages and economic levels is unlimited. The city of Battle Creek, Michigan, for example, is currently experimenting with placing computer stations in public places and training all residents in accessing information (Glenn, 1989). Computers are also increasingly being used in adult literacy instruction; adults learning to read appear to be both "interested in and comfortable with computers" (Lewis, 1988b, p. 7; see also Turner, 1988). The uprising in China's

Tiananmen Square in which students exchanged critical information with students abroad through fax machines is another
example of technology's potential. Naisbitt and Aburdene (1990)
argue that technology is "empowering." In their opinion, "there
are fewer dictators on the planet today because they can no
longer control information. . . . Computers, cellular phones, and
fax machines empower individuals, rather than oppress them,
as previously feared" (pp. 303–304).

The Convergence of Demographics,
Economics, and Technology

Although demographics, economics, and technology have been
presented here as separate dimensions of the American sociocultural context, these forces are closely entwined with each other.
Advances in technology, for example, are interrelated with
changes in the economic structure. Automation and robotics
displace production workers but create other jobs. To some extent technology in the home frees women to enter the work force.
The need to be competitive in the world market leads to further
technological sophistication. Demographics and economics are
clearly related. The baby boom cohort that is now entering the
labor force, for example, is creating a "promotion squeeze. . . .
Some career ladders have become severely congested, forcing
people to look at a number of possible alternatives, all of which
have ramifications for adult education" (Cross, 1981, p. 6). As
another example, the growing number of older adults in our
society is having several effects on the economy. Some are being asked to retire early to make room for younger workers;
with increased longevity and good health, some are pursuing
second or third careers; some employers, especially those in the
service sector, are recognizing the human resource potential of
this group and are actively recruiting older workers.

Embedded in this convergence of demographics, economics, and technology is a value system based on the political and
economic structure of capitalism. Beder (1987, p. 107) explains
how these three forces are linked within the value system: "The
beliefs undergirding the capitalist system emphasize material

values. The health of the system is gauged in terms of national wealth as embodied in the gross national product, and social equality is assessed in terms of economic opportunity—the potential of members of the underclasses to amass more income. Hence, the political and social systems become directed toward . . . economic productivity, and economic productivity under the rationale of human capital theory becomes the predominant rationale for all publicly funded social interventions including adult education." This value system directly shapes adult education in the United States in several ways. First, economic productivity becomes "the dominant rationale for all public subsidy of adult education" (p. 109). Second, social justice becomes equated with economic opportunity in that "the just society is a society that provides opportunity for members of the underclasses to amass more income and material goods" and adult education "helps learners acquire the skills and knowledge" to do so (p. 109). The emphasis is on productivity and efficiency, both of which are enhanced by advances in technology. Thus technology, in the service of economic productivity, converges with changing demographics in shaping the adult learning enterprise.

One manifestation of the convergence of demographics, economics, and technology in adult education is the blurring of the field's content and delivery mechanisms. For example, adult education has been variously divided into formal, non-formal, and informal learning activities (Coombs, Prosser, and Ahmed, 1973). Formal learning takes place in educational institutions and often leads to degrees or credit of some sort. Non-formal learning refers to organized activities outside of educational institutions such as those found in learning networks, churches, and television. Informal learning refers to the experiences of everyday living from which we learn something. Today, many formal providers offer learning experiences that are noncredit, leisure-oriented, and short-term. Likewise, nonformal learning and informal life experiences can be turned into formal, credit-earning activities. Gross (1977), for example, lists eighteen nonformal resources for learning that he calls "the invisible university." The list includes learning groups, arts centers, free universities, tape cassettes, games, and so on.

Another blurring can be noted in higher education (Apps, 1989). Once composed of learners eighteen to twenty-two years old, the student body has grayed along with the population. In fact, "demographers predict that 49 percent of the students enrolled in institutions of higher education in 1992 will be twenty-five years old or older" (Apps, 1988, p. 35). Similar subjects may be taught at the local community college for credit and at the public adult school for noncredit. The part-time adult student taking a course during the day at a college is an adult learner as much as the sixteen-year-old studying for a high school diploma in a local evening class. There is also a blurring between higher education and business and industry. Many postsecondary institutions have business institutes that provide training and development services to business. Conversely, a growing number of private companies such as McDonald's Hamburger University and the Rand Graduate Institute are offering accredited degrees (Eurich, 1985).

Finally, a blurring of content and delivery is found in such popular slogans as "workplace literacy," "learning-to-learn," "critical thinking," and "media literacy." Educators, employers, and society at large are focusing attention on developing the skills needed to be productive and informed members of a fast-changing and highly technical society. With the erosion of boundaries in the content and provision of adult learning, we may be witnessing the emergence of what has been called the learning society. Taking human beings rather than educational institutions as its beginning point, the learning society is a response to the social context. Jarvis (1983) concludes that "it may be possible to detect its emergence as rapidly changing levels of technology provide people with the social conditions necessary for, and make people aware of, the opportunities to extend their learning throughout the whole of their lives" (p. 51).

Summary

Adult learning does not occur in a vacuum. What one needs or wants to learn, what opportunities are available, the manner in which one learns — all are to a large extent determined by the society in which one lives. This chapter has discussed several characteristics of American society today that are shaping the nature of learning in adulthood. Demographics, economics, and technology are three forces affecting all of society's endeavors, including adult learning. With regard to the American population, adults outnumber youth, there are more older adults, adults are better educated, and there is more cultural and ethnic diversity among the population than ever before. Economically we have entered a world economy in which "individuals become 'linked' into an international order . . . by virtue of economic and material interdependence" (Beder, 1987, p. 106). Technology has contributed to, if not caused, the shift to an information society creating dramatic changes in the work force. Although we have treated them separately, these three forces are interactive and firmly embedded in the American capitalist value system. Adult education both reflects and responds to the forces prevalent in the sociocultural context. Among the implications discussed in the chapter were the field's responsiveness to special groups of people, the economic productivity rationale behind much of adult education, the potential of technology for enhancing or impeding learning, and the blurring of content and delivery in current adult education.

Two

Learning in Formal Settings

For most people, learning in adulthood brings to mind classroom scenes in formal institutional settings. The classroom context has come to be equated with learning whether those classrooms are in schools, in the workplace, or in a local community organization. As Kidd (1973) has astutely observed: "The schools and the universities have . . . standardized the ways in which learning is carried on. The most obvious example of this is in the building of classrooms. A visitor to the schools of North America might soon form the opinion that the Almighty has decreed, or a law has been passed, ordering that education must be carried out in a rectangular room and that learning only happens where there are . . . students and one teacher" (p. 242).

National studies of who participates in adult learning activities (see Chapter Four) further underscore the tendency to equate adult learning with formal settings. The National Center for Education Statistics (NCES), for example, which provides triennial surveys of participation, defines adult education as "any course or educational activity taken part-time" (U.S. Department of Education, 1986, p. 1). Consequently, the vast majority (92 percent) of the learning reported in these surveys has been in the form of courses sponsored by a variety of institutions and agencies. In a similar vein, a recent national study of participation undertaken by the American Society for Training and Development and the U.S. Department of Labor includes only learning that takes place in formal settings (Carnevale and Gainer, 1989).

Numerous writers have described the vast array of formal settings that provide learning opportunities for adults. (See Darkenwald and Merriam, 1982; Brookfield, 1986; Merriam and Cunningham, 1989; Boone, Shearon, and White, 1980; Craig, 1987.) For some of these institutions adult learning is the primary mission, while for others it is seen as one way to fulfill their institution's goals. One of the most useful typologies of organizations has been given by Darkenwald and Merriam (1982), who outline four categories of organizations that provide learning opportunities for adults: independent adult education organizations (such as proprietary schools and community-based agencies); educational institutions (such as public schools, colleges, and universities); quasi-educational organizations (such as museums and community organizations); and noneducational organizations (such as business and industry, the armed forces, and correctional facilities). The first category, independent adult education organizations, "played a larger role in the education of the public [in the past] than such organizations do today," they say (p. 155), whereas noneducational organizations are increasingly becoming involved in the education of adults (Carnevale and Gainer, 1989). In fact, as demonstrated by a recent study, "employers deliver learning to more people than does the entire U.S. higher-education system" (Carnevale, 1989, p. 27).

Despite the variety of descriptions of adult learning in different types of settings, few have discussed the effect that these settings, both as distinct units and collectively, have on that learning. This chapter begins by considering the process of learning in formal settings. Following this review the discussion shifts to specific organizational factors—people, structure, and culture—that affect this process. We then demonstrate how these factors—especially the structural components, such as time, standard operating procedures, and facilities, depending on their configuration—can either enhance or impede learning.

The Process

Adult learning in most formal settings occurs under the direction of an educator or trainer who takes on the role of mediating the ways in which people approach their learning. This means that the instructor is usually responsible for planning, implementing, and evaluating the learning that takes place. The most often used models for designing these learning experiences are set in a systems framework (Caffarella, 1988b; Gagne, 1987; Kemp, 1985). Within these models, it is usually the educator's responsibility, sometimes in concert with a content specialist, to determine the learning objectives, the formats and techniques, and the evaluation criteria. Although most instructional design and program planning models include a formal assessment of learners' needs, often this assessment is done superficially if at all ("Employee Training in America," 1986; Caffarella, 1988b).

Once learners enter the learning situation, they may be allowed to modify the objectives and format for a particular activity, but usually within very limited parameters. In addition, evaluation of learning activities often focuses on institutional variables rather than the learning itself (Caffarella, 1988b; Kirkpatrick, 1987; Brandenburg, 1982). An example of this is the "happiness indicators," administered at the end of many education and training events, which allow participants to evaluate such programs as to the instructors' ability, the food, and the registration procedures. It is not that these aspects are unimportant; rather, that the participants learned anything is more often assumed than overtly measured.

This highly structured approach to adult learning in formal settings is illustrated in Marsick's (1987, 1988, 1990) description of workplace learning. She has summarized the process elements of the predominant form of current workplace learning as follows:

1. It is behaviorally oriented with performance outcomes that can be observed, quantified, and criterion-referenced. . . .

2. Learning is designed on a "deficit" model that measures individuals against standard, expert-derived norms. . . .

3. Problem solving emphasizes objectivity, rationality, and step-by-step procedures.

Figure 2.1. Instructional Situations Based on Direction
and Support Needed by Learners.

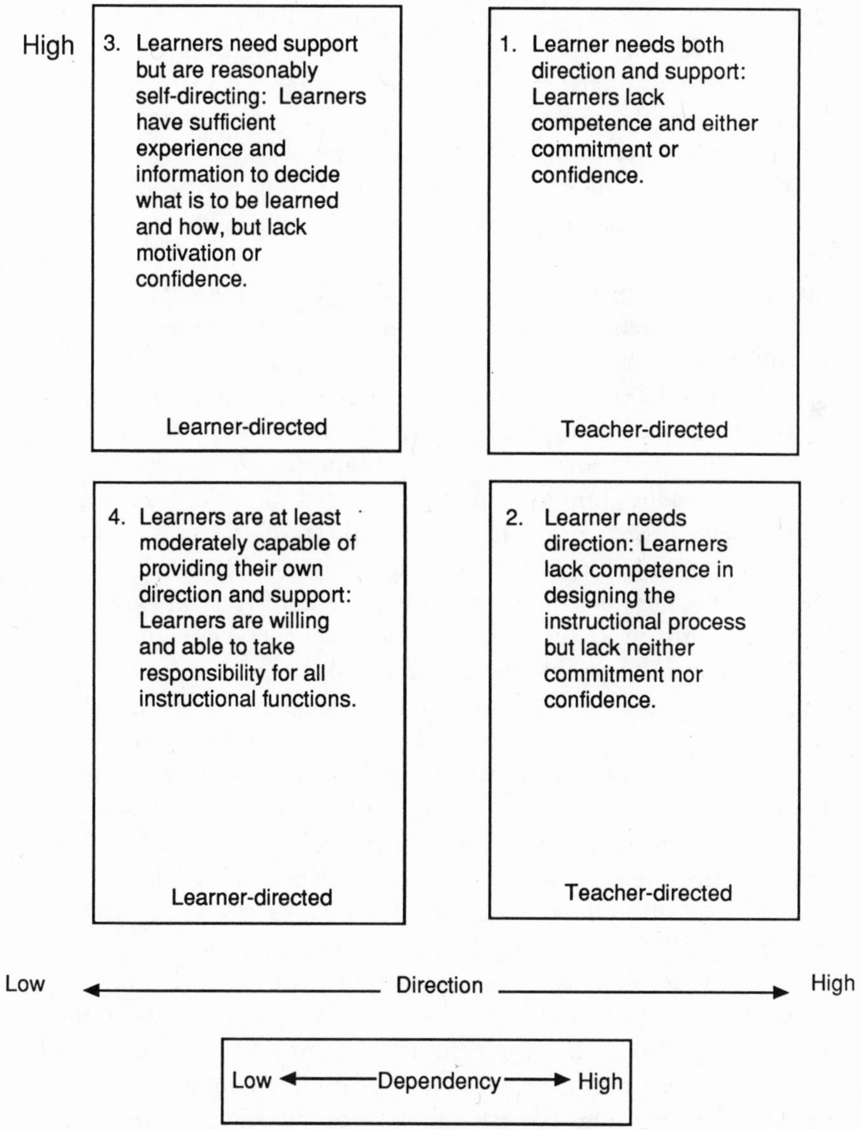

High

3. Learners need support but are reasonably self-directing: Learners have sufficient experience and information to decide what is to be learned and how, but lack motivation or confidence.	1. Learner needs both direction and support: Learners lack competence and either commitment or confidence.
Learner-directed	Teacher-directed
4. Learners are at least moderately capable of providing their own direction and support: Learners are willing and able to take responsibility for all instructional functions.	2. Learner needs direction: Learners lack competence in designing the instructional process but lack neither commitment nor confidence.
Learner-directed	Teacher-directed

Low ◄─────────────── Direction ───────────────► High

Low ◄────Dependency───► High

Source: Pratt, 1988, p. 167. Adapted with permission.

Organizational Factors

Educators of adults, as just noted, "are not independent agents developing programs in ways they alone believe to be most appropriate. Rather, their conception of a target audience, how best to serve it, and what resources are available are conditioned by their particular institutional contexts" (Cervero, 1989, p. 64). In one university, adult students are viewed as a unique, but accepted part of the student body. This is reflected in the way the university has structured the courses and in the attitudes and actions of faculty. All courses are offered during both the day and evening hours as a normal part of university operations, and student services are an around-the-clock operation. Faculty acknowledge the varying backgrounds of their students and use this diversity to enrich their teaching and the students' learning. These faculty actively encourage students to regard one another as resources. In contrast, another university views its adult student population as a necessary but not entirely welcome part of the overall student group. It offers some courses in the evening but expects all students to attend day classes if they want to complete a degree. Any courses offered off-campus, even if taught by regular faculty, carry a special designator of "C" (for continuing education) and can only be used for degree credit if approved by the student's adviser. In addition, only day courses and university-related leadership activities are considered when determining which students can be given special honors such as honor society initiations and university awards.

Three major factors affect the learning climate of an organization: people, structure, and culture. (See Brookfield, 1986; Cervero, 1988; Knowles, 1980; Lovell, 1980; Kidd, 1973; Robinson, 1979; Darkenwald, 1989.) The people factor includes those who are actively involved in the learning process or can influence that process in some way. As Brookfield (1986) has astutely observed: "Every education and training program comprises something of a psychosocial drama, a configuration of unique personalities. The personalities of the chief actors in this drama—the programmer, the administrators concerned, the support staff, the institutional head, the learners—all shape the form and process of the resultant program" (p. 277). Most of us can probably recall at least one learning situation where we felt cheated because a handful of talkative participants monopolized the time and we never got to the material we really wanted to learn. Or perhaps, even more frustrating, we remember the unfilled promises made about a specific course in terms of what we would learn and what the instructor actually taught.

The structural characteristics of the institution itself include its mission, the resource base, the standard operating procedures, the facilities, the flow of communication, and the way authority is exercised. (See Cervero, 1988; Lovell, 1980; Sork and Caffarella, 1989; Caffarella, 1988b.) Of these, the most noticeable features are usually the physical facilities and the standard operating procedures. Knox (1986) offers a useful set of guidelines that address these structural factors. His suggestions range from selecting "facilities that participants are likely to find hospitable and encouraging of sharing" (p. 132) to helping participants feel welcomed and becoming acquainted with one another. Contrast this useful advice to what many of us have found in reality: classrooms that are drab, with uncomfortable seating and lighting, coupled with a demeaning and sometimes even hostile atmosphere.

The culture of the organization represents the third major factor that affects learning in formal settings. Institutional culture is defined as a system of shared beliefs and values that interact with an organization's people, structure, and control system to shape management style and behavioral norms (Ernest, 1985). Although institutional culture comprises a number of variables, such as the history and traditions of the organization, Deal and Kennedy (1982) suggest that "values are the bedrock of any corporate culture" (p. 21). These values constitute "a philosophical position on what the organization thinks is important. In a way, the values can be considered the organization's personality, and this can set one institution apart from another" (Caffarella and O'Donnell, 1987a, p. 4). The university culture is epitomized by the ideal of academic freedom, for example, while corporate America is oriented toward profits. According to Peters and Waterman (1982), the successful organization possesses a distinctive culture that determines whether or not it can respond quickly to the needs of its customers—in this case, adult learners.

The three major factors that affect the learning climate of an organization—people, structure, and culture—"are not independent of each other but interact to a greater or lesser extent dependent upon circumstances" (Lovell, 1980, p. 123). One person, for example, might elect to enroll in a graduate program within commuting distance versus relocating to the graduate school of her choice. This decision may mean that the structural and cultural factors of that program may not meet all her needs; therefore she must either be able to change parts of the system or adapt her own learning needs and style to those of the institution. If a large number of students have learning needs that differ from what is traditionally offered by the school, the institution may eventually have to alter that program or even the institution itself. This has happened in a number of institutions of higher education as part-time adult students have become the norm on some campuses. (See Apps, 1988; Schlossberg, Lynch, and Chickering, 1989.) Although all three factors are important in understanding the learning climate of an organization, the structural variables and the people variables have received the most attention in the literature. These factors will be explored further in light of whether they enhance or inhibit learning in formal settings.

Factors That Enhance or Inhibit Learning

Many educators of adults believe that these organizational factors—people, structure, and culture—can either facilitate or deter learning. This belief has been succinctly stated by Knowles (1980): "The quality of learning that takes place in an organization is affected by the kind of organization it is. This is to say that an organization is not simply an instrumentality for providing organized learning activities to adults; it also provides an environment that either facilitates or inhibits learning" (p. 66). As we shall see in the following sections, some of our intuitive notions about the power of organizational factors have been confirmed, though in-depth exploration of these factors has been limited (Williams and Willie, 1990).

Enhancing Adult Learning. Facilitation of learning by organizations has most often been addressed in terms of the physical environment and the emotional or psychological climate — primarily the structural and people factors. (See Knowles, 1970, 1980; Kidd, 1973; Munson, 1984; Finkel, 1984, 1986; Laird, 1985.) Kidd (1973), for example, advocates an environment that is welcoming and supporting, a place where "rules are made and administered for the welfare of the learner and not the ease and comfort of the personnel in the educational institution" (p. 235); Finkel (1984, 1986), by contrast, specifically addresses how physical facilities should be designed for higher levels of adult learning. Knowles's (1980) description of an educative environment is one of the more encompassing ones. Grounded in the democratic philosophy, Knowles outlines four basic characteristics of educative environments for all types of organizations attempting to help people learn: "(1) respect for personality; (2) participation in decision making; (3) freedom of expression and availability of information; and (4) mutuality of responsibility in defining goals, planning and conducting activities, and evaluating" (1980, p. 67). Knowles also suggests that an organization must be innovative in addition to being democratic if it is to provide a climate conducive to learning.

Few data-based research studies have investigated this notion of educational climate as a source for the enhancement of adult learning in formal settings. Darkenwald and colleagues (Darkenwald, 1987, 1989; Darkenwald and Valentine, 1986; Darkenwald and Gavin, 1987; Beer and Darkenwald, 1989), for example, grounded in social environment theory, have conceptualized the major dimensions of a positive or growth-enhancing environment for adults involved in formal classroom learning. "Classroom" is interpreted by these researchers in the broadest sense to include such activities as workshops, conferences, and training programs as well as the more traditional classroom situations such as formal courses (Darkenwald, 1989). The learning environment, from their perspective, is defined as the "personality" or psychosocial climate of the classroom "created by the characteristics and interactions of students and teachers" (Darkenwald, 1989, p. 67). Through the development and field testing of the Adult Classroom Environment Scale (ACES), Darkenwald and colleagues have identified seven dimensions, made up primarily of people and structural factors, that influence learning in the classroom environment. Among these seven dimensions are the affiliative relationships among students, teachers' support for students, the task orientation of class members and teachers, and the students' influence over class topics and activities. (See Darkenwald, 1987, 1989, for a description of how the scale was developed, the different available forms, and a complete list of variables and specific test items.) Although these dimensions reflect in many ways Knowles's characteristics of an educative environment, they have been much more clearly delineated by Darkenwald and colleagues than by Knowles.

The Adult Classroom Environment Scale has been used in a number of studies of adult learning. Beer and Darkenwald (1989), for example, compared male and female perceptions of classroom social environments. Assessing a sample of 439 adult students enrolled in an urban community college, they found that women did "perceive more Affiliation and a greater degree of Involvement in the classroom than [did] men" (p. 40). Although these findings do not lend themselves to a cause-and-effect explanation, the study does raise interesting questions about the effect of gender on adult learners' reactions to the learning environment.

More recently, the present form of ACES (the Student Ideal Form) has been challenged as a result of two factor analyses of the scale (Langenbach and Aagaard, 1990). On their first test of factor analysis (see Langenbach and Aagaard for a complete description of their methodological procedures), all but fifteen of the original forty-nine items in the original ACES loaded clearly into a five-factor solution versus the seven dimensions cited by Darkenwald (1987, 1989). Three of Darkenwald's dimensions were supported by this first factor analysis (Affiliation, Teacher Support, and Organization and Clarity), although the latter two were subsumed under a single factor, Teacher Activities. Moreover, three other factors were identified: Student Prerogative, Teacher Domination, and Student Attitudes. In addition to supporting the five factors identified in the first factor analysis, a sixth factor (Unrelated Discussion) was also tentatively identified. Langenbach and Aagaard contend that this revised version of the Adult Classroom Environment Scale "will yield more theoretically sound and interpretable data on perceptions of adult classroom environments" (p. 102). It should be noted that Darkenwald (1987), in reviewing an earlier version of the findings of Langenbach and Aagaard, argues that as the ACES essentially measures a unitary dimension (a positive or growth-enhancing classroom environment) "factor analysis is not appropriate for assessing its internal validity" (p. 131).

Using a different approach—ethnography—Ennis and others (1989) have also focused their research efforts on the social climate of adult learning situations. These researchers examined the components of the social system that influence the quality of the learning experiences in an elective program for university adult students. By means of interviews with instructors and students, as well as class observations, data were collected in three areas: perceptions of personal efforts to establish a particular climate, perceptions of interactions with peers and the instructor by students, and descriptions of each class session. The findings revealed that "shared decision making and communication patterns were instrumental in the quality of the adult learning experience" (p. 76). It was also suggested that a sense of mutual trust was a common element in shared decision making and communication. Indeed, "learners reported that an openness on the part of the instructor increased their desire to discuss problems or topics of interest. Moreover, they indicated that these discussions expanded their understanding of the content and assisted them in placing the information within a relevant context in their own lives" (p. 85). These findings (illustrating again the people and structural factors), like the work of Darkenwald and colleagues, confirmed some of the basic tenets of Knowles's description of an educative environment.

An alternative approach to describing a positive educational environment is to explain how this environment can be established. This is the approach taken by Apps (1988) and Schlossberg, Lynch, and Chickering (1989). Although both studies address changing higher-education environments for adult learners, the key elements of their approaches may apply to all institutions. Apps (1988) recommends the transformational process as one way institutions can become more responsive to adult learners: "The transformation mind-set includes a way of looking at situations, at questions, at problems, at solutions, that does not stop with the obvious. We constantly ask questions such as the following: What are the assumptions and values underlying a particular statement? Are there additional alternatives we can consider? Is there another way of doing things, perhaps a way that does not immediately come to mind? Are we asking the right questions?" (p. 55). The process is built on "the premise that what we assume about something or someone influences our perceptions and in turn our actions toward that something or someone" (p. 56). We need not be aware of these assumptions for them to influence our work with adult learners.

The transformational process (Apps, 1973, 1988) includes five phases: (1) developing awareness—recognizing that something is wrong or different; (2) exploring alternatives—searching for new ideas from other institutions and acknowledging that change is needed; (3) making a transition—leaving the old approaches behind (or dramatically changed) and adopting a new way; (4) achieving integration—putting the pieces from the transition phase back together; and (5) taking action—putting the new ideas into operation. This process therefore allows for movement, dynamic and fluid, back and forth and between and among the phases, with the possibility that more than one phase may occur simultaneously. The process can be applied at the instructional, program, or institutional level. For example, at any of these levels educators could examine their assumptions about adults as learners, the basic purposes of adults learning in their organization, and the teaching and learning approaches used (Apps, 1985).

Schlossberg, Lynch, and Chickering (1989) approach the establishment of environments conducive to adult learning in a somewhat different manner. They have described four basic elements that must be addressed more or less concurrently to facilitate change in the current environment. Recognizing the major obstacles to change—such as inadequate information about adult learners and traditional organizational structure—is the first element: "Especially helpful in dealing with these obstacles—and the resistance they represent—is distinguishing among conceptual issues, political issues, and feasibility issues" (p. 230). Do the ideas make sense? Are they consistent with our best knowledge about adults as learners? If so, who will benefit from the ideas and who might be threatened? And, finally, once the political reality has been addressed, are there resources to implement the idea?

The second basic element is undertaking a systematic assessment of the situation: the need for change, potential solutions, and the climate for change. The basic motive for this assessment should be an increased understanding of the adult learners and how they can best be served. The starting point for this assessment is an analysis of the climate for change and who should be involved in the process. Understanding the basic principles of change—and acting accordingly—is the third element. Within this framework they hold that "the main *force* in effecting change at institutions is the change team itself" (p. 237). This team must have linkages to people and to information, operate in an open manner, and take responsibility for the change process. The final element is carrying out professional development activities with staff who work with (or have decision-making power over) programs that involve adult learners. These programs should serve as models of good practice.

Barriers to Adult Learning. Turning now to the way in which institutions inhibit learning, Cross (1979, 1981) has provided us with the most illuminating categories of barriers to learning: situational, dispositional, and institutional. She defines the institutional barriers, which are structural in nature, as those barriers erected by organizations that provide learning opportunities for adults. These barriers "can generally be grouped into five areas: scheduling problems; problems with location or transportation; lack of courses that are interesting, practical, or relevant; procedural problems and time requirements; and lack of information about programs and procedures" (1981, p. 104). Although Cross conceives of the institutional barriers as primarily affecting full-time learners in colleges and universities, these barriers have also been applied to other formal settings.

This wider application has been noted by Darkenwald and Merriam (1982) and Long (1983), among others. Darkenwald and Merriam have subdivided Cross's institutional category into institutional and informational barriers. They expand her notion of informational barriers to include both the "institutional failure in communicating information on learning opportunities to adults . . . as well as the failure of many adults, particularly the least educated and poorest, to seek out or use the information that is available"—thus adding the people factor to the equation (Darkenwald and Merriam, 1982, p. 137). Long (1983), on the other hand, is in agreement with Cross's three basic categories, although he divides the institutional barriers into two major types, administrative and instructional. Long's administrative variables are somewhat similar to Cross's five areas—such as when the learning activity was offered (time of day, season of year) and kinds of courses. His second institutional factor, instruction, includes such areas as teacher experience, ratings, and performance, which again introduces the people factor.

More research has been conducted on the organizational factors that inhibit learning than on those that facilitate it, although again the research has focused primarily on structural factors. The trend has been to examine why adult learners drop out of formal learning programs or choose not to participate in the first place. One notable exception to this tendency has been a study of learning programs in prison settings by Goldin and Thomas (1984) that we review at the conclusion of this section.

Boshier (1973) developed one of the earliest comprehensive models of educational participation and dropout that included institutional variables. It was his premise that "both participation and dropout stem from an interaction of internal psychological variables and external environmental variables" (p. 256). Thus it is the congruence between the participants and their educational environment that determines whether adults will participate and then persist in learning activities. Specifically his model suggests "that educators need to have a regard for environmental aspects which are formal (e.g., the stated requirements of the institution) and informal (e.g., the reception given enrolling students by office staff, arrangements for dining, informal study, etc.)" (p. 279).

Although there is little evidence of a link between the variables that affect dropout and those that affect participation, the importance of the setting is still a key to explaining why adults choose not to participate in organized adult learning or drop out once they do (Garrison, 1985, 1987a; Scanlan and Darkenwald, 1984). Darkenwald and colleagues have had the most consistent line of data-based research in identifying the barriers to participation by adults in formal learning activities. This research includes the development of the Deterrents to Participation Scale (DPS) to assess barriers to learning in specific institutional settings (Scanlan and Darkenwald, 1984). Using the DPS with a sample from the health professions, Scanlan and Darkenwald (1984) identified six factors that act as major deterrents to participation in formal adult learning activities. Two of the factors—lack of quality and work constraints—contain what Cross (1981) and others have termed institutional barriers. These variables, primarily structural in nature, include such ideas as the "program sponsor has a poor reputation" (quality factor), "methods of instruction used are unsatisfactory" (quality factor), and "programs were scheduled at inconvenient times" (work constraints).

With a newly developed version of the Deterrents to Participation Scale (DPS-G), Darkenwald and Valentine (1985) have expanded the research in this arena and "sought to identify the factors that deter the general public from participation in adult education" (p. 177). Although a different set of six factors emerged from this study, the institutional variables (again primarliy structural in nature) within these factors were somewhat similar. Again, the institutional variables were subsumed under two factors: lack of course relevance ("the courses available did not seem interesting"; "the courses available were of poor quality") and time constraints ("the course was scheduled at an inconvenient time"; "the course was offered at an inconvenient location"). These two variables (inconvenient scheduling and location) were assigned the greatest importance by the respondents, while those included in the factor "lack of course relevancy" were given a moderate to high degree of importance. Because of the different findings yielded by this study of the general adult population and the earlier study of health professionals, the authors suggest that "modified or specially developed DPS instruments are needed to measure deterrents for distinctive subpopulations" (p. 185). They caution that further theory building with regard to deterrents to participation requires rigorous, empirical analysis of the deterrent construct with different populations. Darkenwald (1988) has in fact furthered this work by replicating in Britain the 1985 study he completed with Valentine. He concludes: "The factors generated from both the U.S. and British data were comparable and represented clearly defined, conceptually meaningful components of the deterrent construct" (p. 130). Therefore, the institutional barriers that inhibit participation of adults in formal learning activities (time constraints and lack of course relevancy) were essentially the same in both the United States and Britain.

As noted earlier, Goldin and Thomas (1984) examined the organizational factors in one specific institution — prisons — that appear to have seriously hampered adult learning programs offered by that institution. They derived their data from open-ended interviews with prisoners, instructors, and prison and educational officials, as well as from field notes and documents from both the host and delivering institutions. With regard to institutional barriers, Goldin and Thomas discovered some that are unique to the prison setting, such as "lockdowns" (when all prisoners are confined to their cells). Yet most of the other barriers, all structural in nature, mirrored those outlined by Cross and others: poor facilities, lack of access to information, scheduling problems, and the prison's restrictive organizational policies and procedures. They conclude that by breaking down and modifying the most detrimental of these practices, it may become possible to have more meaningful adult learning in prison settings.

Clearly further study needs to be completed before we can pinpoint with certainty which organizational factors enhance or inhibit adult learning in a formal setting. First, we must refine these factors and develop additional instruments to measure them — especially the categories of factors proposed in this chapter: people, structure, and culture. Once that task is completed, we can address the components that make up each of the factors. Second, we need a better understanding of how the various factors interact so we can define the key ingredients that either block or enhance learning. And third, we need to determine whether the discrepancy between learners' expectations and the actual environment affects learning outcomes.

Moreover, in conceptualizing these studies of organizational factors we need to consider whether the learning in these settings is voluntary or mandated. Do the adults freely choose to learn within a specific organizational context, or does the organization require that they participate? Although much organized adult learning is voluntary, there are some setttings, such as the workplace, where learners may have no real choice whether or not they partake of learning activities offered by the organization. These learners are in fact sent to training or adult education programs with the expectation that they will learn something useful. Are the factors that facilitate and inhibit learning in these formal settings different from those in which learners voluntarily choose that setting for learning?

Summary

Adult learning in formal settings comprises a vast network of activities. These opportunities are offered by a wide range of organizations — from traditional institutions such as public schools and colleges to museums and the workplace. The process of learning in these formal settings is most often instructor-directed; the learners themselves have little say in either the design or content of the learning experience.

Three major factors shape this context for learning: people, structure, and culture. It is not entirely clear, however, what specific components make up these factors. Most seem to be structural variables, such as the institution's standard operating procedures and flow of information. Less often addressed is the interplay of the people involved in the learning setting and the overall culture of the organization. Nor is it clear how these factors facilitate or inhibit learning in formal settings. Most of this work has focused on factors that deter adults from either entering the learning situation or dropping the activities once they have started. The problems most often cited by learners in this regard involve scheduling, inconvenient locations, lack of courses that are interesting or relevant, time requirements, and the lack of information.

Few researchers have seriously addressed the issue of what constitutes a positive environment for learning. Certainly more attention needs to be given to delineating just how people, structure, and culture interact to shape the formal learning context. That there has been recent interest in looking more closely at the context — in this case formal learning settings — in which adult learning takes place is encouraging. An awareness of context can lead to better understanding of the learning that does occur, which in turn will improve the practice of adult education in this setting.

Three

Learning as
a Self-Directed
Activity

Learning outside the confines of formal education and training programs, learning on one's own, is the way most adults go about acquiring new ideas, skills, and attitudes. Yet educators of adults have often overlooked this context for learning or considered it less important than learning that takes place in formal settings under the direction of a teacher or instructor. The term that has been used most consistently in describing learning on one's own is self-directed learning (Caffarella and O'Donnell, 1989). Self-directed learning from this perspective is a form of study in which learners have the *primary* responsibility for planning, carrying out, and evaluating their own learning experiences. Although some authors (see Gibbons and Phillips, 1982; Willen, 1984) have excluded self-directed learning in formal settings, we contend that this form of study can take place both inside and outside of institutionally based learning programs. For the most part, however, being self-directed in one's learning is a natural part of adult life.

Brenda has just learned that she has breast cancer. Once over the initial shock, she decides to take an active role in planning her treatment. So that she can speak intelligently with the myriad of medical personnel she knows she must face, she gathers

Note: Portions of this chapter are based on a monograph titled *Self-Directed Learning* by R. S. Caffarella and J. M. O'Donnell (Nottingham, England: Department of Adult Education, University of Nottingham, 1989).

as much information as she can about the disease from a number of sources, including the American Cancer Society, her local Reach for Recovery program, and an oncology nurse who is the close friend of a friend. Moreover, she learns of a local support group for women with cancer and decides to join for both information and emotional solace. Her husband and grown daughter have joined her in her fight, and both are reaching out to a number of different sources for advice and counsel.

George and Sally G., as they enter their fifth decade, start planning for their retirement. They spent about three months working with a financial planner and their attorney on money matters. In addition, they have gathered information from a variety of sources about a number of areas from health care to housing. They also took a trip to Florida to see for themselves if they might like to move there—they talked with real estate salespeople, toured a number of prospective communities, and visited three couples who had recently moved to the area.

Learning on one's own, as seen in these two scenarios, does not necessarily mean learning alone. Rather, adults often use other people as helpers and resources in their self-directed learning activities. This chapter explains what it means to learn on one's own. First we review the recent resurgence of interest in self-directed learning as a form of study. This overview is followed by a discussion of how the process of learning on one's own may differ from the majority of learning experiences in formal settings. Locating resources, as we shall see, is a key aspect of self-directed learning. The chapter concludes with a brief discussion of how educators can assist adults in becoming more effective learners on their own.

Self-Directed Learning as a Form of Study

Cyril Houle (1984), in *Patterns of Learning,* makes the point that self-directed study has always been the paramount means of learning but it is constantly being rediscovered. Kulich (1970), in a much earlier historical overview of the adult self-learner, reinforces this notion by tracing the theory and practice of self-learning back to the days of the early Greek philosophers. The resurfacing of interest in self-directed learning was fostered by Houle's landmark study, *The Inquiring Mind* (1961), and by the work of Allen Tough (1967, 1978, 1979). Reflecting back on *The Inquiring Mind,* Houle (1988) observes that "when some people began to think that it might be interesting or significant to deal directly with the learning desires or processes of the individual, the idea was greeted with apathy or scorn, particularly so far as self-directed study was concerned" (p. 89).

This sentiment did not deter Tough in his quest to understand this form of study; rather, it served as one of the major motivators for his work. According to Houle (1985), Tough's original research (1967) was inspired by his desire to challenge Coolie Verner's (1964) view, among others, that self-directed learning should not be considered adult education. Tough provided the first comprehensive description of self-directed learning as a form of study. Drawing on a study of the learning projects of sixty-six people from Ontario, Canada, he found that 70 percent of all learning projects were planned by the learners themselves (Tough, 1979). He defined a learning project as "a highly deliberate effort to gain and retain certain definite knowledge and skill, or to change in some other way. To be included, a series of related learning sessions (episodes in which the person's primary intention was to learn) must add up to at least seven hours" (Tough, 1978, p. 250).

Tough's model became the basis for numerous studies that have verified the existence of self-directed learning (Brookfield, 1984; Caffarella and O'Donnell, 1987b, 1988a) in a variety of populations ranging from mothers with young children (Coolican, 1973) to farmers (Bayha, 1983) and physicians (Richards, 1986). Although the findings of these studies differ in terms of the percentage of adults who participate in this self-directed form of study, participation seems almost universal (Cross, 1981). Indeed, Tough (1978) has estimated that approximately 90 percent of the population participate in at least one self-directed learning activity per year. The typical learner is involved with five distinct areas of knowledge or skill and spends an average of 100 hours per project.

Why do people prefer to learn primarily on their own

rather than enroll in a formal program of study? Penland (1979) explored this issue in a national study of adult learning in the United States and found that the reasons the respondents gave for planning their own learning placed the emphasis on having individual control over that learning, both in terms of their personal learning style and the learning process itself. They wanted the freedom to set their own learning pace and structure, as well as the flexibility to change learning strategies as needed. In contrast, the traditional reasons (lack of time to engage in a group learning program, problems of transportation) given for not enrolling in formal study were ranked very low in importance in terms of their motivation for engaging in self-directed learning. It seems apparent, then, that control, freedom, and flexibility are the major motivators for engaging in self-directed learning. The question then becomes: Is the process of learning different in self-directed learning—and if so, how?

The Process

How adults learn on their own has been a major area of inquiry for researchers interested in self-directed learning. Until quite recently, it was assumed that the process of self-directed learning was similar in nature to the formal learning process. Learners were seen as planning and carrying out their self-directed learning activities in a fairly linear pattern: establishing goals and objectives, locating resources, choosing learning strategies, and the like (Tough, 1979; Knowles, 1975). Within the last decade, alternative descriptions of the process of self-direction have begun to emerge, which paint a very different picture. Adults engaging in self-directed learning do not necessarily follow a definite set of steps or a linear format (Spear and Mocker, 1984; Danis and Tremblay, 1987; Spear, 1988; Berger, 1990). Rather, many variables, from circumstances and happenstance to motivational issues, determine how people learn on their own. The next section traces the ways in which conceptualization of the process has changed over time.

The Work of Tough and Knowles. The process of how adults go about learning on their own was first described by Tough

(1967, 1979) and Knowles (1975). Tough's list of thirteen steps is based on his background research and experience, interviews with learners (Tough, 1967, 1979), and what he has termed logical analysis. His list (1979, pp. 95–96) represents key decision-making points about choosing what, where, and how to learn·

1. Deciding what detailed knowledge and skill to learn
2. Deciding the specific activities, methods, resources, c equipment for learning
3. Deciding where to learn
4. Setting specific deadlines or intermediate targets
5. Deciding when to begin a learning episode
6. Deciding the pace at which to proceed during a learning episode
7. Estimating the current level of one's knowledge and skill or one's progress in gaining the desired knowledge and skill
8. Detecting any factor that has been hindering learning or discovering inefficient aspects of the current procedures
9. Obtaining the desired resources or equipment or reaching the desired place or resource
10. Preparing or adapting a room (or certain furniture or equipment) for learning or arranging certain other physical conditions in preparation for learning
11. Saving or obtaining the money necessary for the use of certain human or nonhuman resources
12. Finding time for the learning
13. Taking steps to increase the motivation for certain learning episodes

Tough assumed that adults have a wide range of abilities for planning and guiding their own learning activities. Based on this assumption he went on to outline ways that adult educators could help learners on their own—especially assisting them in both locating and using a wide variety of resources for planning and actually carrying out the self-directed learning activities. Tough also proposed strategies that institutions might adopt to help adults become more competent self-directed learners. Among these were sponsoring group programs to enhance these skills, incorporating these competencies into existing courses of study, and establishing centers of self-education where people could receive help in analyzing their strengths and weaknesses and working on specific learning projects.

Knowles (1975) has outlined a somewhat similar set of steps. His five-step model of self-directed learning consists of (1) diagnosing learning needs, (2) formulating learning goals, (3) identifying human and material resources for learning, (4) choosing and implementing appropriate learning strategies, and (5) evaluating learning outcomes (p. 18). Knowles's thinking about self-directed learning is grounded in his conceptualization of andragogy (1980), which has as one of its five hallmark assumptions the idea that learners, as they mature, become increasingly self-directed. Knowles stresses that self-directed learning is not an isolated process, but often calls for collaboration and support among learners, teachers, resource people, and peers (1975). He, like Tough, outlines ways that educators of adults can help people become more competent learners on their own. Specifically, he recommends that teachers of adults become primarily facilitators of learning and assist learners to work their way through the learning process from a procedural rather than a content point of view. Knowles's idea of facilitation has not been without its critics, most notably Brookfield (1986, 1988a).

In essence, the process of learning on one's own has been conceptualized as similar to the way in which we plan and carry out instruction for adults in formal institutional settings (Caffarella and O'Donnell, 1988a, 1989). It has been viewed primarily as a linear process that moves rather logically from assessing needs and deciding what one is going to learn to setting goals, locating resources, choosing strategies, and carrying out and evaluating the learning itself. Recently, however, contrary to these formal models of self-directed learning, researchers have discovered that adults do not necessarily follow a definite set of steps in self-directed learning. (See Spear and Mocker, 1984; Danis and Tremblay, 1987, 1988; Spear, 1988; Berger, 1990.)

Alternative Descriptions of the Process. Spear and Mocker (1984) offered the first alternative explanation of how learners organize their own learning efforts. Drawing on a study of seventy-eight adults with less than a high school education, they found that "self-directed learners, rather than preplanning their learning projects, tend to select a course from limited alternatives which happen to occur in their environment and which tend to structure their learning projects" (p. 4). They labeled this phenomenon the "organizing circumstance" and explained the process as follows: (1) The triggering event for a learning project stems from a change in life circumstances; (2) the changed circumstance provides an opportunity for learning; (3) the structure, method, resources, and conditions for learning are directed by the circumstances; and (4) learning sequences progress as the circumstances created in one episode become the circumstances for the next logical step.

Spear (1988), grounding his work in social learning theory, has moved beyond his and Mocker's notion of the organizing circumstance in further delineating the process of self-directed learning. In a preliminary review of his data, the result of an exploratory study of ten training and development personnel, he found that the process of self-directed learning could be reduced to seven principal components (pp. 212–213):

Knowledge

1. Residual knowledge $K_{(r)}$: knowledge the learner brings to the project as a residue from prior knowledge
2. Acquired knowledge $K_{(a)}$: knowledge acquired as part of the learning project

Action

1. Directed action $A_{(d)}$: action directed toward a known or specific end
2. Exploratory $A_{(e)}$: action that the learner chooses without knowing what the outcomes may be or with certainty that any useful outcome will ensue
3. Fortuitous action $A_{(f)}$: action that the learner takes for reasons not related to the learning project

Environment

1. Consistent environment $E_{(c)}$: includes both human and material elements that are regularly in place and generally accessible

2. Fortuitous environment $E_{(f)}$: provides for chance encoun-
    ters that could not be expected or foreseen and yet affect
    the learner and the project

After further analysis of the data, Spear proposed that
each self-directed learning project is composed of sets or clusters
of these elements. For example, one learning cluster could be
described as follows. Susan B., who is part of an informal study
group on adult development (a consistent environment), has
decided that she would like to learn more about the writings
on women's development, a subject she has become familiar with
through graduate study and independent reading (residual
knowledge). She decides to attend a series of lectures offered
by the local women's center (directed action) on the topic and
finds most of these lectures to be useful (acquired knowledge).
At the end of one lecture, she decides some refreshment might
be appropriate and stops at a nearby coffee shop with a friend
(fortuitous action). By chance they encounter that evening's
presenter discussing her session with two staff members from
the center and are invited to join their lively exchange (exploratory action).

Spear concluded from this analysis that self-directed learning projects do not generally occur in a linear fashion—that is,
one cluster of activities does not necessarily bear any relation
to the next cluster. Rather, information gathered through one
set of activities (one cluster) is stored until it fits in with other
ideas and resources on the same topic gleaned from one or more
additional clusters of activities. Therefore, a successful self-
directed learning project is one in which a person can engage
in a sufficient number of relevant clusters of learning activities
and then assemble these clusters into a coherent whole. Spear
concludes: "The learner is perhaps in greatest control when the
assembling of the clusters begins and decisions are made regarding what knowlege is of most and least importance" (1988, p.
217).

Danis and Tremblay (1987, 1988) and Berger (1990) came
to similar conclusions. Danis and Tremblay studied ten long-
term adult learners and focused on preplanning learning projects

and the linear nature of the planning process in general. They found that their respondents were able to specify learning goals only when they had mastered certain knowledge or skills, and that in general these learners went about learning on their own using multiple approaches as opposed to using only one approach. They did note that the impact of random events stood out, in that these learners took advantage of any opportunities offered them. In contrast to Mocker and Spear's findings, the initial motivation for these learners came not from a particular life circumstance but from an interest, a challenge, or simple curiosity. These differences in initial motivation may stem from the populations studied: Danis and Tremblay's subjects had been engaged in long-term self-directed learning projects (the average was 14.9 years), whereas no specification of this nature was given for Mocker and Spear's subjects.

Like Danis and Tremblay, Berger (1990), who studied twenty Caucasian males with no formal degrees beyond high school, found little evidence that her subjects had preplanned their self-directed learning activities. Most participants in her study did not even make a conscious decision to start a learning project, but rather gradually became involved through a particular circumstance such as having family or friends interested in a specific topic or a chance event like visiting an art show. Berger also noted, as did Danis and Tremblay and Spear and Mocker, that her subjects' learning projects were anything but linear in nature. Rather, her subjects "constantly redefined their projects, changed course, and followed new paths of interest as they proceeded" (p. 176). In essence, the majority of her respondents adopted a trial-and-error approach with an emphasis on hands-on experience and practice, guiding themselves by both their successes and their mistakes as they moved on to new levels of learning.

A Holistic Picture of the Process. The actual process of learning on one's own is probably a blending of the ideas from Tough's and Knowles's earlier work with those of later writers. In essence, self-directed learning probably occurs both by design and by chance — depending on the interests, experiences, and actions

of individuals and the circumstances in which they find themselves (Penland, 1981; Spear, 1988; Berger, 1990). The process
is triggered by the needs or interests of the individual learner,
although this does not in any sense imply a formal assessment
of needs by the learner or an outside resource person. How
learners address these needs and interests depends on their internal motivation (Tough, 1979), the circumstances in which
they find themselves (Penland, 1981; Spear and Mocker, 1984;
Spear, 1988; Berger, 1990), their ability to carry out the learning activities (Tough, 1979; Knowles, 1975, 1980; Caffarella
and Caffarella, 1986), their knowledge and experience of the
content to be learned (Brookfield, 1988a), and simple happenstance (Gibbons and others, 1980; Danis and Tremblay, 1987).
How the process of learning on one's own continues to evolve
depends on the continuing interaction of these variables.

Returning to Brenda, we can follow her trek as a self-
directed learner in her battle with cancer. In the initial stages
of her fight she has gathered information from a number of
sources (the American Cancer Society, her physicians, a friend
who is an oncology nurse, and a local support group) on the
treatment alternatives and the resources associated with each
of those options. She decides on surgery with aggressive follow-
up treatment, but for her this means going to a major medical
center located in another part of the state. With the help of her
family and friends, she learns as much as possible about the area
and the support services for both her and her husband while
she is undergoing treatment. Brenda has also tried to understand the effect her disease might have on her present job situation and how it will affect her family's financial status. Once
her initial treatment phase is completed, Brenda launches a
somewhat different set of learning activities to help her deal with
her continuing chemotherapy treatments and the long-term control over the disease. Again this process has included active involvement in a support group, learning how to meditate, and
intensive soul-searching of her career and family commitments.
Although the learning process has often been painful for Brenda,
she believes she has learned a great deal from the experience
and now volunteers her time to counsel cancer patients and their

families. In addition, she is often asked to conduct educational programs for local community organizations. Brenda's continuing self-directed learning efforts will depend on a number of interacting forces—whether she has a recurrence of the disease (circumstance, happenstance), wants to learn more about the disease (interests, actions) and desires to continue her volunteer work (interests, experiences, actions).

Locating Resources—a Key Aspect of Learning on One's Own

Locating useful resources to help in the planning and carrying out of self-directed learning projects has often been cited as a key aspect of learning on one's own. (See Tough, 1978, 1979; Caffarella and O'Donnell, 1988b; Houle, 1984, 1988; Penland, 1979; Brockett and Hiemstra, 1991.) It has been customary to divide these resources into three major categories: human resources (such as professionals and friends); nonhuman resources (books, magazines, computer programs); and group resources (hobby clubs, self-help groups). (See Tough, 1978; Penland, 1979.) Here are some examples of specific resources used by sample groups:

- Adults from both urban and rural areas, representing a wide range of socioeconomic and educational backgrounds, most frequently cited books, experts, and magazines as the resources they use most. The use of tools and raw materials ranked fourth, while friends and family members were ranked next (Peters and Gordon, 1974).
- Learning cliques are a potent source of professional knowledge (Beder, Darkenwald, and Valentine, 1983).
- Farmers use commercial radio and university field days as important learning resources (Bayha, 1983).
- Nurses predominantly use informal discussion with peers and reading as their resources. Learning materials are obtained from resources in the employing agency (Kathrein, 1981).
- Books, pamphlets, and newspapers are primary sources of information for the older adult (Hiemstra, 1976).

- Participants use their fellow "enthusiasts," many of whom are found in voluntary associations and societies, as resources and supports for learning (Brookfield, 1981; Caffarella and O'Donnell, 1988a).
- Physicians most often use medical textbooks, journals, and informal conversations with colleagues as learning resources (Richards, 1986).
- Knowledgeable friends and relatives, books, and travel are cited as extremely important sources by a national sample of adults from the United States (Penland, 1977).

Implicit in this list of resources is the idea that learning on one's own does not necessarily mean learning in isolation (Knowles, 1975; Brockett and Hiemstra, 1991). Learners often seek out other people, both as individuals and as groups, to assist them in their efforts. Candy (1987b) describes work by Tremblay outlining the characteristics of the ideal helper. To assist a person in learning on his or her own, the helper must have some expertise in the subject and the learning process itself. In addition, the person should be genuinely interested in the learner and be able to communicate that interest in a warm, caring, and empathic way. Therefore, the relationship is more than just a technical association and may take time to establish and nurture.

Although we have a fairly complete list of the types of resources learners use in their self-directed learning projects, we do not have a clear description of how these resources are located and judged to be useful by learners. Apparently some people take a very active role in seeking out these resources, while others tend to use whatever they can find in their immediate environment (Spear and Mocker, 1984; Berger, 1990). The impact of technology on locating resources adds another interesting dimension to the ways in which adults can choose to go about learning on their own (Brockett and Hiemstra, 1991; Mills and Dejoy, 1988; Garrison, 1987b) — for example, a variety of data bases are now accessible through the personal home computer.

Roles of the Educator

A number of writers have assumed that educators should assist adults pursuing this form of learning. (See Tough, 1979; Knowles,

1975; Hiemstra, 1980; Hiemstra and Sisco, 1990; Penland, 1979.) Essentially three types of assistance have been discussed in the literature: assisting learners with individual projects as content or learning process experts; incorporating ways for learners to be more self-directed as part of the formal instructional process; and fostering formal institutional and governmental policies that recognize the value of this form of learning and encourage practices that could better assist people to learn on their own.

The notion that educators of adults should advocate more learner-centered and learner-controlled instruction has raised considerable controversy. (See Knowles, 1975; Brookfield, 1986, 1988a; Candy, 1987a, 1987b; Pratt, 1988.) Should instructors in formal settings, from business and industry to higher education, encourage adult learners to have more control over the learning process and content? Or by doing so are they abdicating their responsibilities as educators? The crux of the argument for more learner control is that learners will have the time and opportunity to think things through on their own — to structure the task of learning as well as decide on the meaning of what is learned. In essence, adult learners would be allowed to express their need to be self-directed in their learning endeavors even within formal settings (Knowles, 1980; Hiemstra and Sisco, 1990). In addition, learners could develop their ability to learn on their own (Gibbons and Phillips, 1982; Caffarella and Caffarella, 1986; Mocker and Spear, 1982). Is this process of giving learners greater control in formal instructional situations more effective than other forms of instruction? Some wholeheartedly endorse this concept as at least as effective as formal modes of instruction (see Knowles, 1980; Hiemstra and Sisco, 1990) while others remain skeptical (see Brookfield, 1988a; Candy, 1987a). As noted in Chapter Two, one of the most recent responses to allowing greater learner control in formal instruction is that it is not an all-or-nothing proposition.

Although they have received little attention, important statements have been made on institutional and governmental policy related to learning on one's own. Candy (1987b) has highlighted "two alternative ways in which organizations can respond: One way is by becoming more flexible and attempting to serve the learning needs as they occur in the community, and the second is by trying to attract some of the vast army of independent learners into various programmed activities" (p. 112). Hiemstra (1980), in particular, has edited a volume on policy recommendations related to self-directed adult learning, while Penland (1979) has called for "a Bill of Rights for adult learners [which] would recognize that a creative and socially relevant individualism is alive and well in self-initiated learning" (p. 178). Although little attention has been paid to policy related to self-directed learning, it is an area in which more research is needed. Quigley (1989a) has recently presented a helpful overview of how to go about influencing social policy in adult education. This movement toward the establishment of formal policy on self-directed learning has not been without its critics, however. Collins (1988), for example, is emphatically opposed to educator intervention in self-directed learning, saying that we only intrude and actually erode further prospects for genuinely autonomous learning.

Summary

Learning on one's own, being self-directed in one's learning, is itself a context in which learning takes place. The key to placing a learning experience within this context is that the learner has the primary responsibility for planning, carrying out, and evaluating his or her own learning. Participation in self-directed learning seems almost universal—in fact, an estimated 90 percent of the population is involved with at least one self-directed learning activity a year.

Until recently, self-directed learning was described in a manner similar to instruction for adults in formal settings. It was conceptualized primarily as a linear process that moved rather logically from assessing needs and deciding what one was going to learn to setting goals, locating resources, choosing strategies, and carrying out and evaluating the learning activity. Within the last decade this picture has begun to change because of observations that adults engaging in self-directed learning do not necessarily follow a definite set of steps or linear format.

Rather, a number of variables determine how people learn on their own: the learner's own motivations, the circumstances in which learners find themselves, the learner's ability to carry out the learning process, previous knowledge and experience with the content to be learned, and happenstance. In essence, self-directed learning occurs both by design and by chance — depending on the interests, experiences, and actions of individual learners and the circumstances in which they find themselves. The learner's ability to locate appropriate and useful resources has often been cited as a key aspect of learning on one's own. Although we have a fairly complete list of the types of resources used, we do not have a clear description of how learners locate these resources and judge them to be useful. One thing, however, is clear: Self-directed learning does not necessarily mean learning in isolation — assistance is often sought from friends, experts, and acquaintances in both the planning and execution of the learning activity.

Thinking about learning in this context, a question has often been raised concerning the role of the educator: Should we change our formal instructional programs to allow adults to take greater control and therefore be more self-directed in the learning process? Should we advocate changes in our present policies and procedures to reflect this context of learning as a key aspect of the adult learning enterprise? Or should we just leave this context to the individual learner?

PART TWO

The Adult Learner

Learning to read at a local education center, learning about a new computer system at your place of employment, learning to tune up a car engine at a vo-tech school, learning how to handle teenagers at a local health clinic — all are considered to be examples of adult education. Despite the diversity of content and sponsoring agents, these instances have one thing in common: the adult learner. The adult learner is at the center of all such learning activities. Understanding who adults are as learners, why they participate or do not participate, what changes they undergo as they age and how those changes interface with learning in adulthood, are important considerations in facilitating meaningful learning encounters. Part Two of *Learning in Adulthood* focuses on the adult learner.

There is no lack of data on who participates in adult learning activities. But it is still difficult to assess what percentage of the adult population participates in what types of activities. Depending primarily on the different definitions of what constitutes a learning activity and the methodological differences in participation studies, estimates of participation range from 13 percent to nearly 90 percent. Beginning with the first large-scale study of participation by Johnstone and Rivera (1965), Chapter Four reviews the major national studies of participation that describe who participates in formal adult learning activities and what they learn. This chapter and the first half of Chapter Five cover some of the same material found in Cross's *Adults as Learners* (1981). Studies of participation since the pub-

lication of her book have been added to give us a better picture
of who participates in adult education and why. A profile of
the "typical" participant is also presented in Chapter Four, as
are some of the sociodemographic variables associated with participation. While studies have revealed common characteristics
associated with participation such as age, previous schooling,
occupation, and so on, only recently have sophisticated research
techniques been employed to assess the importance of these variables in predicting future participation. These studies are reviewed in Chapter Four.

The question of why adults do or do not participate in
learning activities is one of the most researched topics in adult
learning. Chapter Five reviews descriptive studies of participation that attend to this question. Also covered here is the research begun by Cyril Houle in his seminal work *The Inquiring
Mind* (1961) on motivational orientations of adult learners. The
second half of the chapter focuses on the question of nonparticipation — why don't adults take advantage of the myriad learning
opportunities available to them? The question is approached
first from the perspective of the barriers adults are likely to
enounter as they pursue learning opportunities. Then it is covered from the perspective of the social structure — that is, whether
or not adults participate in a learning activity may have more
to do with their positions in society and their social experiences
than with their individual needs or motivation.

Research has shown that adults are often motivated to
participate in learning activities by changes in their lives (Aslanian and Brickell, 1980). Chapter Six explores the developmental
characteristics of adults that are most clearly related to learning. The study of adult development has become a major topic
of interest over the last few decades with a resulting burgeon-
ing of information and data-based research. In selecting the information from this large body of research that is most relevant
to learning in adulthood, three areas were chosen for coverage:
physical changes in adulthood, psychological changes, and sociocultural factors. In essence, we discover that what is presently
known about development in adulthood — and especially how

this knowledge is applied to learning—consists of fragmented facts, ideas, concepts, and theories from a variety of perspectives that have yet to be brought together into a holistic picture of adulthood. Perhaps when an integration of the physical, the psychological, and the sociocultural facets of adulthood is achieved, we will truly understand the adult life experience and its relationship to learning.

Four

Characteristics
and Objectives
of Learners

Residents of Battle Creek, Michigan, will soon be able to go to computer stations at their local library, museum, school, business, or other public place and via satellite have access to two thousand information data bases nationwide (Glenn, 1989). This is an experimental effort to make the entire community a learning and information center and all of its residents lifelong learners. But who is this adult who will attend a workshop to learn how to access the system and later go to one of these sites to find out more about a recently diagnosed illness, or how to build a greenhouse, or where to go for the family vacation? Financial supporters of this project, planners and instructors, and other interested communities are going to want to know *who* is participating and *what* they are learning.

These have always been key questions for the field of adult education. Literally hundreds of studies of participation have been conducted since the 1920s. The scope of the questions as well as who is asked depends on the sponsoring agency and its purpose in conducting the study — from a local program wishing to augment its current offerings to the federal government collecting data to inform policy recommendations. This chapter discusses the major national studies of participation and reviews the conclusions that can be drawn from a comparison of their respective findings. This analysis extends Cross's synthesis in *Adults as Learners* (1981) and is informed by Courtney's (1991) recent work on participation.

61

The continuing fascination with participation in adult education can be at least partly explained by the nature of the field itself. Adult education is a large and amorphous field of practice. There are no neat boundaries such as age, as in the case of elementary and secondary education, or mission, as in the case of higher education. Adult education with its myriad content areas, delivery systems, goals, and clienteles defies simple categorization, funding formulas, or understanding. One way to grasp something of the field is to find out who is involved in the activity itself—hence, studies of participation. This strategy to define the field was begun back with the Carnegie Corporation's desire to promote a learning society. Before such a goal could be operationalized, the corporation's steering committee found it necessary to study the scope of adult education providers and their participants (Rose, 1989). After the formation of the American Association for Adult Education (AAAE) in 1926, several more studies were funded by the Carnegie Corporation (Courtney, 1984). (For a review of early surveys of participation, see Courtney, 1991.) Finding out who participates and what is being studied continues to be one means of describing the field.

Another reason for the great interest in participation is the voluntary nature of adult education. Unlike preadult education, adult education has historically been largely a voluntary activity. Not only is there curiosity about who this volunteer is, but without the volunteer learners there would be a much smaller enterprise of adult education. Providers of adult education need to know who is participating, why they are participating, and what conditions are likely to promote greater participation. Conversely, knowing who is *not* involved can be important information for providers who wish to attract new learners. Interestingly, the report of the first national study of participation is titled *Volunteers for Learning* (Johnstone and Rivera, 1965).

Finally, knowledge about participation is useful to policymakers and those who provide funding. At the federal level, for example, funding for literacy and other programs is a function of who is now participating in conjunction with the perceived needs of nonparticipants. Along with current numbers and rates of participation of various segments of the adult population, of course, other sociopolitical and economic factors play important parts in federal policy formation, not the least of which is the desire to maintain a stable democratic society.

The First National Study

In 1962 an "inquiry into the nature of adult education in America" was funded by the Carnegie Corporation and carried out by researchers Johnstone and Rivera at the National Opinion Research Center (NORC) in Chicago (1965, p. xxv). The study sought to describe participation in formal and informal educational activities, assess attitudes and opinions held by adults concerning education, describe the organizations delivering adult education in a typical urban community, and focus on the educational and work experiences of young adults aged seventeen to twenty-four. The findings of this study have provided a baseline against which the findings of subsequent studies have been compared.

Since comparisons are made, it is important to know how adult education and adult are defined for each study. As mentioned earlier, participation studies define the scope of the field (a stated purpose of the NORC study). Realizing the import of this function, Johnstone and Rivera struggled to come up with a definition of an adult educational activity that was broad enough to capture systematic efforts at learning but not so broad as to include "a host of activities . . . which would fall beyond the range of any reasonable or workable definition of adult education" (1965, p. 26). They decided that an adult education activity would have as its main purpose the desire to acquire some type of knowledge, information, or skill and that it would include some form of instruction (including self-instruction). They thus measured involvement as a full-time adult student, as a part-time participant in adult education activities, and as a participant in independent self-education. An adult was defined as anyone either twenty-one or over, married, or the head of a household (p. 31). Interviews with a random national sample of nearly twelve thousand households formed the data set.

Using these definitions of adult and adult educational activity, Johnstone and Rivera estimated that 22 percent of American adults participated in "one or more forms of learning" between June 1961 and June 1962 (p. 1). They also discovered
that what adults were learning was largely practical and skill-
oriented rather than academic: "Subject matter directly useful
in the performance of everyday tasks and obligations accounted
for the most significant block of the total activities recorded.
Together, the vocational and home and family life categories
alone represented 44 percent of all formal courses studied and
47 percent of the subjects people had studied on their own" (p. 3).

This landmark study also identified the major demographic and socioeconomic variables characteristic of participants. Age and formal schooling were delineated as the major
correlates to participation in adult education. Johnstone and
Rivera's often quoted profile of the typical adult learner has held
up, with minor deviations, in all subsequent national studies
of participation. Their profile is as follows: "The adult education participant is just as often a woman as a man, is typically
under forty, has completed high school or more, enjoys an above-
average income, works full-time and most often in a white-collar
occupation, is married and has children, lives in an urbanized
area but more likely in a suburb than a large city, and is found
in all parts of the country, but more frequently in the West than
in other regions" (p. 8).

NCES Studies of Participation

Beginning in 1969 the National Center for Education Statistics
(NCES) undertook a set of triennial surveys of participation of
adults in education. The results of six surveys are available
(1969, 1972, 1975, 1978, 1981, 1984) and can be loosely compared with each other to reveal participation trends. Since there
were changes in methodology and sample design in the 1978
survey (NCES, 1980a), comparisons among the six surveys must
be viewed with caution. Nevertheless, given our premise that
participation surveys help to define the field of adult education,

it is important to note how the major variables are defined, which in turn influences responses to surveys.

In 1969, participants were defined as "persons beyond compulsory school age (seventeen and over) who are *not* enrolled full-time in a regular school or college program but who are engaged in one or more activities of organized instruction" (NCES, 1974, p. 2). Adult education was equated with organized instruction, "including correspondence courses and private tutoring; usually at a set time and place; ordinarily under the auspices of a school, college, church, neighborhood center, community organization, or other recognized authority; and generally with a predetermined end result which may or may not be a certificate, diploma, or degree" (p. 2). In 1975, NCES enlarged its list of providers to include vocational and technical institutes, cooperative extensions, and media (radio, television, and newspapers). By the 1984 survey, definitions of both adult and adult education were fairly broad: "Adult education is defined as any course or educational activity taken part-time and reported as adult education by respondents seventeen years old and over" (U.S. Department of Education, 1986).

The percentage of the nation's adults participating in organized adult education has increased slightly according to the NCES survey results—from 10 percent in 1969 to 14 percent in 1984 (see Table 4.1). These rates differ from Johnstone and Rivera's estimate of 22 percent, but their rate included full-time students and self-instruction. Their participation rate of 15 percent for part-time involvement only is more in line with NCES estimates.

Table 4.1. NCES Overall Participation Rates.

Year	Rate
1969	10%
1972	11%
1975	12%
1978	12%
1981	13%
1984	14%

Source: Hill (n.d.).

Johnstone and Rivera's profile of the typical adult learner has held up with minor changes across NCES's triennial surveys. Participants in adult education are more likely to be younger, better educated, have higher than average income, be employed full time in white-collar jobs, live in suburbia, and be from the West. Since 1978 women have had a higher rate of participation than men (approximately 55 percent). The 1984 survey reveals that while a greater percentage of participants come from the South (31 percent), followed by the North Central (28 percent), West (24 percent), and Northeast (17 percent) regions, the *rate* of participation—that is, the numbers of adults who participate from an eligible population—is still greatest for the West. The distribution of participants by age, race, school years completed, income, and labor force status can be seen in Table 4.2.

As in the Johnstone and Rivera study, most adults are involved in adult education for practical reasons. In the 1984 survey, 64 percent of the participants were involved in adult education to get a new job or advance in their present job. Some 35 percent indicated non-job-related reasons for their participation. Business courses were most popular for both men and women. See Table 4.3 for a breakdown of the types of courses taken by participants in the 1984 survey.

In summary, the who and what of participation seem to have changed little between the first national study and the latest available NCES data some twenty years later. Despite concern with the middle-class bias in participation, it seems unlikely that the profile of the typical adult learner or the rate of participation will change significantly in the years to come. In a late 1970s study projecting future rates of participation, for example, O'Keefe (1977) estimated that rising levels of education and the "baby boom" involvement in adult education could result in a rate of 17.5 percent participation in the 1980s and presumably thereafter. In another projection, Chimene (1983) used NCES data and calculated that nearly 16 percent of American adults would be involved in organized forms of adult education by 1996. Keep in mind that these participation rates reflect NCES's rather narrow definition of adult education. As we shall see in the following section, broader definitions result in higher participation rates.

Table 4.2. Adult Education Participation by Selected Characteristics: 1984 (numbers in thousands).

Characteristic	Population 17 Years Old and Over[a]	Adult Education Participants					
		Total No.	%	Men No.	%	Women No.	%
Age							
Total	172,583	23,303	100	10,446	100	12,857	100
17-24 years	31,962	3,674	16	1,556	15	2,118	17
25-34 years	39,929	8,030	34	3,738	36	4,292	33
35-44 years	30,081	5,761	25	2,636	25	3,125	24
45-54 years	22,222	3,103	13	1,405	13	1,698	13
55-64 years	22,057	1,869	8	819	8	1,050	8
65+ years	26,331	866	4	291	3	575	5
Race/ethnicity							
White	139,777	20,429	88	9,201	88	11,228	87
Black	18,628	1,506	6	622	6	885	7
Other	4,472	571	2	263	3	309	2
Hispanic	9,706	796	3	360	3	436	3
School years completed							
Elementary: 0-8	21,100	493	2	240	2	254	2
High school: 1-3	26,197	1,397	6	592	6	804	6
4	66,224	6,991	30	2,839	27	4,153	32
College 1-3	30,287	6,022	26	2,545	24	3,476	27
4	17,173	4,542	19	2,039	20	2,502	20
5+	11,602	3,858	17	2,190	21	1,669	13
Annual family income							
Under $5,000	13,016	797	3	271	1	526	2
$5,000-7,499	11,562	712	3	270	1	442	2
$7,500-9,999	10,308	742	3	297	1	446	2
$10,000-12,499	12,079	1,089	5	411	2	678	3
$12,500-14,999	10,509	1,028	4	369	2	659	3
$15,000-17,499	10,353	1,253	5	524	2	729	3
$17,500-19,999	9,422	1,255	5	572	2	683	3
$20,000-24,999	17,431	2,625	11	1,117	5	1,508	6
$25,000-29,999	15,090	2,503	11	1,210	5	1,292	6
$30,000-34,999	13,839	2,505	11	1,197	5	1,309	6
$35,000-39,999	10,287	1,919	8	928	4	992	4
$40,000-49,999	12,643	2,626	11	1,247	5	1,379	6
$50,000-74,999	11,981	2,543	11	1,211	5	1,333	6
$75,000-over	5,112	1,011	4	519	2	491	2
Not reported	8,951	695	3	302	1	393	2
Labor force status							
Employed	104,464	18,929	81	9,448	90	9,480	74
Unemployed	7,977	859	4	374	4	485	4
Keeping house	31,131	2,178	9	12	0[b]	2,166	17
Going to school	6,866	524	2	202	2	322	3
Other	22,144	813	3	407	4	405	3

Note: Details may not add to totals due to rounding.
[a]U.S. Bureau of the Census, Current Population Survey, May 1984.
[b]Less than 0.5 percent.
Source: U.S. Department of Education, 1986.

Table 4.3. Adult Education Courses by Sex of Participants:
1984 (numbers in thousands).

Courses	Total No.	%	Men No.	%	Women No.	%
Total[a]	40,752	100	17,770	100	22,981	100
Business	8,981	22	4,329	24	4,652	20
Engineering	5,899	15	4,030	23	1,869	8
Health care	5,101	13	1,648	9	3,453	15
Education	2,875	7	863	5	2,011	9
Philosophy/religion	2,703	7	1,028	6	1,674	7
Physical education	2,324	6	684	4	1,640	7
Language and literature	2,167	5	828	5	1,338	6
Arts	2,149	5	509	3	1,640	7
Social sciences	2,080	5	1,230	7	850	4
Life sciences	1,331	3	609	3	722	3
Health education	1,204	3	346	2	858	4
Home economics	947	2	66	0[b]	882	4
Personal services	842	2	302	2	540	2
Agriculture	430	1	321	2	109	1
Interdisciplinary studies	357	1	143	1	214	1
Unable to classify and not applicable	1,362	3	833	5	529	2

Note: Details may not add to totals due to rounding.

[a]Participants reported taking 43.1 million adult education courses. However, because of the survey form design, detailed information was obtained on only 40.8 million courses. Though participants could report the total number of courses taken the year ending May 1984, the survey form was designed to obtain detailed information on up to four courses taken per participant. If a participant took five or more courses (as 5 percent did), there was no way to collect detailed information on the fifth, sixth, or seventh course. Thus course information is based on the 40.8 million courses for which detailed data are available.

[b]Less than 0.5 percent.

Source: U.S. Department of Education, 1986.

Other National Studies

Who participates in adult education and what do participants learn? These key questions have been addressed in three other national studies. The first was conducted by the Commission on Nontraditional Study. Founded in 1971, this commission focuses on the learner rather than the institution, "encourages diversity of individual opportunity rather than uniform prescription, and deemphasizes time, space, and even course requirements in favor of competence and, where applicable, performance" (quoted in Cross, Valley, and Associates, 1974, p. ix). Information from the commission's study was meant to inform leaders of nontraditional programs and others who plan programs for adults. Included in this study was a random sample of persons between eighteen and sixty years of age who were living in private households and were not full-time students. Since the focus was on learning, participants were asked if they had received instruction through classes, courses, on-the-job training, private lessons, television, and the like or had instructed themselves in a subject or skill within the previous twelve-month period (Carp, Peterson, and Roelfs, 1974). The study also differentiated between learners — those who had actually received instruction — and would-be learners — those who reported an interest in some kind of further learning.

According to Carp, Peterson, and Roelfs, 31 percent of the population is engaged in some form of adult learning and 77 percent report an interest in learning about some subject or skill in the future. Other aspects of the typical participant are consonant with the Johnstone and Rivera and NCES surveys. Learners tend to be younger, better educated, white, employed full time, and so on (Carp, Peterson, and Roelfs, 1974). In terms of what participants are studying, however, there are significant differences among the studies. In the Carp, Peterson, and Roelfs study there were eight broad categories of general education, vocational subjects, agriculture, hobbies and recreation, home and family living, personal development, religion, and public affairs; 42 percent of learners were involved in hobbies and recreation and 35 percent in vocational subjects. The authors caution against making too much of comparisons, however, since questions and categories were not identical.

Another national study yielding still another rate of participation was conducted by the College Entrance Examination Board (CEEB) and reported by Aslanian and Brickell (1980). A sample of 1,519 adults over twenty-five was drawn, of which 744 or 49 percent reported having learned something formally or informally in the year prior to the study. In contrasting the 744 learners with the 775 nonlearners, learners were found to be younger and better educated; they also had higher incomes, were employed, lived in urbanized areas, were white, were engaged in professional and technical work, and were single or divorced. Courtney (1984, p. 56) notes that this study's sample of adults contains a disproportionate number of "better-educated, white-collar workers," which may explain the high rate of participation.

A third national study conducted by Penland (1979) had a considerably different focus than the other studies reviewed in this chapter. Penland was interested in corroborating Tough's (1979) findings that more than 90 percent of adults are engaged in independent learning projects. (See Chapter Three for a detailed discussion of this line of inquiry.) Briefly, Tough felt that adults were engaged in learning as part of their everyday lives—learning that was not necessarily institutionally based, and not easily recognized by the learners themselves due to the association of learning with formal instruction. Consequently, Tough and Penland asked adults to think about major learning activities that were clearly focused efforts to gain and retain knowledge or skill. A learning project had to have occurred over at least a two-day period totaling at least seven hours of learning. Respondents in both studies were given a list of things people learn about—a foreign language, gardening, raising children, and so on. Penland's 1,501 respondents were selected from the U.S. population by means of a modified probability sample (Penland, 1979). He found that "almost 80 percent (78.9) of the population of eighteen years and over perceive themselves as continuing learners whether in self-planned or formal courses" and "over three-quarters (76.1 percent) of the U.S. population had planned one or more learning projects on their own" (p. 173). Furthermore, of the nine areas of study, personal development and home and family ranked highest in popularity, followed by hobbies and recreation, general education, job, religion, voluntary activity, public affairs, and agriculture/technology.

National studies of participation by Johnstone and Rivera, NCES, Carp, Peterson, and Roelfs, Aslanian and Brickell, and Penland reveal participation rates ranging from 14 percent (1984 NCES study) to 78.9 percent (Penland). Other differences emerge with respect to what adult learners are studying. At the same time, the profile of the typical adult learner has remained remarkably consistent across studies. In the following section we discuss factors that may account for these differences in participation rates. The chapter concludes with a profile of the typical participant.

Variations in Participation Rates

The variability in participation rates can be explained to a large extent, if not wholly, by the way in which concepts are defined and data are collected. Deciding who is to be interviewed mandates that some parameters be drawn around the definition of adult. And while chronological age is widely recognized as a poor indicator of "adult" status from a psychosocial perspective, it is almost always used in research where adult views and behavior are sought separately from those of preadults. The actual age selected seems somewhat arbitrary. Hence Penland (1979) used eighteen to define adult, NCES surveys set seventeen as a bottom limit, Aslanian and Brickell surveyed adults twenty-five years and older, and the Commission on Nontraditional Study, while using eighteen as the bottom limit, inexplicably established sixty years as the upper limit. Johnstone and Rivera set still another age, twenty-one, as their base. Their definition does incorporate other notions of adulthood, however, in that respondents could be under twenty-one but head of household or married and still be interviewed. Their sample also included persons over twenty-one living on a military base or in a school residence or dormitory. Thus, unlike other studies, they counted full-time adult students in higher education.

What gets counted as an adult education activity, in addition to who gets counted, varies widely from study to study. The NCES surveys, focusing on formal, institutionally sponsored instruction, have had the most restricted definition. But even as their scope of delivery systems was broadened in the 1975 survey to include vocational and technical institutes, cooperative extensions, and media as sources of instruction, participation rates have not substantially increased. Courtney (1984)

speculates that while "adult education was no longer synonymous with what went on in officially sanctioned institutions,"
estimates consistent with each other suggest "that the public did
have a definite idea of what could be considered educational activity, even if all of the possible categories are not made explicit"
(p. 47). Even so, most analysts consider the NCES participation rates (14 percent in 1984) to be low. The higher rates of
participation reported by Johnstone and Rivera (22 percent),
Carp, Peterson, and Roelfs (33 percent), and Aslanian and
Brickell (49 percent) reflect broader definitions of an adult education activity. Most notably, these studies included self-instruction that typically takes place in noninstitutional settings. Brookfield (1986) argues that "we should conceive adult learning to
be a phenomenon and process that can take place in any setting. Indeed, it will often be the case that the most significant
kinds of adult learning that are identified as such by adult learners themselves occur in settings not formally designated as adult
educational ones. Such settings include families, community action groups, voluntary societies, support networks, work groups,
and interpersonal relationships" (p. 4).

Penland's estimate of 78.9 percent participation lies at the
opposite end of the spectrum, but his study was designed to tap
the informal learning projects undertaken by adults. Any sustained effort to learn anything was counted in Penland's study.
As Courtney (1984, p. 59) observes, this represents a shift in
focus from "talking about 'adult education,' with its apparent
restriction to organized forms of learning occurring within some
kind of institutional arrangement, to 'adult learning,' a phenomenon that knows no boundaries." It might be noted that Penland's estimate is less than Tough's (90 percent), upon whose
work Penland's study is based.

Differences in sampling and methods of data collection
may also contribute to the wide range of participation rates. For
example, while both the Johnstone and Rivera and the Carp,
Peterson, and Roelfs studies were based on a national probability sampling of households, Johnstone and Rivera had a
higher response rate — due perhaps to better screening of respondents and to fieldworkers interviewing individual respondents

versus having respondents complete a self-administered questionnaire in the other study (Courtney, 1984). In contrast to these two studies, Penland and others who have investigated self-directed learning structure the interviews so that they are almost certain to uncover significant involvement in learning: "Lists of self-directed learning projects, definitions of major learning efforts, lists of individuals who typically assist in the conduct of self-directed learning, lists of reasons for starting learning projects, various prompt sheets — all these have been presented to self-directed learners in an attempt to elicit information about their learning efforts" (Brookfield, 1986, p. 54).

As a final example of how sampling can affect results, Aslanian and Brickell's study, which purports to be a national random sample, has a higher percentage of better-educated, white-collar workers than is found in the general population: "While 28 percent of the U.S. adult population had some college experience or had graduated by 1977, in Aslanian's study this figure was a remarkably high 44 percent" (Courtney, 1984, p. 55). Since more education correlates with greater participation, their 49 percent participation rate could very well be a function of sampling. A recent study of participation using a national data base of longitudinal data gathered on 18,000 high school seniors underscores the link between sampling, education, and participation (Cervero and Kirkpatrick, 1989). The high rate of participation (56 percent) found in this study was partly explained by the fact that the sample did not include the 25 percent of the age cohort that did not reach their senior year in high school.

In a critique of participation research, Rockhill (1982) writes that it suffers from three difficulties: "These include (1) loss of the human perspective in favor of statistical accuracy; (2) definition from 'above' — from the perspective of the researcher rather than the field; and (3) value imposition, which represents a problem in construct validity" (p. 5). With regard to the first difficulty, interest in statistical measures of participation loses sight of individual learners: "Statistics that tabulate data such as education, income, occupation, and attitude provide correlations but leave no sense of person, let alone the meaning of correlations" (p. 6). The definitional dilemma hinges on the fact that adult education cannot be equated with level of schooling, a program, or a set of institutions. We thus get definitions in the research that range from NCES's institutionally based definition to Tough and Penland's broad learning project definition.

Rockhill's third point, related to value imposition, is that constructs are used in the research derived from the literature rather than from the perspective of the people being studied. "It is often assumed," she notes, "that if one doesn't participate in education as defined by the particular study, one is not a learner. . . . In defining people as non-learners, the false notion that people become educated only through educational programs is perpetuated" (1982, p. 7). She calls for research from the participant's perspective, research that employs a qualitative rather than quantitative methodology. More recently, Bagnall (1989) has called for a shift in the focus of participation studies from documenting the *presence* of learners in an education event to investigating the learner's *involvement* in the event and the extent of the learner's *control* over the event. Questions of involvement and control will necessarily mandate the use of interpretive or critical research paradigms (Bagnall, 1989).

The Typical Participant

Different rates of participation can be accounted for to a large extent by how the adult learner and his or her educational activities are defined and counted. Adults who engage in educational activities, however many of them there are, appear to have much in common. The profile of the typical adult learner first advanced by Johnstone and Rivera in the 1960s has changed little. Compared to those who do not participate, participants in adult education are better educated, younger, have higher incomes, and are most likely to be white and employed full time. This profile of the average participant should be viewed with a great amount of caution since it represents an aggregate of statistics and thus tends to obscure substantive differences among individuals. Darkenwald and Merriam (1982) note, for example, that "adults who take part in literacy or job-training programs are very different from those who engage in part-time study in universities," and these differ even further from the "average" participant (p. 120). Moreover, the profile is derived by combining vastly different forms of participation. A piano lesson, learning to read, taking a credit course in physics, participating in an employer-sponsored class on job safety—all would be considered participation. It is quite possible, however, that different learning activities have different sociodemographic and motivational roots.

Several analyses of participation data have been undertaken to assess the predictive strength of variables associated with participation. Using the 1975 NCES survey data, Anderson and Darkenwald (1979) studied eleven variables associated with participation and persistence in American adult education. Their analysis revealed that when the eleven variables were combined, "only 10 percent of the variance associated with participation and persistence could be accounted for statistically. In other words, 90 percent of whatever it is that leads adults to participate in and drop out from adult education has not been identified by this or by other similar studies" (p. 5). Individual variables such as age, sex, race, income, and education, although correlated with participation, do not necessarily explain participation.

Interestingly, the Anderson and Darkenwald analysis may itself be an artifact of methodological problems. Dimmock (1986) has criticized the measurement-related assumptions underlying Anderson and Darkenwald's regression analysis. Using log-linear analysis, which is based on assumptions more consonant with the realities of participation, Dimmock found some very different results regarding sociodemographic variables and participation. Using a specific form of participation (science-related activities) and a national probability sample of 1,635 adults, she was able to substantially explain participation through sociodemographic variables. Age, education, other forms of participation, and interest in science or technology, for example, accounted for 78 to 83 percent of the variance related to visiting science and technology museums. Dimmock argues that participation can be understood if researchers use a more focused definition of participation and an appropriate analytic technique "substantively compatible with the theory to be analyzed" (p. 86).

Another analysis of sociodemographic variables and participation was conducted by Hawk (1988). Using the May 1981 Current Population Survey (CPS) data and samples of individuals in selected metropolitan areas, Hawk attempted to identify the factors that influence adults to continue their education by taking formal course work on a part-time basis. Hawk found that 11.3 percent of adults were participating part time in continuing education activities; for both men and women, prior education, age, and professional employment status distinguished participants from nonparticipants; family income was estimated to be more important than price of the course in determining the probability of enrollment for men, while the opposite pattern emerged for women — for both sexes, however, price and income were less important than other characteristics. Hawk was also interested in finding out the extent to which the statistical technique of discriminant analysis could predict participants from nonparticipants by using ten different socioeconomic variables (such as age, race, price of course, and family income). Using discriminant analysis with these variables, Hawk was able to classify respondents into one of four categories (nonparticipant, career entry, career enhancement, and personal enrichment). For example, he was able to correctly classify 83.7 percent of the women and 73.7 percent of the men in his sample as either nonparticipants or career-oriented participants (pp. 15–16).

In yet another study, Cervero and Kirkpatrick (1990) explored the notion that previous education, which has been shown to be the strongest correlate of participation, may be an empty or intermediary variable — that other factors are antecedent to the amount of formal education. Using longitudinal data collected on more than 18,000 men and women who were high school seniors in 1972, Cervero and Kirkpatrick were able to determine that the father's level of education, combined with the senior's attitude toward education, type of high school program, and rank in high school class, were able to predict participation in learning activities for the same sample of adults at age thirty-two. Study participants' educational attainment was found to be an unnecessary variable in explaining noncredit forms of participation.

In summary, one could ask how these technical research attempts to explain participation relate to everyday concerns of practice. It seems clear that as more sophisticated statistical techniques are employed by researchers in adult education, the field is bound to gain a greater understanding of the role that sociodemographics plays in predicting participation. Moreover, taking greater care in determining who gets counted and what gets classified as adult education may bring about more congruence in findings across various studies of participation. At least we will be better able to explain widely divergent estimates of involvement in learning activities. This knowledge in turn will be helpful to a range of interested parties — from local programs that want to attract various constituencies to their offerings to federal and state funding agencies that need accurate information to formulate policy.

Summary

The question of who participates in adult education activities has intrigued the field since its founding in the 1920s. Such studies, undertaken as a means of clarifying the nature of adult education, have helped to define the parameters of the field. The traditionally voluntary nature of the field has also inspired studies to assess who is volunteering to learn what and for what reasons. Such information is important to program developers, to teachers and counselors of adults, and to policymakers at state and federal levels.

While there were numerous studies of participation in the forty years between the inauguration of the field and the 1960s, it was not until 1965 that the first national study of participation was published. Johnstone and Rivera's study, with its care in defining participation and selecting methods of data collection and analysis, remains a benchmark contribution to this literature. Subsequent triennial surveys by the National Center for Education Statistics (NCES) and studies by the Commission on Nontraditional Education (Carp, Peterson, and Roelfs, 1974),

Aslanian and Brickell (1980), and Penland (1979) have contributed in their own ways to this literature, although a puz-
zling array of participation rates has been one result of these
studies. Differences in participation rates ranging from 14 percent to nearly 80 percent can be explained by how the authors
of these studies delineated who would be counted, what would
be asked, and how the data would be analyzed. Finally, while
these studies have revealed common sociodemographic correlates to participation such as age, previous education, occupation, and so on, only recently have sophisticated methodological techniques been employed to assess the relative importance
of these variables in predicting future participation.

Five

Why Adults
Do or Do Not
Participate in
Learning Activities

Adults are busy people. Most spend at least eight hours a day working and often again as many hours attending to family, household, and community concerns. Why do as many as 23 million of these adults enroll in adult education classes, seek private instruction, or engage in independent learning projects? Curiosity about what motivates adults to participate in adult education—and, more recently, what deters them from participating—has prompted considerable writing and research in the field. Teachers, counselors, programmers, and policymakers all have a keen interest in understanding why people do or do not participate in adult learning activities. The first half of this chapter presents findings from the major national studies of participation and reviews work related to learners' motivations. The second half explores nonparticipation from both a psychological and a sociological perspective.

National Surveys

The simplest way to find out why adults participate in education is to ask them. Hundreds of local, state, and national studies have done just that. In most studies respondents are presented with a list of reasons why people might participate and asked to indicate which ones apply to them. Most respondents report multiple reasons for participation. If asked to indicate the main reason (as they were in the NCES surveys), however, they cite job-related motives.

In the first major national study of participation (Johnstone and Rivera, 1965, p. 143), respondents were asked this question: "In which of the following ways had you hoped the course would be helpful to you?" The eight reasons and their relative importance are as follows:

Becoming a better-informed person	37%
Preparing for a new job or occupation	36%
For the job I held at that time	32%
Spending my spare time more enjoyably	20%
Meeting new and interesting people	15%
Carrying out everyday tasks at home	13%
Getting away from the daily routine	10%
Carrying out everyday tasks away from home	10%

When asked if there were other reasons not listed, 10 percent indicated that there were. These "other" reasons look a lot like those already cited, however, such as "home or family life role" and "other work or job-related reasons." Keep in mind that giving respondents a list of reasons from which to choose predetermines, for the most part, the results. The question then arises as to whether there are other reasons not considered at the time of the interview. And sometimes predetermined reasons are difficult to interpret. Johnstone and Rivera (1965, p. 144) comment on this issue with regard to the 37 percent who indicated they had enrolled "to become a better-informed person": "Since becoming better informed could be a meaningful rationale for studying practically anything, of course, the meaning of the responses to this item is not clear." This caveat aside, it is clear from this first major study that "over and above the desire to become better informed . . . vocational goals most frequently direct adults into continuing education" (p. 144).

In 1972 the Commission on Nontraditional Study sought to update Johnstone and Rivera's study although different measures and definitions were used (see Chapter Four). Using a list of twenty rather than eight alternative reasons for learning, they found that 55 percent participated to "become better informed" while 43 percent engaged in learning either to get a new job or to advance in their present job (Carp, Peterson, and Roelfs, 1974). Again it is difficult to interpret what respondents might have meant by becoming "better informed."

The triennial surveys of participation conducted by the National Center for Education Statistics (NCES) differ from the foregoing studies by asking people to check their "main reason" for taking a particular course. Job-related reasons were the most frequently cited for all six surveys (1969, 1972, 1975, 1978, 1981, 1984). A full 64 percent of the 1984 participants indicated that getting a new job, advancing in the job, and other job-related reasons accounted for their participation in adult education. Some 35 percent engaged in learning for personal and social, general education, and other non-job-related goals (U.S. Department of Education, 1987).

National surveys of participation are also interested in relating the "why" of participation to sociodemographic characteristics such as sex, age, race, education, and income. Cross (1981) has observed that "the reasons people give for learning correspond consistently and logically to the life situations of the respondents" (p. 91). For example:

> People who do not have good jobs are interested in further education to get better jobs, and those who have good jobs would like to advance them. Women, factory workers, and the poorly educated, for example, are more likely to be pursuing education in order to prepare for new jobs, whereas men, professionals, and college graduates are more likely to be seeking advancement in present jobs. Men are more interested in job-related learning than women are, and young people are far more interested in it than older people are. Interest in job-related goals begins to decline at age 50 and drops off sharply after age 60. Those who are not currently participating in learning activities (most

often the economically disadvantaged and poorly
educated) are even more likely to express an interest
in job-related education than are their more advantaged peers, who can afford the luxury of education for recreation and personal satisfaction [1981,
pp. 91–92].

Approaching people's reasons for participating in adult
education from a somewhat different angle, Aslanian and Brickell (1980) of the College Entrance Examination Board sought
to test the hypothesis that life transitions motivate adults to seek
out learning experiences. They found that 83 percent of the
learners in their sample could describe some past, present, or
future change in their lives as reasons for learning. The other
17 percent were engaged in learning for its own sake — that is,
to stay mentally alert — or for the social aspects or because learning is a satisfying activity. Those going through transitions such
as marriage, retirement, job changes, birth of children, and so
on were able to identify specific events such as getting fired or
promoted that triggered their transition. The authors noted seven
kinds of transitions; those relating to career and family accounted
for 56 percent and 16 percent of the learners, respectively. The
other transitions, in descending importance, concerned leisure
(13 percent), art (5 percent), health (5 percent), religion (4 per-
cent), and citizenship (1 percent). Specific events that precipitated transitions were almost totally related to career (56 per-
cent) or family (36 percent). "To know an adult's life schedule,"
the authors conclude, "is to know an adult's learning schedule"
(pp. 60–61).

The survey studies just reviewed have been helpful in
delineating the myriad reasons adults give for participating in
learning activities. They also reveal that these reasons are fairly
predictable given an adult's life situation. Since most adult
learners are employed and derive much of their identity from
their work, it is not surprising to find that at least half of them
are involved in education for job-related reasons. Other investigations have sought to go beyond these self-reported data in

trying to understand the why of participation by asking whether there are certain categories of learners in adult education. These studies are discussed in the following section.

Motivational Orientations of Learners

Interest in categorizing the various reasons given for participating in adult learning has spurred a line of inquiry in addition to the survey studies. Courtney (1991), drawing from personality and life cycle research, traces how the concept of motivation became a research focus from the 1960s on. He notes the underlying assumptions of this approach: "Those who appear eager and willing to participate in organized learning activities are distinguishable from those who are not by an underlying attitude which sees education as a positive force, to be equated with happiness, and finds in it also a mechanism for solving 'acute' problems. However, . . . the person must be in a situation calling for the solution of a particular problem. This could mean situations such as obtaining promotion at work, changing jobs, or taking on new responsibilities in the family or the community, or it could refer to the need to learn a new set of work skills, such as might arise in situations like divorce or unemployment" (chap. 3).

The first significant study in this line of research was undertaken by Houle and published in *The Inquiring Mind* (1961). Choosing a small select sample of twenty-two adults "conspicuously engaged in various forms of continuing learning" (p. 13), Houle conducted in-depth interviews in which he explored his subjects' history of learning, factors that led them to be continuing learners, their views of themselves as learners, and so on. An analysis of the interview data revealed three separate learning orientations held by the adults in his sample. The now famous typology consists of *goal-oriented* learners who use education as a means of achieving some other goal, *activity-oriented* learners who participate for the sake of the activity itself and the social interaction, and *learning-oriented* participants who seek knowledge for its own sake.

For Houle, the goal-oriented learners were easiest to understand because they saw education as a means of responding to a personal need: "The need or interest appeared and they satisfied it by taking a course, joining a group, reading a book, or going on a trip" (1961, p. 18). The learning-oriented adults had always had the "itch to learn." Most "were avid readers and had been since childhood. The fundamental purpose which lay back of all their considerable educational activity was quite simply the desire to know. . . . Most had long been aware of their own preoccupation with learning" (pp. 24-25, 38). Finally, activity-oriented learners seemed to be motivated by social contact or just the idea of doing something: "Mostly their reasons were particular and tied to specific or personal circumstances: loneliness, seeking to escape a spouse or to find one, piling up credits, carrying on a tradition of their family or culture; . . . some had been engaged in education so long they had forgotten why they had started in the first place" (pp. 20-22). Houle was careful to point out that these were not pure types: "The best way to represent them pictorially would be by three circles which overlap at their edges" (p. 16). This notion of overlap becomes important in later research built on Houle's typology.

Houle's research stimulated a number of studies attempting to affirm or refine the original typology. Sheffield (1964), for example, used Houle's interview transcriptions to develop an instrument to measure adults' learning orientations. Through factor analysis he came up with five orientations, two of which he said could be subsumed under two of Houle's original types. Burgess (1971) and Boshier (1971) also developed scales in which the items have been shown to cluster into between five and eight factors.

By far the most extensive work has been done with Boshier's forty-eight-item Education Participation Scale (EPS), later refined to forty items. Developed and used at first by Boshier in New Zealand, it was subsequently used by Morstain and Smart (1974) with 611 adults in evening credit courses at a college in New Jersey. Their six-factor solution extended Houle's typology somewhat. The six factors are:

1. Social Relationships—this factor reflects participation in order to make new friends or meet members of the opposite sex.
2. External Expectations—these participants are complying with the wishes or directives of someone else with authority.
3. Social Welfare—this factor reflects an altruistic orientation; learners are involved because they want to serve others or their community.
4. Professional Advancement—this factor is strongly associated with participation for job enhancement or professional advancement.
5. Escape/Stimulation—this factor is indicative of learners who are involved as a way of alleviating boredom or escaping home or work routine.
6. Cognitive Interest—these participants, identical to Houle's learning-oriented adults, are engaged for the sake of learning itself.

While it is not hard to see Houle's typology represented in these factors, Cross (1981) cautions that there is an important difference in the two approaches: "Houle was classifying groups of people, whereas Morstain and Smart were identifying clusters of reasons. The implication from Houle's typology is that people are consistently motivated by characteristic orientations to learning throughout their lives, whereas the Morstain and Smart approach makes more room for multiple reasons to exist within the same individual and for motivations to change from time to time" (pp. 87–88).

     The most extensive test of Houle's typology was conducted by Boshier and Collins (1985) using EPS data from 13,442 learners in Africa, Asia, New Zealand, Canada, and the United States. Cluster analysis, rather than factor analysis, was used to analyze the data because the technique is more congruent with Houle's original conceptualization of three separate but overlapping orientations. Using the items on the EPS and the six factors from Morstain and Smart, Boshier and Collins were able to effect a three-cluster solution "loosely isomorphic with

Houle's typology" (p. 125). They found that "Cluster I consisted of the Cognitive Interest items and was congruent with his learning orientation." Cluster II, the activity orientation, "was multifaceted and composed of items normally labeled Social Stimulation, Social Contact, External Expectations, and Community Service" (p. 125). Cluster III consisted of the Professional Advancement items and thus resembled Houle's goal orientation. The authors note that while their three-cluster solution is "loosely isomorphic," the grouping of items to make up the activity cluster that matches Houle's typology is "overly generous." They conclude that "Houle's intuition has been partly collaborated; two of the six clusters were as he described them" (p. 127).

One criticism of this line of research is that Houle's orientations are reduced to specific scale items when in fact "an orientation is not simply a set of attitudes, values, and beliefs. It stands as an integration of thoughts and action" (Courtney, 1984, p. 181). For example, "the learning-oriented are defined as such because of patterns of [participation] and not simply because of attitudes or beliefs about learning. In fact, it would not really make any sense to say that someone held the attitudes of a learning-oriented type but rarely . . . engaged in an educational pursuit. It is indeed the very integration of thought and action, belief and social life, which allows us to conclude that such and such a person is learning-oriented" (Courtney, 1984, pp. 181–182).

Despite the limitations of this line of research (see Courtney, 1984, Courtney, 1991, and Long, 1983, for other criticisms), if nothing else it has become evident that learners' reasons for participating in adult education are many, are complex, and are subject to change. The search for an underlying motivational structure related to participation is likely to continue, however, for it holds the potential for better understanding the phenomenon of adult learning.

Barriers to Participation

Knowing why adults do participate in adult education does not tell us why many do not. That is, we cannot assume that those who are not participating are happily employed and satisfied with their family, community, and leisure activities. In fact, one of the field's biggest mysteries is why more adults—especially those who might benefit the most—are not involved in adult education. This question has prompted research into why adults do not participate in adult education.

The two most often cited reasons for nonparticipation are lack of time and money. These are socially acceptable reasons for not doing something, of course, and probably very legitimate reasons for adults who are busy people trying to become or stay economically solvent. Johnstone and Rivera (1965) in their national study of participation found that 43 percent cited cost as a reason for not attending adult education courses and 39 percent said they were too busy. By the CNS study in 1972 these figures had jumped to 53 percent and 46 percent, respectively (Carp, Peterson, and Roelfs, 1974). The cost factor has not consistently emerged as the major obstacle in other studies, however. In an investigation by Dao (cited in Houle, 1980, pp. 150–151), 278 employees of seventeen profit-making organizations were given a long list of reasons for nonparticipation and were asked: "How often do you believe each reason influences people not to participate in educational activities?" Their responses yielded nine clusters of reasons for nonparticipation:

1. Not enough time to participate in educational activities
2. Individual and personal problems (including cost)
3. Too difficult to succeed in educational activities
4. Against the social norms to participate in educational activities
5. Negative feelings toward the institution offering instruction
6. Negative experiences with educational activities
7. Results of educational activities not valued
8. Indifference to educational activities
9. Unawareness of educational activities available

Dao found that the first and ninth clusters (time and unawareness) were the main reasons not to participate in continuing education activities. Cluster 7 was next in influence, followed by clusters 2, 3, 5, 6, and 8. "These latter five," Houle writes (and

it might be noted that cost is in cluster 2), "were not differ-
entiable in level and had only a moderate degree of influence"
(1980, p. 151). Finally, in a recent discriminant analysis of
participation using national census data, Hawk (1988, p. 14)
found that while price of an educational activity was a more
important consideration for women than men, and women paid
less for education than men did, "for both sexes, the price and
income variables were found to be less important than other
personal characteristics in determining the probability of enrollment." The differentiation between men and women that
Hawk found is consonant with NCES data on source of payment for adult education courses. In 1984, some 39 percent of
men but 53 percent of women indicated the source of payment
to be "self or family"; other categories were public funding,
business or industry, and other sources (U.S. Department of
Education, 1986).

Reasons why adults do not participate have been clustered
by several researchers into types of barriers. Johnstone and
Rivera (1965) first did this with their list of ten potential barriers, which they clustered into two categories: external or situational barriers and internal or dispositional barriers. They then
linked these barriers to different sex, age, and socioeconomic
categories. Older adults cited more dispositional barriers while
younger people and women were more constrained by situational barriers. The researchers noted that "persons of lower socioeconomic circumstances face both kinds of obstacles" (p. 221).

Cross, using data from the Commission on Nontraditional
Study, grouped twenty-four nonparticipation items into three
categories of barriers: situational barriers relating to a person's
situation at a given time; institutional barriers consisting of "all
those practices and procedures that exclude or discourage working adults from participating in educational activities"; and dispositional barriers arising from a person's attitude toward self
and learning (Cross, 1981, p. 98).

Yet another typology of barriers is proposed by Darkenwald and Merriam (1982). Like Cross, they cite situational and
institutional barriers. Her "dispositional" barriers they have labeled "psychosocial" obstacles: beliefs, values, attitudes, and per-

ceptions about education or about oneself as a learner. Thus, "don't like school" and "afraid I can't keep up" are examples of psychosocial barriers. Darkenwald and Merriam have added a fourth category, informational, which reflects the lack of awareness as to what educational opportunities are available.

Working with different colleagues, Darkenwald has gone beyond the three-part or four-part barrier typologies in developing a scale of deterrents to participation that can be factor analyzed to reveal the structure of reasons underlying nonparticipation. A Deterrents to Participation Scale (DPS) assessed the factors underlying nonparticipation of allied health professionals (Scanlan and Darkenwald, 1984). A generic form of the DPS (called DPS-G) was then developed to use with a sample of the general adult public (Darkenwald and Valentine, 1985). Of the 2,000 New Jersey households sent the scale, 215 people responded by assessing on a 5-point Likert scale how important each of thirty-four items was as a reason for not participating in an educational activity. Responses were factor analyzed and a "six-factor solution was selected as the conceptually most meaningful representation of the data, accounting for 53 percent of the scale variance" (p. 181). The six factors are lack of confidence, lack of course relevance, time constraints, low personal priority, cost, and personal problems (such as child care, family problems, personal health). The authors compared these factors to Cross's categories of barriers and concluded that this factor structure differed "substantially from the earlier intuitive conceptualization proposed by Cross" (p. 187). In a later analysis of the same data, Valentine and Darkenwald (1990) derived a typology of adult nonparticipants. According to their analysis, the adult nonparticipants in the general public cluster into five distinct groups. People are deterred from participating either by personal problems, lack of confidence, educational costs, lack of interest in organized education, or lack of interest in available courses.

The Deterrents to Participation Scale has also been used with low-literate adults (Hayes and Darkenwald, 1988; Hayes, 1988) and with Air Force enlisted personnel (Martindale and Drake, 1989). One hundred sixty adult basic education (ABE) students in seven urban programs responded to a specially designed version of the DPS. Five factors, rather than six, best described this sample's reasons for nonparticipation in the past: low self-confidence, social disapproval, situational barriers, negative attitude to classes, and low personal priority (Hayes and Darkenwald, 1988). Using individuals' scores on these five factors, Hayes then built a typology of ABE students and was able to classify students into six types. She concludes that "low-literate adults should not be treated as a homogeneous group in respect to their perception of barriers to participation; accordingly, an undifferentiated approach to recruitment and program planning in ABE appears to be inappropriate" (Hayes, 1988, p. 8). Interestingly, although they used a sixty-two-item scale rather than the DPS to measure motivation to participate, Beder and Valentine (1990) also found six distinct subgroups of learners among their sample of Iowa ABE students. In another sample of Iowa adults who had not completed high school and who had never attended ABE classes, Beder (1990) found that thirty-two items representing reasons for nonparticipation could be condensed into four factors: low perception of need, perceived effort, dislike for school, and situational barriers.

Martindale and Drake used the DPS-G with a sample of 966 Air Force enlisted personnel, approximately two-thirds of whom were nonparticipants. Their analysis revealed eight factors rather than six: lack of course relevance, lack of confidence, cost, time constraints, lack of convenience, lack of interest, family problems, and lack of encouragement. They interpret their findings as being congruent with other studies using the scale but note that the "Lack of Interest and Lack of Course Relevance factors were more clearly separated than in previous studies, and the Lack of Convenience and Lack of Encouragement factors added new dimensions to the construct of deterrents to participation in adult education" (1989, p. 73).

Viewing participation from the perspective of barriers lends another dimension to the field's attempt to understand why some adults participate in adult education and others do not. Martindale and Drake suggest that this construct could also be "an important part of a dynamic participation model. Such a model could include motivational, deterrent, and other environmental and dispositional forces yet to be determined. The development of a full model could help solve many adult education problems and help develop programs to provide education to those who are most deterred" (1989, p. 74). (See Chapter Twelve for a discussion of models.)

A Sociological Perspective

The question of why adults do or do not participate in adult education has been studied in North America almost exclusively from a psychological perspective. That is, the *individual's* motivation, attitudes, beliefs, behavior, position in the life cycle, and so on have formed the unit of analysis. This has not always been the case, however, as Courtney (1991) points out in his historical analysis of participation research. From the first systematic studies of participation in the 1920s until the 1960s, participation was viewed from a sociological perspective. Courtney reminds us that a popular topic among researchers was social participation, of which adult education was a component:

> Two of their most significant findings at this time were also findings of adult education surveys. . . . Forms of participation were interrelated and reflected the hierarchical structure of the community. Those who partook of the more organized forms of cultural life were an overlapping population. . . . Those who turned up in some forms of adult education could also be found in others. In a later study, London (1963) spoke of this as a "general participation syndrome."
>
> Social participation was also bound up with socioeconomic status. It was highest among power and cultural elites; the laboring classes tended to avoid formal associations when seeking opportunities for learning and leisure; while the poorer and least-well-off classes tended to shun even these less structured modes, effectively cutting themselves off from any source of organization and power [Courtney, 1985, p. 132].

With the publication of Houle's (1961) study of the learning orientations of individual learners, interest shifted from studying participation in terms of the "tendencies of large groups and classes" to "the decisions of individual men and women and the motives behind those decisions" (Courtney, 1985, p. 133).

While certainly the study of participation from a psychological perspective has not waned, there has been a reintroduction of sociological concepts and theories in the study of several areas of adult education including participation. For the first time ever in the history of decennial handbooks of adult education, for example, the 1990 edition has a chapter on "The Sociology of Adult and Continuing Education" (Rubenson, 1989). Much of this research and writing is coming from Europe, most notably Great Britain. This perspective has been made more accessible through publications, research exchanges, and joint conferences.

Sociological analyses of participation have been put forth by Keddie (1980), Westwood (1980), Jarvis (1985), Quigley (1990), and Courtney (1991), to name a few. In a recent study by Nordhaug (1990), for example, participation in Norwegian adult education was analyzed, not from the individual participant's perspective, but from variables such as material resources and population density related to the structure of municipalities. In sociocultural analyses, psychological factors are important but participation is not merely a matter of motive or intent by participants: "It is something that is clearly related to both the individual's position in the social system and also to his position in the life cycle" (Jarvis, 1985, p. 209). The learner "may well be constrained by social factors of which he is unaware, so that the sociological correlations are important" (p. 210). For the most part adult education, like other forms of education, exists to maintain rather than change the social system. Jarvis has delineated six functions of adult education consonant with this view, each of which helps explain why adults do or do not participate. The six functions are:

1. Maintenance of the social system and reproduction of existing social relations: Adult education, whether for job entry, adapting to technological change, or continuing professional

education, integrates or socializes individuals into the system; its mode of delivery perpetuates class differences.

2. Transmission of knowledge and the reproduction of culture: By transmitting the dominant culture, adult education "reproduces the cultural system which, in itself, is a force for the retention of the status quo rather than social change" (p. 139).

3. Individual advancement and selection: In some cases adult education may function as a means of social mobility, but "those who are socially mobile upwards may experience a degree of isolation . . . because they have not necessarily acquired the culture of the class that they have entered" (p. 140). Furthermore, men and younger adults are more often the recipients of sponsored mobility, thus perpetuating society's age and gender-based differences.

4. Second chance and legitimation: This function of adult education reinforces the status quo since "the structures of the social system remain unquestioned" while giving the "appearance of greater equality of opportunity" (p. 143).

5. Leisure-time pursuit and institutional expansion: This function perpetuates the status quo since leisure education can only be engaged in by those who have the cultural capital — that is, the time and money — to pursue it. Furthermore, it has the latent function of retaining "stability in the social system at a time when many people do not have work to occupy their time and their minds" (p. 147).

6. Development and liberation: This function can be viewed from an individual or a social perspective. Certain forms of development can result in the individual fitting "more easily into the niche prepared for him" (p. 148); in reality, both development and liberation are aims rather than consequences of adult education.

Given these functions of adult education, the variables that correlate with participation and nonparticipation can be better understood. Thus the middle-class bias found in all studies of participation can be explained by the idea that adult education is organized by the middle class and the presentation of knowledge is middle class both in language and content. Furthermore, previous school experiences select out "those who were labeled as successful in education" (Jarvis, 1985, p. 204). The variables of age, sex, and educational background, which are also correlated with participation, can be understood as reproductions of the divisions of labor in society (Jarvis, 1985). In a similar vein, Keddie (1980) makes the point that what we consider to be "problems" in adult education—attracting more participants from the lower socioeconomic classes, for example— are really society's problems: "That is, change will depend on seeing that the 'problems' lie within the nature of the provision adult education makes and not in those who do not avail themselves of the resources it offers" (p. 63).

In summary, if one looks at social structure rather than individual needs and interests, one discovers some very different explanations why adults do or do not participate in adult learning activities. These competing perspectives imply different strategies for increasing participation. If one holds that individual interests and motivation account for participation, then recruitment efforts would center on responding to an adult's perceived learning needs and stimulating motivation. If, on the other hand, participation or nonparticipation is seen as a function of the social structure, then one would work toward changing society in ways that would facilitate participation. (A more thorough discussion of social issues in the provision of adult learning opportunities can be found in Chapter Fourteen.)

Summary

Why adults do or do not participate in adult education is an important question having implications for both theory and practice. The amount of research on this question mirrors the field's interest in the nature of the enterprise. As a result, nearly all surveys of participation have asked respondents to cite their reasons for participating and the barriers preventing participation. These surveys demonstrate "a certain faith in the capacity of people to analyze their own behavior" and are "highly useful in identifying different barriers," but they "probably underestimate the importance of dispositional barriers in adult learning. Respondents are more likely to say that the cost of education is a more formidable barrier to learning than their own disinterest" (Cross, 1981, p. 108).

The work on motivational orientation beginning with Houle's study has sought to provide a richer picture of the motives underlying participation. Houle's tripartite typology of goal-oriented, activity-oriented, and learning-oriented learners stimulated dozens of investigations into the learning orientations of adults. Most notable has been Boshier's research climaxing in a meta-analysis of over thirteen thousand learners who had filled out his EPS scale. For the most part, Houle's typology has been sustained (Boshier and Collins, 1985).

In a similar approach, barriers to participation have been investigated using various forms of the Deterrents to Participation Scale (DPS) developed by Darkenwald and colleagues (Darkenwald and Valentine, 1985; Hayes and Darkenwald, 1988; Scanlan and Darkenwald, 1984). Between five and eight factors have been delineated to explain why adults do not participate in adult education.

Finally, explanations of participation have been advanced from a sociological rather than a psychological perspective. In these analyses, people's decisions to participate have less to do with needs and motives than with their position in society and the social experiences that have shaped their lives.

Six

Adult Development
and the Learning
Experience

That children change as they age is well understood and anticipated; only within the last few decades has it become equally
clear that adults also change as they age. It is not unusual to
hear someone talk about their "age-thirty transition," their "midlife crisis," or their "biological clock" running out. What has become problematic is separating facts, ideas, and theories about
adult development from the popularized and fictionalized ver-
sions of research findings and then linking those findings to learning in adulthood. Efforts to integrate development and learning
have focused on why and how we physically age, our psychological makeup, and the major role transitions play in our lives.
(See Aslanian and Brickell, 1980; Chickering and Associates,
1981; Cross, 1981; Knox, 1977; Merriam, 1984; Schlossberg,
1984; Tennant, 1988.) There has also been some exploration
into how our thinking processes themselves may change in adulthood. (See Caffarella, Loehr, and Hosick, 1989; Peters and Lazzara, 1988; Salthouse, 1988.) This chapter explores the changes
adults undergo as they age and explains how these changes relate to learning in adulthood.

The concept of development itself is most often equated
with change. (See Heckhausen, Dixon, and Baltes, 1989;
Perlmutter and Hall, 1985.) Some view this change as an orderly progression, while others find little that is preprogrammed
(Sugarman, 1986). The goal of development is likewise con-

troversial. Some think that adults move toward closely specified goals such as self-actualization (Maslow, 1970) or a fully integrated sense of ego (Loevinger, 1976). Others (Riegel, 1973; Tennant, 1988) view development as more dialectical in nature, with no specific end other than continued growth and change as a response to the ever shifting dimensions of our lives.

Most of the work in adult development has been driven by the psychological tradition and focuses on the individual's internal process of development. Out of this tradition have grown the most prevalent theories of development, which have conceptualized it as a patterned or ordered progression tied to chronological time. Some theorists, such as Havighurst (1972) and Levinson (1978, 1986), have been highly specific, tying each developmental period to a particular age, while others (Erikson, 1963, 1982; Vaillant, 1977) have left the age frame open-ended and speak rather of life periods such as young adulthood and middle age. Although the psychological framework for development is most often cited, other perspectives on adulthood such as physical aging are equally important, especially when thinking about learning. Moreover, recent years have seen a growing awareness (though some might term it a resurfacing of interest) of the social and cultural forces, such as social class and ethnic background, that affect adult development (Dannefer, 1984; Jarvis, 1987a; Featherman and Lerner, 1985). A number of authors (such as Dannefer and Perlmutter, 1990) have even called for the creation of "a new perspective that . . . draws equally on biology, psychology, and social science, as well as on the humanities" (Levinson, 1986, p. 13) to fully understand the complex and intricate patterns of development in adulthood.

This chapter discusses the developmental characteristics of adults from three major perspectives: physical aging, psychological changes, and sociocultural factors. Each perspective will be explained through illustrative theories and ideas; the major focus is on how the broad themes of learning and development are intertwined. In conclusion we present recent conceptualizations of how these three major perspectives could be integrated into a holistic picture of adulthood.

Physical Aging

Physical aging is a fact of life, though rarely a welcome one. When we ask groups of adults to describe physical changes that have happened to them over the last five to ten years, there is usually a collective sigh and mumblings about weight gain, loss of energy, and the like. It is not a subject most people care to discuss. Yet, with advances in nutrition and health care, our overall outlook for continued health and well-being has never been better. As Erikson (1982) has so keenly observed, we have moved from an elite of elderlies to a mass of elderlies.

Although our life expectancy has almost doubled since the beginning of this century, from approximately forty to seventy-five years, our capacity to live longer does not mean we have been able to halt the normal process of aging—those time-related physical changes in vision and hearing, for example, that happen to all of us (Culter, 1981; James, 1989). The upper limit of life expectancy, usually given as 110 years, has not changed. Rather, our increased longevity stems from overcoming some of the problems related to secondary aging—aging that results from disease or abuse of the physical body. Improved nutrition, hygiene, and medical discoveries have accounted for most of this increased longevity, "primarily by reducing the likelihood of illnesses and injuries that bring a person to an 'untimely' end" (Schaie and Willis, 1986, p. 369).

Since most bodily functions reach their maximum capacity and efficiency in young adulthood, this period is for many adults a time of optimal health, physical strength, and endurance (Schaie and Willis, 1986; Merriam, 1983). Decline in the actual functioning of the major biological systems is slow. The fourth decade tends to be the physiological turning point in most adults, although the effects of these changes may not be detected until the fifth or sixth decade of life (Rossman, 1980; Perlmutter and Hall, 1985; Bee, 1987). The most obvious changes are the ones we see when we return to our twenty-fifth high school reunion. Suddenly our classmates look middle-aged. We see gray and thinning hair, more wrinkles, and different contours of the body. Yet these changes, although noticeable, really have little effect on our physical functioning, unless we take to heart the negative stereotypes society has placed on "looking old." Less obvious to the eye are the more pervasive internal changes. For example, most adults will experience changes in their vision, their cardiovascular systems, their bones and connective material, and their reproductive function sometime in their forties.

It is in the fifties and sixties, when the degenerative biological process overtakes the regenerative process, that the process of senescence gains momentum and begins to have a major effect on all structures and functions of the body. Although as adults we will all experience many major changes in our physical beings as we grow older, the effect of these changes on our capacity to learn is still largely unknown. In fact, such changes may prove to be very minor, except in cases of underlying disease processes. Three specific physical changes that have been shown to affect learning in adulthood are discussed in the following paragraphs — changes in two of the senses, changes in the central nervous system, and changes as a result of major disease processes.

Senses. Deterioration in our ability to see and to hear can create problems with the learning process, although the problems stemming from these physical changes are most often evident in formal learning settings. Specific changes in vision are well documented. One of the most notable changes is the ability to perceive small detail, such as words on the printed page and computer screen. This loss of close vision starts to decline for most people between the ages of forty and fifty and results primarily from the lens becoming more dense and thus losing its elasticity. By the age of seventy-five poor visual acuity is common, although most problems can be corrected with eyeglasses (Schaie and Willis, 1986).

A second major sight-related change concerns light: As people age they need more illumination to see both near and far (Cross, 1981; Bee, 1987). This results from a combination of lens and pupil changes that allow less light and a different quality of light to reach the eye (Perlmutter and Hall, 1985). The lens, in addition to becoming less flexible as noted above,

also becomes less translucent and yellower, while the pupils become smaller. The latter change in the pupils also makes those
past the age of seventy less responsive to sudden changes in illumination such as oncoming headlights (Perlmutter and Hall,
1985; Bee, 1987).

While changes in vision happen primarily at set periods
in life, hearing loss is a progressive but gradual process throughout adulthood. Most adults, however, will not notice any dis-
cernible change until their fifties, when sounds, especially in the
high-frequency range, become more difficult to hear. This loss
is most often noted by males, as hearing loss more often affects
males than females at this age. Even greater hearing losses are
noticed in the seventh decade: An estimated 45 percent of the
population has some detectable amount of hearing difficulty by
the age of seventy-five and 75 percent by the age of eighty. (See
Perlmutter and Hall, 1985; Bee, 1987; Schaie and Willis, 1986.)
According to Bee (1987, p. 89), "The basic cause of this loss
appears to be gradual degeneration of the auditory nerves and
structures of the inner ear."

One of the obvious results of this loss of hearing is the
inability of some older adults to understand the spoken word.
This lack of understanding may be total for those who become
completely deaf, but most often it means the loss of pieces of
words and phrases, so that the meaning may be altered for the
listener. As many grandchildren have observed, asking their
grandparents one question often elicits an answer to a totally
different question. While some hearing losses can be compensated for with the use of hearing aids or by adding such devices
as amplifiers in large meeting rooms, such adjustments do not
often help those with major hearing losses. Those with acute
hearing loss and the people who interact with them often become frustrated with the whole communication process, and
adults with serious hearing losses often become increasingly isolated from others.

The aging of the eyes and ears "serves as a good example
of how the effects of aging need not interfere greatly with the
capacity for learning" (Cross, 1981, p. 156). Except for major
degenerative and other disease processes, corrective measures
such as the wearing of eyeglasses and teaching people to find

alternative ways of communicating can help ensure the best use of the vision and hearing that remain. Adults learning on their own have fewer problems than those who choose to learn in formal settings. For the most part, our institutions do not take into consideration the physical differences of adult learners. Both teachers and learners must ensure that the educational environment is conducive to all adult learners — ensuring, for example, that all buildings are accessible to people with mobility problems and that classrooms are adequately illuminated.

The Nervous System. The central nervous system, consisting of the brain and the spinal cord, forms the primary biological basis for learning. We have only limited knowledge, however, about how changes in this system affect learning in healthy adults as they age. (See Schaie and Willis, 1986; Perlmutter and Hall, 1985; Boucouvalas, 1988b.) For example, both the weight and the number of cells in the brain decline as a person grows older and the connections between these cells become less numerous (Takeda and Matsuzawa, 1985; Bee, 1987), and yet we do not know what impact, if any, these changes have on the learning process.

The most consistent finding related to changes in the central nervous system has to do with decline in reaction time as people age. (See Knox, 1977; Cross, 1981; Schaie and Willis, 1986.) Reaction time is usually measured as the time it takes a person to complete a psychomotor task, such as putting together a puzzle or responding to a specific stimulus by hitting a light button. This decrease in speed can be sizable — from 20 percent for simple tasks to as much as 50 percent on more complex ones (Welford, 1984). Numerous explanations have been posited for this change, such as overall cell deterioration and the lessened coordination of the body's arousal system with actual brain activity (Schaie and Willis, 1986). Not only are the physiological causes unclear, but it has also been found that such factors as the nature of the task and a person's previous experience with it also affect one's reaction time (Knox, 1977; Salthouse, 1988; Shuell, 1986). Additional implications of the slowing of reaction time with regard to memory and other intellectual processes are discussed in Chapters Eight and Nine.

Disease Processes. As one grows older, it becomes difficult to distinguish between the normal or primary aging processes and those physical changes that are disease-related. Although changes in health can affect our ability to learn at any age, the greatest effect is felt in older adulthood, where it has been estimated that after the age of seventy somewhere between 75 and 86 percent of the elderly have chronic health problems. The most common problems stem from cardiovascular disease, cancer, and arthritis (Perlmutter and Hall, 1985; Schaie and Willis, 1986; Bee, 1987).

Although other health impairments may affect the learning process, two specific disease processes affect learning profoundly, depending on the severity and stage of the disease. The first is cardiovascular disease, especially when it results in a stroke or cerebrovascular accident in which the blood supply is cut off to a part of the brain. This can lead to a loss of memory and aphasia, restricting the ability to reproduce verbal speech. Moreover, other physical changes such as loss of mobility can occur, depending on which part of the brain is affected. If the stroke is mild, full or at least partial functioning may be restored so that people can once again communicate normally and be cognizant of the world around them. In the case of massive brain damage, chronic organic brain disorder might result—the second class of health problems that, even in their milder forms, affect learning. The major cause of chronic brain dysfunction is Alzheimer's disease (Perlmutter and Hall, 1985). Alzheimer's disease often develops so slowly that it may take years to recognize, although certain forms of the disease appear to develop more rapidly. The cause of this disease process is not known, but its effects become very apparent over time. Symptoms range from impaired memory and disorganization of thought to changes in judgment and emotion and finally the inability to care for oneself at even a rudimentary level.

In addition to these direct effects, disease processes indirectly influence adults' ability to learn. Pain and fatigue often accompany both acute and chronic illnesses, leaving one with little energy or motivation to engage in learning activities. Different medications and treatments may affect the way one thinks and behaves, although often these side effects go unrecognized.

Moreover, the financial drain on resources may be enormous, particularly in coping with chronic illness, leaving little support for learning activities of any kind, especially those that are institutionally sponsored.

Psychological Changes

The psychological perspective encompasses a broad array of ideas on how adults develop over the life span. The focus of this framework is how development occurs within the individual and in interaction with the environment. The material can be divided into three major categories: intellectual development, cognitive development, and personal development (often referred to as personality or stage/phase theories). As the categories of intellectual and cognitive development are fundamental to understanding learning in adulthood, they are discussed in depth in Chapters Eight and Ten respectively. Here we focus on the third category: personal development. For a more integrated view of how these three categories of the psychological domain of development — personal, intellectual, and cognitive — inform what we know about adult learning, see a recent review of the literature by Tennant (1990).

A number of diverse concepts have been placed in the category of personal development, including the theories of ego development (Erikson, 1963; Loevinger, 1976), general personality development (Levinson and others, 1978; Gould, 1978; Vaillant, 1977), moral development (Kohlberg, 1973; Gilligan, 1982), and faith development (Fowler, 1981). The common theme in this vast array of work is the changing nature of the internal self as we develop. Many of these theorists bind this change to time, either chronological age or a more generalized movement through one's life. Some, such as Erikson (1963) and Vaillant (1977), see these changes unfolding as a result of an internal preprogrammed ground plan termed the epigenetic principle; others (Schlossberg, 1984; Brim and Ryff, 1980) think the changes are tied to specific life events such as marriage, birth of children, and death of a loved one.

The literature on personal development is grounded primarily in cross-sectional clinical studies and qualitative biographies obtained through in-depth interviews. A notable exception to this line of research has been the series of studies of personality using traditional personality inventories, such as the Edwards Personality Preference Schedule and Cattell's 16PF. These studies, although valid and reliable in relation to what they measure, are primarily trait-oriented and "none is linked to any developmental theory of adulthood" (Bee, 1987, p. 253). In addition to the limited nature of the research designs, the samples, except in a few notable studies (Neugarten and Associates, 1964; Haan and Day, 1974), have been relatively small and highly selective. Subjects of the most often quoted studies have been primarily Caucasian and middle class. There also appears to be a male bias to many of the theories that is related either to the subject pool chosen or to the gender of the researcher (Gilligan, 1982; Caffarella and Olson, 1986). Therefore, theory building in personal development is at best tentative and at worst highly biased toward one segment of the population.

A number of authors (see Cross, 1981; Bee, 1987) have attempted a synthesis of the literature from this line of research and theory building. The resulting consensus is that this material is both highly complex and often contradictory. How we move on this path of development—and the end point of development, if there is one—is open to question. Some view adults as fully developed when they become highly autonomous human beings, people who are able to respond to life as distinct human entities (see Maslow, 1970; Kohlberg, 1973). Others believe we must rely not only on ourselves but others in order to function effectively (see Gilligan, 1982; Erikson and others, 1986; Kegan, 1982). In essence, more work must be done before we can describe with any accuracy the salient patterns of internal self-development for adults across the life span.

Although this material on personal development is somewhat tenuous and at times unclear, adult educators such as Knox (1977), Cross (1981), Merriam (1984), Daloz (1986), and Tennant (1990) have proposed a number of useful ideas on how this material can help us understand learning in adulthood. We especially like Daloz's notion of using these developmental theories as alternative maps of how adults can develop—without saying which specific roads should be taken or whether in some cases this developmental journey should be taken at all (Daloz, 1986, 1988b). This best fits our stance—that there is no right or best way of developing as we age. With this caveat in mind, we offer three concepts from the literature on personal development that have salient value in gaining a clear picture of adulthood: sequential patterns of change, life events, and transitions (Merriam, 1984).

Sequential Patterns of Development. Many developmental theorists view development in adulthood as a series of stages that adults pass through as they age. As noted earlier, often these periods of development have been related to chronological time—either specific age periods such as those proposed by Levinson (Levinson and others, 1978; Levinson, 1986) and Gould (1978) and the earlier work of Bühler (1968) and Frenkel-Brunswick (1963) or broad age parameters such as young, middle, and older adulthood (Erikson, 1963, 1982, 1986; Vaillant, 1977). This latter framework has led a number of educators to propose a link between age-appropriate tasks and behavior and the fostering of learning activities for adults. Havighurst (1972) was one of the earliest writers to link these ideas into what he termed the "teachable moment." The idea of the teachable moment is grounded in the concept of developmental tasks—tasks that arise at a certain period in a person's life, such as selecting a mate, starting a family, and getting started in an occupation. Although the timeframe and some of the tasks suggested by Havighurst are somewhat dated, the idea of specific life tasks giving rise to a teachable moment is not (Knox, 1977; Hentges, 1983). This key idea undergirds many program planning models, for example, the ones proposed by Knowles (1980) and Caffarella (1988b). Specifically Knowles views developmental tasks as producing "a 'readiness to learn' which at its peak presents a 'teachable moment'" (1980, p. 51) and outlines his own list of "life tasks" for young, old, and middle-aged adults.

Other developmental writers, such as Kohlberg (1973), Loevinger, (1976), and Kegan (1982), also describe stages of development, but they do not link them to specific ages. Rather, these writers speak of levels, positions, and ultimate developmental goals. The stages of development explored by these researchers are hierarchical in nature; each stage is a distinct and qualitatively different period. The movement is from relatively simple to complex ways of thinking about oneself and the world, each stage becoming more comprehensive and flexible. As Daloz (1986) states, "What is exciting about this family of theory is that it asserts that growth involves more than becoming a well-adjusted member of society. . . . It also means coming to see one's own culture from a critical stance and establishing loyalties that go beyond one's immediate community" (p. 47).

Cross (1981) proposes that "if one accepts a hierarchy of developmental stages, and if one believes that the role of educators is to help each individual develop to the highest possible level, then the role of educators is to challenge the learner to move to increasingly advanced stages of personal development" (p. 240). One way of accomplishing this is to assist adult learners in examining the basic assumptions upon which they operate in order to help them "redefine and reshape them at increasingly higher levels of development" (p. 240). The process of facilitating adult learning in this manner has been best described by Daloz (1986, 1988b) and Brookfield (1986, 1987). Daloz, who has directly linked his work with developmental theory, clearly uses the work of Kegan (1982) and others as the foundation for his notions of helping learners through their "transformational journeys" through formal mentoring and teaching activities. Yet Daloz adds a note of caution to those who assume that education is about helping adults make fundamental changes in their worldviews and thus their lives: "It is finally clear to me that not all students grow from their education. Some people find a point of equilibrium and remain there, resting. And, despite the best efforts of their teacher, may stay there the rest of their lives. . . . Yet in their refusal they have much to teach us. . . . Most adults are richly enmeshed in a fabric of relationships which hold them as they are, and many of their friends and relations do not wish them to change. . . . Sometimes it is just plain simpler to stay right where they are, or at least to appear that way" (1988b, p. 7).

Life Events. One alternative to the major paradigm of development as a set of linear stages is the concept of life events (Hultsch and Plemons, 1979; Brim and Ryff, 1980). In this alternative framework, "life events are benchmarks in the human life cycle," markers that give "shape and direction to the various aspects of a person's life" (Danish and others, 1980, as quoted in Sugarman, 1986, p. 131). Unlike the stage and phase theorists, those who describe life events as providing key growth periods do not usually connect these life events to specific age periods, although some events seem to be more tied to age than others (Hughes, Blazer, and George, 1988). There are two basic types of life events: individual and cultural (Hultsch and Plemons, 1979). Individual life events, such as birth, death, marriage, and divorce, are events that define one person's specific life. Societal and historical happenings that shape the context in which a person develops, such as wars, the women's movement, and natural catastrophes, make up the cultural life events.

A number of markers have been used to classify these events. (See Reese and Smyer, 1983; Brim and Ryff, 1980; Sugarman, 1986.) Among the most salient are *timing* (the event is congruent with either personal or societal expectations of when it should happen); *cohort specificity* (the event may affect only certain generations or it may affect different cohorts of people in different ways); and *probability* (normative being high, nonnormative being low). In addition to being viewed as milestones, life events are also seen as processes (Sugarman, 1986; Reese and Smyer, 1983) that may begin well before the event itself happens and continue well beyond it. The sequence of this process is not necessarily smooth or continuous. In the case of certain disease processes such as cancer, for example, the prognosis may be terminal with the resulting event being death. The process of dying is much more than just the day of death and often takes unplanned twists and turns prior to death itself. There is also a time needed after the event of death for survivors to assimilate the loss and make sense out of a seemingly different world. The notion of life events as a process is often equated with the idea of transitions (Schlossberg, 1984), which is discussed in more detail later in the chapter.

Knox (1977) and Brookfield (1987), among others, propose

that engaging in learning activities is one way in which adults
cope with life events. According to Knox (1977), "When a change
event occurs, the need for some adaptation produces, for some
adults at least, a heightened readiness to engage in educative
activity. The resulting activity may be directly or indirectly
related to the change event, and the relation may or may not
be recognized by the individual" (p. 539). Aslanian and Brickell (1980) found that indeed most adults do "learn in order to
cope with some change in their lives" (p. 111) and concluded
that this learning is tied to a triggering event. Their results also
substantiate Knox's earlier observations that the learning resulting from these triggering events is not always related to the event
itself. For example, a divorce (the triggering event) may motivate a woman to return to school (the learning activity) so she
may become more employable and therefore self-sufficient.
These triggering events were most often related to career and
family changes, such as moving to a new job or becoming preg-
nant. Finally, in a recent study of work, love, and learning in
adult life, Merriam and Clark (forthcoming) found that life
events occurring in a person's work life, such as being promoted
or receiving an award, or personal life, such as becoming a parent or coping with the death of a loved one, are also sources
of learning. Furthermore, respondents identified the learning
related to these events as highly significant, to the point, in some
cases, of bringing about a change in their worldview.

Transitions. Transitions are a concept that is used both by de-
velopmentalists who speak in terms of life stages (such as Levinson and others, 1978, 1986) and those who address the life events
paradigm (such as Schlossberg, 1984). Transitions are viewed
as "the natural process of disorientation and reorientation that
marks the turning points of the path of growth . . . involving
periodic accelerations and transformations" (Bridges, 1980, p.
5). Adults continually experience transitions, whether anticipated or unanticipated, and react to them depending on the type
of transition, the context in which it occurs, and its impact on
their lives. Schlossberg (1987, 1989) specifically describes how
people in transition have both strengths and weaknesses — re-

sources and deficits—to cope with the transition. She divides them into "four major categories, the four S's: situation, self, supports, and strategies" (1987, p. 75). How does the person assess the transition—as positive, negative, or indifferent? What are the person's inner strengths for dealing with the transition? What kinds of internal and external supports does the person have? And, finally, does the person have a wide repertoire of strategies for coping with the transition?

Although movement through a transition cycle is not an orderly or sequential process, Sugarman (1986) has identified seven stages that accompany a wide range of transitions: (1) immobilization—a sense of being overwhelmed or frozen; (2) reaction—a sharp swing of mood from elation to despair depending on the nature of the transition; (3) minimization—minimizing one's feelings and the anticipated impact of the event; (4) letting go—breaking with the past; (5) testing—exploration of the new terrain; (6) searching for meaning—conscious striving to learn from the experience; and (7) integration—feeling at home with the change. Bridges (1980) stresses that the fourth stage, letting go of the past, is often overlooked. We want to get on with the change rather than deal with the loss of the way we were before. When first having a child, for example, we must let go of what being childless was all about.

Again, a number of educators have linked the concept of transition to learning in adulthood. Aslanian and Brickell found that as adults reassess their lives, they come to "the realization that they will have to learn something new if they are going to make the transition successfully" (1980, p. 52). Therefore, unlike the triggering event where the learning may or may not relate to the event itself, the learning activity must be directly related to the kind of change an adult is making. As with triggering events, learning is most often related to transitions involving career and family, although other spheres such as leisure pursuits and health are also important.

Schlossberg (1984) has suggested areas of knowledge and skill that would be useful for people in transitions, including exploration of the transition event and process, problem-solving techniques, and skills for coping with the transition. Moreover, she believes that helpers are needed to assist adults in transition in examining their present situation and future scenarios from differing perspectives. Daloz (1986) and Brookfield (1986, 1987) have provided more specific guidance for how this could be done in a learning environment. Daloz, for example, thinks a mentor relationship is especially powerful when adult learners encounter a new transition in their lives.

Sociocultural Factors

Understanding how social and cultural factors influence development in adulthood is being given more recognition in the developmental literature than ever before. (See Bronfenbrenner, 1979; Palmore, 1980; Gutmann, 1982; Datan, Rodeheaver, and Hughes, 1987; Perlmutter and Hall, 1985; Thompson, 1988; Dannefer and Perlmutter, 1990.) The assumption underlying this perspective "is not to discover universals, not to make predictions that will hold good over time, and certainly not to control; but, instead, to explicate contexts and thereby to achieve new insights and new understandings" (Neugarten, 1984, as quoted by Datan, Rodeheaver, and Hughes, 1987, p. 163). Bee, for example, has listed how adult lives differ in our society for working-class and middle-class people. Adults with higher social status, compared to those of lower status, have the following characteristics (Bee, 1987, p. 51):

- They are less likely to experience periods of unemployment in their adult lives.
- They are healthier and live longer.
- They have more stable and satisfying marriages.
- They are, in general, more satisfied with their lives.

She goes on to say that although social class does not necessarily determine how adults will live out their lives, the effect of one's social class "probably shapes the choices, opportunities, and obstacles an adult is likely to face, as well as the way in which those choices and obstacles are met" (p. 51).

Dannefer (1984), in his thoughtful essay on adult development and social theory, offers us the clearest description of adult development as a socially organized and produced phenomenon. He outlines three major principles that define a sociological stance to development: seeing human beings as open and unfinished and thus able to be influenced by the environment; accepting the complexity and diversity of the social environment organized by levels and classes; and understanding the symbolic nature of the social environment, such as the "taken-for-granted ideas about 'normal development,' including age-linked stereotypes" (p. 107), defined by society as a whole and the smaller groups in which we interact.

As an example of interpreting data from this perspective, Dannefer gives two distinct explanations why middle-age adults may be less satisfied in their careers than both younger and older adults. The first interpretation, drawn from a study by Kalleberg and Loscocco (1983), is that during this midlife period adults' career satisfaction may be affected by the search for greater meaning in life, which in turn may lead to a midcareer identity crisis. Although Dannefer agrees that this explanation is plausible, he says it is based on assumptions about age-linked psychological change. What is not posited by these authors, he points out, is an alternative explanation focusing on social conditions that may produce the same effect. He then cites two such factors that could "reduce job satisfaction or perhaps even produce an identity conflict that results in reduced job satisfaction: issues of career achievement or 'success' and the broader social comparison of one's own perceived circumstances with those of others" (p. 110). In conclusion, Dannefer proposes that development in adulthood may be affected at least as much by sociological factors as by innate psychological forces.

The investigation of social roles has been a major focus of the sociological perspective, which views change as a product of lifelong socialization experiences (Brim, 1968). Social roles are defined as both a position and its associated expectations determined primarily by normative beliefs held by society (Whitbourne and Weinstock, 1979). Examples of these various positions include parent, spouse, worker, child, and friend. Changes in one's social position result from modifications of these roles (such as redefining the role of parent when both parents assume full-time employment) and the taking on of new roles (such as wife to widow or paid worker to retired person). These changes may be initiated by the individual or by others — a parent might ask an older child to take on the role of worker to help pay for her college expenses, for example, or a change in legislative policy might give a specific group in society, such as minorities or women, more control over their own lives. This focus on social roles has fostered a number of research traditions in such subjects as career development (Bray and Howard, 1983; Super, 1985) and marriage and family roles (Hill and Mattessich, 1979) that are found in most major texts on adult development. (See Perlmutter and Hall, 1985; Schaie and Willis, 1986; Bee, 1987.)

A second major strand of research from the sociological perspective is framed in what Dannefer has termed the symbolic nature of the environment, which is exemplified by the work of Neugarten and colleagues (1973, 1976, 1979). Neugarten suggests that theory should be built around the expected timing of life events in adulthood. A summary of Neugarten's work is offered by Merriam (1984): "Within every social system, expectations develop as to the appropriate times certain events should occur. Each person becomes aware of the 'social clock' that suggests the best time to leave home, to marry, retire, and so on. . . . Neugarten (1976) goes on to argue that the events themselves do not necessarily precipitate crisis or change. What is more important is the timing of these events. If they occur off-time, that is, outside the 'normal, expectable life cycle' (being widowed in young adulthood or fired close to retirement, for example), they are much more likely to cause trauma or conflict" (pp. 21–22). From this vantage point, the study of adult development then becomes a study of the timing of life events construed from socially constructed beliefs, whereas in the psychological tradition the focus is on the life events themselves, both as markers and processes.

Another important view of adult development, one which is not as yet well developed, is the cross-cultural perspective. (See Gutmann, 1982; Perlmutter and Hall, 1985; Turnbull, 1983.) Considered from this framework are the ethnic differences both within, between, and among cultures grounded in racial diversity, religion, and national identity. Membership in an ethnic group creates its own "traditions, values, and beliefs, as well as its own expectations about sex roles, child rearing, the family, and aging" (Perlmutter and Hall, 1985, pp. 475–476). For example, the roles of women are viewed very differently in Iran and other Middle Eastern cultures than they are in North America.

Although a vast number of cross-cultural studies have been completed in the anthropological tradition, this material has rarely been incorporated into the adult developmental literature. There have, however, been some notable exceptions. Erikson (1978), for example, in an edited book of essays, has provided us with an excellent sampling of adulthood in other cultures. These essays, primarily linked to the religious orientation of each cultural grouping, give a diverse picture of how the adult life cycle is depicted according to one's religious traditions. Another example of cross-cultural material on adulthood can be found in the vivid descriptive studies of Coles and Coles (1978, 1980) of women from all walks of life. Through a biographical approach, the story is told of "the daily battles, the losses, the small victories, the long, burdened marches across time and space" (1978, p. 273) of black, Chicano, Eskimo, and Pueblo Indian women, among others. Coles and Coles conclude that the interwoven factors of gender, race, and social class have had a major impact on these women's lives: "The enemy is a given social order, yes; an economic system, yes; but also and quite distinctly—or as George Eliot might want to say quite definitely—a certain number of men" (1978, p. 232).

Application of the sociocultural perspective of development to learning in adulthood has been limited. This is not surprising, considering that most of the adult development literature has been framed in the psychological tradition. Kidd (1973) and Knox (1977), for example, briefly explore how changes in roles can be related to learning activities. Specifically, Kidd has outlined a taxonomy suggested by Malcolm Knowles at a UNESCO seminar in Hamburg in 1972 that takes into account not only roles but also the competencies related to those roles. The

implied assumption underlying this taxonomy is that learning
programs could be built to address these competencies for adults
going through role changes or wishing to become more competent in their present roles. A sampling of that taxonomy follows:

Role	Competencies
Family member	Maintaining health, planning, managing, helping, sharing, buying, saving, loving, taking responsibility
Worker	Career planning, technical skills, giving and using supervision, getting along with others, cooperating, planning, delegating, managing
Citizen	Caring, participating, leading, decision making, discussing, acting, having perspective

Although some of these competencies may be outdated, the idea
that learning in adulthood is related to appropriate role taking,
as defined by society's expectations, has a long history from the
early citizenship education for immigrants to present-day government job training programs. Even learning on our own may
be driven by what society expects of us.

Another link to the sociocultural perspective is found in
the participation studies. The best example of this is the socioeconomic status (SES) variable proposed as part of Darkenwald
and Merriam's (1982) model (see Chapter Twelve). Defined as
educational attainment, occupational status, and income, "adult
SES is portrayed as the first and dominant influence in a sequence of variables affecting the probability that an individual
will participate in adult education" (p. 142). At least part of this
proposed variable, educational attainment, has proved to be one
of the best predictors of participation in adult learning activities (Cross, 1981).

The most comprehensive integration of the sociocultural
framework of development into research and theory related to
adult learning has come from Jarvis (1987a). Approaching learn-

ing from a macro-perspective, Jarvis contends "that learning is not just a psychological process that happens in splendid isolation from the world in which the learner lives, but is intimately related to that world and affected by it" (p. 11). His justification for this position is built upon two major assumptions. The first is that most people, through their socialization processes, take on, at least in part, the knowledge, values, beliefs, and attitudes of the society in which they live. Second, Jarvis views the person as "a reflection of the sum total of experiences that the individual has in society" (p. 13). He then proposes a complex model of adult learning, the key ingredient of which is the experiences of the learner. This model maps out nine different ways that adults respond to their experiences and three possible classes of response: nonlearning responses, nonreflective learning, and reflective learning. (See Chapter Thirteen for a more detailed description of the model.) The value of Jarvis's work does not necessarily lie in the model itself, although it is a useful starting point for further study. Rather, Jarvis has challenged educators of adults to view learning from a quite different perspective.

Creating New Perspectives on Development

The challenge to create new paradigms of adult development reflecting a more holistic picture of adult life has received greater attention in the literature within the last decade. Observations by long-term scholars of development (Levinson, 1986; Datan, Rodeheaver, and Hughes, 1987; Dannefer and Perlmutter, 1990; Sinnott, 1981) and those who have studied adulthood for the first time (Bryant, 1989) make us cognizant of the incompleteness of our narrow definitions of adulthood whether from the psychological, the physiological, or the sociocultural perspective. As put so eloquently by Bryant (1989): "One need only look at the plights of those in even very recent history who were out of sync with their time, the forerunners of new criteria for normal adult development — the women who could not be patently subservient to men, the men who could not be independent of emotions, the oldsters who persist in physical and sex-

ual vigor. . . . It seems virtually impossible that psychologists
and sociologists could concurrently accommodate the changes
that these individuals represent. What they can do is only observe, compute and rhapsodize over statistics, and inject some
of their own thought and personal dispositions" (pp. 3–4). A
few attempts have been made to respond to the call for a more
integrated theory of adult development, one that regards adults
as physical, emotional, and spiritual beings who live and grow
within a wider societal context. Three recent models of adult
development, those proposed by Baltes (1982), Peck (1986), and
Peters (1989a), are illustrative of this new wave of theory building.

Baltes (1982) introduced one of the earlier models that
emphasized a "multicausal and interactive view" (p. 18) of adult
development. Drawing on the work of Havighurst, Neugarten,
and others, he hypothesized that biological and environmental
forces constitute the basic determinants for development. These
are then influenced by three major sets of factors: normative
age-graded influences (forces normally correlated with age); normative history-graded influences (events that are widely experienced by one age group of people); and nonnormative influences
(factors significant to one particular person). The interaction
of these influences results in developmental changes over the
life span. Baltes hypothesizes that the relative significance of these
three developmental influences may vary at different points in
the life span — "for example, age-graded influences may be especially important . . . in old age, whereas history-graded and
nonnormative influences may predominate in early and middle
adulthood" (Schaie and Willis, 1986, p. 22). Baltes has also
stressed the need for "new development-specific" research methodologies to address the more interactive and complex models
of adult development. In his view this lack of appropriate methodological tools has continued because the traditional focus in
"research methodology has been oriented toward such features
as optimal prediction (rather than representation of change) and
interindividual differences (rather than patterns of intraindividual
change)" (Baltes, 1982, p. 21).

Drawing from the research on women's adult experiences,
Peck (1986) has proposed a second model describing women's

development. This model, which incorporates primarily social and psychological principles, "seeks to describe factors affecting the way in which a woman's sense of self is defined and redefined during the adult years . . . and emphasizes the impact of relationships upon the woman's self-definition" (p. 277). A woman's self-definition is the product of two major factors: social-historical time, defined as the context (political, social) in which a woman functions at any given point in time, and the sphere of influence, defined as the sum of relationships in which a woman is involved (family, friends, work). This sphere of influence is bidirectional, as a woman is influenced by others and at the same time influences them. The process of development is viewed as a spiraling funnel that may expand as a person moves through life. The key to this movement is a woman's ability to change her web of relationships. Therefore, the model captures what the literature has termed the importance of attachment or interconnectedness that many women feel throughout their life cycle. (See Gilligan, 1982; Baruch, Barnett, and Rivers, 1983; Caffarella and Olson, 1986.) Although the model specifically addresses women's development in adulthood, its major premise — the importance of relationships in adulthood — may apply as well to men. To date, no studies have been published that either verify or dispute this premise or the model itself.

The final illustrative model is one proposed by Peters (1989a) as part of a framework for extensive education programming through the adult's life span. The model brings together the biological, psychological, and sociological aspects of adult development. One of the model's key elements is the changing nature of the life structure, consisting of the task-related subsystems of work, other, and self. "Work" refers to the job-related activities in which the person engages. "Other" includes the many relationships adults have, such as family, friends, and social acquaintances. "Self" represents the individualized nature of each person. It is the interrelationship of these subsystems that depicts "who the person is" at a particular time in his or her life (Peters, 1989a, p. 86). Internal forces (psychological, biological) and external forces (social expectations, economic conditions) make up the second major element in the model. These forces influence the choices people make about their work, their relationships with others, and how they see themselves as individuals. Young adults, for example, especially males, often concern themselves with building and maintaining a career; therefore the work subsystem would predominate with lesser attention paid to the other aspects of life. A person's life structure does not remain stable but changes as a result of both the internal and external forces and the individual's choices. It is the reconfiguration of this life structure that is assumed to be the "essence of development" (p. 86). No verification studies of the model have been completed. In addition to mapping out the model itself, Peters has outlined specific implications for educational programming in terms of both the needs assessment process and the educational strategies for learning.

Although application of these integrated models to learning in adulthood has been limited, the message conveyed by the theorists is clear: To fully understand development in adulthood, one must move beyond explanations fostered only by one or two perspectives. Educators of adults must be mindful of the impact of single-perspective theories "on shaping and maintaining conventionally held views about what it means to be a mature and healthy adult" (Tennant, 1988, p. 65). Therefore, we must continue to widen our applications of adult developmental theory beyond those ideas fostered predominantly by the psychological tradition.

Summary

Adult developmental theory and research offer a rich array of material from which numerous implications can be drawn about learning in adulthood. This chapter has reviewed the developmental characteristics of adults from three perspectives: physical aging, psychological change, and sociological factors. With regard to physical aging, all adults experience some changes as they age. Many of these changes, such as weight gain, graying hair, and wrinkles, while unwelcome and unsettling perhaps, have no effect on learning. The changes that can affect learning, such as deterioration of sight and hearing, changes in reaction time, and cardiovascular disease, vary widely from person to person. That is, not all adults will lose their hearing, be unable to complete a task in a specified time, or be impaired by a stroke. Furthermore, we know that adults compensate for physical changes such that learning may not seem affected at all.

Psychological changes in adulthood have been charted by a number of researchers. This work can be loosely grouped into three categories: that which focuses on sequential patterns of development, life events, and transitions. The sequential development theories of Levinson, Gould, Erikson, Kohlberg, and others attempt to delineate the common themes of adult life according to what age or stage of life one is in. The characteristics and concerns of a particular stage of life have been linked to learning through what Havighurst (1972) called the "teachable moment." An alternative to the sequential pattern approach is the life event framework. Life events are happenings that shape the context of people's lives and also precipitate learning. Transitions have been connected to both the sequential pattern and the life event paradigms, but they have also been studied in their own right and have been linked to adult learning by several authors.

The third perspective reviewed in this chapter focuses on how social and cultural factors influence development in adulthood. From this perspective, change in adulthood is determined as much by the sociocultural context as by individual maturation. Socialization experiences and social roles are key concepts in understanding change and its relationship to learning. Emerging research from this perspective has quite naturally led to cross-cultural comparisons of change and development in adulthood.

The material on adult development presented in this chapter was selected for its relevance to learning in adulthood. This information is obviously somewhat fragmented, since it represents a variety of perspectives that have yet to be integrated into a holistic picture of adulthood. Nevertheless, the more we know about adult learners, the changes they go through, and how these changes motivate and interact with learning, the better we can structure learning experiences that both respond to and stimulate development.

PART THREE

The Learning Process

Understanding learning in adulthood is like piecing together a puzzle—there are many parts that must be fitted together before a total picture emerges. The individual learner and the context in which the learning takes place are key pieces of this puzzle. A third piece is the learning process. To be better learners ourselves, and to be better facilitators of other people's learning, we need to understand how learning occurs and whether or not adults learn differently than children. Do adults have different capabilities and ways of processing material? If so, how do these differences affect the adult's ability to learn? These crucial questions are addressed in the following chapters.

Part Three opens with a chapter reviewing four traditional theories of learning. Beginning with the earliest developed orientation to learning, behaviorism, the chapter goes on to review cognitivism, humanism, and social learning theory. These orientations offer very different explanations of learning. Each also encompasses several individual theorists who are closely aligned in terms of their assumptions—for example, a behaviorist orientation includes the theories of Thorndike, Hull, Skinner, Tolman, and Guthrie. These four orientations are assessed for their contribution to our understanding of learning in adulthood.

Chapter Eight focuses on the concept of intelligence. Beginning with the early work of Thorndike, researchers and educators alike have sought to understand the nature of adult intelligence and how it might be affected by the aging process.

This chapter traces the development of the concept of intelligence, highlighting the theories that have helped to clarify the nature of adult intelligence. In general, the movement has been from viewing intelligence as a single general trait to a more multifaceted construct. Also explored are the means of assessing intelligence in adulthood and the shortcomings of the present measurement tools. The relationship of intelligence to memory, information processing, and cognition is so complex that researchers have yet to agree on their definition of the concepts let alone how the various processes may interact.

Chapter Nine focuses on memory and cognition. After reviewing how memory works, we turn to the different components of memory, short-term and long-term memory, and how age may or may not affect an adult's ability to remember. Other important aspects of cognition are schema theory, how prior knowledge and experience affect learning, and the differences between cognitive style and learning style. Although the major work in cognition has been done with children and computers, many educators have generalized the findings to include learning in adulthood without the necessary verification studies. Therefore, the focus of this chapter is on work primarily oriented toward adult learning. In exploring this material, the importance of the social and cultural context of learning emerges as a major variable that affects cognition in adulthood.

The last chapter in Part Three explores cognitive development in adulthood—that is, how adults' thinking patterns change over time. Beginning with a discussion of the pioneering work of Piaget, we then present alternative models of adult cognitive development. Dialectical thinking, characterized by the acceptance of alternative truths and ways of thinking about similar phenomena in adult life, is explored as one of the major schemas of mature adult thought. Among the works discussed are those of Riegel, Basseches, Perry, and Labouvie-Vief. Finally, we consider one of the hallmarks of adult thought: wisdom.

Seven

Key Theories
of Learning

Learning, so central to human behavior yet so elusive to understanding, has fascinated thinkers as far back as Plato and Aristotle. Indeed, the views of these two men underpin much modern-day research on learning conducted by psychologists and educators. The fact that so many people have thought about, investigated, and written about the process of learning over the years suggests the complexity of the topic. Learning defies easy definition and simple theorizing. This chapter reviews some of the major ways learning has been studied and delineates the contributions these orientations have made to our understanding of learning in adulthood.

Originally, learning was within the purview of philosophical investigations into the nature of knowledge, the human mind, and what it means to know. As mentioned above, Plato and Aristotle's views about how we know something underlie contemporary learning theory. Plato believed that the physical objects in our everyday world have corresponding abstract forms that we can come to know "by reflecting on the contents of one's mind" (Hergenhahn, 1988, p. 31). Aristotle, on the other hand, believed that all knowledge comes through the senses; these sense impressions can be pondered upon "to discover the lawfulness that runs through them" (p. 33). Plato's "rationalism" can be seen in Gestalt and cognitive psychology; Aristotle's "empiricism" is particularly evident in early behavioral psychology. Later philosophers presented variations on these two basic positions, ranging from Descartes's separation of mind and body to Kant's notion of innate mental faculties.

It was not until the nineteenth century that the study of the mind, of how people know, and, by extension, of behavior, became "scientifically" investigated. Hergenhahn (1988) writes that Hermann Ebbinghaus "emancipated psychology from philosophy by demonstrating that the 'higher mental processes' of learning and memory could be studied experimentally" and that many of his findings on learning and memory published in 1885 are still valid today (p. 42). Another pioneer, Wilhelm Wundt, set up the first psychological laboratory in Leipzig in 1879 and investigated how experience was assimilated "into the knowledge structures one already had" (Di Vesta, 1987, p. 206). By the turn of the century, systematic investigations into human learning were well under way in both Europe and North America.

Learning and Learning Theories

Although learning has been defined in a variety of ways, most definitions include the concepts of behavioral change and experience. A common definition from psychologists, especially those who were investigating the phenomenon until the 1950s, is that learning is a change in behavior. This definition, however, fails to capture some of the complexities involved — such as whether one needs to perform in order for learning to have occurred or whether all human behavior is learned. The notion of change still underlies most definitions of learning, although it has been modified to include the *potential* for change. Likewise, the idea that having an experience of some sort, rather than learning as a function of maturation, is important. Thus a reasonable definition of learning would be: "Learning is a relatively permanent change in behavior or in behavioral potentiality that results from experience and cannot be attributed to temporary body states such as those induced by illness, fatigue, or drugs" (Hergenhahn, 1988, p. 7). Or as stated more simply by Maples and Webster (1980): "Learning can be thought of as a process by which behavior changes as a result of experiences" (p. 1).

Learning as a process (rather than an end product) focuses on *what happens* when the learning takes place. Explanations of what happens are called learning theories, and it is these theories that are the subject of this chapter. There are, however, many explanations of learning, some more comprehensive than others, that are called theories. How the knowledge base in this area is divided and labeled depends on the writer. Hilgard and Bower (1966), for example, review eleven learning theories and then note that they fall into two major families: stimulus-response theories and cognitive theories. Knowles (1984) uses Reese and Overton's (1970) organization in which learning theories are grouped according to two different worldviews: mechanistic and organismic.

Since there is little consensus on how many learning theories there are or how they should be grouped for discussion, we have organized this chapter according to orientations that present very different assumptions about learning and offer helpful insights into adult learning. With these criteria in mind, four basic orientations have been selected for discussion: behaviorist, cognitivist, humanist, and social learning. As Hill (1977) has observed: "For most of us, the various learning theories have two chief values. One is in providing us with a vocabulary and a conceptual framework for interpreting the examples of learning that we observe. These are valuable for anyone who is alert to the world. The other, closely related, is in suggesting where to look for solutions to practical problems. The theories do not give us solutions, but they do direct our attention to those variables that are crucial in finding solutions" (p. 261). For the four orientations examined in this chapter, the following topics are covered: the major proponents, the view of the learning process itself, the purpose of education, the role of the teacher, and the ways in which these theories are manifested in adult learning. A summary of this information can be found in Table 7.1 at the end of the chapter.

The Behaviorist Orientation

Behaviorism is a well-known orientation to learning that encompasses a number of individual theories. Founded by John

B. Watson in the early decades of the twentieth century, behaviorism loosely encompasses the work of such people as Thorndike, Tolman, Guthrie, Hull, and Skinner (Sahakian, 1984). What characterizes these investigators is their underlying assumptions about the process of learning. In essence, three basic assumptions are held to be true. First, observable behavior rather than internal thought processes is the focus of study; in particular, learning is manifested by a change in behavior. Second, the environment shapes one's behavior; what one learns is determined by the elements in the environment, not by the individual learner. And third, the principles of contiguity (how close in time two events must be for a bond to be formed) and reinforcement (any means of increasing the likelihood that an event will be repeated) are central to explaining the learning process (Grippin and Peters, 1984).

Edward L. Thorndike, a contemporary of Watson, is "perhaps the greatest learning theorist of all time" (Hergenhahn, 1988, p. 55). A prolific researcher and writer, "he did pioneer work not only in learning theory but also in the areas of educational practices, verbal behavior, comparative psychology, intelligence testing, the nature-nurture problem, transfer of training, and the application of quantitative measures to sociopsychological problems" (p. 55). His major contribution to understanding learning has come to be called connectionism, or the S-R theory of learning. Using animals in controlled experiments, Thorndike noted that through repeated trial-and-error learning, certain connections between sensory impressions or stimuli (S) and subsequent behavior or responses (R) are strengthened or weakened by the consequences of behavior. Thorndike formulated three laws of learning to explain his findings. The Law of Effect states that learners will acquire and remember responses that lead to satisfying aftereffects. The Law of Exercise asserts that the repetition of a meaningful connection results in substantial learning. The Law of Readiness notes that if the organism is ready for the connection, learning is enhanced; if not, learning is inhibited (Hergenhahn, 1988). While these laws were modified by Thorndike himself and later researchers, they are nevertheless still applied widely in educational settings.

Thorndike's connectionism became refined and expanded

upon by his contemporaries and by those who followed. Pavlov, for example, working in Russia, added concepts of reinforcement, conditioned stimulus, and extinction to the basic notion of the stimulus-response connection. Guthrie stated that one law of learning based on contiguity is all that is needed to make learning comprehensible: "Whatever you do in the presence of a stimulus, you do again when that stimulus is re-presented" (Grippen and Peters, 1984, p. 61). Tolman introduced the notion that learning occurs in relation to purpose and that there are intervening variables between a stimulus and a response. Hull expanded Tolman's concept of intervening variables and proposed that a response depends on such factors as habit, strength, drive, and motivation. Important as the work of these researchers was (see Hergenhahn, 1988, or Sahakian, 1984, for detailed discussions), behaviorism was most developed as a theory of learning by B. F. Skinner.

Skinner's major contribution to understanding learning is known as operant conditioning. Simply stated, operant conditioning means "reinforce what you want the individual to do again; ignore what you want the individual to stop doing" (Grippen and Peters, 1984, p. 65). Reinforcement is essential to understanding operant conditioning. If behavior is reinforced or rewarded, the response is more likely to occur again under like conditions. Behavior that is not reinforced is likely to become less frequent and may even disappear. Within this framework, even something as complex as personality can be explained by operant conditioning. Personality, according to Skinner, is a "repertoire of behavior imported by an organized set of contingencies"—in effect, a personal history of reinforcements (1974, p. 149). Skinner's research concentrated on positive and negative reinforcement schedules, the timing of reinforcements, and avoidance behavior. In essence, his work indicates that since all behavior is learned, behavior can be determined by arranging the contingencies of reinforcement in the learner's immediate environment. Behaviorists since Skinner have taken into account certain aspects of the human organism but still emphasize that it is environment which controls behavior, "not some mechanism within the individual" (Grippin and Peters, 1984, p. 71).

The behaviorist orientation to learning underlies much educátional practice, including adult learning. Skinner in particular has addressed the application of his theory to educational issues. As he sees it, the ultimate goal of education is to bring about behavior that will ensure survival of the human species, societies, and individuals (Skinner, 1971). The teacher's role is to design an environment that elicits desired behavior toward meeting these goals and to extinguish behavior that is not desirable. Several educational practices can be traced to this type of learning. The systematic design of instruction, behavioral objectives, notions of the instructor's accountability, programmed instruction, computer-assisted instruction, competency-based education, and so on are solidly grounded in behavioral learning theory. Adult vocational and skills training—in which the learning task is broken into segments or tasks and there is a 'correct response,' which is rewarded"—in particular draws from behaviorism (Cross, 1981, p. 233). Thus the behavioral orientation to learning has had a profound effect on our educational system. It has also been challenged by theorists from two radically different perspectives: cognitivism and humanism.

The Cognitive Orientation

The earliest challenge to the behaviorists came in a publication in 1929 by Bode, a Gestalt psychologist. He criticized behaviorists for being too particularistic, too concerned with single events and actions, and too dependent on overt behavior to explain learning. Gestalt (a German word meaning pattern or shape) psychologists proposed looking at the whole rather than its parts, at patterns rather than isolated events. Through the research of Gestaltists Wertheimer, Kohler, Koffka, and later Lewin (Hergenhahn, 1988), Gestalt views of learning rivaled behaviorism by the mid-twentieth century. These views have been incorporated into what have come to be labeled as cognitive or information-processing learning theories.

Perception, insight, and meaning are key contributions to cognitivism from Gestalt learning theorists. According to cognitivists, "The human mind is not simply a passive exchange-terminal system where the stimuli arrive and the appropriate response leaves. Rather, the thinking person interprets sensations and gives meaning to the events that impinge upon his consciousness" (Grippen and Peters, 1984, p. 76). Learning involves the reorganization of experiences in order to make sense of stimuli from the environment. Sometimes this sense comes through flashes of insight. Hergenhahn (1988, p. 252) summarizes the learning process according to Gestalt psychology: "Learning, to the Gestaltist, is a cognitive phenomenon. The organism 'comes to see' the solution after pondering a problem. The learner thinks about all the ingredients necessary to solve a problem and puts them together (cognitively) first one way and then another until the problem is solved. When the solution comes, it comes suddenly, that is, the organism gains an *insight* into the solution of a problem. The problem can exist in only two states: (a) unsolved and (b) solved; there is no state of partial solution in between." A major difference between Gestaltists and behaviorists, therefore, is the locus of control over the learning activity. For Gestaltists it lies with the individual learner; for behaviorists it lies with the environment. This shift to the individual — and in particular to the learner's mental processes — is characteristic of cognitivist-oriented learning theories.

A cognitive psychologist who clarified the focus on internal cognitive processes was Jean Piaget (1966). Influenced by both the behaviorist and Gestalt schools of thought, Piaget proposed that one's internal cognitive structure changed partly as a result of maturational changes in the nervous system and partly as a result of the organism interacting with the environment and being exposed to an increasing number of experiences. His four-stage theory of cognitive development and its implications for adult learning are discussed more fully in Chapter Nine.

Currently, a number of research and theory-building efforts take as their starting point the mental processes involved in learning. These efforts include information processing theories, work on memory and metacognition, theories of transfer, mathematical learning theory models, the study of expertise, computer simulations, and artificial intelligence. Converging with cognitive learning theory are theories of instruction that attempt to unite what is known about learning with the best way to facilitate its occurrence. Ausubel, Bruner, and Gagne are good examples of how the understanding of mental processes can be linked to instruction.

Ausubel (1967) distinguishes between meaningful learning and rote learning. He suggests that learning is meaningful only when it can be related to concepts which already exist in a person's cognitive structure. Rote learning, on the other hand, does not become linked to a person's cognitive structure and hence is easily forgotten. Also unique is Ausubel's notion of "reception" learning. New knowledge is processed by the learner "only to the extent that more inclusive and appropriately relevant concepts are already available in the cognitive structure to serve a subsuming role or to provide definitional anchorage" (1967, p. 222). He suggests the use of "advance organizers" to prepare a person for new learning (1968). Ausubel's work can be seen as an antecedent to current research on schema theory wherein schemata—structures that organize the learner's worldview—in turn determine how new experiences are processed (Di Vesta, 1987; Greeno, 1980).

Ausubel emphasizes the importance of the learner's cognitive structure in new learning. Bruner, whose views are often contrasted with Ausubel's, emphasizes learning through discovery. Discovery is "in its essence a matter of rearranging or transforming evidence in such a way that one is enabled to go beyond the evidence so reassembled to additional new insights" (Bruner, 1965, pp. 607–608). According to Knowles (1984), Bruner's instructional theory is based on a theory about the act of learning that involves "three almost simultaneous processes: (1) acquisition of new information . . . ; (2) transformation, or the process of manipulating knowledge to make it fit new tasks; and (3) evaluation, or checking whether the way we have manipulated information is adequate to the task" (p. 25).

Linking the acquisition and processing of knowledge to instruction has probably been most thoroughly developed by Gagne and Briggs (1979). They contend that there are eight different types of knowledge, each of which has appropriate instructional procedures. The eight types of learning are signal learning, stimulus-response, motor training, verbal association, discrimination learning, concept learning, rule learning, and problem solving (Gagne and Briggs, 1979). Kidd (1973, p. 182) points out that the work of Gagne and others has been an important influence on the "learning how to learn" concept. This concept has been explored in some depth by Smith (1982, 1987), who has been particularly interested in applying it to adult learning. According to Smith: "Learning how to learn involves possessing, or acquiring, the knowledge and skill to learn effectively in whatever learning situation one encounters" (1982, p. 19). Three subconcepts are involved: learners' needs, a person's learning style, and training, which is organized activity, or instruction, to increase competence in learning. In addition to Smith's work on learning how to learn, the cognitive orientation can be seen in two other areas that have particular relevance for adult learning. First, interest in cognitive development in adulthood has been the subject of recent research (see Chapter Ten); second, the study of learning processes as a function of age (see Chapters Eight and Ten) draws from the cognitive focus on learning.

In summary, cognitively oriented explanations of learning encompass a wide range of topics. What unites these various approaches is the focus on internal mental processes that are within the learner's control. Di Vesta (1987, p. 229) has summarized recent directions in cognitive learning: "It is apparent that the current cognitive movement, rather than seeking the general all-encompassing laws for controlling and predicting behavior, as did the earlier grand theories of learning, is directed toward miniature models of specific facets of cognition, such as models of discourse analysis, models of comprehension, ways of aiding understanding and meaningful learning, the nature of the schemata, the memory system, the development of cognitive skills, and the like."

The Humanist Orientation

In contrast to behaviorist theories that concentrate on observable behavior shaped by environmental forces, as well as cog-

nitivist theories that deal with the mental processing of information, humanist theories consider learning from the perspective of
the human potential for growth. The shift to the study of the affective as well as cognitive dimensions of learning was in part informed by Freud's psychoanalytic approach to human behavior.
Though most would not label Freud a learning theorist, aspects
of his psychology such as the influence of the subconscious mind
on behavior, as well as the concepts of anxiety, repression,
defense mechanism, drives, and transference, have found their
way into some learning theories. Sahakian (1984), in fact, makes
the case for psychoanalytic therapy as a type of learning theory.

Despite Freud's focus on personality, humanists reject the
view of human nature implied by both behaviorists and Freudian
psychologists. Identifying their orientation as a "third force,"
humanists refuse to accept the notion that behavior is predetermined by either the environment or one's subconscious. Rather,
human beings can control their own destiny; people are inherently good and will strive for a better world; people are free to
act, and behavior is the consequence of human choice; people
possess unlimited potential for growth and development (Rogers,
1983; Maslow, 1970). From a learning theory perspective, humanism emphasizes a person's perceptions that are centered in
experience, as well as the freedom and responsibility to become
what one is capable of becoming. These tenets underlie much of
adult learning theory that stresses the self-directedness of adults
and the value of experience in the learning process. Two psychologists who have contributed the most to our understanding of
learning from this perspective are Abraham Maslow and Carl
Rogers.

Maslow (1970), considered to be the founder of humanistic
psychology, proposed a theory of human motivation based on
a hierarchy of needs. At the lowest level of the hierarchy are
physiological needs such as hunger and thirst, which must be
attended to before one can deal with safety needs—those dealing with security and protection. The remaining levels involve
belonging and love, self-esteem, and, finally, the need for self-
actualization. This need can be seen in a person's desire to become all that he or she is capable of becoming. The motiva-

tion to learn is intrinsic; it emanates from the learner. For Maslow self-actualization is the goal of learning and educators should strive to bring this about. As Sahakian (1984) notes, learning from Maslow's point of view is itself "a form of self-actualization. Among the growth motivations was found the need for cognition, the desire to know and to understand. Learning is not only a form of psychotherapy . . . , but learning contributes to psychological health" (p. 438). While self-actualization is the primary goal of learning, there are other goals (p. 439):

1. The discovery of a vocation or destiny
2. The knowledge or acquisition of a set of values
3. The realization of life as precious
4. The acquisition of peak experiences
5. A sense of accomplishment
6. The satisfaction of psychological needs
7. The refreshing of consciousness to an awareness of the beauty and wonder of life
8. The control of impulses
9. The grappling with the critical existential problems of life
10. Learning to choose judiciously

Another major figure writing from a humanist orientation is Carl Rogers. His book *Freedom to Learn for the 80's* (1983) lays out his theory of learning, which he sees as a similar process in both therapy and education. In fact, his "client-centered therapy" is often equated with student-centered learning. In both education and therapy, Rogers is concerned with significant learning that leads to personal growth and development. Such learning has the following characteristics (p. 20):

1. Personal involvement—the affective and cognitive aspects of a person should be involved in the learning event.
2. Self-initiated—a sense of discovery must come from within.
3. Pervasive—the learning makes a difference in the behavior, the attitudes, perhaps even the personality of the learner.
4. Evaluated by the learner—the learner can best determine whether the experience is meeting a need.

5. Essence is meaning—when experiential learning takes place, its meaning to the learner becomes incorporated into the total experience.

Quite clearly, Rogers's principles of significant learning and Maslow's views have been integrated into much of adult learning. Knowles's theory of andragogy (see Chapter Thirteen) and much of the research and writing on self-directed learning (see Chapters Three and Eleven) are grounded in humanistic learning theories. Moreover, humanistic theories have the potential for designing a true learning society, since "there is a natural tendency for people to learn and that learning will flourish if nourishing, encouraging environments are provided" (Cross, 1981, p. 228).

A Social Learning Orientation

The fourth and final set of learning theories to be discussed in this chapter draw from, yet differ significantly from, the behaviorist, cognitivist, and humanist orientations. Quite simply, social learning theory posits that people learn from observing other people. By definition, such observations take place in a social setting—hence the label "observational" or "social" learning (Lefrancois, 1982). Just *how* the learning occurs has been the subject of several investigations.

Miller and Dollard in the 1940s were the first to explore how people learn through observation. Drawing from stimulus-response and reinforcement theory, they argued that people do not learn from observation alone—rather, what has been observed must be imitated and reinforced. "If imitative responses were not made and reinforced, no learning would take place. For them, imitative learning was the result of observation, overt responding, and reinforcement" (Hergenhahn, 1988, p. 321). Their ideas were of course totally congruent with the behaviorist orientation to learning. Their main contribution was to demonstrate that "social-personality phenomena could be described and explained with the more objective and reliable concepts of a learning theory" (Phares, 1980, p. 412). Not until the 1960s, however, with the work of Bandura, did social learning theory break from a purely behaviorist orientation.

Bandura focused more on the cognitive processes involved in the observation than on the subsequent behavior. Central to his theory is the separation of observation from the act of imitation. One can learn from observation, he maintains, without having to imitate what was observed (Hergenhahn, 1988). In fact, the learning can be vicarious: "Virtually all learning phenomena resulting from direct experiences can occur on a vicarious basis through observation of other people's behavior and its consequences for the observer" (Bandura, 1976, p. 392). In addition to being cognitive and vicarious, Bandura's observational learning is characterized by the concept of self-regulation. He contends that "persons can regulate their own behavior to some extent by visualizing self-generated consequences" (p. 392).

Observational learning is influenced by the four processes of attention, retention or memory, behavioral rehearsal, and motivation (Hergenhahn, 1988). Before something can be learned, the model must be attended to; some models are more likely than others to be attended to such as those thought to be competent, powerful, attractive, and so on. Information from an observation then needs to be retained or stored for future use: "Symbols retained from a modeling experience act as a template with which one's actions are compared. During this rehearsal process individuals observe their own behavior and compare it to their cognitive representation of the modeled experience" (Hergenhahn, 1988, p. 327). Finally, the modeled behavior is stored until a person is motivated to act upon it.

Bandura's theory has particular relevance to adult learning in that it accounts for both the learner and the environment in which he or she operates. Behavior is a function of the interaction of the person with the environment. This is a reciprocal concept in that people influence their environment, which in turn influences the way they behave. This three-way interactive model is pictured by Bandura as a triangle (Bandura, 1986; Staddon, 1984). Learning is set solidly within a social context.

The importance of the social situation in learning has been

further developed by Rotter (1954) whose theory includes strands from behaviorism, cognitivism, and personality theory. Rotter's theory is framed by seven propositions and attendant corollaries that delineate relationships among the concepts of behavior, personality, experience, and environment. Rotter's theory assumes "that much of human behavior takes place in a meaningful environment and is acquired through social interactions with other people" (Phares, 1980, p. 406). Key to understanding "which behavior (once acquired) in the individual's repertoire will occur in a given situation" (p. 407) are the concepts of expectancy and reinforcement. Expectancy is the likelihood that a particular reinforcement will occur as the result of specific behavior: "The way in which the person construes or psychologically defines the situation will affect the values of both reinforcement and expectancy thereby influencing the potential for any given behavior to occur" (p. 408). Phares notes that research on the ways in which expectancies "generalize and change" has been a major contribution to our understanding of the learning process (p. 426).

Several useful concepts emerge from social learning theory. For example, the motivation to engage in adult learning activities might be partly explained by Rotter's (1954) notion that "people tend to ascribe their successes and failures to internal or external causes. Thus, there appear to be a personality type whose *locus of control* (Rotter's terminology) is external and another type that is more internally oriented" (Lefrancois, 1982, p. 266). Another connection to adult learning is the importance of context and the learner's interaction with the environment to explain behavior. That is, explanations of learning may need to focus on more than overt behavior, mental processes, or personality. Studying the interaction of all these factors may result in a more comprehensive explanation of how adults learn. Moreover, Bandura's work on observational learning and modeling provides insights into social role acquisition and the nature of mentoring, a topic recently explored in depth by Daloz (1986).

Summary

Learning, a process central to human behavior, has been of interest to philosophers, psychologists, educators, and politicians for centuries. Beginning in the late nineteenth century, the systematic investigation of this phenomenon has resulted in many explanations of how people learn. This chapter has reviewed some of these theories. Since there are dozens of learning theories and volumes written describing them, we have explored different *orientations* to learning, any of which might include numerous learning theories. The behaviorist, cognitivist, humanist, and social learning orientations were chosen for their diversity and for their insights into learning in adulthood. Table 7.1 summarizes these four orientations. Since each is based on different assumptions about the nature of learning, the strategies one might use to enhance learning will depend on one's orientation. Instructors and program developers can use this review of major learning theories to identify their own theory of learning and discover the strategies for facilitating learning that are most congruent with their theory.

In brief, behaviorists define learning as a change in behavior. The focus of their research is overt behavior, which is a measurable response to stimuli in the environment. The role of the teacher is to arrange the contingencies of reinforcement in the learning environment so that the desired behavior will occur. Findings from behavioral learning theories can be seen in training and vocational adult education.

In contrast to behaviorists, researchers working from a cognitivist perspective focus not on external behavior but on internal mental processes. Cognitivists are interested in how the mind makes sense out of stimuli in the environment — how information is processed, stored, and retrieved. This orientation is especially evident in the study of adult learning from a developmental perspective. The major concerns are how aging affects an adult's ability to process and retrieve information and how it affects an adult's internal mental structures.

Also in contrast to behaviorism is the humanistic orientation to learning. Here the emphasis is on human nature, human potential, human emotions and affect. Theorists in this tradition believe that learning involves more than cognitive processes and overt behavior. It is a function of motivation and involves choice and responsibility. Much of adult learning theory, especially the concepts of andragogy and self-directed learning, are grounded in humanistic assumptions.

Table 7.1. Four Orientations to Learning.

Aspect	Behaviorist	Cognitivist	Humanist	Social Learning
Learning theorists	Thorndike, Pavlov, Watson, Guthrie, Hull, Tolman, Skinner	Koffka, Kohler, Lewin, Piaget, Ausubel, Bruner, Gagne	Maslow, Rogers	Bandura, Rotter
View of the learning process	Change in behavior	Internal mental process (including insight, information processing, memory, perception)	A personal act to fulfill potential	Interaction with and observation of others in a social context
Locus of learning	Stimuli in external environment	Internal cognitive structuring	Affective and cognitive needs	Interaction of person, behavior, and environment
Purpose of education	Produce behavioral change in desired direction	Develop capacity and skills to learn better	Become self-actualized, autonomous	Model new roles and behavior
Teacher's role	Arranges environment to elicit desired response	Structures content of learning activity	Facilitates development of whole person	Models and guides new roles and behavior
Manifestation in adult learning	• Behavioral objectives • Competency-based education • Skill development and training	• Cognitive development • Intelligence, learning, and memory as function of age • Learning how to learn	• Andragogy • Self-directed learning	• Socialization • Social roles • Mentoring • Locus of control

The fourth and final orientation discussed here is social learning. This perspective differs from the other three in its focus on the social setting in which learning occurs. From this perspective learning occurs through the observation of people in one's immediate environment. Furthermore, learning is a function of the interaction of the person, the environment, and the behavior. Variations in behavior under the same circumstances can be explained by idiosyncratic personality traits and their unique interaction with environmental stimuli. Social learning theories contribute to adult learning by highlighting the importance of social context and explicating the processes of modeling and mentoring.

Eight

Age and Intelligence

The old adage that "you can't teach an old dog new tricks" still pops up in the minds of both instructors of adults and adult learners themselves as they set forth on new learning ventures. The image of the office worker who exclaims she is "just too old to use that newfangled computer" is still a reality. So, too, is the young trainer, fresh out of graduate school, who secretly believes she will never be able to teach this entrenched office staff anything, let alone how to use a new computer system. This powerful myth — that adults lose their ability to learn as they age — still prevails, although for the most part it has not been substantiated in the literature.

Intelligence is defined in a number of ways. From the perspective of the casual observer, intelligence is often equated with "being smart" — that is, being able to act intelligently when dealing with everyday life. But there is also another definition of intelligence that most adults have carried with them since their elementary school days — intelligence is a specific measurement of the ability to learn. Although many adults may not actually know their IQ scores, they often have vague recollections of being labeled an "average student," with some perhaps being "above average" and others "below." This view of intelligence as a measurable quality has predominated in the study of intelligence over the life span (Schaie and Willis, 1986).

Beginning with the early work of Thorndike, researchers have sought to understand the nature of adult intelligence and how it might be affected by the aging process. This chapter traces the development of the concept of intelligence in adulthood. Highlighted in the next section are representative theories that have been used to clarify the nature of adult intelligence. This discussion is followed by an examination of how intelligence in adulthood is assessed. The chapter concludes with a review of what happens to intelligence as people age.

Concept of Intelligence

Intelligence has most often been studied from what has been termed the psychometric tradition. This tradition, which will be addressed fully in the next section, assumes that intelligence is a measurable construct. Some who have studied intelligence, such as Binet and Stern (Schaie and Willis, 1986; Hayslip and Panek, 1989), describe it as a single factor termed the "general ability" or "*g*" factor. This means that a person's "performance on many different types of tests (vocabulary, arithmetic, object assembly, block design) can be explained in terms of a *single* underlying ability" (Hayslip and Panek, 1989, p. 197). Therefore, scores from diverse tests or subscales can be combined to form an overall general score or index of intelligence quotient (IQ). Other models of intelligence (such as those of Thurstone and Thurstone, 1941; Guilford, 1967; Gardner, 1983) favor the notion of multiple factors of intelligence. "The 'purest' tests of these factors are sometimes administered as tests of the 'primary mental abilities'" (Schaie and Willis, 1986, p. 290) consisting of spatial ability, perceptual speed, numerical ability, verbal relations, words, memory, and induction. Another recent research trend has been to explore whether intelligence is related to competence for everyday living (see Sternberg, 1985, 1990c; Sternberg and Wagner, 1986; Schaie, 1987).

The Early Work on Adult Intelligence. The first extensive study of adult intelligence was completed by E. L. Thorndike and colleagues (1928). This pioneering work, grounded in the idea that intelligence consists of a number of factors, challenged the fundamental notion that learning ability peaks very early in life. Using primarily laboratory or schoolroom tasks, Thorndike measured the speed of the performance of people from fourteen to

fifty years of age on a variety of tasks from memorizing poetry
to acquiring an artificial language (Kidd, 1973). Thorndike concluded from his many studies that, "in general, teachers of adults
of age twenty-five to forty-five should expect them to learn at
nearly the same rate and in nearly the same manner as they
would have learned the same thing at twenty" (1928, pp. 178–
179). In reflecting on Thorndike's work, Kidd (1973) noted two
major contributions. The first was to raise the ceiling of the
downhill slide of a person's ability to learn from twenty years
of age to forty-five. Second, and even more important, Thorndike "helped stimulate colleagues to reject traditional views and
formulas" (p. 79) about learning in adulthood. Other noted
studies of adult intelligence (Jones and Conrad, 1933; Miles and
Miles, 1932) of the same era reached similar conclusions, "although they found that the decline begins at a later age and the
rate of that decline is not as sharp as in 'Thorndike's curve'"
(Cross, 1981, p. 158).

     Another strong influence on our view of intelligence in
adulthood was the work of Wechsler (1958). Wechsler created
one of the most often used instruments to measure adult capacity for learning, the Wechsler Adult Intelligence Scale (WAIS).
This scale, which is described in greater detail later in the chapter, consists of a variety of timed and untimed subtests ranging
from tests of vocabulary to object assembly. Wechsler himself
believed, after numerous administrations of the test, that one's
mental ability as a whole declines with age in a similar fashion
to the rest of one's body (Kidd, 1973; Schaie and Willis, 1986).
On closer examination of both earlier and later WAIS test
results, however, it became apparent to both Wechsler and others
that the decline in intellectual functions was not equal for all
tasks: "In general, scores on performance tests [did] show a loss,
but not on the verbal tests" (Kidd, 1973, p. 81). One key was
that "the subtests in which older subjects do poorly are all
'speeded' tests" (Schaie and Willis, 1986). These conflicting
results raised numerous questions about the true nature of adult
intelligence that are still being debated today. Are verbal tests
more appropriate measures of intelligence in adulthood than
performance tests? Is a timed task as valid as an untimed task?

Another early voice that echoed these concerns about the conventional measures of adult intelligence was that of Lorge. In a series of articles published in the 1940s, Lorge (1944, 1947) highlighted a number of problems with the research on adult intelligence up to that time. Among these were the "relationship of previous education and skills to measurement of adult intelligence; the factorial composition of adult intelligence tests; . . . and the standardization and norming of adult intelligence" (Lorge, 1944, p. 438). His most serious criticism, however, was that "conventional speeded tests bias the results against adults" (Cross, 1981, p. 158). Lorge went on to demonstrate through his own work "that power tests (those deemphasizing speed) do not show the same decline as speeded tests" (Cross, 1981, p. 158). Although Lorge's work has not been totally confirmed, it did give reason to view adult intelligence as a somewhat different construct.

Cattell's Theory of Fluid and Crystallized Intelligence. One of the major changes in thinking about adult intelligence is grounded in the work of Cattell (1963, 1987). Although Cattell had presented his ideas about the existence of the crystallized (G_c) and fluid (G_f) abilities in the early 1940s, "it was not until 1965 that Cattell's doctoral student, John Horn, more or less popularized the theory based upon research with a wide variety of adults" (Hayslip and Panek, 1989, p. 200). Cattell conceptualized intelligence as consisting of two primary factors, each with differing origins. The first factor, fluid intelligence, "has more of the characteristics that used to be equated with the old 'innate' biologically determined concept of the IQ, whereas crystallized intelligence is influenced more heavily by education and experience" (Cross, 1981, p. 161). Both kinds of intelligence, however, "involve some similar processes such as perceiving relationships among items, abstract reasoning, concept formation, and problem solving" (Schulz and Ewen, 1988). In measuring these two forms of intelligence, fluid intelligence is most often associated with tests that assess such abilities as memory span and adaptation to new situations. These tests also tend to be speeded and at least labeled as "culture-fair" tests. In contrast, crystallized

intelligence is more likely to be assessed by nonspeeded measures "calling for judgment, knowledge, and experience—tests
such as vocabulary, general information, and arithmetic reasoning" (Cross, 1981, p. 161).

The consensus has been that fluid intelligence tends to
peak in early adolescence (approximately age fourteen), whereas
crystallized intelligence "generally increases and/or remains stable over most of the adult years" (Hayslip and Panek, 1989, p.
200). Recently there has been debate about whether the loss of
fluid intelligence is inevitable as we age. Baltes and Willis (1982),
for example, assuming that fluid abilities are more than neu-
rophysiological in nature and therefore amenable to training,
have been researching ways to improve the fluid abilities of older
adults. If this conceptualization of intelligence as two distinct
factors is accepted—which it is not in all circles (Guilford, 1967;
Schaie and Willis, 1986; Hayslip and Panek, 1989)—the result
is a rather stable and positive view of adult intelligence. The
basic premise, that what is lost in our fluid intelligence can be
at least partly regained through training or compensated for by
our crystallized intelligence, has a sense of "commonsense credi-
bility." As observed by Cross (1981), research tends to confirm
this sense: "On the average people seem to perform best in their
youth on tasks requiring quick insight, short-term memorization, and complex interactions. As people get older, they accumulate knowledge and develop perspective and experience
in the use and application of it" (p. 162). This same idea has
been aptly summarized by Knox—as adults age, they may "sub-
stitute wisdom for brilliance" (1977, p. 421).

Guilford's Structure of Intellect Model. In contrast to the two-
factor model of fluid and crystallized intelligence proposed by
Cattell, Guilford's model (1967) consists of 120 theoretical factors clustered into three major categories. These categories, seen
as independent of each other, include (1) contents, referring
to the type of material being tested such as verbal, numerical,
and behavioral; (2) operations, which are the basic mental processes such as memory, reasoning, and creative thinking; and
(3) product, referring to the form of information that results

from the interactions of the other two categories (from single units to complex patterns of information). A key assumption underlying the model is that the mental operations used on a particular task are as important as the nature of the task itself. Guilford's model offers researchers an alternative frame of reference about the human intellect upon which hypotheses can be generated about new factors of intelligence (Guilford, 1967; Huyck and Hoyer, 1982). Therefore, the model continues to provide a major building block for expanding our thinking about the fundamental nature of human intelligence.

Some, however, have expressed reservations about the theory's utility: "While Guilford's theory of intelligence has generated a great deal of research, the structure of intellect model has for the most part yet to be integrated into adult developmental research on intelligence" (Hayslip and Panek, 1989, p. 198). The noted exception has been the studies on "divergent thinking" (the ability to produce alternative ideas or solutions). For example, in cross-sectional comparisons of the creative process and products of younger versus older adult women, Alpaugh, Parham, Cole, and Birren (1982) found a decline in divergent thinking abilities with age. They hypothesized that the older creator may rely "more on previous experiences than on present divergent thinking abilities, whereas younger creators draw more heavily on divergent thinking" (p. 112). Even though Guilford's model has not been used often by researchers of intelligence in adulthood, we believe the model, especially the notion of both the multiple and interacting factors of intelligence, may prove useful in future research and theory building on adult learning.

Gardner's Theory of Multiple Intelligences. In a similar vein, Gardner (1983, 1990) has proposed the "theory of multiple intelligences." From his perspective, the concept of intelligence has been too narrowly limited to the realm of logical and linguistic abilities, primarily by the way intelligence has been measured. Rather, he argues, "there is persuasive evidence for the existence of several relatively autonomous human intellectual competencies . . . that can be fashioned and combined in a multiplicity of adaptive ways by individuals and cultures" (pp. 8–9). From a number of unrelated sources, such as studies of prodigies, brain-damaged patients, and normal children and adults, Gardner has identified seven different forms of intelligence. (See Gardner, 1983, for a complete description.) These forms include "not only the standard academic ones of linguistic, logical-mathematical, and spatial (the visual skills exhibited by a painter or architect) but also musical, 'bodily-kinesthetic,' and two 'personal' intelligences involving a fine-tuned understanding of oneself and others" (Levine, 1987, p. 54).

In introducing this new theory, Gardner (1983, p. 280) stresses that "the idea of multiple intelligences is an old one" recognized even in early Greek times. In Gardner's framework, our tendency to label people as being in general bright, average, or dull just does not fit. Rather, a person may exhibit high intelligence in one or two areas, such as music and math, and yet demonstrate only average intelligence in other respects. In other words: "You can be smart in one thing and stupid in something else" (Levine, 1987, p. 54). This thinking seems to reflect similar themes emphasized by those studying cognitive processes (see Chapter Nine) to the effect that rules of learning may be more subject-specific than general in nature.

Gardner, in proposing this theory of multiple intelligences, is interested in both theory building within the purviews of cognitive and developmental psychology as well as examining the theory's educational implications. It is his hope that this conceptualization of intelligence may prove useful to policymakers and educators alike. Thus far the applications of his work have primarily concerned preschool and school-age children (Gardner and Hatch, 1989; Gardner, 1990), although it appears to have a definite utility for the study of learning in adulthood. Therefore, as in the case of Guilford's work, we see significant value in integrating Gardner's ideas into our study and practice of learning in adulthood.

Sternberg's Triarchic Theory of Intelligence. Sternberg (1985, 1986a, 1988, 1990c), like Gardner, has broken from the tradition of framing intelligence as primarily a measure of formal "testlike" problem solving to one that includes problem solving for everyday life. Unlike the "schooling world" where problems are usually highly definitive and structured, real-world issues tend to be both ill defined and contextualized. Therefore, Sternberg contends that most present-day theories, especially the measures of intelligence, address only the "schooling" kind of intelligence and almost totally ignore the notion of practical intelligence. Building on his earlier study of the componential theory of intelligence, which was grounded primarily in the information-processing framework, Sternberg has proposed a new triarchic theory of human intelligence.

According to Sternberg (1985, 1986a, 1990c), the triarchic theory is composed of three subtheories: a componential subtheory describing the internal mental mechanisms and processes involved in intelligence, an experiential subtheory focusing on how a person's experience with a set of tasks or situations may affect his handling of those tasks; and a contextual subtheory emphasizing the role of the external environment in determining what constitutes intelligent behavior in a situation. The first part of the subtheory, the mental mechanisms of intelligence, is posited as universal: "Although individuals may differ in what mental mechanisms they apply to a given task or situation, the potential set of mental mechanisms underlying intelligence is claimed to be the same across all individuals, social classes, and cultural groups" (Sternberg, 1986a, pp. 23–24). The other two parts of Sternberg's theory, which emphasize the experience of the learner and the real-world context, are seen as having both universal and relativistic components. The universal aspect has to do with the areas being studied within each of these subparts of the theory (such as the processes of automation, environmental adaptation, and shaping). These processes are seen as important no matter what the cultural milieu or the person's experience with the tasks or situations chosen to measure these aspects. The relativistic nature of these parts of the theory comes from the recognition that what constitutes intelligent behavior is not the same for all groups of people. As Sternberg puts it: "Parts of the theory are culturally universal, and parts are culturally relative" (1986a, p. 24).

Sisco (1989) offers an excellent overview of how Sternberg's triarchic theory may apply to adult learning. From Sisco's
perspective, "one of the most significant implications would appear to be something that many adult educators have believed,
at least implicitly, for a long time now: that human intelligence
is much more than performance on standardized tests and
achievement in schools" (p. 287). In taking this view, Sternberg
and Gardner offer similar observations — that intelligence consists
of not only the academic abilities, such as verbal and logical-mathematical skills, but also the capacity to perform in the everyday
world. Sternberg's notion of practical intelligence — "intelligence
as it operates in real-world contexts" (1986a, p. 301) — seems
especially useful in the pursuit of gaining a clearer picture of
adult intelligence.

A second major implication, cited by Sisco (1989), stemming from Sternberg's work is the notion that intelligence can
be taught. Although, as noted earlier, others have posited this
idea, (see, for example, Baltes and Willis, 1982), Sternberg has
offered the most comprehensive blueprint of a training program
for enhancing intellectual skills. (See Sternberg, 1986a, 1988.)
In this program, targeted at the high school and collegiate level,
Sternberg offers applied examples of each subtheory along with
practical exercises. According to Sisco, the main strengths of
this program are that "it is based on a theory that has been sub-
jected to fairly extensive and rigorous empirical testing . . . ,
focuses on academic as well as practical intelligence . . . , [and]
has assessment tools for measuring training effects" (p. 287).
In summary, it appears that Sternberg's work on intelligence,
like that of Guilford and Gardner, may be very useful in in-
forming both the theory and practice of learning in adulthood.

Assessment of Intelligence

Intelligence, as noted earlier, has been defined primarily from
the psychometric tradition. This means that in defining the concept of intelligence, emphasis has been placed on being able to
develop testable items that can measure a person's intellectual
abilities. Intelligence as a measurable construct was grounded

in the practical need to assess the potential scholastic success of young children (Schaie and Willis, 1986). The tradition of using tests that primarily measure academic abilities, whether those tests are designed for children or adults, is still predominant today. As Gardner (1983) has observed, most current intelligence tests "have predictive power for success in schooling, but relatively little predictive power outside the school context, especially when more potent factors like social and economic background have been taken into account" (p. 16). Thus those who were seen as "whiz kids" are not necessarily the same people who are judged to be highly successful in later life. Although efforts are currently under way by R. J. Sternberg (personal letter, 1990) to develop a test of "practical intelligence," we do not yet have a definitive instrument that can assess a person's ability to learn within the everyday context of life. (See Gardner, 1983; Sisco, 1989; Smith, Dixon, and Baltes, 1989.)

The use of intelligence testing with adults has not been as prevalent as the testing of children. The first widespread testing of adults was by the army in World War I with the administration of the Army Alpha Tests of Intelligence. Other uses of intelligence tests with adults, which are still predominant today, include assessing people in the workplace for job placement and in clinical settings for appropriate treatment plans. In addition, intelligence tests have been used in research to determine how intellectual abilities change as people age. The two tests of adult intelligence most often used in both research and practice are the Wechsler Adult Intelligence Scale (WAIS) and the Primary Mental Abilities (PMA) test. The most recent version of the PMA is the Schaie-Thurstone Adult Mental Abilities Test (STAMAT) (Schaie, 1985, 1987).

The WAIS is the most widely researched and used measure of adult intelligence (Knox, 1977; Schaie and Willis, 1986). Consisting of eleven subtests grouped into verbal and performance scales, the WAIS provides a measure of overall general intelligence. The verbal portion of the test relies heavily on language skills, such as word definitions and general information items, although two subtests of this scale also address basic numerical abilities. Responses to the performance scales are based on nonverbal skills such as locating missing parts of a picture or reconstructing block designs. The majority of the verbal tests are not timed; those in the performance category are all timed exercises. Several of the WAIS subtests are often grouped together for measuring Cattell and Horn's constructs of fluid and crystallized intelligence. Knox (1977), drawing on an earlier study of the relationship between the WAIS and achievement scores of 207 adult learners (Knox, Grotelueschen, and Sjogren, 1968), has commented that scores on the WAIS can "usually provide a helpful estimate of adult learning ability to perform verbal learning tasks in educational settings. . . . It is less clear that they provide an accurate estimate of adult learning ability related to social effectiveness, such as modification of occupational performance" (p. 413). Knox's observations are similar to those of other critics who argue that present measures of intelligence do not assess the totality of intelligence in adulthood (Gardner, 1983; Sternberg, 1986a, 1990c; Sternberg and Wagner, 1986).

Interest in the second test of adult intelligence, the Primary Mental Abilities test, is often associated with the work of Schaie and colleagues on intelligence and aging (Schaie, 1979; Schaie and Willis, 1986). The underlying assumption of the PMA, grounded in the work of Thurstone and Thurstone (1941), is that intelligence is really several distinct abilities and not a single general trait. Purported to measure five relatively independent factors, the PMA test battery consists of five subtests: (1) verbal meaning, which is the ability to understand ideas expressed in words; (2) space, describing the ability to think about an object in two or three dimensions; (3) reasoning, involving the ability to solve logical problems; (4) number, the ability to handle arithmetic problems; and (5) word fluency, concerning the speed and ease with which words are used (Schaie, 1979). The PMA subtests, all of which are timed, can be reported as a composite score that constitutes an overall index of intellectual ability. Like the WAIS, the PMA appears to assess academic abilities related to formal schooling such as verbal and reasoning ability. In a challenge to this idea, Willis and Schaie (1985) found that at least in later adulthood certain of the primary mental abilities do predict competent behavior in specific situations—for example, "competence in active situations was predicted both by spatial ability and inductive reasoning, and competence in passive situations was predicted by verbal ability" (Schaie and Willis, 1986, p. 290). To these researchers, the findings suggest "a strong relationship between the 'building blocks' of intelligence and abilities on real life tasks" (Schaie and Willis, 1986, p. 290). Only further study will tell whether the PMA and other intelligence tests of this nature can actually be used as adequate predictors of everyday intelligence.

In using intelligence tests with adult learners, it is important to understand, as highlighted by the discussions of the WAIS and the PMA, that we are making a judgment about the nature of intelligence. Do we see intelligence as one major general trait, or is it a set of highly diverse abilities? Is intelligence primarily a measure of academic potential, or does intelligence, especially intelligence in adulthood, also encompass the ability to handle new learning within the context of everyday life? If the accepted concept of intelligence is widened to include both the academic and the practical elements, are the present pencil and paper measures sufficient to assess intelligence? Our response would be: Probably not.

In thinking about future means of assessing intelligence in adulthood, two major issues have surfaced. First, as alluded to in the preceding paragraph, we must develop tests that can in fact measure both academic and practical notions of intelligence. This effort would include further study of present measures, such as that undertaken by Willis and Schaie (1985), as well as the development of new instruments (Baltes, Dittmann-Kohli, and Dixon, 1984). Sternberg, for example, is undertaking such a task (Sisco, 1989; Sternberg, 1990c). Second, we must pay more attention to revising and designing tests that are "age-fair." These measures would take into account "tests of adult intelligence relevant to competence at different points in the lifespan" (Schaie and Willis, 1986, p. 292), just as current tests take into account primarily the competencies needed for academic activities. Research in this arena has just begun. The further development of intelligence tests suited for adult learners will require much time and effort.

Age and Intellectual Abilities

Does intelligence decline with age? The responses to this question are still mixed and often controversial. The classic school of thought contends that intelligence enters a process of irreversible decline in the adult years, although the hypothesized onset of that decline has been extended from the early twenties to at least the age of fifty or sixty. Others say that "intelligence is relatively stable through the adult years, with the brain providing more than enough capacity for anything we would want to contemplate until serious disease sets in late in life" (Schaie and Willis, 1986, p. 293). Still others contend that intelligence declines in some respects, remains stable in others, and may even increase in some functions (Baltes, Dittmann-Kohli, and Dixon, 1984). What creates such a confusing picture of adult intellectual abilities? Botwinick (1977) cites four key factors upon which the controversies rest: one's definition of age or aging; definitions of intelligence; types of tests used to measure intelligence; and research methods and their pitfalls. All of these factors are discussed in this section, along with current research and practice.

What Is Meant by Age and Aging. Whether or not one believes that intelligence declines with age depends on "where in the age spectrum one chooses to look" (Botwinick, 1977, p. 580). Are we talking about adults in early, middle, or later adulthood? In reviewing data on early and middle adulthood, our response would be that intelligence does not decline with age. (See Schaie and Hertzog, 1983; Baltes, Dittmann-Kohli, and Dixon, 1984; Schaie and Willis, 1986.) In fact, some intellectual functions, no matter what testing procedures are employed, seem to increase. The answer to whether intelligence declines in later adulthood is not so clear-cut. (See Horn and Donaldson, 1976; Baltes, Dittmann-Kohli, and Dixon, 1984; Hayslip and Panek, 1989.) Most agree there is some decline in functioning after the age of sixty, but just what this decline is and, more important, its practical effect on learning ability are still unknown. For example, there does appear to be a drop in intelligence within a few years of death. This phenomenon, labeled the terminal drop, might account at least in part for the decrease in the intellectual functioning of older adults as opposed to the usual explanation that intellectual impairment is a universal condition of advancing age (Troll, 1982; Labouvie-Vief, 1990). In line with this observation, few studies have addressed the intellectual abilities of healthy adults much beyond the age of sixty-five or seventy. In one recent longitudinal comparison (Field, Schaie, and Leino, 1988) of subjects ranging in age from seventy-three to ninety-three, it was found that although many of the subjects showed some decline in abilities, more than half displayed no such change, even at the oldest age levels.

Definitions of Intelligence. As we noted in our discussion of the nature of intelligence, there is no universal agreement as to what intelligence really is. Therefore when we speak about changes in intellectual ability as we age, a key question must be answered: What do we mean by intelligence? When intelligence is defined as a unitary property, the research tends to confirm that indeed intelligence does decline as we age, although again, as noted earlier, the point of departure for that decline often varies (Schaie and Willis, 1986). Yet when intelligence is defined as a multifaceted entity, the response tends to be that some of our abilities decline while others remain stable or even increase (Schaie, 1979, 1987; Baltes, Dittmann-Kohli, and Dixon, 1984; Sternberg and Berg, 1987). The best example of this kind of thinking is seen in the study of fluid and crystallized intelligence, where it is hypothesized that fluid intelligence decreases with age whereas crystallized intelligence first increases and then remains relatively stable (Horn, 1982). Intertwined with this idea of multidimensional intelligence is an even more fundamental question: Are the primary factors that have been identified as the building blocks of intelligence, such as verbal and numerical abilities, the foundations upon which all intellectual skills are developed for a lifetime? Or are different kinds of intellectual abilities, such as those needed for everyday learning, of greater importance for learning in adulthood? (See Gardner, 1983; Scribner, 1984; Sternberg, 1986b, 1990c; Sternberg and Wagner, 1986; Schaie, 1987; Sternberg and Berg, 1987; Labouvie-Vief,

1990.) These are questions for which no clear answers are yet forthcoming.

Types of Tests. Behind every intelligence test is a definition of intelligence, whether given directly or implied by the test's author. Thus it is apparent that generalizations about intelligence and the aging process are also affected by the test used. As noted earlier, most research on the effects of intelligence and aging have been conducted using either the WAIS or the PMA. The question then arises whether either of these two measures captures a holistic picture of adult intelligence. Some would say that they do (Schaie, 1979, 1987; Sternberg, 1990a, 1990c; Schaie and Willis, 1986), while others have raised serious questions about their validity for adult learners (Sternberg, 1986b, 1990a, 1990b; Sternberg and Wagner, 1986). Another criticism of both these tests has been their inclusion of timed items. All of the PMA subtests are timed, while in the WAIS about half of the subtests are timed. Is a timed test, especially one involving perceptual motor function, a valid measure of intelligence, especially for older adults? Some would choose to eliminate this factor of speed as an important intellectual property. Moreover, questions have been raised about the language of the test items, which may be biased toward a younger age cohort and therefore inappropriate for all age groups.

Research Methods. The research designs employed in investigating changes in intelligence over the life span have generated the most discussion in the literature. Results of cross-sectional studies, those which compare one-time test scores of different age groups (twenty, forty, and sixty years old, for example) have been misinterpreted to show that as we age our intelligence declines. (See Botwinick, 1977; Knox, 1977; Schaie and Willis, 1986.) Findings from longitudinal studies, however, usually support a very different conclusion. Based primarily on the readministration of intelligence tests over time to the same group of people, the longitudinal investigations demonstrate little, if any, overall decline in scores (at least until the age of sixty) within a particular age group. (See Knox, 1977; Schaie and Willis, 1986.) Botwinick (1977), reflecting on this problem of research designs, has observed that "the cross-sectional method may spuriously magnify age decline, and the longitudinal method may minimize it" (p. 582). In cross-sectional investigations, the background and experiences of the different cohorts being studied may cloud the results due to such factors as formal educational attainment and health. Moreover younger cohorts, especially those in their twenties, may be much more "testwise" than people in their sixties and seventies. In longitudinal studies, on the other hand, "there is a problem of selective dropout, with lower-ability adults tending to die off earlier or to be unavailable for retesting some years later" (Cross, 1981, p. 161).

     In response to this problem, researchers have adopted alternative designs to control some of the biases inherent when only a simple cross-sectional or longitudinal design is used. (See Baltes, Reese, and Nesselroade, 1977, and Schaie and Willis, 1986, for a description of these designs.) Schaie and his associates best exemplify the work that has been done using these alternative designs. (See Schaie, 1979; Schaie and Labouvie-Vief, 1974; Schaie and Parham, 1977; Schaie and Hertzog, 1983.) Over a twenty-one-year period they tested and then retested four separate groups of adults ranging in age from twenty-two to seventy at the first administration of the tests (the PMA and the Test of Behavioral Rigidity). With four cross-sectional studies in addition to longitudinal data, they were able to do a number of different analyses (for example, cross-sectional and cohort-sequential). In essence they found that the cross-sectional data "showed the typical pattern of intellectual decline" (Schaie and Willis, 1986, p. 298), while the longitudinal data suggested little if any decline of practical importance until after age sixty (Schaie and Hertzog, 1983). Schaie and associates attributed the differences found when using these two research designs to cohort variation — differences between the generations versus difference in the ages of the subjects. These cohort variations are in turn attributed to higher educational levels of succeeding generations and overall better nutrition and health care that may have resulted in superior physiological brain functioning.

     Schaie's (1979) overarching conclusion from this vast array

of data is that "reliable decrement until very old age (and by that I mean the late 80s) cannot be found for all abilities or all individuals" (p. 104). Rather, these studies "suggest once again the tremendous range of individual differences. Some adults show decrement on some abilities quite early in life, but others maintain their function into old age" (p. 105). Although his conclusions appear to be well founded, they are not accepted in all circles (Horn and Donaldson, 1976; Horn, 1982).

A New Perspective

A promising resolution of this ongoing controversy of whether adults lose their intellectual abilities as they age has been set forth by Baltes, Dittmann-Kohli, and Dixon (1984). Drawing on present trends in research on intelligence and other areas of study such as biology, sociology, and personality theory, they offer eight propositions aimed at guiding future research and practice. "On the most general level," they say, "the propositional framework acknowledges stability, growth, and decline as coexisting features of intellectual development" (p. 34). Specifically, these authors view adult intelligence as stable, at least for functioning in the "average range" until at least the age of sixty. If a decline in functioning does exist, it applies primarily to the "maximum" or more difficult levels of functioning rather than the average potential that each of us possesses. There is also evidence for the possibility of growth in intellectual abilities; these changes are most likely to involve those functions associated with previous experience or accumulated knowledge. In addition, the propositions emphasize "the need to consider the developmental pragmatics of intellectual functioning" (p. 31). Within this framework, the life situations and goals of adults as they age must be given more consideration when building theories of adult intelligence. In highlighting the need to consider the more practical side of intellectual functioning, these authors are in agreement with the work of such theorists as Gardner (1983) and Sternberg (1986a, 1988).

Illustrating how their propositional scheme could be used to promote theoretical development, Baltes, Dittmann-Kohli, and Dixon (1984) have outlined two new models of intellectual development. Both models emphasize the multiple pathways of intellectual development, the possible occurrence of growth in some areas and decline in others, and the ability of individuals to modify this process. The first model, the dual-process approach, describes two distinct but interrelated processes: the mechanics of intelligence and the pragmatics of intelligence. The mechanics of intelligence refers to the basic cognitive operations and structures "associated with such tasks as perceiving relationships, classification, and logical reasoning" (p. 63). The pragmatics of intelligence refers to the adaptive functions of intelligence — that is being able to act intellectually within a number of different contexts based on our accumulation of both generalized and specialized knowledge. Development of the mechanics of intelligence is more prominent in the first third of life, while "intellectual pragmatics appears to be the centerpiece of intelligence during adulthood and old age" (p. 64). In many ways, these two general processes mirror the three subtheories of the triarchic theory proposed by Sternberg (1986a, 1988). The mechanics of intelligence might be equated to Sternberg's componential subtheory, while the pragmatics of intelligence encompasses aspects of both the contextual and experiential subtheories.

Selective optimization with compensation characterizes the second model proposed by Baltes and colleagues. At the heart of this model is the assumption that people, in adjusting to the aging process, can selectively choose those areas of the intellect they wish to enhance and thus engage in compensatory efforts, if necessary, to ensure continued success and perhaps even mastery of these abilities. This model has both psychological as well as sociological facets. From the psychological perspective, it allows people to use their storehouse of knowledge and intellectual functions in new and creative ways. The sociological factors enter with the support and resources provided by people's referent groups and society in general, which allow them to continue to grow and develop. For example, providing elderhostels and free tuition at higher-education institutions could be termed support resources for older adults in pursuing both specific and general areas of intellectual interest. In exploring this model further, there is a need for "investigation of compensatory cognitive skills" (1984, p. 68). How, for example, do compensatory skills evolve? What differentiates these abilities from the basic intellectual functions?

Summary

Intelligence has been defined primarily by the psychometric tradition, which assumes that intelligence is a measurable quality. First conceptualized as a single factor of general ability, the construct has been broadened to include the notion that there are multiple forms of intellectual ability. The development of adequate tools to measure these multiple abilities of adult learners is still in its infancy. The present tests focus primarily on academic abilities versus the practical intelligence needed for everyday adult life.

Whether adults lose their intellectual abilities as they age is still open to question for a number of reasons, including a lack of consistent research methodologies and tools. The most common response to this important issue is that adult intelligence appears relatively stable, at least until the sixth or seventh decade. If a decline in functioning does exist, it appears to apply primarily to the maximum versus average levels of functioning. In reflecting on the issue of aging and intelligence, remember that myths promote powerful images, whether the myth is grounded in fact or fiction. It has been difficult for educators and researchers alike to give up the stereotype that young equals sharp and older means dull. Until both groups are willing to consider learning abilities beyond those measured by our traditional intelligence tests, the stereotype of the old dog and the new tricks, especially for older adult learners, is likely to continue. Perhaps this stereotype should be replaced by a slightly expanded adage: "And so we come to the general conclusion the old dog can learn new tricks but the answer is not a direct and simple one. . . . He is less likely to gamble on the results, particularly when he is not convinced that the new trick is any better than the old tricks, which served him so well in the past. He may not learn the new trick as rapidly as he did in the past, but learn it he does. Further, the best evidence seems to indicate that if he starts out as a clever young pup, he is very likely to end up as a wise old hound" (Bischof, 1969, p. 224).

Nine

Memory, Cognition, and Learning Styles

Educators of adults often puzzle over the issue of whether adults learn any differently than children. There are those among us who believe that adults do process information differently and, therefore, we should structure our practice, especially our teaching, accordingly. There are others who are openly skeptical about these purported differences and continue to ask for further clarification and elaboration. One area of research, the study of cognition, has been especially useful in helping us clarify our views on how adults learn. Cognition is defined as the study of how people receive, store, retrieve, transform, and transmit information (Stillings and others, 1987). Often studied from an interdisciplinary perspective, the major work in cognition has been done with children in primarily formal educational settings and with computer learning (for example, artificial intelligence). Many educators, however, have generalized the findings from this work to include all forms of learning in adulthood without the necessary verification studies.

The work with adult populations related to cognition has been primarily in the area of memory and aging. This chapter highlights that work along with other key concepts that provide insight into adults as learners. After presenting an overview of the information processing framework for memory that lies at the heart of the study of cognition, we review recent work on memory and aging. Next we explore the idea of scheme theory and the role of prior knowledge in learning, two important areas for educators of adults to understand. The chapter concludes with a discussion of cognitive and learning style theories and the importance of context in both memory and cognition. Since the topics addressed in this chapter are complex in nature, only a basic discussion is provided for each theme. By highlighting these key topics we hope to encourage the reader to investigate important but unexplored areas of learning in adulthood.

Human Memory

Fear of memory loss is a common concern of people as they age. Parents often observe how much more easily their children can remember such simple things as telephone numbers and zip codes, while many older adults seem to remember childhood events vividly but often have difficulty remembering what they had for lunch that day. These observations and images foster the idea that memory loss is a normal result of aging and thus is something we all must accept. Are these perceptions of memory loss accurate, and if so what effects do they have on learning in adulthood? Often memory functions are equated with learning or are seen as one of the primary mental processes associated with learning (Long, 1983). If adults do suffer major changes, especially decline, in their memory functions, it follows that the learning process may also be impaired. To understand how memory can be affected by the aging process, we first need to examine how the process of memory itself is conceptualized.

Since the 1960s, human memory has been studied primarily from the "information processing" approach (Craik, 1977; Salthouse, 1985): The mind is visualized as a computer, with information being entered, stored, and then retrieved as needed. Conceptualizing where people store or file what they learn, termed the structural aspect of memory, was the first major focus of study from this perspective. Three categories have been used to describe the different structures of memory: sensory memory, short-term (or primary) memory, and long-term (or secondary) memory. (See Schaie and Willis, 1986; Di Vesta, 1987; Schulz and Ewen, 1988.) Each of these three forms of memory is described somewhat differently by different authors. In general, though, the structural model emphasizes that each form of memory has a distinct capacity in which information is filed for a period of time. Both sensory and short-term memory have very small capacities and brief storage times (milliseconds in sensory memory, about one-half minute in short-term memory), while long-term memory has an enormous capacity and can store information for a lifetime. Recently researchers have visualized these structures as a continuum with the focus on the "processes that account for how material is transferred from one store to another" (Hayslip and Panek, 1989, p. 234).

Emphasized in the process aspect of information processing are "the mental activities that we perform when we try to put information into memory (learn), or make use of it at some later date (remember)" (Schulz and Ewen, 1988, p. 134). Usually the memory process is divided into three phases (Schaie and Willis, 1986; Poon, 1985). The encoding or acquisition phase is the initial process in which the information is entered into the system. Filing this material for future use is termed the storage or retention phase. The final phase, retrieval, describes how you get material out of storage when needed. Two of the most common methods of retrieval are recall and recognition. Recall requires bringing forth "to-be-remembered" information, while recognition involves choosing from a group of possible answers. As we well remember from our school testing days of essay versus multiple-choice exams, "recall is considered to be a more demanding test of retrieval than is recognition" (Schulz and Ewen, 1988, p. 138).

A number of alternatives have been proposed for how the structural components fit within the process model. (See Craik, 1977; Poon, 1985; Salthouse, 1985; Schaie and Willis, 1986; Hayslip and Panek, 1989.) The most common explanation is that information from our environment is registered within sensory memory via our visual, auditory, and tactual senses (termed sensory registers). Material is then selectively transferred or encoded into short-term memory. The control system of selective attention determines what is important enough to be moved into the short-term memory store. There is considerable flexibility with what can be done with the information in short-term memory. It "can be used as a cue to retrieve other information from long-term memory, it can be elaborated, it can be used to form images, it is used in thinking, it can be structured to be placed in long-term or secondary memory, or if nothing is done with it, it can be discarded" (Di Vesta, 1987, p. 211). As the functions of short-term memory are complex and the storage time and capacity are small, two major control processes are used to sort and file the data: chunking and automatization. Chunking essentially is organizing the information in groups or patterns (a phone number in three chunks, 804-467-1331, for example), while automatization allows for a chunk of information to become so familiar that a person can handle it without really thinking (McKeachie, 1988). The material structured in short-term memory for long-term memory is then encoded into that memory bank for permanent storage by highly organized episodes (by time and place) or by meaningful relations to earlier stored material. This type of processing is often referred to as deep processing versus the shallow processing done at the short-term level (McKeachie, 1988; Schaie and Willis, 1986). The information is then retrieved as needed from this long-term storage.

Memory and Aging

A great deal of research from the information processing framework has been conducted on the topic of memory and aging. (See Poon and others, 1980; Salthouse, 1985, 1986; Rybash, Hoyer, and Roodin, 1986.) The general consensus from this work is that certain memory functions indeed decline with age. A number of authors have cautioned, however, that because of methodological considerations and the variables being studied, this work must be interpreted with care. The vast majority of it has focused on comparing young adults (usually introductory psychology students) with older adults by using cross-sectional designs (Bee, 1987). These two factors combined make it difficult to generalize across age groups because of subject and cohort bias (Perlmutter and Hall, 1985; Salthouse, 1985). Moreover, most of this research has been conducted primarily in laboratory settings using memory tasks and activities, such as repeating back nonsense words and lists of random numbers. The primary criticism leveled against this type of research on memory is that these tasks and "skills are taken out of the context of everyday life. . . . There is as yet no way to determine the importance of these factors in life situations, so at present we do not know if—and how—the interaction of the factors affects performance" (Perlmutter and Hall, 1986, p. 208). A response to this criticism in recent years has been to design "ecologically valid" research that takes into account the everyday learning demands of adults. (See Hayslip and Panek, 1989; Rogoff and Lave, 1984; Rybash, Hoyer, and Roodin, 1986; Schulz and Ewen, 1988.) With these limitations in mind, we offer a summary of this research on memory in adulthood.

Sensory and Short-Term Memory. In general, few clearly defined changes have been found in both sensory and short-term memory as people age. As there are fairly major changes with age in both vision and hearing, one would expect to see these changes reflected in sensory memory. Yet only minor deficits have been found—although it is often difficult with present testing procedures to distinguish between age-related physiological decline in the senses themselves, especially hearing, and actual decrements in the process of sensory memory (Schulz and Ewen, 1988). Short-term memory is also relatively stable (Craik, 1977; Poon, 1985), especially in relation to storage capacity and simple tasks. Some studies have demonstrated, however, that when memory tasks become more complex or are speed-related, older people may be at a disadvantage in relation to short-term memory processing (Bee, 1987; Schulz and Ewen, 1988).

Long-Term Memory. It is in long-term memory that age deficits are more commonly found. (See Hayslip and Panek, 1989; Craik, 1977; Rybash, Hoyer, and Roodin, 1986; Salthouse, 1982.) Four major differences have surfaced in long-term memory for older versus younger learners. These include changes in the encoding or acquisition of material, the retrieval of information, the level of processing, and the speed of processing. Few changes have been noted in the storage or retention capacity of long-term memory over the life span.

The question that often surfaces in reviewing the processes related to long-term memory is whether it is more difficult for adults as they age to get information into the system (to encode it) or get it out (to retrieve it). The response to this question appears to be both. It is not at all clear which part of the process creates more difficulty (Bee, 1987; Schulz and Ewen, 1988). Encoding problems are most often associated with the organization of information. Specifically, older adults appear to be less efficient at organizing new material. Yet "when older subjects are given clues ahead of time about what they will later have to remember, or are shown how to organize the material in an effective way, the age differences in [at least the area of] recall decline" (Bee, 1987, p. 125).

On the retrieval side, changes are most often noted in the recall versus recognition of information. In tests of recall, for example, major differences have been demonstrated for older and younger people, whereas in recognition activities the differences are small or nonexistent (Poon, 1985). The general conclusion from this work is that "older subjects have a lot of information in memory storage that they cannot get to in difficult retrieval tasks, such as recall" (Schaie and Willis, 1986, p. 341). Another aspect of retrieval that is often taken as a given is that older persons can retrieve "ancient memories" better than younger people — along with the accompanying myth that older people can clearly remember events in their distant past but have trouble recalling recent events. Rather, it appears that this reversal of memory strengths — remote memories are stronger than recent memories — is a natural phenomenon that occurs at all ages, not just with older people. We all seem better able to recall occurrences that happened to us in the distant or far past than in the very recent past (Schaie and Willis, 1986).

With regard to the level and speed of processing, older adults appear to process more information at a shallower level and with less speed. Why do older adults appear to process information less deeply than younger adults? The primary hypothesis is that they have a lessened capacity to pay attention to diverse stimuli in the environment (Craik, 1977; Craik and Rabinowitz, 1984). The reasoning is as follows: "Older adults must therefore expend more mental effort to process information more deeply, with the result being they are less likely to do so" (Schulz and Ewen, 1988, p. 153). This notion of less depth of processing for older adults is not well accepted in all circles (Salthouse, 1982).

In terms of the speed of processing, adults do seem to have more difficulty with speeded tasks (as was also noted with short-term memory). When tests for memory tasks are paced — meaning that the time given per item or between items is fixed — age deficits definitely show an increase (Salthouse, 1982, 1985; Hayslip and Panek, 1989). Salthouse accounts for at least part of these differences in speeded tasks as a slowing of both the encoding and retrieval processes.

In summary, in relation to secondary memory it appears that older adults may not acquire or retrieve information as well as do younger adults, nor do they organize information as effectively. They also may not process information as deeply, and the speed at which they process that information may be slower. Again, it must be stressed that this line of research has limited generalizability because of the samples, the memory activities tested, and the separation of the research from the real world of the adult learner.

Real-Life Memories. In response to some of the criticisms of memory research just cited, a different approach has been taken by placing memory tasks in the context of everyday adult lives. This strand of research, which fosters what has been termed ecological validity, has received very little attention, "primarily because it is untidy and affected by so many different variables" (Perlmutter and Hall, 1985, p. 226). The term *ecological validity* assumes that the tasks being studied are meaningful to the person and accurately reflect real-life adult experiences. These studies have been done primarily through "memory for text" formats (Hultsch and Dixon, 1984) that include reviews of sentences, paragraphs, and stories versus single words and symbols. Less prevalent is research on memory skills for everyday activities such as keeping appointments and remembering what items to buy at the grocery store. These studies also address some of the other concerns voiced by scholars of the contextual approach, such as the person's needs and motivation, the specificity of the task, and situational variables. One thing at least is evident: When a contextual approach is used, less decline is found in memory processes as we age.

As noted earlier, the assumption underlying the research is that memory capacities and skills form one of the keystones of how adults learn. Formal memory training, the most structured approach to building memory skills, has been shown to be useful in helping older adults cope with memory deficits. (See Poon, Walsh-Sweeney, and Fozard, 1980; Rybash, Hoyer, and Roodin, 1986.) This training has most often focused on the teaching of encoding strategies, such as practicing rehearsal of information or fostering the use of mnemonics (devices for helping people improve their memory). For example, Yesavage (1983) taught older adults to improve their name/face recall by using visual imagery as a mnemonic. Moreover, Perlmutter and Hall (1985) have suggested teaching adults about metamemory—the understanding of the way the memory system works. A number of authors have suggested ways to integrate training in memory skills into formal learning programs for adults: providing both verbal and written cues, such as advance organizers and overheads, when introducing new material to students; reviewing at the beginning of each session key material covered at previous sessions; and giving opportunities to apply the new material as soon after the presentation as possible. (See Knox, 1977, 1986; Jones and Cooper, 1982; Di Vesta, 1987, for a thorough discussion of these ideas.)

Adults learning on their own may also find it helpful to use memory aids in their learning activities (Rybash, Hoyer, and Roodin, 1986). These can come in many forms—from structured checklists for learning a new skill to personal note taking on items of interest. For example, someone might jot down in a pocket notebook interesting new words she encountered each day. She could then practice using these words until they became a natural part of her vocabulary.

Biology and Memory

Before leaving the topic of memory and aging, it should be mentioned that the newest frontier of research in this arena focuses on the anatomical and chemical basis of memory and learning. (See Long, 1983; Boucouvalas, 1988b; Cattell, 1987; Farley, 1988). Although the majority of this work is still in its infancy in terms of having practical relevance to adult learning, its impact is likely to be felt as we move toward the twenty-first century (Boucouvalas, 1988b; Hannay and Levin, 1987). Viewing the devastation of the memory and learning capacity of a person with advanced Alzheimer's disease brings home to each of us the innate and yet almost mystical ways in which the brain functions.

The brain, the storehouse of memories, is in the words of Frank Farley, "a wonderful gismo" (1988, p. 15). Weighing approximately three and a half pounds, "it is one of the most complex electrical systems in nature and certainly vastly more complex than any manmade computer" (Hannay and Levin, 1987, p. 1). Scholars from the neurosciences have contributed most to our knowledge of how the brain functions (Boucouvalas, 1988b). This knowledge has been built primarily from studies of animals and humans in which damage has occurred to part or all of a structure or set of structures within the brain, resulting in a marked behavioral change. As the neuroscientist must wait in most cases for a naturally occurring problem (produced by trauma or stress) when studying human subjects, it has been difficult to control for a variety of important factors in this research such as age, genetic history, gender, time since onset of injury or disease, and socioeconomic background. Therefore, inferences from this work about how the brain actually functions in healthy adults have often been contradictory and unclear. Newer technologies, however, such as computed tomography (CT scan), positron emission tomography (PET), and magnetic resonance imaging (MRI), all of which are noninvasive procedures, offer a great deal of promise for further exploration of how the brain operates (Gur, 1987).

One of the major educational applications of brain research to memory and learning has been related to brain hemisphere differences and specializations (Witelson and Swallow, 1987). The idea that our brains are divided into two hemispheres, or halves, is a popularly accepted idea. Indeed, it has led some educators to design full programs for the left versus the right brain. By the end of the program, they claim, people can more fully develop their untapped right or left brain potential. Although there are indeed hemispheric specializations, Springer (1987) points out that "we have no basis for believing that presenting stimuli or tasks for which one hemisphere is specialized builds up that hemisphere at the expense of the other. Moreover there is very little evidence to support the claim that the right hemisphere is specialized for creativity. . . . [Rather], by all our current measures, including the newest ones, both hemispheres are active and involved in any situation" (p. 28). Farley (1988, p. 16), citing the work of Levy (1983), summarizes the things we know for certain about hemispheric specialization of the brain:

- In the vast majority of right-handers, speech is almost entirely confined to the left hemisphere.
- Right-hemisphere processes add emotional and humorous overtones important for understanding the full meaning of oral and written communications.
- The two hemispheres differ in their perceptual roles, but both sides are involved in the creation and appreciation of art and music.
- Both hemispheres are involved in thinking, logic, and reasoning.
- The right hemisphere seems to play a special role in emotion. If students are emotionally engaged, both sides of the brain will participate in the educational process regardless of subject matter.

As Farley points out, this relatively short list is hardly a basis upon which a full curriculum of instruction should be constructed. The point of disagreement between the neuropsychologists and the right/left brain advocates is not whether people vary in the way they approach learning or their natural learning ability but on "the presumed link between these differences and brain asymmetry" (Springer, 1987, p. 28).

A second major application from this line of research to learning has been centered on the chemical functioning of the brain (Long, 1983; Cattell, 1987). As noted by Long (1983), "information concerning the association between certain chemical substances and brain functions as manifested in memory continues to accumulate" (p. 77). This is not necessarily a new trend, for chemical substances have long been used in mind-altering experiences such as religious ceremonies of earlier tribal societies. Cattell (1987) notes that most foreign chemicals such as alcohol, lead, and LSD "merely reduce effective abilities" (p. 244), while the natural biochemicals (like thyroxin and adrenaline), if below normal in amount, can inhibit functioning. He goes on to add that at this point there is "no magic 'elixir' for intelligence" (p. 244), no smart pill, although the idea is intriguing. Yet perhaps current experiments with drug trials for Alzheimer's disease and other dementias may lead to a better understanding of how chemicals can positively affect the processes of memory and learning.

The study of memory, as noted earlier, has received the most attention in the literature, but there are other areas of research that can help us understand learning in adulthood. Among the most useful ideas have been scheme theory, the role of prior knowledge and experience in learning, the notions of cognitive style and learning style, and the importance of acknowledging the context of learning. Each of these areas will be discussed in the remaining sections of the chapter.

Scheme Theory

In studying cognition, the emphasis is on what learners know versus how they behave. This knowing involves both the acquisition of knowledge, discussed in the section on human memory, and the actual structure of that knowledge (John-Steiner, 1985; Shuell, 1986; Cervero, 1988). In this perspective, considerable importance is placed on prior knowledge as well as new knowledge being accumulated. Since it is assumed that most adults have a greater store of prior knowledge than children, understanding the role that this knowledge plays in learning is critical. In thinking through the possible connections of prior knowledge to learning in adulthood, scheme theory provides a very useful framework. (See Di Vesta, 1987; Glaser, 1987; Rumelhart, 1980; Rumelhart and Norman, 1978.)

Scheme theory describes how knowledge is packaged and organized in long-term memory and how this packaging "facilitates the use of knowledge in particular ways" (Rumelhart, 1980, p. 34). These schemata (the singular is scheme), which may be embedded within other schemata or stand alone, are filled with descriptive materials and are seen as the building blocks of the cognitive process. Schemata are not just passive storehouses of experience, however; they are also active processes whose primary function is to "provide the basis for the assimilation of new information" (Di Vesta, 1987, p. 213). We all carry around with us our own individualized set of schemata that reflect both our experiences and our worldview. Therefore, as adult learners each of us comes to a learning situation with a somewhat different configuration of knowledge and how it can be used. For example, some participants in a seminar on adult development may bring to that learning experience a firm belief that what Gail Sheehy (1976) described in *Passages* is what adult development is all about. After all, the "age-thirty transition" was a really difficult time, just as Sheehy described it would be. Others may have a very different set of life experiences (as a lesbian, perhaps, or the adult child of an alcoholic) that may lead them to question much of what is described as "normal" developmental patterns of adulthood. Therefore, each learner in the seminar may not only come with a different scheme set but also depart having learned very different material—even though all were exposed to basically the same ideas.

In categorizing schematic types, two kinds of knowledge are most often distinguished: declarative knowledge and procedural knowledge (Anderson, 1982, 1983). Declarative knowledge is what we know about things and often is represented as facts (Shuell, 1986); procedural knowledge, by contrast, "is our knowledge about how to perform" various skills and tasks (Cervero, 1988, p. 40). We may be able to describe two or three different models for instruction (declarative knowledge), for example, but when we try to put these models into action (procedural knowledge), we may fail miserably. As the question is open whether learning facts or knowing how to perform comes first, the scenario just described could also be reversed: A person may be an excellent instructor and yet have no specific knowledge of instructional models.

According to Rumelhart and Norman (1978), three different modes of learning fit the scheme framework: *accretion,* meaning the daily accumulation of information that is usually equated with learning facts; *tuning,* which includes slow and gradual changes in current schemata; and *restructuring,* involving both the creation of new schemata and reorganization of those already stored (see Figure 9.1). Most current models of memory reflect only learning by the accretion or fact-gathering process (Shuell, 1986). Educators, however, are well aware that most learning in adulthood goes far beyond the simple memorization of facts. The expectation is that adults will somehow be able to put those facts to good use in their everyday living, whether as workers, parents, spouses, friends, and so on. Therefore, the processes of tuning and restructuring of information, as well as both declarative and procedural knowledge, become vital in adult learning. The general processes of problem solving and critical thinking are good examples of the importance of these constructs. Specifically, in most problem-solving situations we are trying to fit new ideas (declarative knowledge) and ways of acting (procedural knowledge) into earlier patterns of thinking and doing (our current schemata). If we are unable to change our earlier thought patterns (that is, fine-tune or restructure them), our chances of being able to frame and act on problems from a different perspective is remote if not impossible.

The Role of Prior Knowledge and Experience

One key assumption underlying scheme theory is that "learning is cumulative in nature—nothing has meaning or is learned in isolation from prior experience. This assumption has a ped-

Figure 9.1. Three Mechanisms by Which Learning Might Occur.

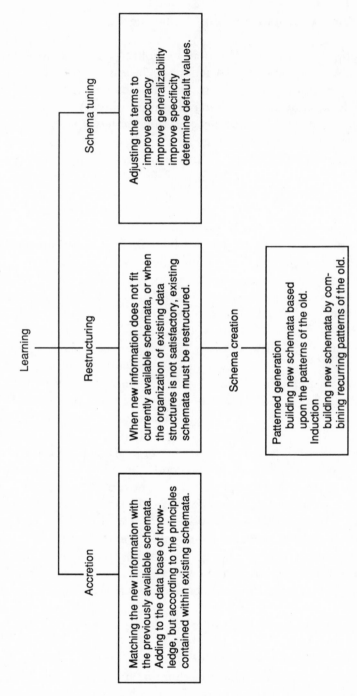

Learning

Accretion

Matching the new information with
the previously available schemata.
Adding to the data base of knowledge, but according to the principles
contained within existing schemata.

Restructuring

When new information does not fit
currently available schemata, or when
the organization of existing data
structures is not satisfactory, existing
schemata must be restructured.

Schema creation

Patterned generation
building new schemata based
upon the patterns of the old.
Induction
building new schemata by combining recurring patterns of the old.

Schema tuning

Adjusting the terms to
improve accuracy
improve generalizability
improve specificity
determine default values.

Source: Rumelhart and Norman, 1978.

igree dating back to Dewey, who said 'no one can think about anything without experience and information about it'" (Cervero, 1988, p. 41). This has led at least one researcher to hypothesize that the importance of prior knowledge and experience in learning new material may account for at least some of the cognitive gains in adulthood (Salthouse, 1988). Flavell (1970, 1985), for example, has addressed directly the idea of experience as it relates to cognition. He contends that "the most important adult cognitive changes are probably the result of life experience" (1970, p. 247). These life experiences include both programmed ones such as adult education and counseling and the everyday experiences of living such as marriage, parenting, work activities, and retirement. These cognitive changes related to life experiences have more to do with judgments, attitudes, and beliefs than with skills or information, and for the most part are highly individualized. This does not mean, however, that there may not be some experience-based adult changes that are more universal in nature and thus some common pattern of cognitive change may exist "associated simply with the fact that one is at a particular point in the life stream" (p. 252). Other writers, such as Knowles (1980), Mezirow (1981), Freire (1970b), and Jarvis (1987a, 1987b), have incorporated this notion of the importance of experience into their theories of learning in adulthood. (See Chapter Thirteen for a detailed overview of each theory.)

In exploring the role of prior knowledge and experience in learning, two additional ideas are important: the amount of that prior knowledge and experience and its nature. In terms of the amount one possesses, the difference between those who know a great deal about a subject (experts) and those who know very little (novices) is a key distinction. (See Chi, Glaser, and Farr, 1988; Salthouse, 1985; Glaser, 1984, 1987.) A person may be an expert in a variety of areas from model railroading to skiing. It appears that experts not only have a greater storehouse of knowledge but also think in different ways than novices. According to Glaser (1984): "The knowledge of novices is organized around the literal objects explicitly given in a problem situation. Experts' knowledge, on the other hand, is organized around principles and abstractions that subsume these objects. . . . In addition, the knowledge of experts includes knowledge about the application of what they know" (p. 99).

One application of this distinction between novice and expert thinkers has been to build computer-based systems for modeling the ways experts solve problems. Peters and Lazzara (1988) have described one way of building such a system and its application to studies of adult reasoning and thinking. Their model is based on two primary elements: "a picture of the problem-solving process that the person uses and a structured record of the person's . . . practices which consists of his/her rule system" (p. 242). These expert systems are in use by the military to train physicians, for example. The further development of expert systems holds the potential for clarifying learning and problem-solving processes in adulthood.

In further examination of the issue of a novice versus expert learner, some authors (Glaser, 1984, 1985, 1987; Glaser and Chi, 1988; John-Steiner, 1985; Shuell, 1986) have speculated that at least some learning processes, rather than being universal, may be specific to certain domains or subject matter — thus making transfer of learning skills across these domains very difficult, if not impossible, for some people. Educators often observe that being an expert in one area does not necessarily translate into being an expert in another, no matter what the learner's motivation. Many graduate students for example, although very perceptive and advanced in their own fields of study, may have a great deal of trouble completing statistical and advanced research design courses. This is especially true of students who are not mathematically inclined. Moreover, some people become experts in carpentry or tracing genealogy, while others view these tasks as beyond their capabilities.

In general, we need to discover more about the differences between the novice and expert learner and "how the transition between novice and expert takes place" (Shuell, 1986, p. 427). A useful starting point has been provided by Glaser (1987), who has listed ten generalizations about those who possess expertise in specialized areas, by Chi, Glaser, and Farr (1988), who have taken a comprehensive look at the nature of expertise, and by John-Steiner (1985), who has traced the thinking patterns of experienced and productive artists, scientists, philosophers, and historians. Understanding these transitions is especially important for educators of adults as we are often asked to assist people in becoming experts in a particular area of study. Moreover, we need to gain a clearer picture of how becoming an expert may be unique for different domains of knowledge — for example, being an expert computer programmer versus an expert carpenter. Studying these questions may help educators of adults to design more effective units of instruction.

Cognitive Style and Learning Style

Another important aspect of cognition related to learning in adulthood is the notion of cognitive style. Cognitive styles are characterized as consistencies in information processing that develop in concert with underlying personality trends. They are reflected in "typical modes of perceiving, remembering, thinking, and problem solving" (Messick, 1976, p. 5) and encompass the ways people see and make sense of their world and attend to different parts of their environment. Some people tend to look at problems from a global perspective, for example, while others are more interested in the specifics. The latter types want facts and figures first; the former want a holistic picture of the situation drawn for them.

A number of cognitive-style dimensions, ranging from field dependence versus independence to cognitive complexity versus simplicity, have been identified through research. (For a complete summary of these dimensions see Messick, 1976, 1984; Knox, 1977; Bonham, 1987.) The outstanding feature of these varying dimensions is their tendency to be bipolar. In contrasting people's cognitive styles, however, we tend to label people as being at either end of the continuum, which is "probably not complex enough to capture the essence of individual differences among human beings" (Bonham, 1988, p. 15). For the most part cognitive styles are considered relatively stable, although some authors have conjectured that changes might be more apparent between middle and old age (Knox, 1977).

Although a great deal of research has been conducted on cognitive styles, "much of the research has been done with children, and it is unclear how or whether the findings translate to adults" (Bonham, 1988, p. 14). Moreover, these studies have not for the most part focused on actual applications to learning. There have been a few exceptions related to adult learning (Tootle, 1985; Simpson and Supapidhayakul, 1986), but "nearly all this literature has approached cognitive performance from only one dimension (for example, field dependence/independence)" (Sisco, 1987, p. 226) versus studying simultaneously a number of different dimensions. Sisco's 1987 study of 119 university adult students is a notable example of a study that moved beyond this unidimensional approach to a multidimensional one. He concludes that it is "possible to test and arrange adult subjects according to performance across seven dimensions of cognitive types," resulting in three "articulated levels or profile types" (p. 230). It is still unclear how this work on cognitive style may relate to helping adults learn more effectively (Knox, 1977; Bonham, 1987). Hiemstra and Sisco (1990) have conjectured that knowledge about cognitive styles might assist instructors in predicting how learners are "likely to perform typical learning tasks such as remembering, selecting, comparing, focusing, reflecting, and analyzing" information (p. 241).

A related yet somewhat different phenomenon is the concept of learning style. The literature describing cognitive style and learning style is somewhat confusing, as some authors use the two terms interchangeably (see Tennant, 1988) whereas others view cognitive style as the more encompassing term (see Kirby, 1979) and still others see learning style as the more inclusive term (see Hiemstra and Sisco, 1990). Clearly there is no common definition of learning style, nor is there a unified theory upon which this work is based. (See Bonham, 1987, 1988; Claxton and Murrell, 1987; Sternberg, 1990b.) The most often quoted definition of learning style in the adult education literature is that given by Smith (1982). In his terms learning style is the "individual's characteristic ways of processing information, feeling, and behaving in learning situations" (p. 24).

It appears that the real difference between this and similar definitions of learning style versus cognitive style lies in the emphasis placed on the learning situation versus the more general notion of how people perceive, organize, and process information. Therefore, when studying learning style the emphasis is usually placed on both the learner and the learning environment (Hiemstra and Sisco, 1990). Claxton and Murrell (1987), for example, say that learning style can be important in working with the diverse array of students entering higher education today. They assume that knowledge and practical applications of this notion can inform teaching practice and highlight issues of faculty roles and the culture of the institution itself. Specifically, they offer four steps that institutions could take to promote a more effective learning and organizational climate through the use of learning-style materials. Among these are "conducting professional development activities for faculty on the use of learning styles in improving teacher and student development functions" (p. 77) and changing job specifications to specify that candidates should have a clear understanding "of teaching-learning practices that recognize individual differences, including style" (p. 78).

Despite the lack of uniform agreement about which elements constitute a learning style, it seems apparent that learning-style inventories, unlike most cognitive-style instruments, have proved useful in helping both learners and instructors alike become aware of their personal learning styles and their strengths and weaknesses as learners and teachers. What must be remembered in using these instruments, however, is that each inventory measures different things, depending on how the instrument's author has defined learning style. In using the variety of learning-style inventories available, it is therefore important to help learners understand how the author of the instrument has conceptualized learning style. (For a review of these instruments see Smith, 1982; Price, 1983; and Bonham, 1987.) It is also important to remember that "learning-style instruments are best used as tools to create awareness that learners differ and as starting points for individual learners' continued investigation of themselves as learners" (Hiemstra and Sisco, 1990, p. 240).

Acknowledging the Context

A major theme emerging from the current literature on cognition in adulthood is how the social and cultural context may affect cognitive functioning. (See Abeles and Riley, 1987; Datan, Rodeheaver, and Hughes, 1987; Dannefer and Perlmutter, 1990; Goodnow, 1990; Heise, 1987; Keating and MacLean, 1988; Rogoff and Lave, 1984; Tennant, 1990.) The underlying assumption of this perspective, similar to that of adult learning in general, is that cognition is more than an internal psychological process (Jarvis, 1987a). The major implications of viewing cognition from this perspective are threefold. First, we may need to reinterpret past and current findings in light of the apparent importance of context in the study of cognition. Illustrative of this "reinterpretation strategy" (Keating and MacLean, 1988) is the criticism of the work on memory and aging, described earlier in this chapter, for its lack of focus on the real-world tasks of adult learners.

Second, we need to look directly for "effects of 'cognitive socialization' in the performance" and measurement of individual cognitive tasks (Keating and MacLean, 1988, p. 313). Cognitive socialization means that we must consider the impact of the family, the educational system, and the culture on what we know and how we come to know it. In the Western industrialized nations, for example, we have come to expect that young and middle-aged adults, for the most part, will display productive mental activities, while old age is equated with a decline in both thinking power and activity. To respond to this observation, we first need to acknowledge that this phenomenon is an important factor in cognitive abilities and describe it more accurately and fully (Chapman, 1988; Goodnow, 1990; Rogoff and Lave, 1984). Moreover, we must develop or reconstruct the present measures that are used in research on cognition and memory either to make them as context free as possible — that is, tasks should be truly universal in nature — or at least acknowledge that the tasks being measured may favor one group over another as one group is more socialized into doing them than the other (Abeles and Riley, 1987; Rogoff and Lave, 1984).

Young adult college students, for example, who often make up one of the subject groups for studies on cognition, tend to be at their prime of life for memorization of facts as their success as students depends on this skill. Middle-aged and older adults, on the other hand, are rarely in situations where they need to memorize anything, especially facts or ideas that do not relate to their everyday life experiences.

And third, we need to expand our way of studying cognition in adulthood. More emphasis has to be placed, as in the study of adult development and intelligence, on interdisciplinary research (Dannefer and Perlmutter, 1990; Goodnow, 1990). Educators of adults could have a special role on these teams — that of linking the theoretical notions of adult cognition with the practical observations of adults in everyday learning situations. (See Caffarella, Loehr, and Hosick, 1989; Merriam, 1987; Salthouse, 1982.) Moreover, the study of cognition in adulthood should be widened beyond the traditional experimental design to include multiple methods such as those of phenomenology, hermeneutics, and case study. Examples of how these alternative approaches have been used in studying adult cognition can be found in the work of Finger (1988), Keating and MacLean (1988), Lave, Murtaugh, and de la Roche (1984), and Mehan (1984).

Summary

Cognition describes how people receive, store, retrieve, transform, and transmit information. Most of the work on cognition in adulthood has focused on memory and aging, with the resulting conclusion that there are some apparent losses, noted primarily in long-term memory, as we age. How this loss in memory affects the everyday learning activities of adults is still unanswered and may in fact have very little overall impact. Other important aspects of cognition reviewed in this chapter were schema theory and how our storehouse of prior knowledge and experience may affect how we learn. In this discussion of prior knowledge and experience, special emphasis was given to the idea of novice and expert learners and how they may learn differently. The differences between cognitive style and learning style were discussed as well, with the resulting observation that further work needs to be done in both these areas to ensure that the concepts are more clearly defined and operationalized. This effort includes translating these concepts into realistic practice not only in teaching/learning transactions but also in the organizational cultures of our institutions. The chapter concluded with an overview of the most recent emphasis in cognitive research—how the social and cultural context may affect cognitive functioning. Special emphasis was placed on reinterpreting past research in light of the context, creating new research designs and ways of measuring cognitive processes, and fostering interdisciplinary study.

Ten

Cognitive Development
in Adulthood

Until the last two decades the notion that qualitative changes in thought processes might occur in adulthood was largely ignored. With the willingness of scholars to reexamine cognitive development models, however, intriguing suggestions about the existence of further stages have begun to emerge. Moreover, other researchers have posited models of cognitive development that may be unique to adulthood.

Cognitive development describes how thinking patterns change over time. This development is often linked to a combination of factors, primarily the interaction of maturational and environmental variables. As in other research traditions on learning, the major studies on cognitive development have been carried out chiefly with children and adolescents. In extending this research to adulthood, the underlying assumption has often been that adults can work to reach a final stage of cognitive development, however that is defined, or if that stage has been attained, work at maintaining that level. Drawing on the writings of Piaget (1972), Riegel (1973), Kramer (1983, 1989), and Perry (1981), among others, this chapter explores the complex phenomenon of cognitive development in adulthood. The idea of wisdom, often posited as the pinnacle of cognitive development, is also discussed.

The Foundational Work

When we speak of cognitive development, Piaget immediately comes to mind. Although Piaget's work is entirely focused on childhood cognitive development, his theory has provided the framework for the majority of work completed with adults. Piaget proposed four invariant stages of development that describe certain configurations of development in an age-gradient fashion. These stages represent "qualitatively different ways of making sense, understanding, and constructing a knowledge of the world" (Tennant, 1988, p. 68). In Piaget's view, children's thought processes move from innate reflex actions (sensory-motor stage), to being able to represent concrete objects in symbols and words (preoperational stage), to an understanding of concepts and relationships of ideas (concrete operational stage), to an ability to reason hypothetically, logically, and systematically (formal operational stage). It was his contention that normal children have the capacity to reach this final stage of formal operations between the ages of twelve and fifteen, later revised upward to ages fifteen to twenty (Piaget, 1972). It is this final stage, characterized by the ability to think abstractly, "which marks the commencement of mature adult thought" (Tennant, 1988, p. 69).

Tennant (1988, p. 77) has noted a number of ways in which Piaget's work has laid the foundation for our understanding of cognitive development in adulthood. Piaget's most salient contributions in this respect are:

- The emphasis on qualitative rather than quantitative developmental changes in cognition (and his related "structuralist" approach to cognitive development)
- The importance attached to the active role of the person in constructing his or her knowledge (with the implication that learning through activity is more meaningful [than passive learning])
- A conception of mature adult thought (that is, formal operations)

In extending Piaget's theory to the study of adult learners, the research has mainly focused on "whether, and how, formal operational thought is generalized, extended, and maintained in adulthood" (Tennant, 1988, p. 79). Another line of research has explored why many adults never reach (or perhaps never seem to use) the formal operations stage. For example, it is estimated that "in Western culture, virtually all adults think easily at the concrete operational level; [while] perhaps half of adults think at the formal operational level" (Bee, 1987, p. 131). Summaries of the application of Piaget's theory to adulthood have been completed by a number of authors including Papalia and Bielby (1974), Long, McCrary, and Ackerman (1979), and Denney (1982). The essence of these summaries is twofold. First, within the Piagetian framework there are diverse explanations for how adult cognition develops and possibly regresses over the life span. And second, as noted above, there appears to be sufficient evidence to question the traditional views that cognitive development ends with the formal operations stage.

In line with this second observation, a number of scholars have proposed new structures or patterns of thinking for adults that are seen as developmentally beyond or different from Piaget's stage of formal operations. Some, as represented by Riegel (1973, 1975, 1976), have proposed different thought processes that may operate simultaneously with the formal system of logical thought proposed by Piaget. Others have posited "fifth stages" such as Arlin's problem-finding stage (1975); while still others have proposed whole new schemes of cognitive development (Perry, 1970; Pascual-Leone, 1983; Belenky, Clinchy, Goldberger, and Tarule, 1986; Rybash, Hoyer, and Roodin, 1986). A sampling of these alternative conceptualizations of cognitive development in adulthood is outlined in the next sections.

Dialectic Thinking

Riegel (1973, 1975, 1976) is one of the earliest and most often quoted theorists of cognitive development who challenged the notion that Piaget's theory adequately represents mature adult thought. According to Riegel (1973), "dialectic conceptualization characterizes the origin of thought in the individual and in society [and] represents a necessary synthesis in the development of thought toward maturity" (p. 350). In essence, dialectic thought explains the contradictory nature of human thought and action. Whereas "formal operational thinking as described by Piaget . . . involves the effort to find fundamental fixed realities — basic elements and immutable laws" — dialectical thinking "attempts to describe fundamental processes of change and the dynamic relationships through which change occurs" (Basseches, 1984, p. 24). Thinking in the dialectic sense allows for the acceptance of alternative truths or ways of thinking about similar phenomena that abound in everyday adult life. One might abhor killing, for example, and yet silently applaud the gentle person who switches off the life-support system of her spouse who is suffering beyond relief from a terminal illness.

Riegel (1973, 1975) proposed a corresponding mode of dialectic operations to stand beside Piaget's formal system (see Figure 10.1). The key to this alternative system is the inclusion of the dialectic or the acceptance of inherent contradictions and ambiguities in thought processes at all developmental levels and not just as part of more mature thought. "The skills and competence in one area of concern, for instance in sciences, might be of the type of formal dialectic operations; those in a second area, for instance in everyday business transactions, might be of the type of concrete dialectic operations," and so on (Riegel, 1973, p. 365). Riegel's basic assumptions are that people do not have to pass through any of the Piagetian levels to reach the higher levels of thinking within the dialectic framework and that people can operate simultaneously on all levels. In proposing this system, Riegel argued that people are not only ready to live with life's inherent contradictions and ambiguities but accept "these contradictions as a basic property of thought and creativity" (1973, p. 366).

A number of other writers, such as Pascual-Leone (1983), Basseches (1984), and Kramer (1983, 1989), have incorporated the notion of dialectic thinking into their work on adult cognitive development. Unlike Riegel, however, some of these scholars view dialectical thought processes as evolving from the formal stages proposed by Piaget, rather than conceptualizing the dialectical thought process as an alternative to the Piagetian sequence. Pascual-Leone, for example, suggests that adult cognitive devel-

Figure 10.1. Schematic Representation of Piaget's Extended Theory of Cognitive Development.

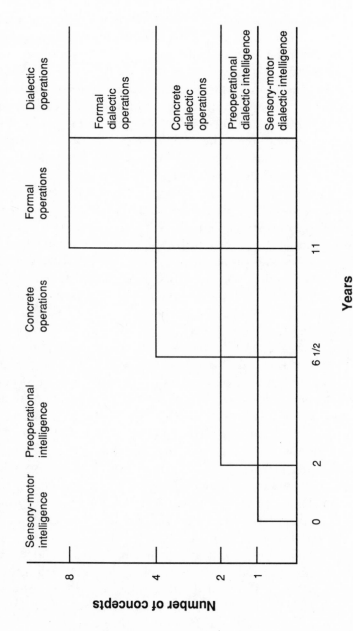

Source: Riegel, 1973. Reprinted by permission of S. Karger AG, Basel.

opment does not stop with formal operational thinking. Rather he posits four distinct stages beyond formal operations: the late formal stage, the predialectical stage, the dialectical stage, and the transcendental stage. He assumes that the structure of formal operations and the stages that precede it are not adequate to handle the everyday contradictions of adult life. These contradictions and conflicts necessitate different forms of thought.

Benack and Basseches (1989) also describe dialectical thinking as a postformal stage of thought. They have operationalized dialectical thought into a "dialectical schemata framework" consisting of twenty-four schemata representing different "moves in thought that dialectical thinkers tend to make" (p. 98). These schemata were abstracted from "writings reflecting dialectic world-outlooks" (Basseches, 1984, p. 72) and interviews with college students and professors about the nature of education. Basseches claims that "some of the dialectical schemata describe steps in dialectical analyses of phenomena. Other schemata describe ways of introducing dialectical perspectives on existence and knowledge into processes of inquiry. Others describe ways of maintaining dialectical movement within one's own thought" (1984, p. 73). Based on his research, Basseches has suggested that there are actually four phases to the development of mature dialectic thinking. (See Basseches, 1984, and Benack and Basseches, 1989, for a full description of these phases.) Both the basic schemata framework and the notions of phases of dialectic thinking call for further investigation.

Kramer (1983, 1989) is representative of theorists who appear to follow the thinking of Riegel (1973) in that she postulates a series of cognitive developmental stages separate from those of Piaget. Kramer's theory is grounded in the assumption that adult thought centers on both relativistic and dialectical operations, with the acceptance of contradiction and different worldviews as hallmarks of adult thinking. She posits a sequence of seven levels of development; the last four stages represent adolescent and adult thought processes. (See Kramer, 1989, for a complete description of these stages.)

Like Riegel, Kramer observes that rudimentary dialectic thinking begins in childhood, but she hypothesizes that mature dialectic thought (termed the stage of dynamic dialecticism) "rarely appears before middle age" (1989, p. 151). This mature dialectic thought is characterized by an awareness that all thought processes are culturally and historically bound and therefore dynamic and constantly evolving. An acceptance of this premise allows people to categorize ways of thinking and yet also accept the inherent contradictions that these different ways of thinking represent. Ways of thinking then become neither inherently good nor bad but rather are seen as unique for different groups of people at specified points in time. Although Kramer's model of cognitive development is not built upon Piaget's stages, she does see each adult stage of the model as "characterized by some degree of abstract thought" (1989, p. 155). Thus "a minimal Piagetian competence of formal operativity" (p. 157) is necessary for fully developed adult thinking. As noted by Kramer and Woodruff (1986), however, "there are still a number of theoretical issues which must be resolved . . . before the existence of such a structurally more advanced stage [dynamic dialecticism] can be forcefully posited" (p. 289).

Alternative Concepts Based on the Writings of Piaget

Moving away from the dialectic framework, other scholars have proposed different models and schemata to explain the development of adult cognition. Some of this work is grounded in the writings of Piaget (Arlin, 1975; Sinnott, 1984; Labouvie-Vief, 1984, 1989), with the emphasis on the notion that changes in cognition may extend beyond or differ from the level of formal operations he proposed. The work of Arlin (1975) and Labouvie-Vief (1980, 1984, 1990) can be taken to represent this line of research and theory building.

Arlin (1975, 1984), drawing on the work of Gruber (1973) on the development of creative thought in adults, has sought to identify a fifth stage of development (beyond that of Piaget's formal operations). She contends that formal thought actually consists of two distinct stages, not one, as proposed by Piaget. In her framework, Piaget's formal operations stage is renamed the problem-solving stage; the focus in this stage is on "the process of seeking a solution of a specific presented task" (Arlin, 1975, p. 603). Arlin then hypothesizes a new fifth stage, the problem-finding stage, characterized by "creative thought vis-à-vis 'discovered problems'" (p. 603) and the ability to generate and respond to important new questions and problems. In postulating these newly organized stages of development, she fully accepts the commonly recognized criteria for a stage model of development with the notions of sequential and hierarchical ordering of development. Therefore, "the relationship between formal operational thinking in the Piagetian sense (problem-solving stage) and the new stage of problem finding should be that all subjects who are successful in problem finding should also be characterized as formal operational thinkers in the Piagetian sense" (p. 603).

Arlin (1975) tested her proposed framework by studying the problem-solving and problem-finding behavior of sixty female college seniors. Although her findings generally support the existence of a distinct fifth stage (at least for some people), the study produced more questions than answers. For example, in further conceptualizing these fourth and fifth stages it is not clear how the patterns of thinking within each stage relate to one another. Further, it is not clear what operations in the problem-solving stage might assist a person in moving into the fifth stage of problem finding.

Labouvie-Vief (1980, 1984, 1990) extends Piagetian theory in a very different way. Suggesting that mature adult cognition does not develop until middle or later adulthood, Labouvie-Vief contends that a different form of thinking, other than formal abstract logic, must be integrated into one's model of adult cognitive development. "While the theme of youth is flexibility, the hallmark of adulthood is commitment and responsibility. Careers must be started, intimacy bonds formed, children raised. In short, in a world of a multitude of logical possibilities, one course of action must be adopted. This conscious commitment to one pathway and the deliberate disregard of other logical choices may mark the onset of adult cognitive maturity" (Labouvie-Vief, 1980, p. 153). In essence, this new form of thinking is "characterized by the ability to fit abstract thinking into the concrete

limitations of life" (Tennant, 1988, p. 79). The "playful exercises of cognitive schemas, [the] endless generating of 'ifs' and
'whens,' no longer may be adaptive, the task then becomes instead an attempt to utilize best one's knowledge towards the management of concrete situations" (Labouvie-Vief, 1980, p. 153).
Therefore, what many have conceived of as a regression in later
life to more concrete thought patterns is rather a positive adaptation to the realities of adult life. One key factor in being able
to adapt to these new ways of thinking is the ability to accept
and even thrive on contradiction. This in turn leads to acceptance of the notion of the inherent relativity of knowledge and
the ability to be self-regulating in choosing one's worldview.

In studying cognitive development in adulthood, Labouvie-
Vief (1990) goes on to postulate that "it may be variables related
[more] to one's social context rather than to one's age that account for particular developmental gradients" in cognition (p.
256). Therefore, if one wishes to discover changes and patterns
in cognitive development, it might be more fruitful to examine
groups of people who share pertinent life events and experiences
versus people of a certain chronological age group. For example, is it age that fosters changes in cognitive patterns? Or is
it a change in life circumstances such as retirement? In posing
this framework, Labouvie-Vief is echoing the sentiments of those
studying personal development. (See, for example, Dannefer,
1984; Dannefer and Perlmutter, 1990; Neugarten, 1976, 1979.)

Although at this point there is relatively little research
(Rogoff and Lave, 1984) that has directly examined such a "sociocultural" hypothesis of adult cognitive development, Goodnow (1990) has proposed a framework to explain how the sociological perspective (which does address the context issue) could
be used to extend the predominantly psychological accounts of
cognitive development. Goodnow argues, using the positions
put forth by four prominent sociologists (Berger, Habermas,
Bourdieu, and Foucault), that basically two "possible grafts"
could be made to the present work on cognitive development.
The first is "the general need to give more attention to the acquisition of values, either as a particular form of knowledge or
as an integral part of every piece of knowledge or skill" (p. 93).

In other words, there is an inherent bias in terms of what social classes or groups of people may be allowed access to certain areas of knowledge. This bias may also influence researchers to value and therefore study one type of cognitive skill development rather than another (say, abstract logic versus social cognition). Second, Goodnow observes that the social context often presents "a relatively benign, neutral, or free market" image (p. 82) despite the notion that the "social world takes an active and managing interest in the ideas people acquire" (p. 93). Goodnow goes on to outline specific ways in which sociologists could work with psychologists to enrich the present research and theory-building efforts in cognitive development.

Other Conceptions of Adult Cognitive Development

In a different vein, other theorists have posited entirely different schemes of cognitive development in adulthood. (See Perry, 1970, 1981; Kitchener and King, 1981; King and others, 1983; Belenky, Clinchy, Goldberger, and Tarule, 1986; John-Steiner, 1985; Rybash, Hoyer, and Roodin, 1986.) Perry (1970, 1981), for example, has offered an alternative map of cognitive development based on his work with college students (young adults). He proposes a nine-stage model of cognitive development, each position representing a qualitatively different way of interpreting learning experiences. As in Piaget's work, each stage is conceptualized as hierarchical and sequential and moves from relatively simple thinking patterns to highly complex ways of perceiving and evaluating knowledge. People move from viewing knowledge in "dualistic" terms as either right or wrong to an acceptance of knowledge and values as "relativistic"—that is, the context of the knowledge is as important as the knowledge itself. Unlike Piaget, Perry places as much emphasis on the transitions between each stage as on the stages themselves: "Perhaps development is all transitions and 'stages' only resting points along the way" (1981, p. 78). Here are some examples of Perry's proposed stages and the transitions between them (see Perry, 1970, 1981, for a complete description):

Position 1: Authorities know, and if we work hard, read every word, and learn Right answers, all will be well.

Transition between positions 1 and 2: But what about those Others I hear about? And different opinions? And uncertainties? Some of our own Authorities disagree with each other or don't seem to know, and some give us problems instead of answers.

Position 2: True Authorities must be Right, the Others are frauds. We remain Right. Others must be different and wrong. . . .

Transition between positions 5 and 6: But if everything is relative, am I relative too? How can I know I'm making the Right Choice?

Position 6: I see I'm going to have to make my own decisions in an uncertain world with no one to tell me I'm Right. . . .

Transition between positions 8 and 9: Things are getting contradictory. I can't make logical sense out of life's dilemmas.

Position 9: This is how life will be. I must be wholehearted while tentative, fight for my values, yet respect others, believe my deepest values right yet be ready to learn. I see that I shall be retracing this whole journey over and over—but, I hope, more wisely [Perry, 1981, p. 79].

Within this schema one can see shades of the more conceptually complex notions of mature dialectic thinking as noted by such writers as Riegel (1973, 1976) and Kramer (1983, 1989), as well as the major theme of becoming more relativistic in one's thought patterns as one matures.

Not only is each stage descriptive of individual cognitive growth, but Perry's stages have also been used to describe how people view instructor's roles and their own roles as learners. Learners at the lower positions, for example, tend to view instructors as authority figures and their job as learners to filter out the right answers from the material presented. Those at the higher end of the continuum view knowledge in a contextual sense and search for relationships between ideas and therefore see instructors more as experts and guides through the process.

Most of the work using Perry's schema has been completed with traditional-age college students, although a few studies (such as Cameron, 1983) have focused on adult learners, again usually in a college setting. One notable exception to this trend has been Kasworm's (1983b) attempt to integrate Perry's work into theory building on self-directed learning. From Kasworm's work and observations made by Perry (1970) and others, it appears that Perry's work may have broad implications across a greater spectrum of learners, but this line of thinking has yet to be extended in any systematic or concerted fashion. Cross (1981), for example, speculating on Perry's theory, foresees the possibility of new and varied stages emerging, especially if the focus of the study is on "adults doing extensive intellectual work" (p. 182).

Belenky, Clinchy, Goldberger, and Tarule (1986), grounded in the assumption that little attention has been paid to women's ways of knowing, as perhaps differentiated from the ways men think, have focused their work on women as learners and knowers. They have interviewed women from formal academic settings and women enrolled in parenting classes; the focus is on women's roles as students and parents rather than in the workplace. From their in-depth interviews of 135 women, "based on the theoretical and empirical work of Perry, Kohlberg, and Gilligan" (p. 14), Belenky and colleagues (1986, p. 15) grouped women's perspectives on knowing into five major categories:

1. Silence—a position in which women experience themselves as mindless and voiceless and subject to the whims of external authority. They are passive, feel incompetent, and are defined by others.
2. Received knowledge—a perspective from which women conceive of themselves as capable of receiving, even reproducing, knowledge from the all-knowing external authorities but not capable of creating knowledge on their own. They listen to the voices of others; their world is literal and concrete, good or bad.
3. Subjective knowledge—a perspective from which truth and

knowledge are conceived of as personal, private, and subjectively known or intuited. The locus of truth shifts to the self; intuition is valued over logic and abstraction; here women begin to gain a voice. Half the women in the study were in this category.

4. Procedural knowledge — a position in which women are invested in learning and applying objective procedures for obtaining and communicating knowledge. This position takes two forms: *separate knowing* — the self is separate from the objects of discourse, making it possible to doubt and reason; and *connected knowing* — there is intimacy and equality between the self and the object of discourse, based on empathetic understanding.

5. Constructed knowledge — a position in which women view all knowledge as contextual, experience themselves as creators of knowledge, and value both subjective and objective strategies for learning. This stage is characterized by the development of an authentic voice.

These categories, which are not necessarily fixed or universal, move from the simple to the complex — from having no voice (being almost mindless) to being able to value and create subjective and objective ways of knowing. Although the authors do not claim that these categories constitute specific stages of cognitive development, they appear to present them as such (Clark, 1990). Further research — with different groups of women and with various research designs — is needed to verify and refine these categories and build a data base demonstrating their developmental nature.

Clark (1990) has noted significant parallels between the findings of Belenky and her colleagues and those of Perry: "Received knowledge parallels the dualistic position; subjective knowledge correlates with multiplicity; and procedural and constructed knowledge has elements of relativism" (pp. 22–23). Still Belenky and colleagues' work (1986) has provided a significant contribution in that it allows women's voices, a metaphor often used in feminist theory, to become an important part of the theory building in cognitive development. As they note, and as

Clark has observed, similar categories have been found in men's thinking, yet there is a quality of uniqueness in the rich descriptions of women's voices presented.

Belenky and colleagues, like Perry, address the role of the instructor, emphasizing the notion of connected teaching: "The connected class provides a culture for growth. . . . The connected teacher tries to create groups in which members can nurture each other's thoughts to maturity" (p. 221). Uncertainty in knowing is both allowed and encouraged, and learners are urged to explore their current knowledge and experience in both objective and personal ways. Therefore, a learning experience can become both objective and personal for both instructor and participants. Daloz (1986) echoes similar notions in his descriptions of effective teaching and mentoring.

Rybash, Hoyer, and Roodin (1986) propose one of the most integrative and comprehensive models of cognitive development: the encapsulation model. Grounded in several approaches to the study of cognition (such as the cognitive-science, information-processing, and psychometric approaches), this model assumes that cognition is composed of three major elements: *processing* (how mental abilities and psychological resources are used to process information); *knowing* (how information is represented, stored, accessed, and used); and *thinking* (how people develop an understanding of their knowledge). As adults age, their "processing" and "knowing" abilities appear to decline with age and their knowledge is likely to become more "expert, intuitive, and domain-specific" (p. 120) versus comprehensive. This "encapsulation" of domain-specific knowledge (specific areas of expertise) results in adult styles of thinking that allow people more time to develop their "thinking" capacities, giving them an opportunity to develop and refine their areas of expertise. Since the number and nature of domain-specific areas of knowledge vary from person to person, adults' thinking patterns tend to become more differentiated as they age. If adults are able to "conceptualize their domain-specific knowledge in a relativistic, dialectic, and open-ended manner, they become capable of (a) solving the ill-defined problems characteristic of real life, (b) finding and identifying new problems and new perspectives from which they may be solved (for example, problem finding), and (c) producing creative and sophisticated works within defined areas of expertise" (p. 121). Rybash, Hoyer, and Roodin (1986) outline nine key areas for future research in adult cognition that emerge from the tenets of the encapsulation model. Among the most salient issues are these: "how domain-specific expertise arises over the course of development" (p. 157); what the different "processing strategies are among novices and experts within various knowledge domains" (p. 157); and how "novices and experts actually employ their knowledge in real life settings" (p. 159). Many of these sentiments have been noted by others as discussed in Chapter Nine.

In contrast to the other theories of cognitive development, John-Steiner (1985) has constructed a fascinating picture of how productive thinkers from a variety of fields, scientists to philosophers, have developed their thinking processes over a lifetime. One hundred creative men and women (almost equally distributed), defined as people who devoted many hours each day to intellectual pursuits, cooperated in this endeavor, which included in-depth interviews as well as letters, journals, biographies, autobiographies, and works in progress. From this vast array of materials, John-Steiner developed highly descriptive "notebooks of the mind" that offer a vision of how these people's thought processes were developed and nurtured, their various forms of thinking (such as visual and verbal thought), and what this all means in "the varied contexts of shared human knowledge" (p. 9).

From this exploration of thinking and the creative process, three major themes emerged. The first is that "immersion and exploration characterize the early stages of development" (p. 206), followed by lengthy and varied apprenticeships. "The role of friendships and collaboration as part of an individual's ability to sustain his or her work and to develop an effective organization of knowledge and purpose" (p. 210) is stressed, although the demands of solitary work and individual creative urges are also noted. The second theme is the different languages of thought (visual thinking, verbal thinking, languages of emotion, scientific thought) that are vividly portrayed by the subjects.

In discussing this theme, the author not only explores the rich diversity of these thought processes but also searches for "shared cognitive dynamics that cut across the many domains of knowing" (p. 9). A predominant thread she finds among most of these experienced thinkers, no matter what language or languages of thought they use, is their ability to continually integrate new, random, and unstable ideas into their more sustained processes of thought. The third theme that emerged is the passion for their task found in these productive thinkers. There is a continuity of concern for a subject tied to "an intense awareness of one's active inner life combined with sensitivity to the external world" (p. 220). The full realization of these people's creativity often came from a painful dialectic between what they already knew and what they came to realize as they developed their life's work. John-Steiner has contributed a unique picture of how productive thinkers' cognitive patterns develop and appear in different domains, and yet in her work can be seen the movement of these people toward highly complex relativistic and dialectical thinking, as described by other theorists, such as Riegel (1973, 1976) and Rybash, Hoyer, and Roodin (1986). In addition, one obvious question, since her subjects were chosen for their intellectual abilities and achievements, is whether John-Steiner's observations are relevant to the average adult learner. Some may not be, especially the notion of the importance of early immersion in the specific content area. Other observations, though, may prove to be applicable to learners in general—for example, the key role of significant others in sustaining cognitive development and the passion for knowing.

A Need for Further Conceptualization

Although there is little empirical evidence to support or refute the idea that adult thought patterns are qualitatively different from those of children, the notion is intriguing. Two things at least are clear: Mature adult cognition involves more than just the ability to think in abstract logical terms, and cognitive development cannot be separated from its social and cultural context. Obviously, there is a need for further study with a variety of different populations and the addition of different paradigms to clarify these adult thought processes and how they develop throughout the life span. (See Keating and MacLean, 1988; Goodnow, 1990; Rybash, Hoyer, and Roodin, 1986.) One result of further study in this area could be a shift from the "dominant (but limited) view of adult thinking which focuses primarily on the gain or loss of specific skills" (Bee, 1987, p. 133) to a further understanding of what does transpire as adults develop thinking patterns that seem to be characterized as much by the acceptance of multiple perspectives and dialectic thought as by formal logical reasoning.

Wisdom: The Hallmark of Adult Thinking

Wisdom is often seen as the pinnacle of adult thinking, yet this concept has received little attention until quite recently in the literature (Clayton, 1976; Clayton and Birren, 1980; Holliday and Chandler, 1986; Boucouvalas, 1987; Taranto, 1987; Sternberg, 1990e). Our concept of wisdom has come primarily from the great philosophers and theologians of both the Eastern and Western worlds. Birren and Fisher (1990) point out that

> The concept wisdom contains within it a dimension that ranges, at one end, from religion and the belief that God alone possesses the ultimate wisdom to a more mundane view that practically minded administrators, leaders, business persons, and others can acquire the necessary experience and shrewdness in the conduct of daily affairs to be termed wise. In other words, people can become wise as they ripen in a particular culture. In particular, there is the notion in our culture that wisdom must ripen, and it is therefore attributed most often to older persons.
>
> Another dimension of wisdom relevant to its attribution to older persons is the fact it involves a changing balance between acting and reflecting. . . . Thus, youth may have capacity to be wise but are too impelled to action to demonstrate this capacity [p. 319].

Psychologists and educators have defined and studied wisdom from a variety of perspectives. Robinson (1990) noted that its definition has changed over time, differing in the ancient Greek, traditional Christian, and contemporary conceptions. Sternberg (1990d) defines it as a metacognitive style, Baltes and Smith (1990) define it as expertise in everyday life, and Meacham (1990) suggests that it is an awareness of the fallibility of knowing; age is explicitly not a component of wisdom; in fact, one may lose it with age. Arlin (1990) links it to cognitive development and associates it with problem-finding ability, while Orwoll and Perlmutter (1990) relate it to personality development, defining it as the integration of cognition with affect, affiliation, and social concerns. These and other definitions point to the complexity of the concept. Most researchers do agree, however, that wisdom is the province of adulthood, although older is not necessarily to be equated with wiser.

Research on wisdom has attempted to delineate its major components and its relationship to age. Following is a discussion of some of the recent studies on wisdom. Clayton (1976, 1982), for example, has explored the dimensions or underlying structure of wisdom in order to build an empirical definition. The participants in her study, consisting of eighty-three well-educated people representing three broad age cohorts, were asked to judge groups of words on whether they were descriptive of wisdom. What emerged was a multifaceted description of wisdom as the integration of affective (understanding, empathy, peacefulness), reflective (introspection and intuition), and cognitive (knowledge and experience) components. Age differences were found in the perceived dimensions of wisdom, in that these dimensions became "more differentiated with the increase in the participant's age" (Clayton and Birren, 1980, p. 117), suggesting that the underlying structure of wisdom may change as a person ages.

Holliday and Chandler (1986), like Clayton (1976, 1982), have sought to provide empirical parameters for the term wisdom in three interlocking studies. They first collected general descriptions of wise people from which they then in a second study formulated a basic description of wisdom. In the third phase of their research, they "examined the influence of the wise prototype on people's information processing strategies" (p. 44). Subjects in their studies, numbering 458 different individuals, represented all age cohorts of young, middle, and older adults. Like Clayton, they concluded that wisdom is a multidimensional construct consisting of more than the objective and context-free aspects of thought. Using Habermas's (1970) framework, Holliday and Chandler propose a tripartite model of wisdom that consists of technical, practical, and emancipatory elements. In their view, "Wise people must be able to solve problems—but not in the abstract sense. The type of problems that wise people presumably deal with appear to have strong practical and emancipatory components. That is, wisdom problems are problems endemic to life and to the human condition. . . . Consequently, the problems typically involve or center on values" (p. 90).

In a somewhat different framework, Sternberg (1986b) sought to discover people's conceptions or implicit theories of wisdom by exploring "the nature and the interrelationships of intelligence, wisdom, and creativity" (pp. 177-178). Through a series of four studies with both laypersons (community volunteers and students) and specialists (college professors from a variety of disciplines), Sternberg found that people not only have implicit theories about intelligence, wisdom, and creativity but use them to evaluate others (p. 185). Moreover, he found differences in the way laypersons and specialists perceived each of the three constructs, including the notion of wisdom.

Laypersons perceived the wise individual to have much the same analytic reasoning ability one finds in the intelligent person. But the wise person has a certain sagacity that is not necessarily found in intelligent people: He or she listens to others, knows how to weigh advice, and can deal with a variety of different people. The wise person is especially able to make clear, sensible, and fair judgments and is perceived to profit from the experience of others and learn from others' mistakes, as well as from his or her own (p. 186). The specialists, on the other hand, tended to emphasize certain aspects of wisdom as more critical than others. The art professors, for example, "emphasize insight, knowing how to balance logic and instinct . . . and sensitivity," while the business professors emphasize such things as "maturity of judgment, understanding of the limitations of one's actions . . . and appreciation of the ideologies of others" (pp. 186–187). Sternberg concludes that the three major constructs of intelligence, wisdom, and creativity are indeed distinct and yet interrelated and, moreover, that we must pay as much attention to wisdom and creativity as to intelligence.

Smith, Dixon, and Baltes (1989), in contrast to Sternberg, frame their work from the perspective that wisdom is a part of intelligence—what they have termed the "pragmatics of intelligence" (see Chapter Eight). They view wisdom as a cognitive expertise in the fundamental pragmatics of life that are "visible in situations related to life planning, life management, and life review. This expertise is reflected in individuals' definition of, judgments about, and solutions to life problems" (p. 311) and is built on a person's store of factual knowledge and experience. In the most global sense they see wisdom as "good judgment about important but uncertain matters" (p. 312). The basis of this wise judgment "is both specialized knowledge about life in general and a repertoire of efficient strategies for applying and adapting that knowledge to many contexts, interpersonal situations, and life tasks" (p. 326).

Smith, Dixon, and Baltes's initial empirical approach (1989) to studying wisdom from this framework focused on situations involving "life planning" decisions (decisions about careers, retirement, family). Intensive interviews were conducted with sixty adults, from three broad age cohorts, as they worked through several fictitious life planning tasks presented by the researchers. Contrary to expectations, the age differences in responses were small and emerged only when the problems were related to age. Both younger and older adults responded more effectively when confronted with problems their age group would normally face. Their results seem to suggest that older does not necessarily mean wiser, at least not for the kind of judgments needed for life planning decisions.

Despite the different perspectives from which wisdom has been studied and the lack of consensus on its precise dimensions, several points of agreement have emerged: "Wisdom has been held to involve access to special types of pragmatic or experientially based knowledge. Somewhat less uniformly, wisdom has also been characterized by its practical nature and orientation to social and interpersonal issues" (Holliday and Chandler, 1986, p. 26). Moreover, wisdom seems to consist of the ability to be reflective and to make sound judgments on the everyday practicalities of life.

In reflecting on this renewed interest in the study of wisdom and how it might enrich learning in adulthood, we were struck by observations made by Dychtwald and Flower (1989) about "the third age"—that part of life beyond the age of sixty, a time of life that more and more people are experiencing as healthy and vital individuals. Dychtwald and Flower contend that this third age allows for "the further development of the interior life of the intellect, memory, and imagination, of emotional maturity, and of one's personal sense of spiritual identity" (p. 53). It is a time for people to give back to society through their wisdom, power, and spirituality "the lessons, resources, and experiences accumulated over a lifetime" (p. 53). They then quote Monsignor Fahey, the director of Fordham University's Third Age Center: "People in the third age should be the glue of society, not its ashes" (p. 53). Their conclusion is clear and dramatic: "Think about it. We know even with the best care overall fitness will decline gradually with the years. While the strength of the senses is weakening, what if the powers of the mind, the heart, and the spirit are rising? If life offers the ongoing opportunity for increased awareness and personal growth, think of how far we could evolve, given the advantage of several extra decades of life!" (p. 52). Mature adult cognition is more than just abstract logic and complex reasoning; it also encompasses the ability to think, feel, and act "wisely" in life. What a gift of knowledge and experience older adults can offer to those of us who are wrestling to understand learning in adulthood.

Summary

Cognitive development refers to the change in thinking patterns as one grows older. Much of the work on cognitive development in adulthood has been grounded primarily in the work of Piaget. One line of research has focused on how Piaget's final stage of formal operational thought is generalized and maintained in adulthood. A more fruitful research tradition has been the conceptualization of "adult" stages of cognition beyond that of formal operations and the positing of different schemata of adult cognitive thought.

Some theorists, represented by Riegel (1973, 1976), Kramer (1983, 1989), and Labouvie-Vief (1980, 1984, 1990), have proposed different types of thought processes that may operate in concert with (or be more advanced than) the formal system of logical thought proposed by Piaget. Two prominent themes that emerge from this work are the dialectic and relativistic nature of mature adult thought. Other researchers have posited entirely new schemes of adult cognitive development. These alternative systems range from the traditional stage theories of development, such as the work of Perry (1970, 1981), to those theories, represented by the work of John-Steiner (1985) and Rybash, Hoyer, and Roodin (1986), that advance a comprehensive and complex view of how adults' thinking processes develop. Again, as in the work that primarily evolved from Piaget's formal system of logical thought, the two basic themes of dialectic and relativistic thought patterns appear in these alternative conceptions. A new perspective on adult cognitive development, one emphasizing the impact of social context on development, has been noted as well. Throughout the chapter we have pointed out the need to broaden the study of cognitive processes beyond the customary psychological framework, a theme stressed in Chapter Nine as well as in the study of adult development described in Chapter Six.

The chapter concluded with a brief overview of the concept of wisdom, often regarded as the hallmark of mature adult thinking. Although often discussed by the great philosophers and theologians, this area of study received little attention until quite recently in the literature on learning. Representative conceptions of wisdom, such as those of Clayton (1976, 1982), Holliday and Chandler (1986), and Sternberg (1986b), were reviewed. Despite the different perspectives from which wisdom has been studied, theorists seem to agree that wisdom involves special types of experience-based knowledge and is characterized by the ability to be reflective in one's thinking and to make sound judgments in everyday life.

PART FOUR

Building
a Theoretical Base
for Adult Learning

The accumulation of facts about a particular field of practice usually leads to thinking about how bits and pieces of information can be pieced together to explain some aspect of practice — the process is known as theorizing. In an article exploring the relationship between practice and theory, Suttle (1982) observes that "while practice deals with the descriptive world, theory attempts to explain that world. Put into an educational context, this difference is ultimately the difference between merely having an assortment of so-called facts at one's disposal and being able to understand what one allegedly knows" (p. 105).

Theorizing about a phenomenon often results in a conceptual scheme in the form of a "framework," "model," or "theory." Part Four of *Learning in Adulthood* highlights theory building in the field of adult learning. Some of these efforts, as in the area of self-directed learning, are in fact tentative frameworks for ordering research — frameworks suggesting future directions for theory. Other efforts can properly be labeled models, if we define model as a visual representation, while others claim to be theories. A theory is a set of interrelated concepts that explain some aspect of the field in a parsimonious manner. Three areas in particular have been the focus of model or theory building: self-direction, participation, and adult learning.

Since Tough's work on adult learning projects published in 1971, self-directed learning and individual learning projects have captured the imagination of researchers and writers both inside and outside the field of adult education. After a phase of descriptive studies of self-directed learning, today more attention is being given to mapping the relationships between self-direction, autonomy, instruction, and learning in adulthood. Chapter Eleven describes the two broadest frameworks being explored for future research and theory building: self-direction in learning as a form of study and self-directedness as a personal attribute of the learner. The ground-breaking work being done by Spear and Mocker, Danis and Tremblay, Brockett and Hiemstra, Candy, and others is highlighting the importance of self-directed learning, autonomy, the centrality of the learner, and environmental circumstances. Underlying much of this effort, especially as reflected in recent work by Candy and Brockett and Hiemstra, is an attempt to bring greater conceptual clarity to the term *self-directed learning.*

More than other areas of adult learning, participation and motivation have been systematically investigated. Beginning with Houle's typology of adult learners published in *The Inquiring Mind* (1961), capturing information on motivation and participation by means of typological frameworks or models has been a popular undertaking. Chapter Twelve reviews models of participation from Houle's work to recent models and frameworks proposed by Miller, Boshier, Cross, Rubenson, Darkenwald and Merriam, and Cookson. As far as we can determine, only Boshier's and Darkenwald and Merriam's models have been tested. This research is reviewed briefly. The chapter includes an assessment of the strengths and weaknesses of all the models.

Chapter Thirteen explores several attempts to formulate a comprehensive theory of learning in adulthood. These theories can be loosely grouped into three categories. First we survey the theories based on characteristics of adult learners. This category includes Knowles's well-known concept of andragogy and Cross's characteristics of adult learners (CAL) model. The second category includes theories based on an adult's life situation. McClusky's theory of margin, Knox's proficiency theory, and Jarvis's model of adult learning are discussed in this section. Changes in consciousness constitute the focus of the third category. Mezirow's perspective transformation and Freire's conscientization contend that changes in perspective or consciousness are the defining characteristic of learning in adulthood. Mezirow's theory in particular has stimulated considerable debate. The chapter closes with an overall assessment of these efforts to explain learning in adulthood.

Eleven

Clarifying
the Nature of
Self-Directed Learning

Since Tough's work on adult learning projects published in 1971, self-directed learning has captured the imagination of researchers and writers both inside and outside the field of adult education. Although learning on one's own has been the primary mode of learning in adulthood throughout the ages, serious study of this phenomenon is fairly recent. Why this apparent dichotomy between the prevalence of this learning mode and the lack of serious study? One response has been that only learning which takes place in formal institutions is relevant to adult educators (Verner, 1964; Houle, 1988). Studying learning within the natural environment of adults' everyday life has not been considered useful or even possible by some. Tied in with this perspective is the role of educators of adults. (See Hiemstra, 1980, 1988a; Brookfield, 1981; Garrison, 1989.) Do we have any business working with learners outside the formal institutional environment? From an even more critical perspective, others have questioned whether self-directed learning is in fact a distinct concept. (See Boshier, 1983; Little, 1979; Brookfield, 1986; Candy, 1987b.) Despite these concerns, the study of self-directed learning has become more prevalent and emerged as a salient strand of research over the last two decades.

Note: Portions of this chapter are based on a monograph titled *Self-Directed Learning* by R. S. Caffarella and J. M. O'Donnell (Nottingham, England: Department of Adult Education, University of Nottingham, 1989.)

This chapter reviews the major research efforts in self-directed learning. Here we provide a framework for ordering future research and theory building in self-directed learning and discuss the major issues that must be addressed as this work moves beyond description into theory. The earlier research in this arena was primarily descriptive in nature (Brockett, 1985b), building on the pioneering work of Cyril Houle (1961) and Allen Tough (1967, 1979). A great deal of emphasis in this work was placed on verifying that adults do deliberately learn on their own and discovering how they go about doing this. Recent work has focused on the learning process itself (Spear and Mocker, 1984; Spear, 1988; Danis and Tremblay, 1987, 1988) and on the characteristics and styles of learners who are self-directed (Chene, 1983; Oddi, 1984, 1986; Candy, 1987b; Bonham, 1989). In discussing this research we have grouped this large array of studies into two broad frameworks. Research that addresses self-directed learning as a form of study is explored first. We then survey those studies that view self-directedness as a personal attribute of individual learners. The chapter concludes with a discussion of the major issues that must be considered in building future research and theory-building agendas in self-directed learning.

Self-Directed Learning as a Form of Study

Self-directed learning has most often been used to describe a form of study in which people take the primary initiative, with or without the help of others, for planning, conducting, and evaluating their own learning activities (Knowles, 1975). The definition that has been used most often by researchers studying self-directed learning from this perspective is the operational definition offered by Allen Tough (1979) in his study of learning projects. A learning project is defined by Tough "as a series of related episodes, adding up to at least seven hours. In each episode, more than half of the person's total motivation is to gain and retain certain fairly clear knowledge and skill, or to produce some other lasting change in himself" (1979, p. 7). Two lines of inquiry within this framework have been verification studies and the work completed on the process of self-directed learning.

Verification Studies. Tough's model of self-directed learning became the basis for numerous dissertations and research studies on the verification of the existence of self-directed learning as a form of study. A range of specific populations has been studied; pharmacists (Johns, 1973), mothers with young children (Coolican, 1974), extension agents (Bejot, 1981), nurses (Kathrein, 1981), farmers (Bayha, 1983), students at all levels (Kratz, 1978; Geisler, 1984; Caffarella and Caffarella, 1986), older adults (Hiemstra, 1976), clergymen (Morris, 1977), and physicians (Richards, 1986). Although there is disagreement on the amount and type of self-directed learning that goes on in the general population, we can say without reservation that the existence of self-directed learning as a form of study has been established (Brookfield, 1984; Caffarella and O'Donnell, 1987b, 1988a).

A number of methodological criticisms have been aimed at these verification studies (Brookfield, 1984, 1986, 1988a; Caffarella and O'Donnell 1987b, 1988a, 1989); the most serious focus on the populations studied and the data collection technique. Although other types of groups have been studied (Brockett, 1985c), the verification studies deal primarily with the middle class (Brookfield, 1984, 1985; Caffarella and O'Donnell, 1987b). Yet McCune (1988), in a recent meta-analytic study of self-directed learning that included both descriptive and quantitative research, contends that "socioeconomic status is sparsely reported in the adult self-direction in learning research," so definite conclusions about this variable cannot be drawn (p. 120). The same is true of the ethnicity of the subjects. McCune goes on to say that the data do suggest that the populations studied have consisted primarily of middle-aged, educationally advantaged females. Her findings are in agreement with earlier observations by Caffarella and O'Donnell (1987b, 1988a) that many times only sketchy descriptions of the subjects have been given. In relation to criticisms of the data collection technique, Tough's interview schedule (and variations thereof) calls for probing and prompting, a technique that has the potential for contaminating the findings. Moreover, the subjects must reflect back on their learning experiences (Boshier, 1983).

Caffarella and O'Donnell (1987b, 1988a) suggest that any further verification studies should examine highly diverse populations — including more subjects with lower levels of formal education and different ethnic and socioeconomic backgrounds — and be representative of various cultural groups. The results of these studies should be compared with those completed with the predominantly highly educated female population. In addition, collecting data by means other than Tough's interview schedule, such as learning diaries (Allerton, 1974; Boshier, 1983), conversational interviews (Brookfield, 1981; Danis and Tremblay, 1987, 1988), and standardized instruments, should be explored. Again the verification data from studies using these alternative methodologies should be compared, with similar subject pools, with data collected using Tough's interview schedule.

The Process of This Form of Study. Although studies in the Tough tradition are often quoted to verify the existence of this form of learning, the heart of this work concerns how adults go about planning and carrying out their self-directed learning and what resources they use in this process. Coupled with the description given by Knowles (1975, 1980), the process of self-directed learning, as outlined in Chapter Three, has been conceptualized primarily as linear — that is, adults decide what they want to learn, formulate goals, and then proceed to select learning activities, resources, and ways to evaluate their learning. Gerstner (1987) observed that, at least for Tough, this linear framework may have developed from his original dissertation on adult self-teachers (Tough, 1966, 1967), which was grounded in the literature addressing teaching and curriculum planning.

The major challenges to the notion that self-directed learning is primarily a linear process, one that mirrors the formal instructional process, have come from four exploratory studies (Spear and Mocker, 1984; Danis and Tremblay, 1987, 1988; Spear, 1988, and Berger, 1990) plus earlier conceptual writings of Penland (1981) and Gibbons and others (1980). In essence, the consensus is that adult learners rarely plan their self-directed learning activities in advance. Rather, they follow numerous paths and use a variety of strategies when learning on their own. The ability to locate appropriate and useful resources is often seen as a key aspect of this process. Although these studies, especially the four data-based studies, have provided us with some provocative questions about the process of self-directed learning, this work is just in its infancy and must therefore be interpreted with caution.

To build a more comprehensive picture of the process of self-directed learning, further study is required: studies done in Tough's tradition but with a broader spectrum of populations; well-designed qualitative studies to give us additional in-depth descriptions of the process; and more quantitatively oriented work emphasizing the verification and expansion of sharply definitive descriptions of the process. One of the more detailed frameworks that have been proposed for this further study is Spear's (1988) cluster analysis procedure, which is grounded in Bandura's (1977) social learning theory. In completing a cluster analysis, detailed accounts of the learning project, obtained through in-depth interviews, are analyzed using the seven interactive elements that make up the learning transaction. (See Chapter Three for a description and example of a cluster of these interactive elements.) It is Spear's assumption, based on his own research, that clusters of elements will begin to emerge — some as separate entities and some as a series of pieces in which one cluster leads to related clusters. Once these clusters are identified, "each individual cluster may be analyzed and understood according to how the elements interact and affect one another. These analyses give insights into the degree of significance respective elements contribute to the project" (Spear, 1988, p. 218). To date, only one research project (Berger, 1990) using Spear's proposed framework has been completed. Although Berger, who analyzed the learning projects of twenty Caucasian males without college degrees, found Spear's framework and categories to be useful starting points for charting her subjects' self-directed learning activities, she also encountered a number of difficulties in applying the model. Among these difficulties were listing the precise learning steps or actions in the order in which they occurred; the lack of attention in the model to changes in attitude and skill building that participants displayed; and the inability at times to differentiate between the categories of elements proposed by Spear. Berger reflected that some of the difficulties in using Spear's framework for the research may have arisen from the long-term nature of most of the learning projects her subjects described. By contrast, in Spear's original pilot test of the model, the adults were engaged in relatively short-term projects. She observed that perhaps the level of detail required by the Spear framework could be gathered only in self-directed learning projects of relatively short duration (under six months) and with more definite starting and ending points.

Peters (1989b) has proposed a second intriguing procedure for clarifying the process of self-directed learning. Grounded in the premise that many self-directed learning activities are undertaken by adults to solve problems in their lives, he outlines "a method for studying self-direction in learning in the context of problem solving processes" (p. 1). The Action-Reason-Thematic (ART) method (see Peters, 1988, for a full description), developed by Peters and Lazzara (1988), consists of cycles of analyses followed by interviews in which the interviewer seeks to discover how people approach solving their problems, including the underlying reasons for taking the actions they did. Here are some specific questions used in this protocol (Peters, 1989b, p. 14):

1. What is the documentary or situational information utilized by a learner in making decisions — the aspects of a situation which the learner attends to or ignores?
2. What are the kinds of additional information which the learner seeks, or which the learner provides out of his own knowledge, given a problem?
3. How does the learner attempt to recast or transform a problem he/she is called upon to

solve in order to relate it to his/her own experience?

4. What are the general or high-level strategies which a learner employs in the conduct of making decisions?

5. What are the short-cuts, precepts, and rules of thumb which guide many of the learner's actions?

It is Peters' contention that many of these questions "address descriptions of self-direction in learning that are missing in current literature" (p. 15).

Three issues have been viewed as especially important to research on the process of self-directed learning: the resources used by learners, the quality of both the process and end product of self-directed learning, and the competencies of learners for this form of study (Caffarella and O'Donnell, 1987b, 1988a). It appears that we now have a basic understanding of the resources used by self-directed learners (Tough, 1979; Penland, 1979; Caffarella and O'Donnell, 1988a, 1989), especially the resources they choose most often. What we need now is further clarification of the usefulness of each type and how educators of adults can assist learners in finding and using these resources (Tough, 1978; Penland, 1979; Houle, 1984, 1988). Above all we need basic descriptive studies exploring why and in what circumstances each resource is used and in clarifying what our roles as adult educators should be in this part of the process.

Although the skills needed by adults to carry out self-directed learning have been identified (Tough, 1979; Knowles, 1975; Caffarella and Caffarella, 1986), these competencies have never been empirically tested for reliability and validity. Nor do we have a clear picture of how adults have acquired or could acquire these competencies. Do they become proficient as a result of family influence? Formal schooling? Work experience? Trial and error? These issues offer a rich area for further study. Moreover, we need a reliable and valid instrument to measure a person's skills related to self-directed learning.

Coolican (1973), Brookfield (1984, 1988a), and Brockett

and Hiemstra (1991) have expressed concern about the overall quality of self-directed learning, both as a process and as a product. How can we both ensure and measure the quality of this form of learning? Caffarella and O'Donnell (1988b, in press) studied one specific group of adult learners, training professionals, in order to discover how they define and evaluate the quality of their self-directed learning experiences. From this context-specific qualitative research they concluded that the learner's control over both the learning project and its evaluation were important elements affecting the quality of the learning experience. Furthermore, the ease with which learners can locate appropriate resources seems to determine whether they label their project a "quality" experience. We need to clarify exactly what quality means for this type of learning from the combined perspectives of the learner and the educator.

Many of the researchers who have studied self-directed learning as a process implicitly assume that although the learner takes primary responsibility for the learning process, the learning act itself can take place in a variety of settings from individual homes to formal classrooms (Tough, 1978, 1979; Knowles, 1975). This has raised the important question in the minds of a number of researchers as to the boundaries of self-directed learning versus organized instruction. Can both forms of learning coexist and complement one another (Hiemstra, 1980; Caffarella and Caffarella, 1986; Kasworm, 1983a), or are they in fact incompatible? Some authors, as noted in Chapter Three, exclude this form of learning as being outside the organized adult education system (Willen, 1984; Candy, 1987b; Gibbons and Phillips, 1982), while others have been willing to accept a blending of the two (Brockett and Hiemstra, 1991; Hiemstra, 1980; Hiemstra and Sisco, 1990; Caffarella and Caffarella, 1986; Brookfield, 1988a). Specifically, Brookfield (1988a) asserts that "any act of self-directed learning must be seen as a complex configuration of differing domains, forms, and methods: Most efforts we undertake to explore an area of knowledge, to acquire certain skills, to become more insightful, involve us in a complicated and dynamic interconnection of reflection, action, individually planned activities, self-directed decision, decisions arrived at collaboratively, decisions imposed upon us from without and so on" (p. 17). Therefore, in his opinion, no act of learning can be described as fully self-directing (Brookfield, 1984, 1988a). Rather, this form of learning can be described only within a self-directed context.

Self-Directed Learning as a Personal Attribute

There has been less focus in the research literature on self-direction in learning as a personal characteristic of the learner. The assumption underlying much of this work is that learning in adulthood means becoming more self-directed and autonomous (Knowles, 1980; Chene, 1983). Kasworm (1983b), for example, proposes that self-directed learning "represents a qualitative evolvement of a person's sense of cognitive definition and developmental readiness for ambiguous and nondefined actions" (p. 8). And Chene (1983) offers three elements that characterize an autonomous or self-directed learner: independence, the ability to make choices, and the capacity to articulate the norms and the limits of a learning activity.

Research into the nature of the self-directed learner asks the who and what questions: Are these learners introverts or extroverts? What is their cognitive style? What personality characteristics do they have in common? What level of education have they achieved? Are they more autonomous than other learners? Basically researchers are trying to gain an understanding of the typical learner's characteristics and style. Specifically they have tried to link a number of different variables with being more or less self-directed in one's learning. Examples of these variables include readiness for self-directed learning (Guglielmino, 1977; Guglielmino and Guglielmino, 1988), educational level (Bejot, 1981; Savićević, 1985), personality factors (Fox and West, 1983; Oddi, 1984, 1986), learning style (Deroos, 1982; Theil, 1984), locus of control (Skaggs, 1981), field independence and field dependence (Pratt, 1984; Brookfield, 1986), life satisfaction (Brockett, 1985b), creativity (Torrance and Mourad, 1978), and autonomy (Chene, 1983; Candy, 1987b; Boucouvalas, 1988a). Their findings, however, are confusing and con-

tradictory at best. Deroos (1982), for example, whose participants consisted of 175 men and women enrolled in a three-year
independent study program for health care professionals, found
that an abstract learning style, based on the Kolb (1984) classification, was related to a person's persistence in self-directed
learning. Theil (1984), on the other hand, whose subjects included thirty men and women from French-speaking associations, found that it was the accommodator style which was
related to success in self-directed learning. From a more conceptual perspective, Pratt (1984) states that people with tendencies toward field independence are more capable of self-directed
learning, while Brookfield (1986) expresses the opposite view
that field dependence is more characteristic of self-directed
learners. Brookfield's view, which is contrary to what most theorists have expressed, is grounded in the idea that "self-directed
learning is equated with the exhibition of critical reflection on
the part of adults" (p. 42) and that the kinds of beliefs (such
as the contextuality and relativity of knowledge) needed for this
kind of thinking are most often seen in field-dependent versus
field-independent learners.

The notion of readiness and the concept of autonomy have
been studied and discussed most often in the professional literature on self-directedness as a personal attribute. The notion
of readiness implies an internal state of psychological readiness
to undertake self-directed learning activities. Guglielmino (1977)
has provided the most widely used operational definition of this
idea. She states that people must possess eight factors to be considered ready to pursue self-directed learning: openness to learning, self-concept as an effective learner, initiative and independence in learning, informed acceptance of responsibility, love
of learning, creativity, future orientation, and the ability to use
basic study and problem-solving skills. These factors undergird
her Self-Directed Learning Readiness Scale (SDLRS), designed
to ascertain adult readiness for self-directed learning. Numerous studies (Torrance and Mourad, 1978; Hassan, 1981; Brockett, 1985b; Caffarella and Caffarella, 1986; Guglielmino and
Guglielmino, 1988) have been completed using this scale.

Use of the SDLRS in research on self-directed learning

has not been without controversy, however. Major questions have been raised by Field (1989, 1991), among others (Brookfield, 1984; Brockett, 1985a, 1985b), as to its basic validity and reliability. Field contends, after thorough examination of the instrument, that "the problems inherent in the scale are so substantial that it should not continue to be used" (1989, p. 138). In addition to methodological concerns, he highlights the scale's conceptual flaws as the fundamental problem. In a tripartite response to Field's work, Guglielmino, Long, and McCune (1989) dismiss most of Field's arguments due to "errors of omission and commission" in Field's research. Specifically, they have criticized Field's analysis of the SDLRS on three major grounds: incorrect interpretation of sources cited, the limited nature of his subject pool for a study of this type, and the statistical procedures used. Only further studies on the SDLRS will put to rest these major differences of opinion.

The relationship of autonomy and self-directedness in learning has been discussed primarily at the conceptual level. Chene (1983), for example, defines the autonomy of the learner as independence and the will to learn. However, she also notes that the learner must have an awareness of the learning process, an understanding of what is conceived as competence in a specific area of study, and the ability to make critical judgments: "[Autonomy] is a structure which makes possible the appropriation of learning by the learner" (p. 46).

Autonomy, however, is not necessarily context-free; there is a relationship between the personal and situational variables that must come into play for a person to be autonomous in certain learning situations. As Candy (1987b, p. 47) observes: "One does not 'become' autonomous in any final or absolute sense." Confidence and commitment enter into each learning situation. Pratt (1988), in agreement with Candy, contends that self-direction is a situational attribute of learners, not a general trait of adulthood. Therefore, adults vary considerably in their desire, capacity, and readiness to exert control over instructional functions and tasks. Pratt goes on to suggest that learners may need more direction when they lack the information to make informed choices. In addition, he points out that self-directed learners must be able to decide on two issues: Do they value having control over their learning? And will they do anything to establish or relinquish that control?

In a similar vein, Boucouvalas (1988a) has challenged the exclusive emphasis on the autonomous self as only a partial explanation of what selfhood is all about. She turns to the concept of homonomy in conjunction with autonomy as complementary dimensions of the growth of self. While autonomy reflects independence and uniqueness, homonomy is "the experience of being part of meaningful wholes and in harmony with superindividual units such as family, social group, culture, and cosmic order" (p. 58). The prime motivations for the autonomous self are achievement and conquest, whereas participation in something beyond the individual self is the motivation for the homonomous (connected) self. Giving wider recognition to this homonomous part of the self may allow for fuller explanations of the collaborative aspects of self-directed learning referred to by Tough (1978, 1979), Knowles (1975), and others in activities such as teamwork, shared resources, and peer networks.

To understand self-directedness in learning as a personal attribute, more in-depth study is required. We need to isolate the variables that appear to assist a person to be more self-directed in his or her learning—from seemingly simple demographic variables such as age, socioeconomic status, and occupation to more complex concepts like autonomy, life satisfaction, cognitive style, and motivation. Varying methodological routes are also required in the further exploration of this area. The first route calls for the quantitative paradigm with a greater emphasis on quasi-experimental and experiential design, including the development of more sophisticated instrumentation (Brockett and Hiemstra, 1991; Field, 1989, 1991; Six, 1989). The most promising new instrument is the Oddi Continuing Learning Inventory (OCLI) (1984, 1986), which identifies self-directed learners according to salient personality characteristics. To date this instrument has not had much exposure, especially in comparison to Guglielmino's Self-Directed Learning Readiness Scale. However, a recent validation study by Six (1989) indicates that the three major dimensions of the OCLI (a general factor; ability to be self-regulating; and avidity of reading) remained stable under different study conditions. But he cautions that before using this scale with populations other than those included in the major validation studies (college undergraduates and graduate students), further validation studies are needed. Moreover, he suggests that further efforts be initiated to improve the measurement properties of the OCLI, such as analysis leading to "simpler and more meaningful factor solutions" (p. 50). In-depth qualitative studies such as those conducted by Danis and Tremblay (1987, 1988) and Berger (1990), the second major methodological route, are also important to give us the rich and detailed descriptions necessary for fully understanding the personal attributes of the self-directed learner.

Future Research and Theory-Building Agendas

Although there has been a vast array of studies on self-directed learning, Candy (1987b, 1989a, 1989b) argues, after a thorough review of the literature, that research on self-direction appears to have become "blocked" or "stalemated" in recent years. He attributes this lack of progress to three causes: the absence of a consistent theoretical base, confusion over what the term itself means, and the use of inappropriate research paradigms in the study of self-direction.

The first cause, the absence of a consistent theoretical base, has resulted, according to Candy, in the failure "to develop a cumulative knowledge base about the phenomenon" (1989b, p. 27). In essence, we have a mass of descriptive data about the process and personal attributes of learners who are self-directed. Three recent attempts to rectify this lack of a conceptual base have been proposed by Long (1989), Brockett and Hiemstra (1991), and Grow (1991). Long suggests that "adult self-directed learning has a number of conceptual dimensions," including sociological, pedagogical, and psychological elements. The sociological dimension captures the idea of the learner's social isolation (that is, adults learning independently on their own), while the pedagogical dimension emphasizes the procedures carried out by the learner (such as diagnosing needs and identifying resources). The psychological dimension refers to the degree to which "the learner, or the self, maintains active control of the learning process" (Long, 1989, p. 3). Long believes that we have paid the least attention in our work to the dimension he views as the most critical in self-directed learning: the psychological dimension. He then proposes a theoretical framework (see Long, 1989) for studying self-directed learning in situations where the learner is involved in group activity. Long's framework has not yet been empirically tested.

Brockett and Hiemstra (1991) suggest an alternative model for capturing and integrating the various elements of self-directed learning. Their model, the Personal Responsibility Orientation (PRO) model, is grounded in a definition of what they term "self-direction in learning," an umbrella concept that refers to two distinct but related dimensions. The first of these dimensions, self-directed learning, centers on the instructional processes of learning whereby learners assume primary respon-sibility for planning, implementing, and evaluating their learning experiences. The authors note that "an educational agent or resource often plays a facilitating role in this process" (p. 13). The second dimension, referred to as learner self-direction, "centers on a learner's desire or preference for assuming respon-sibility for learning" (p. 13). In the PRO model, Brockett and Hiemstra provide a framework for linking these two major dimensions of self-direction (self-directed learning as an instruc-tional method and self-direction as a personality characteristic) "through the recognition that each emphasizes the importance of learners assuming personal responsibility for their thoughts and actions" (p. 27). Although they agree that the individual learner is central to the idea of self-direction, they also regard the context, or social milieu, in which that learning activity tran-spires as important. The PRO model appears to offer a great deal of promise in helping researchers formulate a more holis-tic concept of self-directed learning.

Grow (1991) proposes a model — the Staged Self-Directed Learning (SSDL) model — that outlines how teachers can assist students to become more self-directed in their learning within the formal learning process. Grounded in the situational leadership model of Hersey and Blanchard, Grow's model describes four distinct stages of learners:

- Stage 1: Learners of low self-direction who need an authority figure (a teacher) to tell them what to do
- Stage 2: Learners of moderate self-direction who are motivated and confident but largely ignorant of the subject matter to be learned
- Stage 3: Learners of intermediate self-direction who have both the skill and the basic knowledge and view themselves as being both ready and able to explore a specific subject area with a good guide
- Stage 4: Learners of high self-direction who are both willing and able to plan, execute, and evaluate their own learning with or without the help of an expert

Within each of these stages Grow outlines possible roles for the teacher or facilitator depending on the learner's stage. He goes on to highlight the problems that may arise when there is a mismatch between the role or style of the teacher and the learning stage of the participants. Grow emphasizes that good teachers individualize their teaching strategies to match the learner's stage of self-direction and allow the students to become more self-directed in their learning. Therefore good teaching is situational in nature. His thoughts on integrating the notion of self-direction into formal instruction are very similar to those of Pratt (1988), Hiemstra and Sisco (1990), and Brockett and Hiemstra (1991).

The second cause of the stalemate in research — the number of different meanings that have been given to the term *self-directed learning* — is at least tangentially related to the first. This is reflected in the variety of labels that have been used in this research effort (see Brookfield, 1984; Caffarella and O'Donnell, 1989). Candy (1989b) postulates that this one term — self-direction in learning — has been used to describe at least three distinct phenomena: "self-direction as the independent pursuit of learning opportunities without institutional support or affiliation (referred to as autodidaxy); self-direction as a way of organizing instruction (learner-control); and self-direction as a personal quality or attribute (personal autonomy)" (p. 27).

More recent definitions of self-directed learning reflect this same sort of categorization. For example, those proposed by Caffarella and O'Donnell (1989) and Brockett and Hiemstra (1991), as noted earlier, define self-direction in learning as being composed of two major dimensions: self-directed learning as a process or method of study and self-directedness in learning as a personal attribute of the learner. Candy (1989b) has reformulated one of his original categories, self-direction as a personal quality, to self-direction as a philosophical ideal, while still retaining the idea of personal autonomy as the key attribute of that category. Unlike the other writers cited here, Candy (1987b) argues that as these two views are not synonymous they should be studied as separate entities and, furthermore, he contends that autodidaxy is not part of the instructional domain at all. By way of contrast, Brockett and Hiemstra's PRO model advocates that further understanding of self-directed learning will come only through the study of how these various dimensions, whether two, three, or more, are linked together. It becomes apparent from this recent work that the debate over the meaning of self-directed learning is not yet over.

Candy attributes the third major cause of the stalemate in research — the inappropriate use of research paradigms — to a "'slippage' between the research paradigms employed and the nature of the phenomenon being studied" (1989b, p. 27). He claims that self-directed learning has been studied primarily from a positivistic paradigm and that the assumptions underlying this paradigm are, if anything, "particularly antithetical to those underlying 'self-direction'" (p. 27). He suggests that a constructivist or interpretive approach (1989a) — such as that used in the earlier studies of Houle (1961) and Tough (1967) and the more recent studies by Danis and Tremblay (1987, 1988) and Caffarella and O'Donnell (1988b) — may be more appropriate to the study of self-directed learning. In this approach, "examining the attitudes and the intentions of learners is essential" (Candy, 1989b, p. 28) if we are to gain a full understanding of what self-direction in learning is all about. Specifically, Candy suggests that in reframing research in self-direction from the interpretive paradigm we should consider four major thematic areas:

"(1) the learner's views of learning in general; (2) his or her intentions or purposes in the situation; (3) his or her attitudes towards direction or assistance; and (4) views of autonomous learning and the development of personal autonomy" (1989b, p. 28). Moreover, he argues that the learner should be studied within the specific situational context in which the learning occurs. He also suggests that it would be useful to conduct research from the point of view of the people who assist adults in their learning.

Brockett and Hiemstra, as well as Candy, consider the learner as the central point for the study of self-directed learning, yet both have cautioned that the context in which this learning takes place is also critical. In viewing the context as important, they are in agreement with others such as Pratt (1988) and Gerstner (1987). The key problem is to operationalize and then describe the interaction between the learner and the context.

Summary

The primary purpose of this chapter has been to explore the research and theory-building efforts in self-directed learning. Although learning on one's own has been the principal mode of learning throughout the ages, serious studies of this phenomenon did not become prevalent until the 1970s and 1980s. The first category of studies addressed self-directed learning as a form of study. Within this framework, we reviewed the descriptive studies verifying the existence of this form of learning. Although a number of criticisms have been made about this work, we can now say without reservation that self-directed learning is indeed a form of study. We have offered suggestions, such as diversifying the sample groups and adopting alternative methodologies, for gaining a clearer picture of this form of study for a wider spectrum of the population. We then surveyed the research on the process of self-directed learning and observed that, in essence, it is more reasonable to think of this process as multidirectional, depending on both the learner and the context, rather than primarily formal and linear. In studying the process of self-directed learning, we highlighted three issues as especially important for future research agendas: the resources used by the learner, the quality of both the process and the end product of that learning, and the competencies that enable a person to carry out this form of study. Again suggestions were made concerning appropriate research methodologies, with an emphasis on gathering more in-depth descriptions of this process from the learner's perspective.

We then explored the second major category of studies — those focused on self-directedness as a personal characteristic of the learner. The notion of readiness and the concept of autonomy have received the greatest attention from scholars studying self-directed learning from this perspective. As this strand of research is fairly recent, there is a need to increase research efforts in this arena. This means defining more clearly those variables which appear to assist adults in being more self-directed in their learning and developing more sophisticated instruments as well as further qualitative studies.

The chapter concluded with a review of the major issues researchers must address in building future agendas for research in self-directed learning. The most salient is the persistent absence of a consistent theoretical framework, resulting in continuing confusion about the meaning of the term *self-directed learning*. This confusion has led some recent writers to adopt the notion of self-direction in learning — as opposed to self-directed learning — to describe this complex web of concepts and practices.

Twelve

Explaining
and Predicting
Participation

How many adults participate in adult education? Who are they? What leads one person, but not the next-door neighbor, to enroll in a class, hire a tutor, or undertake a learning project? These questions have haunted adult educators since the field's formal beginnings in the 1920s. Hundreds of studies have given us various estimates as to the number of participants and lists of reasons why adults do or do not participate. We also have some idea which sociodemographic variables are most often associated with participation. What the field is still searching for is a theory that explains and predicts the phenomenon of participation.

The search may be in vain, however, as some agree with Rubenson that a phenomenon as complex as participation "requires not a single theory but a conjunction of a variety of theories" (1982, p. 62). In Rubenson's opinion, there can never be a single comprehensive theory on participation. At least three theoretical models are necessary: for adult education as a societal process, for the individual's conceptual apparatus, and, in addition, for the links between these levels (p. 62). While the field does not yet have a comprehensive theory of participation, what it does have are several models, some of which emphasize the psychological and some of which link the individual with socioenvironmental forces. Six models of participation are discussed in this chapter. Three of them (Miller's, Boshier's, and Rubenson's) have been critiqued elsewhere by Cross (1981); her own chain-of-response model of participation, presented as a separate model in this chapter, in fact grew out of a synthesis of these three models. Courtney's (1991) thorough study of the history of participation research also provides a detailed analysis of the models reviewed here. The models presented in this chapter are generally considered to apply to participation in formal learning activities rather than informal or self-directed learning. (See Chapter Eleven for a discussion of efforts in this area.) The chapter closes with an overall assessment of model-building efforts in participation.

Miller's Force-Field Analysis Model

One of the earliest efforts to explain participation was presented in a monograph by Harry Miller in 1967. Miller attempted to link the motivational needs hierarchy of Maslow (1954) with Lewin's (1947) force-field theory. According to Maslow's hierarchy, fundamental needs of survival, safety, and belonging have to be met before status, achievement, and self-realization needs can be addressed. In applying this scheme to adult education, Miller hypothesized that adults from lower socioeconomic classes would participate for job-related and basic skills reasons, whereas participants from higher social classes would seek education to satisfy achievement and self-realization needs. This tendency was also related to one's place in the life cycle—younger people would be more interested than older people in achieving economic security and establishing a social network for belonging needs. Not until later in life can one attend to self-actualizing needs: "It is a rare person who begins to think about the meaning of his life and the value of self-hood before he reaches his 40s" (Miller, 1967, p. 7).

From Lewin, Miller drew the idea that both negative and positive forces act upon the individual. The direction and sum total of these forces determine an adult's motivation to participate in adult learning activities. Miller depicted these forces by arrows; wider arrows meant a stronger force. Most of his monograph consists of figures depicting this force-field analysis for four social classes (lower lower, working, lower middle, and upper middle) and four content areas (vocational, family, citizenship, and self-development). Figures 12.1 and 12.2 show how the force-field analysis works. In Figure 12.1 the negative forces are much more powerful than positive forces for lower-lower-class participants. The horizontal line is drawn at a low level in the field, indicating a low motivational level for participation for this group. In Figure 12.2 there are eight positive forces of varying strength, making the level of motivation to participate quite high.

Miller (1967) also made four predictions about participation: (1) when both personal needs and social forces are strong in the direction of an educational objective, participation will be high; (2) strong personal needs in concert with nonsupportive social factors will result in a low level of participation with individual exceptions; (3) weak personal needs in conjunction with strong social forces will lead to high initial involvement, followed by high dropout; and (4) if personal and social forces conflict, "the participation level will depend on the strength of the social force in the given situation, but there will be a considerable amount of tension within the program itself" (p. 4). These predictions seem to explain certain known facts about participation. Middle-class adults who are both personally and socially motivated toward education have high levels of participation. At the same time the high dropout rate in adult basic education programs may be the result of low personal need but strong social pressure to participate. Finally, there are always exceptional people so personally motivated that they excel in continuing education despite strong negative social forces (Miller's second prediction).

While Miller's model seems to have promise for explaining and predicting participation, it has yet to be tested. It has also been criticized as being simplistic. While personal and social needs may be in conflict, for example, he fails to consider conflicting forces within each category (Long, 1983). A person may be anxious to learn Spanish, for instance, but at the same time be afraid of failing. Linking Maslow's hierarchy of needs to social class has its problems as well. Certainly there are barriers to middle-class participation, although his model shows

Figure 12.1. Education for Vocational Competence:
Lower-Lower–Class Level.

Positive Forces

Negative Forces

1. Survival needs

2. Changing technology

3. Safety needs of female culture

4. Governmental attempts to change
   opportunity structure

5. Action-excitement orientation
   of male culture

6. Hostility to education and to
   middle-class object orientation

7. Relative absence of specific,
   immediate job opportunities
   at end of training

8. Limited access through
   organizational ties

9. Weak family structure

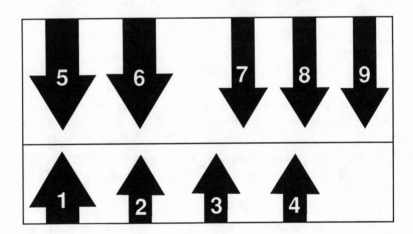

Source: Miller, 1967.

Figure 12.2. Education for Vocational Competence:
Upper-Middle–Class Level.

Positive Forces

1. Satisfied survival and safety needs

2. Strong status needs

3. Strong achievement needs

4. Change forces in professions
and business

5. Growth of professional and executive
positions in the economy

6. Familiarity with education

7. Acceptance of middle-class career values

8. Strong organizational identification

Negative Forces

9. Threats to executive groups
implicit in changing
definition of business roles

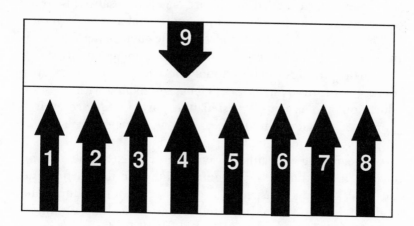

Source: Miller, 1967.

only one (see Figure 12.2). Furthermore, a great many middle-class adults participate in education for job-related reasons; economic security is at least as great a motivator for the middle classes as for the lower. Likewise, there is little evidence to support the idea that self-actualization as a motivator is exclusive to the highest socioeconomic classes.

Boshier's Congruency Model

Like Miller, Boshier (1973) explains participation in terms of the interaction between personal factors and social factors. According to Boshier, "the model asserts that 'congruence' both within the participant and between the participant and his educational environment determine participation/nonparticipation and dropout/persistence" (p. 256). Drawing from Maslow, Boshier posits that people are either primarily growth-motivated or deficiency-motivated. A growth-oriented person has satisfied basic needs in Maslow's hierarchy and is "inner-directed, autonomous, open to new experience, willing to be spontaneous, creative, and free from deterministic attitudes" (p. 256). In contrast, deficiency-oriented people are engaged in satisfying lower-order needs, are more at the mercy of social and environmental forces — indeed, "are more afraid of the environment" (p. 256). In Boshier's model (see Figure 12.3) the starting point for predicting participation is the individual and whether or not this person is growth-motivated or deficiency-motivated with regard to education. ("It is not suggested that participants are entirely growth or deficiency-motivated; the 'deficiency' may apply to only one aspect of behavior"; p. 258.)

Beginning with either orientation, participation and dropout are "a function of the magnitude between the participant's self-concept and key aspects (largely people) of the educational environment" (p. 260). Intra-self incongruence refers to differences between one's self and one's ideal self. In Boshier's model this is followed by perceived congruence between the self and other students, the self and the teacher, and the self and the institutional environment. The cumulative effect of these discrepancies is mediated by social and psychological variables

Figure 12.3. Boshier's Model to Explain Dropout from Adult Education Institutions.

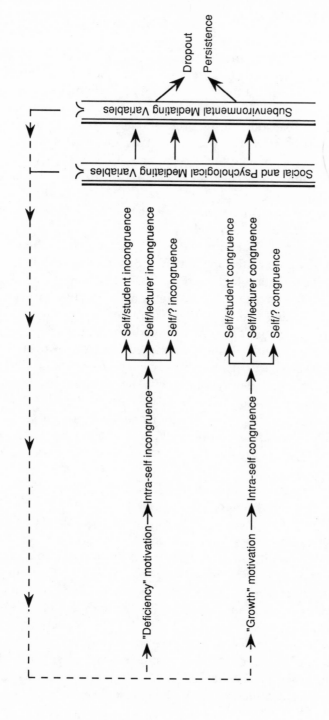

Source: Boshier, 1977, p. 91.

such as age, sex, and social class and subenvironmental variables such as transportation and class size. The arrows in the
model suggest that these two groups of mediating variables have
had an effect on the person's orientation in the first place.

Unlike some of the other models discussed in this chapter, Boshier's has been tested. Using an instrument designed
to assess discrepancy scores between self/ideal self, self/other students, and self/teacher, Boshier attempted to predict dropout
using a sample of 1,372 university continuing education students. He confirmed his hypothesis that those with high incongruence scores are more likely to drop out. The cumulative discrepancy scores accounted "for over 30 percent of the variance
in the dropout criterion" (p. 275). Boshier suggests that "dropping out of an adult education class is associated with student/
educational environment incongruence" and that "incongruence
initially resides within the participant and is 'projected' or 'generalized' . . . onto or into the adult education situation" (p. 274).
In a second study Boshier attempted to link growth-motivated
or life-space participants and deficiency-motivated or life-chance
participants to socioeconomic class and factors from the Education Participation Scale (EPS). Deficiency or life-chance individuals, he hypothesized, are from the lower classes and are
involved in satisfying Maslow's lower-order needs; life-space participants are motivated by self-actualizing needs and are of the
higher social classes. This test of the "mediating" variables in
his model proved inconclusive (Boshier, 1977).

A more recent test of the model by Garrison (1987a) analyzed Boshier's incongruency variables together with a variety
of other socioeconomic and psychological variables using a sample of 110 adult learners enrolled in tenth-grade math classes.
Compared with Boshier's 30 percent, only 16.4 percent of the
persistence/dropout variance was explained in this study. Using discriminant analysis, Garrison was able to predict persistence and dropout for 77.3 percent of the subjects. But "while
93 percent of the persisters were correctly predicted, only 20.8
percent of the dropouts were predicted correctly. Certainly the
implication must be that reasons for dropout are many and complex, thus making prediction of dropout very difficult" (Garrison,

1987a, pp. 218–219). A similar conclusion was reached several decades ago in a study by Knox and Sjogren (1965) of achievement and withdrawal in university adult education courses.

In summary, Boshier's model is based on the assumptions that participation and persistence in adult education are determined by how people feel about themselves and the match between the self and the educational environment. These are provocative notions that warrant further testing. As with Miller's model, however, there is a sense in which the model takes a rather basic notion and then, in linear fashion, tries to account for a far more complex reality. Drawing on some of the same assumptions underlying the congruency model, Boshier (1986) has proposed another model of participation to characterize present and future North American adult education. This model takes three concepts into account: learners' motivation, need, and orientation to future-centeredness (that is, learning that deals with known situations, as opposed to learning in novel situations). For a discussion of Boshier's proposal, see Bagnall (1990).

Rubenson's Expectancy-Valence Model

Rubenson's 1977 model of participation draws from psychological motivation theories and, like Miller's and Boshier's models, has its individual and environmental aspects. The decision to participate is a combination of the negative and positive forces within the individual and the environment. Expectancy consists of the expectation of being successful in an educational situation and the expectation that this success will have positive outcomes. Valence relates to the value a person puts on being successful; one could be positive, negative, or indifferent. While one might expect to succeed in a word processing class and this success would allow one to enter the work force, such an acquired skill might disrupt the power relationships within the family unit.

The individual is the center of Rubenson's model because everything depends on a person's perception of the environment and the value of participating in adult education. People develop these perceptions through being socialized by family, school, and work. The greater participation of middle-class adults might be explained by this concept of socialization: "As a consequence of socialization, . . . adult education has become a part of the value system of some groups but not of others" (Long, 1983, p. 209). As can be seen in Figure 12.4, structural factors in the environment—such as the values of people important to one's self-definition, accessibility of educational programs, and so on—directly affect how one sees the environment. Running parallel with socialization and structural factors are the person's current needs. Again, it is how one experiences these needs that determines whether one has a positive, negative, or neutral valence toward the proposed education.

Rubenson's model addresses the three key areas listed at the beginning of this chapter: There is attention to societal process through his socialization and structural components; the individual's conceptual apparatus is deemed crucial in perceiving needs, the environment, and the value of education; and these two dimensions combined lead to a determination of one's participatory behavior. The model has yet to be systematically tested.

Cross's Chain-of-Response Model

Drawing upon a synthesis of the common elements in Miller's, Boshier's, and Rubenson's models, Cross has proposed "a conceptual framework designed to identify the relevant variables and hypothesize their interrelationships" (1981, p. 124). She assumes that participation in a learning activity is the result of a chain of responses to both psychological and environmental factors. As in Boshier's model, the chain of responses (COR) begins with the individual as depicted in Figure 12.5. Self-evaluation (A) is one's assessment whether achievement in an educational situation is possible. This evaluation combines with attitudes about education (B). Echoing Boshier's notion of growth-motivated or deficiency-motivated learners, Cross comments on the linking of points A and B: "There is a relatively stable and characteristic stance toward learning that makes some people eager to seek out new experiences with a potential for growth while others avoid challenges to their accustomed ways of thinking or behaving" (p. 126). Point C—the importance of goals and

Figure 12.4. Rubenson's Paradigm of Recruitment.

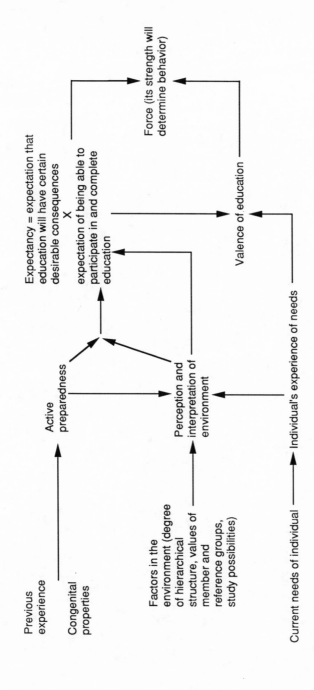

Source: Rubenson, 1977, p. 35. Reprinted by permission.

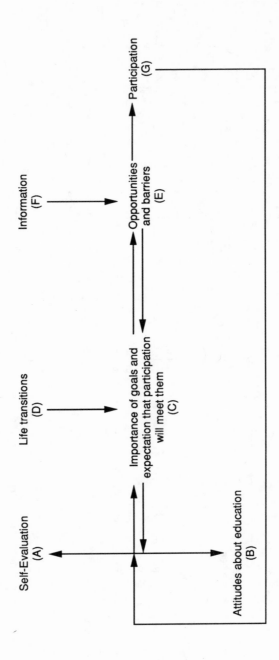

Figure 12.5. Cross's Chain-of-Response Model for Participation in Adult Education.

Source: Cross, 1981, p. 124.

the expectation that participation will meet them—is equivalent to Rubenson's notions of expectancy and valence. Expectancy is closely related to points A and B "in that individuals with high self-esteem 'expect' to be successful" (p. 126). Positive attitudes and self-evaluation usually result in expecting to succeed, thus making motivation to participate relatively high at this juncture in the model.

Cross's COR model is the first to incorporate life events and transitions. Life transitions (D) are those events and changes that all adults encounter as they move through the life cycle. Graduation, marriage, retirement, and so on precipitate transitions that, according to one study, account for 83 percent of the motivation to participate in adult education (Aslanian and Brickell, 1980).

Points E and F are environmental factors that may decide whether one participates in education. Barriers can be overcome and opportunities taken advantage of if one has the information needed to proceed (point F). "Without accurate information, point E in the model is weak because opportunities are not discovered and barriers loom large" (p. 127). If responses all along the chain are positive, the result will be participation (point G). Cross says that the model is not really as linear as these steps might suggest. It is also a reciprocal model in that participation in adult education (G) can affect how one feels about education (B) and oneself as a learner (A).

While Cross's model does have environmental components, it is primarily a psychological model with its focus on the individual progressing through the chain-of-response. For Cross, the psychological factors are most important: "If adult educators wish to understand why some adults fail to participate in learning opportunities, they need to begin at the beginning of the COR model—with an understanding of attitudes toward self and education" (p. 130).

Darkenwald and Merriam's Psychosocial Interaction Model

Cross's, Boshier's, and Rubenson's models of participation emphasize the individual's orientation, perception, and motivation

in the decision whether or not to participate in an adult education activity. Darkenwald and Merriam's model emphasizes
"social-environmental forces, particularly socioeconomic status,
not because individual traits or attitudes are unimportant but
because less is known about their influence on participation"
(1982, p. 142). Their model has two major divisions: preadulthood and adulthood. In the preadulthood phase, individual and
family characteristics, particularly intelligence and socioeconomic status, determine the type of preparatory education and
socialization a person undergoes in becoming an adult. The
adult's socioeconomic status is the direct result of these preadulthood experiences. Prior education in particular is linked to social class and to participation in adult education. See Figure
12.6 for a graphic display of these preadulthood factors.

The adulthood phase consists of six components, each of
which can have a high, moderate, or low value. The socioeconomic status (SES) of adulthood appears first in the chain of
adulthood factors and has a "dominant influence" in determining the probability of participation (p. 142). The second of these
six components—learning press—is directly related to SES.
Learning press, which is unique to this model, is defined as "the
extent to which one's total current environment requires or encourages further learning. High learning press is related to high
SES (and low to low) in that learning press is determined by
general social participation (e.g., participation in civic, cultural,
religious, and recreational activities and organizations), occupational complexity (e.g., technical, professional, and managerial
employment), and life-style (e.g., personal taste, leisure-time
preference)" (Darkenwald and Merriam, 1982, p. 142). The
other adulthood components of the model are perceived value
and utility of adult education, readiness to participate, participation stimuli, and barriers. Participation stimuli are specific
events that prod adults into considering an educational activity.
They are the triggers to transition studied by Aslanian and Brickell (1980). The arrow between this component and learning press
indicates the "direct relationship between the intensity of one's
learning press and the frequency and intensity of the participation stimuli one experiences" (p. 144). For example, an event

Figure 12.6. Psychosocial Interaction Model of Participation in Organized Adult Education.

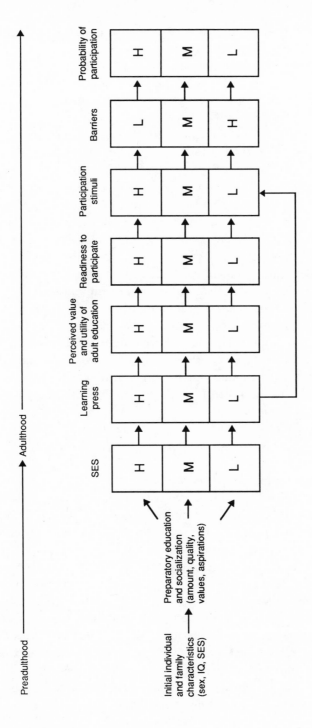

Source: From *Adult Education: Foundations of Practice*, by Gordon Darkenwald and Sharan B. Merriam. Copyright © 1982 by Harper & Row, Publishers, Inc. Reprinted by permission.

such as retirement is more likely to trigger participation for someone of higher SES because such a person probably sees learning as a positive activity, is likely to be involved in other forms
of participation, and so on.

Cervero and Kirkpatrick (1990) have tested aspects of the
Darkenwald and Merriam model using the data set of the National Longitudinal Survey of the High School Class of 1972
(NLS). Data have been collected from 18,000 randomly selected
high school seniors six different times (1972, 1973, 1974, 1976,
1979, and 1986). Independent variables from the 1972–1979
data set were selected to represent the two early-life variables
in Darkenwald and Merriam's model: individual and family
characteristics, on the one hand, and preparatory education and
socialization on the other. Educational attainment at age twenty-
five was also used as an independent variable. Dependent variables of credit/noncredit and a composite measure of participation (respondents who had participated in either credit or noncredit courses) were formed using the 1984 data set. Cervero
and Kirkpatrick found that the preadulthood variables explained
a significant amount of participation for both credit and noncredit activities.

Cookson and the ISSTAL Model

The last model to be discussed is the ISSTAL model that Cookson (1986) adapted from Smith's (1980) social participation
model. ISSTAL stands for interdisciplinary, sequential specificity, time allocation, life span. It is interdisciplinary in that it
includes concepts from several disciplines; sequential specificity relates to the causal interconnectedness of variables leading
to participation; time-allocation and life-span assumptions have
to do with viewing participation in adult education as but one
form of an adult's overall social participation. Cookson explains
that social participation tends to fit into lifelong patterns: "Accordingly, relative to others within the same cohort, people who
exhibit higher levels of [participation in adult education] in their
thirties may be expected to display similarly higher levels in their
forties, fifties, and sixties" (p. 132).

As can be seen in Figure 12.7, variables predicting participation are on a continuum. The further left on the continuum, "the more general, transsituational its impact and the greater probability that its effects will be mediated by subsequent and consequent variables. Conversely, the further right a variable is placed . . . the more situation/role specific its influence" on participation (p. 132). Thus contextual factors including climate, topography, culture, and social structure affect participation but are mediated by subsequent personal variables. Social background and social role refer to sociodemographic characteristics such as age, education, and occupation. Next in the ISSTAL model are personality and intellect. These factors are fairly stable and predispose a person to certain types of behavior, including social participation. Even more specific in their influence on participation are attitudinal dispositions and retained information. Attitudinal variables are composed of values, attitudes, expectations, and intentions in "dynamic interaction" with personality traits and intellectual capacity and "are posited as contributing to the motivation of the individual" (p. 136). The information variable is similar to the same variable in Cross's model but is more complex. For Cookson, information includes awareness of educational opportunities, beliefs about the value of participation, and plans—that is, "cognitions about decisions to respond" (p. 138). Situational variables reflect the person's immediate situation and have the most specific influence on the decision to participate. Through these variables, Cookson says, "the complex and interactive effects of all previous and more enduring variables in the ISSTAL model are processed and transmitted" to participation (p. 138).

Cookson has tested this model in two studies conducted in British Columbia (1987a). Fifty-eight measures of social position, personality characteristics, attitudinal disposition, beliefs and opinions, and situational variables were used to predict participation of two groups of adults: Fifty male low-income heads of household were interviewed about their participation in adult education for one study, and four hundred men and women in public evening school classes were given a participation questionnaire. Of the fifty-eight independent variables used to predict

Figure 12.7. Cookson's Adaptation of the ISSTAL Model for Participation in Adult Education.

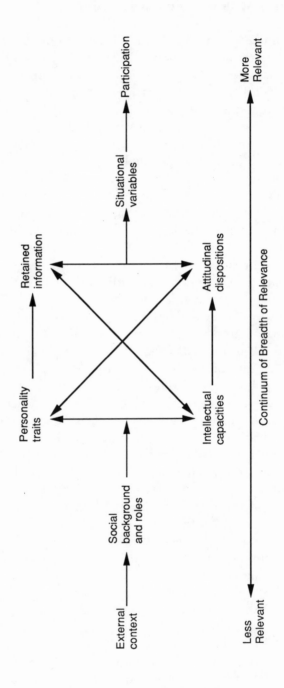

Source: Cookson, 1986, p. 130.

participation, none proved significant in the study with male household heads and only three were significantly related to participation in the questionnaire study. Cookson concludes that since participation in adult education is complex and multidimensional, "it may be more manageable to mount more modest studies which touch on overlapping portions of the ISSTAL model variable categories" (1987a, p. 213).

Assessment of Model-Building Efforts

It has been nearly twenty years since Boshier noted the crippling effect of the "absence of testable theory" on participation and dropout research (1973, p. 255). Since then there have been numerous efforts at a comprehensive explanation of participation in formal learning activities. Several such explanations in the form of models have been reviewed in this chapter. Some observations can be made about the models themselves as well as the state of theory building overall.

Each model presented is an attempt to account for the research on who participates and why, as well as stimulate new research directions. All the models posit an "interaction between the individual and his or her environment" (Cross, 1981, p. 123). The relative weight of these two factors varies from model to model—from the emphasis on the individual's orientation in Boshier's model to the external context and social background stressed in the ISSTAL model. Moreover, most of these models attempt to explain participation in institutionally sponsored learning activities—this is, after all, what most educators are interested in. "People interested in attracting nonparticipant segments of the general population or allaying dropout" need a framework to translate research findings into administrative action (Boshier, 1973, p. 255). Of the six models reviewed here, only Cross's seems capable of explaining participation in self-directed learning activities. Bagnall (1989, p. 256) points out that these models assume the learner's physical presence, which in Bagnall's framework is only one way to think of participation. Participation can also be thought of as involvement (the extent to which the learner is actively engaged in the learning event) and control (the extent to which the learner controls the content, goals, or outcomes of the event).

There are unique features in the different models, each of which holds promise for contributing to an overall understanding of participation. Rubenson, for example, makes use of member and reference groups whose norms determine one's perceptions of the usefulness of education. Fingeret's (1983) research on illiterate adults, in which she explores the effects of their membership in a social network, lends support to the validity of this concept for explaining participation. That is, many illiterates may fail to join literacy classes because their literacy needs are met through an exchange of goods and services and the groups with whom they identify do not promote education as a means of dealing with their literacy needs. Cross includes life transitions as an important determinant of participation. This component takes into account the research on adult development and in particular the potential of periods of change in the adult life cycle for precipitating learning needs. Aslanian and Brickell (1980), discovering that 83 percent of the learners were participating in adult education because of some past, present, or anticipated change in their lives, provide strong support for the life transition component in Cross's model. Unique to Darkenwald and Merriam's model is "learning press," which includes general social participation, occupational complexity, and lifestyle — all of which, in combination, press one in varying intensity toward further learning.

Finally, Cookson's adaptation of the ISSTAL model includes an intellectual capacity factor. He notes that when operationalized in terms of intelligence test scores, there is a relationship to persistence in adult basic education programs (Cookson, 1986). The practical considerations involved in obtaining such a score, however, may mitigate against its use in predicting persistence. Valentine and Ehringhaus (1989), for example, although they were not testing the relationship between intelligence and persistence, sought to assess the utility of a test of cognitive ability for designing remedial instruction in adult basic education. They found such a score to be "relatively unimportant" and concluded that the "predictive yield" was virtually non-existent compared to reading and math achievement measures.

The differences among the models are, in Cookson's opinion, cause for concern. In reviewing the models of Miller, Rubenson, Boshier, Cross, and Darkenwald and Merriam, he says: "Of the eighteen factors identified by one or more of the five models, seven factors were named in two, and ten factors were named in different single models. It may be concluded, on the basis of this comparison, that the models constituted virtually independent and unrelated efforts to provide explanations—rather than incrementally developed formulations moving toward a more comprehensive explanation of adult education participation" (1987b, p. 27). One might ask to what extent this area of adult education has advanced in its theory building in the last twenty years if one takes Cookson's comments to heart. That is, the isolated attempts that have been made do not seem to be moving the field toward a comprehensive explanation of this phenomenon. On the other hand, a comprehensive theory may not be possible given the complexity of the topic.

Yet another way of looking at the state of theory building in participation is to note that one of the current models of participation may in fact emerge as a valid and reliable explanation of participation. As of this writing, however, only three of the models have begun to be tested (Boshier's, Darkenwald and Merriam's, and ISSTAL) and these tests have yielded contradictory or inconclusive results. Careful attention to operationalizing complex variables such as personality traits, structural factors in the environment, learning press, and so on, combined with more sophisticated data analysis, might eventually result in a good explanatory model of participation that will be of use to researchers and educators alike.

Summary

Participation is one of the more thoroughly studied areas in adult education. We have a sense of who participates, what is studied, and what motivates some adults and not others to enroll in a

course or undertake an independent learning project. This accumulation of descriptive information about participation has
led to efforts to fit the pieces together in the form of models that
try to convey the complexity of the phenomenon. Models are
visual representations of how concepts related to participation
interact to explain who participates and perhaps even predict
who will participate in the future. Six models of participation
were reviewed in this chapter.

Miller's (1967) force-field analysis model links Maslow's
hierarchy of needs with Lewin's force-field theory. In this model,
participation is a function of one's socioeconomic class and place
in the life cycle (survival needs of lower-class adults and self-
actualization needs of older adults, for example). The balance
of positive and negative forces that are based on class and life
cycle determine an adult's overall motivation to participate in
learning activities. Boshier's (1973) congruency model is somewhat similar to Miller's in that participation is explained by the
interaction between internal and external motivating factors.
The key to Boshier's model is the notion of congruency — that
is, participation and subsequent persistence in the activity depend on the level of congruence between one's view of the self
and the educational environment. Rubenson's (1977) expec-
tancy-valence model weds perception of the environment and
the value of participation with positive and negative forces within
the individual and the environment. Rubenson attends to the
importance of socialization in that a person's perceptions are
developed in the contexts of family, school, and work. Cross's
(1981) chain-of-response (COR) model, a synthesis of the foregoing three models, consists of six factors such as attitudes about
education, life transitions, and information. How people respond
to these factors determines whether or not they participate in
a learning activity.

The fifth model reviewed in this chapter, Darkenwald and
Merriam's (1982), emphasized socioenvironmental factors, particularly socioeconomic status. It has two major divisions: preadulthood and adulthood. Preadulthood factors play a major
role in determining participation as an adult. There are six com-

ponents in the adulthood phase, each of which can have a high, moderate, or low value in determining the probability of participation. The last model reviewed is Cookson's (1986) ISS-TAL model. In this model seven different variables are placed on a continuum from less relevant to more relevant. Less relevant variables are more likely to be affected by subsequent variables and have less direct effect on the decision to participate.

The value of these models in explaining or predicting participation has yet to be determined through research and testing. Nevertheless, they do constitute a contribution to the literature on participation in that they attempt to map the interaction of variables that have been shown to influence a person's decision to participate and subsequent perseverance in the activity. While the interaction is conceptualized in diverse ways in the different models, the models can help educators and others to become aware of the importance of certain factors in the explanation of participation—factors perhaps not noticed previously—and appreciate the vexing complexity of the phenomenon itself. Such an appreciation may well preclude a simplistic approach to increasing participation in adult learning activities.

Thirteen

Toward
Comprehensive Theories
of Adult Learning

How easy it would be to explain adult education to legislators,
public school personnel, educators, and the general public if we
had but a single theory of adult learning—a theory that differentiated adults from children, that included all types of learning,
and that was at once elegant and simple. But just as there is
no single theory that explains human learning in general (see
Chapter Seven), there is no single theory of *adult* learning. Nor
is there likely to be one. Nearly twenty years ago Kidd observed
that "no such magical or scientific theory is likely to arise or
be formulated" (1973, p. 188). Brookfield (1986) compares the
search to the quest for the Holy Grail, and Cross states flatly
that there will be not one but "many theories useful in improving our understanding of adults as learners" (1981, p. 112).

What we do have at this point are suggestions, constructs,
tentative formulations, and models, rather than fully developed
theory. Houle (1972), for example, has developed a model or
"system" as he calls it, for analyzing activities that take place
in various learning situations. Kidd (1973) proposes adopting
the concept of "mathetics" in an effort to focus our research efforts
on learning rather than teaching. This chapter examines the

Note: Much of the material in this chapter is based on an earlier article by Sharan B. Merriam titled "Adult Learning and Theory Building: A Review" in *Adult
Education Quarterly,* 1987, *37* (4), 187–198.

theory-building efforts that we do have. Each theory reviewed here focuses on adult learning and adheres to a broad definition of theory as a set of interrelated concepts or principles that attempt to explain a phenomenon. If a theory helps us to understand how adults learn, we should be able to predict when and how learning will take place and, as educators, arrange for its occurrence. Adult learning theory can be divided into three categories: those anchored in adult learners' characteristics, those based on an adult's life situation, and those that focus on changes in consciousness.

Theories Based on Adult Characteristics

The best-known theory of adult learning is andragogy, defined by Knowles (1980) as "the art and science of helping adults learn" (p. 43). It is based upon five assumptions, all of which are characteristics of adult learners:

1. As a person matures, his or her self-concept moves from that of a dependent personality toward one of a self-directing human being.
2. An adult accumulates a growing reservoir of experience, which is a rich resource for learning.
3. The readiness of an adult to learn is closely related to the developmental tasks of his or her social role.
4. There is a change in time perspective as people mature — from future application of knowledge to immediacy of application. Thus an adult is more problem-centered than subject-centered in learning (Knowles, 1980, pp. 44–45).
5. Adults are motivated to learn by internal factors rather than external ones (Knowles, 1984, p. 12).

From each of these assumptions (the fifth was added after the original four), Knowles draws numerous implications for the design, implementation, and evaluation of learning activities with adults. This theory, or "model of assumptions" as Knowles also calls it (1980, p. 43), has given adult educators "a badge of identity" that distinguishes the field from other areas of education, especially childhood schooling (Brookfield, 1986, p. 90). Many would agree with Bard (1984) that andragogy "probably more than any other force has changed the role of the learner in adult education and in human resource development" (p. xi).

It has also caused more controversy, philosophical debate, and critical analysis than any other concept proposed thus far. One of the early points of criticism was Knowles's original inference that andragogy, with all its technological implications for instruction, characterizes adult learning and that pedagogy, with another set of implications, characterizes childhood learning. He later clarified his position by stating in essence that andragogy–pedagogy represents a continuum and that the use of both techniques is appropriate at different times in different situations regardless of the learner's age (Knowles, 1980, 1984). Since andragogy now appears to be situation-specific and not unique to adults, technically it does not qualify as a theory of adult learning.

As a theory to explain how adults learn, andragogy has been critiqued on other grounds. Hartree (1984) observes that it is not clear whether Knowles has presented a theory of learning or a theory of teaching, whether adult learning is different from child learning, and whether there is a theory at all—perhaps these are just principles of good practice. The assumptions, she notes, "can be read as descriptions of the adult learner . . . or as prescriptive statements about what the adult learner *should* be like" (p. 205). Because the assumptions are "unclear and shaky" on several counts, Hartree (1984) concludes that while "many adult educators might accept that the principles of adult teaching and conditions of learning which he evolves have much to offer, and are in a sense descriptive of what is already recognized as good practice by those in the field, conceptually Knowles has not presented a good case for the validity of such practice. . . . Although he appears to approach his model of teaching from the point of view of a theory of adult learning, he does not establish a unified theory of learning in a systematic way" (pp. 206–207).

Brookfield (1986), who also raises the question of whether andragogy is a "proven theory," assesses to what extent a "set of well-grounded principles of good practice" can be derived from andragogy (p. 98). He argues that three of the assumptions are problematic when drawing inferences for practice: Self-direction is more a desired outcome than a given condition, and being problem-centered and desiring immediate application can lead to a narrow reductionist view of learning. Brookfield finds only the experience assumption to be well grounded (p. 98).

Davenport and Davenport (1985) review the use of the term *andragogy* and chronicle the history of the debate as to whether it is in fact a theory. They note that andragogy has been classified "as a theory of adult education, theory of adult learning, theory of technology of adult learning, method of adult education, technique of adult education, and a set of assumptions" (p. 157). They are a bit more optimistic than other critics for andragogy's chances of possessing "the explanatory and predictive functions generally associated with a fully developed theory" (p. 158). For them the issue can be resolved through empirical studies that test the underlying assumptions.

A few studies have attempted to do just that. At least three studies have focused on the relationship between andragogical assumptions and instruction. Beder and Darkenwald (1982) asked teachers who taught both adults and preadults if their teaching behavior differed according to the age of the students. Teachers reported viewing adult students differently and using more andragogical techniques. Gorham (1985), however, actually observed teachers of adults and preadults. She found no differences in how a particular teacher instructed adults or preadults, although teachers claimed that they did treat the two age groups differently. Beder and Carrea (1988) found that training teachers in andragogical methods had a positive and significant effect on attendance but no effect on how teachers were evaluated by the students. Yet another study draws from Knowles's assumption that adults are self-directing and thus like to plan their own learning experiences. Rosenblum and Darkenwald (1983) compared achievement and satisfaction measures between groups who had planned their course and those who had it planned for them. No differences were found in either achievement or satisfaction.

A second attempt at theory building that rests on characteristics of adults is Cross's characteristics of adults as learners (CAL) model. Cross (1981) offers it as "a tentative framework to accommodate current knowledge about what we know about adults as learners" (p. 234). Based on differences between children and adults, it consists of two classes of variables: personal characteristics and situational characteristics. As can be seen in Figure 13.1, personal characteristics include physical, psychological, and sociocultural dimensions. These are continua and reflect growth and development from childhood into adult life. Situational characteristics focus on variables unique to adult participants—for example, part-time versus full-time learning and voluntary versus compulsory participation.

Cross believes that her model incorporates completed research on aging, stage and phase developmental studies, participation, learning projects, motivation, and so on. The model can also be used to stimulate research by thinking across and between categories. It might be asked, for example, whether there is a "relationship between stage of ego development and voluntary participation in learning" or whether transition points

**Figure 13.1. Characteristics of Adults as Learners:
A Conceptual Framework.**

Personal Characteristics

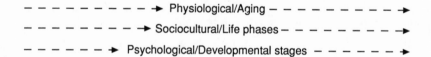

— — — — — — — — — ➤ Physiological/Aging — — — — — — — — — ➤
— — — — — — — — — ➤ Sociocultural/Life phases — — — — — — — — — ➤
— — — — — — — ➤ Psychological/Developmental stages — — — — — — ➤

Situational Characteristics

Part-time learning versus full-time learning
Voluntary learning versus compulsory learning

Source: Cross, 1981, p. 235.

in development "generate extra amounts of volunteer learning" (p. 248). Rather than suggesting implications for practice, as Knowles's andragogy does, Cross's model offers a "framework for thinking about *what* and *how* adults learn" (p. 248).

Although the CAL model is intended to be a comprehensive explanation of *adult* learning, the variables may be too broadly defined: What situational characteristics when combined with which personal characteristics lead to explaining different types of learning, for example? Probably a more serious problem with the model is its focus on the *characteristics* of adults, which tells us little about how adults actually learn or if they learn differently than children. Furthermore, the personal characteristics can apply to children as well as adults since they are on continua reflective of growth from childhood into adulthood. Nor do the situational characteristics neatly divide between children and adults. Some adult learners are full time and some participate because of mandatory continuing education requirements; some preadults are part-time learners and some learning is done on a voluntary basis. The CAL model has yet to be empirically tested.

Theories Based on an Adult's Life Situation

Andragogy and the CAL model are explanations of adult learning emanating from the characteristics of adult learners. The three theories reviewed in this section — McClusky's theory of margin, Knox's proficiency theory, and Jarvis's model of the learning process — are anchored in an adult's life situation with its attendant experiences, roles, and responsibilities.

McClusky presented his theory of margin in a 1963 publication followed by discussions of application in 1970 and 1971. Adulthood is a time of growth, change, and integration in which one constantly seeks balance between the amount of energy needed and the amount available. This balance is conceptualized as a ratio between the "load" of life, which dissipates energy, and the "power" of life which allows one to deal with the load. The energy left over when one subtracts load from power McClusky called "margin in life." He describes how the theory works: "Margin may be increased by reducing Load or increasing Power, or it may be decreased by increasing Load and/or reducing Power. We can control both by modifying either Power or Load. When Load continually matches or exceeds Power and if both are fixed and/or out of control, or irreversible, the situation becomes highly vulnerable and susceptible to breakdown. If, however, Load and Power can be controlled, and, better yet, if a person is able to lay hold of a reserve (Margin) of Power, he is better equipped to meet unforeseen emergencies, is better positioned to take risks, can engage in exploratory, creative activities, is more likely to learn, etc., i.e. do those things that enable him to live above a plateau of mere self subsistence" (1970, p. 83).

This theory, he argues, helps to explain the dynamics of adult learning. A learning situation requires the expenditure of resources—that is, "a necessary condition for learning is access to and/or the activation of a Margin of Power that may be available for application to the processes which the learning situation requires" (1970, p. 84). The situational focus of this theory is reflected in his recognition that "adjustments of Load to Power become matters of overarching concern as a person accumulates and later relinquishes adult responsibilities and modifies the varying roles which the successive stages of the life cycle require" (1970, p. 84). Using the theory of margin as a conceptual framework, Main (1979) studied adult learning and teaching. Its greatest application, however, has been with middle-aged and older adults. Using an instrument developed to measure margin in life, Stevenson (1980) compared the load, power, and margin patterns of independent older adults, nursing home residents, and young and middle-aged adults. Baum (1980) tested the theory using a randomized sample of 100 widows.

McClusky's theory has appeal in that it speaks to the everyday events and life transitions that all adults encounter (see Chapter Six). It is perhaps a better counseling tool than it is an explanation of adult learning. In fact, there is a striking similarity between McClusky's power, load, and margin concepts and the components of Schlossberg's model for counseling adults in transition. In her model, one assesses the ability to work through a transition by assessing the relative strength of four factors: the situation, the self (internal strengths), external supports, and strategies one has developed to handle stress (Schlossberg, 1984, 1987). While certainly life events and transitions precipitate many (and some would say the most potent) learning experiences, McClusky's model does not directly address learning itself but rather *when* it is most likely to occur. One might also question whether "a necessary condition for learning" (McClusky, 1970, p. 84) is a reserve of energy or margin of power. This may seem to apply more readily to formal learning situations; informal learning can occur under conditions of stress or, in McClusky's terms, when load is greater than power.

Knox's (1980) proficiency theory also speaks to an adult's life situation. Adult learning, he writes, is distinctive on at least two counts: "the centrality of concurrent adult role performance" (p. 383) and the "close correspondence between learning and action beyond the educational program" (p. 384). Proficiency, as defined by Knox, is "the capability to perform satisfactorily if given the opportunity," and this performance involves some combination of attitude, knowledge, and skill (1980, p. 378). At the core of his theory is the notion of a discrepancy between the current and the desired level of proficiency. This concept of proficiency helps explain "adult motivation and achievement in both learning activities and life roles. Adults and society expect that individual adults will be proficient in major life roles and as persons generally" (1985, p. 252). A model representative of the theory contains the following interactive components: the general environment, past and current characteristics, performance, aspiration, self, discrepancies, specific environments, learning activity, and the teacher's role.

The set of interrelated concepts in Knox's proficiency theory hinge upon what he defines as being the purpose of adult learning (whether self-directed or in organized programs): "to enhance proficiency to improve performance" (1980, p. 399). Knox's theory is not well known by adult educators, perhaps because its publication has been in sources outside the field of adult education. Its emphasis on performance would also appear to limit its application to learning that can be demonstrated by enhanced performance. More problematic is the model's mixture of learning, teaching, and motivation. Knox writes that the theory "suggests fundamental relationships among essential aspects of adult learning and teaching which constitute an interrelated set of guidelines for helping adults learn, with an emphasis on motivation" (1985, p. 252). How one tracks the interaction of ten components (or "essential aspects of adult learning and teaching") to arrive at an explanation of how adults learn is far from clear.

The third theory of adult learning reviewed in this section is offered by Jarvis (1987a). It too begins with an adult's life situation or, more correctly, with an adult's experience: "Even miseducative experiences may be regarded as learning experiences . . . *all* learning begins with experience" (p. 16). Some experiences, however, are repeated with such frequency that they are taken for granted and do not lead to learning — such as driving a car or household routines. At the start of the learning process are experiences that "call for a response" (p. 63). Like Knox's and McCluskey's theories, Jarvis's model is based on a discrepancy between biography (all that a person is at a particular point in time) and experience — an incident that a person is unprepared to handle. This "inability to cope with the situation unthinkingly, instinctively, is at the heart of all learning" (p. 35).

For Jarvis, all experience occurs within a social situation, a kind of objective context within which one experiences life: "Life may be conceptualized as an ongoing phenomenon located within a sociocultural milieu which is bounded by the temporality of birth and death. Throughout life, people are moving from social situation to social situation; sometimes in conscious awareness but on other occasions in a taken-for-granted manner" (p. 64). Jarvis's model of the learning process begins with the person moving into a social situation in which a potential learning experience occurs. From an experience there are nine different routes that a person might take, some of which result in learning, and some of which do not. Presumption, nonconsideration, and rejection do not result in learning. The six other responses (preconscious, practice, memorization, contemplation, reflective practice, and experimental learning) represent six different types of learning. The nine responses form a hierarchy: The first three are nonlearning responses, the second three are nonreflective learning, and the final three are reflective learning. These latter three, Jarvis says, are the "higher forms of learning" (1987a, p. 27). Of the nonlearning responses, one can respond in a mechanical way (that is, presume that what has worked before will work again); one can be too preoccupied to consider a response; or one can reject the opportunity to learn. The nonreflective learning responses can be preconscious (that is, a person unconsciously internalizes something); one can practice a new skill until it is learned; or learners can acquire information "with which they have been presented and learn it, so that they can reproduce it at a later stage" (p. 33). The three higher forms of learning call for more involvement. Contemplation is thinking about what is being learned and does not require a behavioral outcome; reflective practice is akin to problem solving; experimental learning is the result of a person experimenting upon the environment.

In his book on the model Jarvis explains how each of the nine responses coincides with the visual representation of the learning process. As in Figure 13.2, a person enters a social situation, has an experience, and can exit (box 4) unchanged by ignoring the event or taking it for granted. One might also go from the experience (box 3) to memorization (box 6) and exit either unchanged (box 4) or changed (box 9). For a higher type of learning, a person might go from the experience to reasoning and reflecting (box 7) to practice experimentation (box 5) to evaluation (box 8) to memorization (box 6) and to being changed (box 9).

More than the theories based on adult characteristics or the other two theories discussed in this section, Jarvis's model does deal with learning per se. The thoroughness of his discussion, which concentrates on explaining the responses one can have to an experience, is a strength of the model. These responses encompass multiple types of learning and their different out-

Figure 13.2. A Model of the Learning Process.

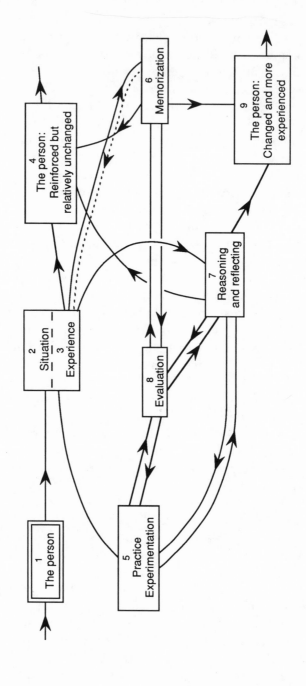

Source: Jarvis, 1987a, p. 25. Reprinted by permission.

comes — a refreshingly comprehensive view of learning. Furthermore, his model situates learning within a social context; learning is an interactive phenomenon, not an isolated internal process. There is some question, however, as to whether his model
is unique to adults. Although it was constructed from research
with adult learners and has been used by Jarvis with adults in
various settings, he himself suspects that "it is as valid for children as it is with adults. . . . There may be a relationship between the frequency of use of these different types of learning
and the age of the learner, [but] no evidence exists at present
that might verify this" (Jarvis, 1987a, pp. 35–36).

Theories Based on Changes in Consciousness

The theories so far discussed attempt to explain the phenomenon of adult learning from the perspective of adult characteristics and adult social roles, responsibilities, and experiences. The
theoretical formulations discussed in this section have a stronger
cognitive focus in that they deal with the mental construction
of experience and inner meaning. Reflection upon the content
of one's environment and one's experiences is a common component of the theories reviewed here. Reflective thought, some
propose, may even be *the* thought structure to emerge in adulthood and "a necessary prerequisite to asking questions, and discovering problems (Allman, 1983, p. 114).

The most developed "theory" in this group is Mezirow's
notion of perspective transformation. Drawing from the writings of the German philosopher Jurgen Habermas, Mezirow
defines three areas of cognitive interest: technical or instrumental, which is task-related; practical or dialogic, which involves
social interaction; and emancipatory, which is characterized by
interest in self-knowledge and insights gained through self-reflection. Recently Mezirow has reduced these three domains to
two: Emancipatory learning is now operative in the technical
and practical domains (1989). It is this emancipatory learning
that Mezirow (1990) equates with perspective transformation:
"Perspective transformation is the process of becoming critically
aware of how and why our presuppositions have come to con-

strain the way we perceive, understand, and feel about our world; of reformulating these assumptions to permit a more inclusive, discriminating, permeable, and integrative perspective; and of making decisions or otherwise acting upon these new understandings. *More inclusive, discriminating, permeable, and integrative perspectives are superior perspectives* that adults choose if they can because they are motivated to better understand the meaning of their experience" (p. 14). Critically reflecting upon our lives, becoming aware of "*why* we attach the meanings we do to reality, especially to our roles and relationships . . . may be the most significant distinguishing characteristics of adult learning" (1981, p. 11). Learning in adulthood is not just adding to what we already know. Rather, new learning transforms existing knowledge into a new perspective and in so doing emancipates the learner. The ultimate result of this type of learning is to become aware of the "cultural assumptions governing the rules, roles, conventions, and social expectations which dictate the way we see, think, feel, and act" (1981, p. 13).

The process of perspective transformation begins with a "disorienting dilemma" to which one's old patterns of response are ineffective. This situation precipitates a self-examination and asessment of one's assumptions and beliefs. A movement begins whereby one revises "specific assumptions about oneself and others until the very structure of assumptions becomes transformed" (1981, p. 8). Mezirow feels that adult educators have a responsibility which "gives adult education its distinctive mission and even its meaning" (1985, p. 148). It is not enough to help learners perform, achieve, and produce. The one significant commitment of adult education is "to help learners make explicit, elaborate, and act upon the assumptions and premises . . . upon which their performance, achievement, and productivity are based" (1985, p. 148).

Mezirow's theory has been criticized by Ekpenyong (1990), Griffin (1987), Clark and Wilson (1991), Collard and Law (1989), and Hart (1990). Ekpenyong (1990) feels that Mezirow's theory has "limited application" (p. 165). A more comprehensive understanding of adult learning, according to Ekpenyong, is to be found in philosopher Thomas Kuhn's notion of paradigm-transition. Griffin argues that Mezirow has presented not so much a theory as a "set of prescriptions for good practice on the part of professional adult educators who are committed to facilitating self-directed adult learning" (1987, p. 183). Indeed, Mezirow (1981) outlines a "charter for andragogy" stressing the adult educator's role as one of "enhancing the learner's ability for self-direction" (p. 21). Clark and Wilson (1991) point out that Mezirow's orientation toward autonomy uncritically reflects the values of the dominant culture in our society — masculine, white, and middle class. In Griffin's (1987) opinion, Mezirow fails to provide an ideological basis for adult education as social policy. Collard and Law (1989) fault Mezirow for his lack of attention to the social context and to social change as the natural outcome of perspective transformation. For Mezirow, however, change need not be just social change; it can also be epistemic (knowledge-related) or psychic (relating, for example, to unresolved childhood dilemmas that influence adult behavior). Mezirow (1989) writes: "Social action may develop, and it is desirable and appropriate that it do so. But this is the learner's decision, not the educator's. . . . Educators do not set out to effect specific political action; this is indoctrination" (p. 173). Hart (1990) contends that Mezirow is too "rationalist" in that "he tries to systematize the areas of 'distortions' requiring . . . fundamental changes or transformations . . . without directly criticizing current economic, social, and political arrangements which are inherently tied to these 'distortions' " (p. 127).

More than the other theories discussed here, Mezirow's perspective transformation deals directly with the process of learning. Furthermore, although some would contest the notion, Mezirow claims that this type of learning is unique to adulthood (1981). The combination of these factors — that is, a theory about learning itself which is perhaps unique to adults — makes Mezirow's theory particularly promising for understanding adult learning. A recent publication by Mezirow and Associates (1990) cites programs that have stimulated critical reflection and offers practical methods for helping adults engage in critical reflection that can result in transformative learning. Only a few research studies have focused on perspective transformation.

Hunter (1980), Cochrane (1981), and Williams (1985) studied perspective transformation related to health practices, withdrawal experiences, and spouse abuse, respectively. Young (1986) was able to change the perspectives of workshop participants (toward a global, future-oriented worldview) with a contextual learning intervention. Boyd and Fales (1983) studied the relationship of reflection to meaning transformation and delineated a process with stages much like the stages of perspective transformation.

One educator who does espouse social change as a necessary corollary to critical reflection is Freire. His "theory" is more precisely a theory of education (of which learning is an important component) in contrast to Mezirow's focus on the learning process itself. Freire is a Brazilian educator whose theory of adult education is set within a larger framework of radical social change. Education for Freire is never neutral; it either oppresses or liberates. Conscientization—"the process in which men, not as recipients, but as knowing subjects, achieve a deepening awareness both of the sociocultural reality which shapes their lives and of their capacity to transform that reality"—is what takes place in an authentic educational encounter (1970a, p. 27). Increasing awareness of one's situation involves moving from the lowest level of consciousness, where there is no comprehension of how forces shape one's life, to the highest level of critical consciousness. Similar to Mezirow's "critical reflectivity" (1981), critical consciousness is marked by a thorough analysis of problems, self-awareness, and self-reflection.

Within Freire's theory of education for social change are components relevant to adult learning situations. He distinguishes between "banking" and "problem-posing" education. In traditional banking education, deposits of knowledge are made into student receptacles; in problem posing, teachers and students cooperate in a dialogue that seeks to humanize and liberate. Central to the learning is a changed relationship between teacher and student. They are coinvestigators into their common reality: the sociocultural situation in which they live. Dialogue is the method by which this sharing takes place and by which consciousness is raised. Generative themes, concerns that are posed by the learners themselves, become the content of a learning situation. The ultimate goal is liberation, or praxis, "the action and reflection of men upon their world in order to transform it" (1970b, p. 66).

Freire has operationalized his theory of education into techniques that have demonstrated success in combating illiteracy, especially in the Third World. Its application in North America has been limited, owing perhaps to the necessary corollary of social change. Some have suggested that conscientization is not comprehensive enough to explain various types of learning that an adult might experience; others contend that the emphasis on active involvement, experiential learning, and dialogue is not new. If taken out of its political context, conscientization shares with perspective transformation the idea that *adult* learning is the process of becoming aware of one's assumptions, beliefs, and values and then transforming those assumptions into a new perspective or level of consciousness. This "awakening . . . proceeds to action, which in turn provides the basis for new perception, new reflection" (Lloyd, 1972, p. 5).

In summary, Mezirow's and Freire's approach to adult learning emphasizes the importance of inner meaning and mental constructs in defining the nature of learning in adult life. More so than the theories based on learner characteristics or adult life position, the formulations described in this section give rise to philosophical and ethical issues: What right do adult educators have to tamper with the worldview (mental set, perspective, paradigm, or state of consciousness) of the learner? How is the goal of educational intervention to be determined? What is the educator's responsibility for the action component of praxis? These questions are addressed in Chapter Fifteen.

Summary

This chapter has reviewed seven different theory-building efforts in adult learning. Knowles's andragogy and Cross's CAL model were discussed together in that they both stress adult learners' characteristics. Three theories—McClusky's theory of margin, Knox's proficiency theory, and Jarvis's model of the learning process—are solidly anchored in the adult's life situation. Finally, Mezirow's perspective transformation and Freire's conscientization were treated together as theories that focus on changes in consciousness.

In assessing the theory-building efforts in adult learning, one can ask how well the seven theories reviewed in this chapter explain learning—in particular, adult learning. One can ask if the theory is comprehensive, that is, includes all types of learning. Rachal suggests that one can also ask how practical the theory is and how universal its application might be (1986).

No single theory fares well when all of these criteria are brought to bear. Each has strengths and weaknesses, most of which have been discussed in this chapter. Four of the theories reviewed here (those of Knowles, Cross, Knox, and McClusky) reveal more about the learner's characteristics, his or her life situation, and the desired outcomes of learning than they do about learning. While these theories help us understand the learner and to some extent the motives for participation, they do little to advance our understanding of the learning process. Three focus on the process of learning itself—Jarvis's, Mezirow's, and Freire's—but only one, Mezirow's perspective transformation, claims to explain learning that is unique to adults. This claim has yet to be supported by research. Indeed, none of the theories is supported by a substantial body of research. Until there is more empirical support, the criterion of universality, or how well predictions derived from theory hold up, is a moot point. Finally, while most of these theories address implications for practice (see especially Mezirow and Associates, 1990), only Knowles' andragogy has been widely *applied* in practice (Knowles and Associates, 1984).

A phenomenon as complex as adult learning will probably never be adequately explained by a single theory. Each of the seven attempts reviewed in this chapter contributes something to understanding how adults learn and, by extension, how educators can enhance the process. At least four components of adult learning can be extracted from these theories: (1) self-direction or autonomy as a characteristic or goal of adult learning; (2) breadth and depth of life experiences as content or triggers to learning; (3) reflection or self-conscious monitoring of changes taking place; and (4) action or some other expression of the learning that has occurred. While one theory to explain all adult learning may never emerge, the process does stimulate inquiry, reflection, and research, all of which will eventually provide us with some of the answers to our questions about adult learning.

PART FIVE

Challenges
in Fostering
Adult Learning

In this final section of *Learning in Adulthood,* we step back and reflect on some important issues in the practice of adult learning. In the four previous sections of this book we reviewed the accumulation of knowledge about learning in adulthood—the context in which it takes place, the learner, the learning process, and theory building. This knowledge only partly, if at all, informs the decisions that educators make in practice. Another kind of knowledge, that which is lodged in values and beliefs, defines practice to a much greater extent. Thus we have chosen to address here some of the societal values that shape the provision of adult learning opportunities (Chapter Fourteen) and some of the ethical issues inherent in the teaching/learning transaction (Chapter Fifteen). Chapter Sixteen, the final chapter, is a summary integrating and synthesizing the wide range of material covered in this book.

Questions of access and opportunity have plagued the adult learning enterprise for most of the modern era and have become even more troublesome in recent years. The gap between the better educated who seek out continuing education and those who do not continues to widen. Government policy and government funding tend to support only those efforts directly related to basic skills and employment. Large segments of the adult population who do not fall into these categories but

267

do not have the resources to continue their own learning go un-
served. Adult learning thus becomes a vehicle for solidifying
a socioeconomic structure contrary to the stated goals of adult
education in our society. Chapter Fourteen examines the rhetoric, which espouses one set of values, and the reality, which
demonstrates another, in the provision of adult learning opportunities. The chapter is organized around three questions: Who
in our society decides what the learning opportunities will be?
To what goals are the learning activities directed? And who benefits from these activities?

　　While Chapter Fourteen examines the larger social issues
involved in the provision of learning opportunities, Chapter
Fifteen shifts to the ethical questions inherent in the learning
transaction. To what extent, for example, should we be concerned with a person's growth and development versus what is
"good" for society? To what extent do we do an injustice by raising expectations that learning to read will lead to a better job
and a better life? Whose responsibility is it to determine the goals
of a learning activity? How much responsibility for planning
and implementing a learning activity should be the teacher's
versus the learner's? What about the outcomes of a learning activity? As everyone knows who has seen the film *Educating Rita,*
the growth that results from learning can be painful, disorienting, and have unintended consequences. This chapter explores
the ethical dilemmas inherent in determining the goals of learning, implementing the learning activity, and accounting for its
consequences.

　　In Chapter Sixteen, the summary chapter, we discuss how
the three primary factors in learning—the context, the learner,
and the learning process—come together to provide us with some
understanding of learning in adulthood. In this chapter we also
assess the extent to which our understanding of learning in adulthood is currently reflected in theory and practice in the field.

Fourteen

The Social and
Political Issues

In a provocative book titled *Learning to Labour: How Working Class Kids Get Working Class Jobs* (1977), author Paul Willis makes the case that there is little hope for working-class youth to move from blue-collar jobs to the middle class. The social structure and the major institutions of family, community, and school act in concert to reinforce class distinctions and status. Many have argued that adult education functions in the same way; certainly there is evidence in the participation literature to support this contention. Not until recently, however, has attention been given to the social issues involved in the provision of learning opportunities for adults. The focus of discussion, research, and writing has been on the individual learner and the individual educator. As Rubenson states, "One gets a picture of the adult educator with a firm grip on the rudder keeping the vessel on the right course. However, no one seems to ask where the wind and the waves are coming from" (1980, p. 13). This chapter tries to find out where the wind and waves are coming from—that is, we shift the focus from the person to the larger setting of society. At any level, from preschool through adult, the provision of learning opportunities is a value-laden, political activity. As a form of social intervention, education is a "deliberate attempt by professionals to change the characteristics of individuals or groups or to influence the pattern of relationships between individuals and/or groups" (Kelman and Warwick, 1978, p. 4). In choosing goals for a learning activity, in defining the target audience and the means of implementation, certain values take precedence over others. Often these values go unexamined or are assumed to be held in common by both the policymakers and the recipients of the intervention. Moreover, one set of values may be advanced in public rhetoric while quite another set may be operationalized in practice. While we may know a good bit about the context of adult learning, learners themselves, and the process of learning, we are rarely able to apply this knowledge directly to a learning situation. Other factors — in particular the values inherent in a social and economic system — shape the learning enterprise as much as theory and research. This chapter explores the rhetoric and reality of certain social issues surrounding the provision of adult learning opportunities. Specifically, three questions are addressed: Who decides what the learning opportunities will be? To what goals are the learning activities directed? And who benefits from these learning activities?

Who Decides?

Asking who decides what the learning opportunities should be is the same as asking who has the power to decide. In theory, at least, it is learners themselves who decide what is to be offered. The voluntary nature of most adult learning reinforces this in that a great many of these activities are characterized by voluntary participation in contrast to the compulsory nature of pre-adult schooling. Adults will not volunteer — or will not stay if they do volunteer — to participate in formal or nonformal learning activities that are not responsive to their needs. And since much of organized adult learning is self-supporting, learners do to some extent decide what is offered. But if learners were the only ones to determine offerings, the entire field of adult education could become a reactive endeavor in which trained personnel become technicians in the service of demanding learners. Furthermore, the provision of learning opportunities would be based solely upon who is willing to pay — resulting in a market-driven rather than an educationally inspired enterprise.

The reality is much more ambiguous. The service orientation of adult education is alive and well, and to some extent learners do influence what is offered. But so do trained adult educators, legislators, employers, and others who may or may not themselves be participants. Nevertheless, the answer to who decides what is to be offered cannot be uncoupled from the question of who finances the various adult learning opportunities. And in North American society, tying these two questions together makes for a very murky answer at best.

The answer is somewhat easier to track in reference to formal adult education — learning that is institutionalized versus nonformal learning that is organized outside the formal system (such as self-help groups and alternative schools). In North America there are many providers of formal learning opportunities including government at all levels, employers, educational institutions, and community institutions such as libraries. Because much of the expenditure for this form of learning is hidden under a variety of budgetary labels — at one time more than 270 federal programs alone had some component of adult learning (Griffith and Fujita-Starck, 1989) — it is difficult to measure the relative financial power of various providers.

To further complicate the matter, what is offered at any particular time "will almost inevitably relate to the pressures generated in the social system. . . . Social pressures act in such a manner as to create an imbalance in the system to which institutions, other than that generating pressure, respond by seeking to restore the system to some form of equilibrium" (Jarvis, 1986, p. 57). Institutions are currently being pressured to respond to the issues of an illiterate work force, for example, and to the health threat of AIDS. This notion of mobilizing institutions in the service of maintaining social equilibrium is but one explanation for understanding shifts in curriculum emphasis. Another explanation has to do with the desire of those in control to maintain a social structure that supports established power relations (Giroux, 1983). This perspective is discussed later in the chapter.

The problem of *who* decides what learning opportunities should be available brings into question the extent to which the public good takes precedence over individual freedom. In the case of AIDS, for example, does the government have the right to send an educational brochure to people's homes? Can employers require employees to attend an educational workshop on AIDS? Actually, federal initiatives in response to social concerns through education have been rather limited. (The recent Literacy Initiative is an exception.) According to the U.S. Office of the Secretary of Education (1978, p. 16): "Education in the United States has traditionally been a local *function,* a state *responsibility,* and a federal *concern.*" With the responsibility at the state level, and especially in a period of decentralization and deregulation, states are making many of the decisions as to how educational dollars are to be spent. States do have some choice in how they respond to these social pressures, of course. In a study of state policies and practices vis-à-vis the provision of adult learning activities, Cross and McCartan (1984) have identified four levels of intervention. The first of these they label the *laissez-faire* approach. Here the state either believes that a free market will best serve the interests of adults or it simply does not wish to get involved. The second stance, and the most prevalent, is *encouragement.* The state takes no direct action but facilitates the involvement of others through "planning and goal setting, collecting data, promoting local cooperation, or establishing task forces" (p. 4). The third option, *intervention,* is rationalized on the basis of the "state's interest in the efficient use of public resources and in protecting citizens against fraudulent or shoddy educational practices" (p. 125). Finally, states may intervene with *direct support and services,* especially if it is more cost-effective or more equitable to offer a service statewide.

     The flip side of the question of public rights in deciding what provisions to offer is the question of individual learning rights. Is there such a thing? Is it related to certain roles such as citizen, consumer, employee? To what extent does our system of adult and continuing education support, neglect, or reject these different learning rights? In contrast to totalitarian forms of government, a democratic form of government such as that found in North America would seem to foster individual learning rights. Do learners, for example, have the right to request support for learning about environmental and consumer issues that in turn makes for a more informed citizenry? If learners have a right to ask for certain educational activities, who is obligated to respond?

In a pluralistic society such as ours, the question of who decides what learning opportunities to offer has no single answer. In reality, decisions are made by those who pay — whether that means the learners themselves, government, employers, or educational institutions. And those who pay are in positions of power and hence determine what is good for the rest of society. Those not in positions of power rarely decide what learning opportunities to offer. Their role is limited to deciding not to participate. How the social situation is defined and by whom are issues inextricably linked to the purpose of providing the learning opportunity in the first place.

For What Purpose?

In *Modern Practice of Adult Education* (1980), Knowles presents a model of practice that is responsive to individual, institutional, and societal needs. Educational objectives are developed by considering each set of needs against the sponsoring institution's philosophy, feasibility measures, and clientele interests. However, this model tends "to ignore the constraints of social structure and to assume that the educational process occurs in relative isolation" (Jarvis, 1985, p. 68). Indeed, the many discussions of goals and purposes of adult education in the literature tend to present the ideal that we perhaps strive for, rather than the reality of what is actually implemented. Darkenwald and Merriam (1982), for example, list the purposes of adult education as the cultivation of the intellect, individual self-actualization, personal and social improvement, social transformation, and organizational effectiveness. Recently Beder (1989) reviewed several typologies of purposes and collapsed the various lists into four major categories: to facilitate change in a dynamic society; to support and maintain the "good" social order; to promote productivity; and to enhance personal growth. Common to most of the lists is the ideal of a democratic society in which the individual can personally benefit through education and where access and opportunity are available to all.

In practice, though, education in most societies functions to preserve society as it is, rather than to change it. "The process of education is powerful," Cunningham writes, because "it is an apparatus for social control" (1988, p. 133). Rather than promoting the democratic ideal of equity, "adult education as now practiced in the United States is elitist by nature" (p. 140). In support of the charge that adult education is an elitist and highly political endeavor, Cunningham points to middle-class participation patterns, to the homogeneous, technically oriented training of adult educators, to a "psychology of individual deficit" as a basis for explaining social inequities, and to the erosion of the voluntary nature of adult education (p. 141). She and others have also argued that not only are most people unaware of this dichotomy between ideals and reality but "inequality is seen not only as inevitable but also necessary and beneficial to all, since individual survival is contingent upon the survival and well-being of society" (Rubenson, 1989, p. 54). That the way things are (even if there are inequities) should seem right and normal is a strategy of the ruling elite to maintain control (Cunningham, 1988; Jarvis, 1986; Rubenson, 1989).

A more comprehensive list of the functions of adult education, one that takes into account the "constraints of social structure," is presented by Jarvis (1985). While several of the functions can be regarded as truly democratic and liberating, Jarvis points out how they can also be used in the service of the status quo. First, adult education maintains the social system and existing social relations. Second, "the education of adults transmits the dominant culture and in the process it reproduces the cultural system which, in itself, is a force for the retention of the status quo rather than social change" (p. 139). A third function is individual advancement and selection, although this is a selective process carefully monitored by the system itself. The fourth function — offering a second chance and legitimation — still promotes the dominant culture since "second chance education actually produces an appearance of greater equality of opportunity and, hence, reinforces the existing social structures" (p. 143). Leisure-time pursuit and institutional expansion, the fifth function, have as a latent function "the retention of stability in the social system at a time when many people do not have work to occupy their time and their minds" (p. 147). Finally, development and liberation can be goals of adult education, although one should be aware that such development and liberation may actually be designed to enable people to fit more easily into the existing social system.

Whatever the stated or actual purposes of a learning activity, adult education is a form of social intervention and very often "begins as an effort to solve a problem" (Kelman and Warwick, 1978, p. 12). What is seen as problematic depends on one's values, social position, and perspective: "Identification of the problem has important ethical implications because it determines selection of the target to which change efforts are directed. Where we intervene depends on where we, with our personal value preferences and perspectives, perceive the problem to lie" (p. 13). In the case of social unrest, for example, "those who identify with the status quo are likely to see the problem as a breakdown of social order, while those who identify with the protesters are more likely to see the problem as a breakdown of social justice" (pp. 12–13).

The identification of "problems" to which adult education attempts to respond tends to be done by those who have a value perspective not necessarily shared by the target population. As Cunningham has noted, much program planning is based on an "individual deficit" model rather than an examination of "the oppressive structures in which people live" (1988, p. 141). Programs are thus designed around learner deficiencies, which may or may not be of concern to the learner. A good example of this problem involves the Lifelong Learning Act passed by Congress in 1976. Testimony by Senator Walter Mondale in support of the legislation reveals what is probably the prevailing view of the purpose of providing learning opportunities to adults: "Lifelong learning offers hope to those who are mired in stagnant or disadvantaged circumstances — the unemployed, the isolated, elderly, women, minorities, youth, workers whose jobs are becoming obsolete. All of them can and should be brought into the mainstream of American life. Lifelong learning is a necessary step toward making the lives of all Americans more rewarding and productive" (quoted in Richardson, 1987, p. 2). Richardson offers one explanation why the act was never funded: "Lifelong learning is a fuzzy, shorthand, politically expedient term, offered as a solution to a clump of ill-defined problems which would be thought about more usefully if they were kept separate: age discrimination, worker alienation, rapid social change, the knowledge explosion, poverty, illiteracy, and a host of related educational and social inequities" (p. 3).

Nevertheless, "adult education is given public support when the public can see the connection between education and the solution to a threatening situation" (Griffith and Fujita-Starck, 1989, p. 172). Most "threatening" are challenges to economic stability and social order. The emphasis may shift with changes in the society's social, cultural, and economic structure. Religious education in Colonial America gave way to a citizenship orientation in the mid-eighteenth century when the development of an informed citizenry was deemed crucial to the success of a new democracy. The late nineteenth and early twentieth centries saw adult education become a vehicle for adjusting to industrialization and acculturating immigrants to American ideals. The present emphasis is on remedial training (especially literacy) and vocational training. Literacy and job skills most directly relate to the nation's economy. Programs addressing these issues are stopgap measures, safety valves, and a means of maximizing human capital in service to the state. In the present situation, Petska observes, "we cannot expect an active, widespread concern for people and for social well-being. Nor can we expect marked changes in an educational system which, despite the occasional claim of freeing human mind and spirit, has a record of binding individuals to societal patterns" (1982, p. 22).

In a recent discussion of social policy models, Quigley (1989b) points out that the market model (rather than a progressive-liberal welfare model or a social redistribution model) has "influenced adult education in recent years with demand for self-financed education; for more competitive, measurable, outcome criteria in basic, higher, and vocational education programs. Today questions of participation are framed as manpower planning and human resource development issues with target groups and economic return as areas of concern" (p. 257).

Apart from the economic linkage, the current emphasis on literacy and job skills in the United States addresses issues of social stability. Thousands of illiterate, unemployed, or underemployed adults with nothing to do and no money to do it with pose a threat to the stability of the social order, not to mention a drain on social resources. So while the rhetoric of adult education suggests some rather lofty ideals for the purposes of the endeavor, the reality suggests much more conservative purposes — maintenance of the status quo and economic return are the two primary orientations of those who decide what learning opportunities are to be offered. The next question of importance, then, is who benefits from these opportunities?

Who Benefits?

Popular rhetoric suggests that everyone — young or old, well-educated or not, rich or poor — can enhance their life situation through learning. And one can certainly find programs that attract or are even targeted for every description of adult and every subject imaginable. Theoretically, every adult can choose to participate in any adult learning activity. The reality of the situation, however, is that the vast majority of adults attracted to continued learning are already well educated, middle class, and white. "A close look at different forms of adult education reveals," Rubenson points out, "that the better an education pays off in terms of income, status, occupation, political efficacy, cultural competence, and similar matters, the greater the differences in socioeconomic status between participants and nonparticipants" (1989, p. 64). According to Rubenson, the least payoff and thus the least socioeconomic difference between participants and nonparticipants can be found in self-directed learning activities such as those investigated by Tough (1979). The greatest payoff can be found in higher and continuing education; there large socioeconomic differences distinguish participants from nonparticipants. Between these two points on a continuum are community-based organizations and employer-sponsored education (Rubenson, 1980).

The democratic ideals of equal opportunity and open access make the current reality of uneven and unequal participation in formal adult learning particularly worrisome to policymakers, educators, and researchers. Numerous studies have been undertaken to find out why a certain segment of our society participates and others do not. Most explanations focus on a person's stated reasons for nonparticipation such as cost, time, transportation, and lack of confidence. When viewed from a social perspective, other explanations emerge. Rubenson argues, for example, that "through socialization within the family, the school, and, later on, in working life, a positive disposition towards adult education becomes a part of some group's habitus but not of others" (1989, p. 64). Jarvis (1985) refers to Bourdieu's concept of "cultural capital" to explain adult education's middle-class bias: "Those most likely to be the recipients of the dominant culture are those who, as a result of birth and upbringing, have already acquired the cultural capital to receive it." In other words: "Those who have already been socialized into a culture that is sympathetic to the dominant culture, or into the dominant culture itself, are more likely to acquire the fruits of education than those who have not" (pp. 138–139). Cultural capital can also help to explain nonparticipation in that the idea can be "used as a *basis for exclusion* from jobs, resources, and high status groups" (Lamont and Lareau, 1988, p. 156).

Society's assumption that adults are not only free to choose among options but capable of choosing wisely rests upon several factors, not all of which actually exist in a given situation. Kelman and Warwick (1978, p. 15) cite six such factors:

1. The structure of the environment provides them with options for choice.
2. They are not coerced by others or forced by circumstances to elect only certain possibilities among those of which they are aware.
3. They are, in fact, aware of the options in the environment and possess knowledge about the characteristics and con-

sequences of each. Though such knowledge may be less than complete, there must be enough to permit rational deliberation.
4. They are psychologically able to weigh the alternatives and their consequences. In practice this means not only possessing information but being able to use it in coming to a decision.
5. Having weighed the relative merits of the alternatives, they can choose among them. Rollo May has argued that one of the pathologies of modern existence is an inability to choose — a deficiency of will. A person who cannot pass from deliberation to choice must be considered less than free.
6. Having chosen an alternative, they are able to act on it. Among the conditions that may prevent them from doing so is a lack of knowledge about how to implement the choice, anxiety about acting at all, or a low level of confidence in their abilities, even when they have sufficient knowledge to act.

Those adults who have been socialized into valuing and acquiring these attitudes and skills will be the ones to take advantage of learning opportunities. Since most providers of such opportunities have themselves acquired the ability to function freely, little effort is expended on trying to understand and provide for other perspectives. The modus operandi of most providers is to offer a set of activities that they assume learners will want. A response, however, is predicated upon the assumptions that the learner knows about the program, can attend at the time offered, and can afford it, that the subculture of the institution is conducive to his or her own, and that what is actually offered corresponds with what he or she needs (Jarvis, 1985). Rubenson argues that "a system of adult education that implicitly takes for granted that the adult is a conscious, self-directed individual in possession of the instruments vital to making use of the available possibilities for adult education — a system that relies on self-selection to recruit the participants — will by necessity widen, not narrow, the educational and cultural gaps in society" (1989, p. 65).

Thus the question of who actually benefits from learning opportunities is somewhat obscured by rhetoric about who *should* benefit. In a society that values freedom and equality, learning opportunities are for everyone to take advantage of regardless of gender, ethnicity, age, race, or socioeconomic class. In reality, however, only a certain segment of the adult population responds to and thus benefits from these opportunities. The reasons for this are certainly complex. From a social rather than individual perspective, a partial answer may lie in the socialization process of prospective learners—a process resulting in values and attitudes that are not necessarily in concert with those who control what is offered.

Responding to the Issues

From the foregoing discussion of who decides, for what purpose, and who benefits, one might conclude that adult education is in the hands of a ruling elite whose interest in self-preservation and self-perpetuation determines the answers. Yet adult educators, policymakers, and others close to the enterprise are themselves functioning with worldviews they have been socialized into. Out of these worldviews come support for social institutions like church and government and for concepts like equality and freedom that are consonant with one's worldview. Social interventions such as adult education are designed to preserve and sustain what is valued. The problem, Cunningham notes, "is that we have difficulty seeing how we ourselves have constructed our world" (1988, p. 135). But since we have constructed our social reality, we can also change it. The responses we suggest in this section reflect our assumptions that while we may be shaped by our social context, we can also act upon it. We believe that adult educators should take a critical stance in examining their own values and assumptions and the extent to which these perpetuate the myths of our practice.

Educators and others are in fact becoming aware that the status quo can be changed and that transformations at both the individual and societal levels can happen. Several recent conferences and newly formed organizations in adult education are rekindling the spirit of social reform that was characteristic of adult education in the early decades of this century. Questions are being raised about the role of adult education in promoting social change. Issues of quality, access, and equity are receiving attention in the literature (see Brockett, 1988a; Collard and Law, 1989; Hayes and Snow, 1989; Quigley, 1989a, 1989b) alongside issues related to programming, budgeting, and needs analysis.

Several writers have suggested what might be done to promote a more equitable system of adult learning. These suggestions fall into two major categories: the development of critical thinking and a critical pedagogy, on the one hand, and the support and promotion of community-based learning activities on the other.

The development of critical thinking within a wide range of activities is seen by many as a means of bringing about change. Brookfield has devoted a book to why it is important and how adults can become critical thinkers in their family, work, and personal lives and in relation to mass media (1987). Deshler (1990) suggests that through analyzing common metaphors (such as those mentioned in Chapter One), we can "exorcize the 'ghosts' of our socialization so that we can freely choose meanings out of which we want to live our lives" (p. 296). Mezirow (1990) too begins with fostering critical thinking in individual learners "before social transformations can succeed. It is also clear that the individual perspective transformation process includes taking action, which often means some form of social action—which in turn can sometimes mean collective political action" (p. 363).

Critical thinking has recently been coupled with literacy training. Critical literacy is more than just acquiring basic skills of reading and computing. According to Cunningham (1988), it "means encouraging expression by the individual through dialogue, writing, and public expression"; it is promoting the skills necessary in "creating knowledge and action" (p. 143). Critical thinking in this sense is more often construed as critical pedagogy, or critical practice, and draws from Freire (1970b), Giroux (1988), and Shor and Freire (1987), among others.

Another arena where the promotion of critical thinking can lead to change is in the training of educators at all levels. Apps (1987), in fact, makes the point that adult educators should not isolate themselves from the rest of the education world. It is important to know what happens educationally in school, in the family, in "everyday living, from going to the movies and from the mass media. . . . Unless we begin to be more concerned about the rest of education . . . the field of adult/continuing education will increasingly be concerned with remedial education" (p. 17). From a critical practice position, Cunningham suggests making sure that the content of all programs "is open to competing ideas" and that professional development programming includes "content that goes beyond nationalist concerns, including such subjects as peace education and global resource sharing" (1988, p. 143). Furthermore, she says, the training of adult educators is too "confined to our technology" without coming to "grips with the purposes of that technology. Two basic ethical questions that should be discussed are (1) who has the power to make decisions on the nature of adult education programs, and (2) who do these programs benefit? To make this point at the basic ethical level in practice is to decide whether our resources should, for example, be addressed to questions regarding andragogy or racism; self-directed learning or sexism; models of evaluation or the emergence of a permanent underclass in our democracy" (p. 140).

Becoming aware of the power of education, and its politically charged nature, is a first step in addressing some of its inequities. Critical pedagogy directly confronts issues of power and control, conflict and oppression, and mandated action to deal with social equalities as they are revealed in learning encounters. (See Ellsworth, 1989, for an example of an attempt to do this.)

The promotion of community-based populist learning activities is a second major strategy in changing the present situation. Because of their nonformal nature, these programs have had little visibility and even less public support compared to formal, institutionally based programs. In many ways, however, they are much more egalitarian in practice and are closer to the ideals of adult education in a democratic society than many formal programs. Examples of such programs are study circles (Oliver, 1987), the National Issues Forum, self-help groups, and community-oriented adult literacy programs (Hayes and Snow, 1989). Typically these groups are citizen entities rather than professionally organized, are voluntary, have as a goal the development of an awareness of their situation, choose to create their own knowledge base rather than accommodate "official" knowledge, and have a strong action component. Hayes and Snow (1989) further differentiate community-oriented programs, in this case literacy programs, from mainstream programs with respect to mission (social change versus individual literacy), instruction (group-devised methods versus standardized curricula), source of problem (flawed society versus flawed individuals), and outcome (group action versus individual achievement).

Every society has "valuables" that are deemed scarce and necessary, such as material wealth, knowledge, skill, and power. Whereas politics is the shaping and sharing of power, education is the shaping and sharing of knowledge and skills. That knowledge is power and education is empowerment is commonly understood. Promoting critical thinking and critical practice and supporting community-oriented programs can bring about social change. Cunningham explains how this can come about: "First, the participant-produced knowledge competes with, confronts, and forces change onto the official knowledge; second, the participants, in recognizing that they have produced and celebrated their own view of the world, empower themselves. . . . This can produce interdependence and informed critical thinkers, as opposed to a dependent and 'coping' underclass" (1988, p. 137).

Summary

This discussion of social issues in the provision of adult learning opportunities began with the premise that the practice of adult education can be better understood by looking at the social context in which it takes place. Learning encounters are shaped by more than the knowlege base derived from research.

The actual and espoused values of the social system in which the learning takes place also shape the learning enterprise. In our society, questions of access and equal opportunity that trouble the adult learning enterprise reflect the disjuncture between the values we promote in our rhetoric and what actually happens in practice. The gap between the better educated who seek out and can afford continuing learning opportunities, versus those who do not, continues to widen. Government policy and government funding tend to support only those efforts directly related to basic skills and employment. Large segments of the adult population do not respond to these initiatives. Those who do participate are already the better educated, the more socially mobile, the ones with higher income. Adult learning thus becomes a vehicle for solidifying a socioeconomic structure contrary to our stated goals of access and equality.

This chapter has explored the gap between the rhetoric and the reality of three factors in the provision of learning opportunities: Who decides what is to be offered; for what purposes is it offered; and for whom is it offered? The chapter concludes by suggesting that adult educators and others encourage the development of critical thinking and critical practice in all of life's activities, including the training of future adult educators, and that popular, community-based activities should be supported.

Fifteen

Ethical Dilemmas
in Teaching and Learning

In "The Story of Gladys Who Refused to Grow: A Morality Tale for Mentors," Daloz (1988b) recounts his experience advising an adult learner who stubbornly resists thinking critically or imaginatively about her life experiences. It becomes clear to him that "not all students grow from their education." Such students "contradict our best hopes and some of our fonder theories." "People like me, " Daloz admits, "prefer to look the other way" (p. 7). Daloz goes on to explain what students like Gladys can teach us about learning in adult life — how the price of change may be too expensive for some. Daloz's encounter with Gladys raises questions about the adult learning transaction, questions that are ethical in nature.

What is the right way to act in the teaching/learning situation? What are the responsibilities of the teacher and the learner? It is clear that in making decisions in everyday practice, one cannot rely solely on the kind of knowledge described in previous chapters on the learner and the learning process. That is, knowing something about how adults learn does not necessarily tell you how to respond to Gladys. This chapter explores some of the ethical issues related to learning — in particular, those present in the teaching/learning transaction. In contrast to the broad perspective of the preceding chapter on social issues, the focus here is on the individual and the learning activity. What both chapters have in common is the notion that values and beliefs, whether societal or individual, shape the adult learning enterprise as much as the official knowledge base reviewed in the earlier chapters of this book.

Adult education is a social activity. It involves people and their interactions with one another — people who have differing views on how things should be done, who feel obligated and responsible in different ways. Conflicting obligations and competing values underlie the ethical dilemmas of practice. Because "ethics is socially defined in the political arena of practice" (Cunningham, 1988, p. 139), the microcosm of the teacher, the learner, and the learning activity is a good place to examine the ethical dimensions of learning in adulthood.

Furthermore, being involved in the provision of formal learning is a moral activity. Regardless of our specific role or the agency or institution that employs us, we are engaged in bringing about change. Education, like public policy, military intervention, community development, or psychotherapy, is a form of social intervention, which is defined as "any act, planned or unplanned, that alters the characteristics of another individual or the pattern of relationships between individuals" (Kelman and Warwick, 1978, p. 3). While most of adult education is a planned activity designed to affect the learner in specified ways, there are often unintended outcomes affecting the people involved or their pattern of relationships. Gladys is a case in point. Her academic experience affected her only marginally; rather, the interaction became an unplanned learning experience for her mentor. Daloz learned that there are good reasons for which adults resist change, reasons that have to do with maintaining rather than altering the pattern of relationships: "Most adults are richly enmeshed in a fabric of relationships which hold them as they are, and many of their friends and relations do not wish to see them change. . . . Change demands a complex kind of renegotiation of relationships among spouses, children, friends, parents, and teachers. Complex enough for young adults in college for the first time, the mix can be boggling for adults. Sometimes it is just plain simpler to stay right where they are, or at least appear that way" (Daloz, 1988b, p. 7).

Thus, adult learning is both a moral activity and a social intervention accompanied by dilemmas over good versus bad and right versus wrong. Ethical dilemmas are grounded in conflicting yet equally legitimate views of what is good and right. Dilemmas are dilemmas because of their complexity. There are no simple answers. An ethical dilemma forces choice between competing courses of action, each with its own values. An ethical dilemma is in fact "a choice that has no totally acceptable resolution" (Sork, 1988, p. 37). This chapter explores ethical dilemmas with regard to three aspects of an adult learning situation: determining the goals of learning, implementing the learning activity, and assessing the consequences of learning.

Setting the Goals

Ethical dilemmas may arise in setting goals for the learning activity. We cover three questions here, which correspond to three aspects of the process. The important question of *who* sets the goals is discussed first. The second question to be considered is *how* the goals are determined. The final question is *what* the goals themselves will be. Usually they will reflect the values and orientation of the person who is in a position to decide on them.

Who Sets the Goals? Several questions are involved in determining the goals of adult learning: Who should decide? How are decisions made? And what should the goals be? As for who decides the goals, there are several possibilities — the teacher, the learner, or both, through negotiation. Goals may also be set by external agencies such as institutions, political bodies, or funding agencies. The literature on adult education recommends at least consulting with prospective learners about the goals of their learning. Ideally, the goals of the learning activity are determined by the learners themselves. In practice, however, the goals are rarely determined by the learners — and for good reasons. They may not know enough about the subject to establish realistic goals, the process may be too time consuming, and the professional is trained to offer just such knowledge. The situation has ethical consequences, as Sork (1988, p. 44) notes in a discussion of program planning: "Although many authors extol the virtues of client involvement in planning, con-

versations with practitioners suggest that such direct involvement is rare. There are practical consequenses of not involving
clients in decision making, but of concern here is the morality
of planning programs *for* rather than *with* adult learners."

As well intentioned as most adult educators are, determining goals for, rather than with, learners conflicts with another
value in the field—that of viewing the adult as an independent,
authentic, responsible being capable of determining his or her
own goal in a learning activity. Gladys set her own goal of
recording her concrete experiences running a nursing home.
Based on his years of experience guiding adults through a liberal
arts program, Daloz had a different goal for Gladys. Both were
forced to come to terms with differing expectations. The dilemma
in setting the goals of the learning experience centers on the
question of who decides what is to be accomplished in a teach-
ing/learning transaction. Both the teacher and the learner in-
vest in the activity. Each has a personal understanding of what
might be accomplished.

How Are Goals Determined? In this, as in numerous other situations, how one decides between conflicting courses of action
depends on one's view of human nature, of the learner, and of
adult learning. Examining what one believes about people,
learners, and learning is part of what distinguishes informed
educators from pure technicians. Good practice in adult education is enhanced by those who not only can make choices
among alternatives but also know why they make the decisions
they do. If one views human beings as higher-level animals
whose behavior is determined by past experiences (a psychoanalytic orientation) and or by environmental engineering (behaviorist), then the choice of who designs and implements the
learning transaction is clear. The choice is also clear, but different, if one believes that people can change the direction of their
lives through individual consciousness and effort (a humanistic
position). One's faith in the potential of people for affecting their
life situation underlies much of adult learning. Kazemek (1984),
for example, makes the point that "how one perceives the adult
nonreader and writer—either as competent and capable of cre-

ative action and intelligent judgment or as incompetent and unable to act meaningfully upon the world — is an ethical matter"
(p. 1).

Even more specific to the teaching/learning transaction
is what one believes about adult learners and the nature of learning itself. "How [instructors] teach, what they teach, and the
way they interact with their students" are influenced by one's
views on the nature of adults as learners (Caffarella, 1988a, p.
106). Literature in the field makes a strong case for viewing adult
learners as different from children: "Adults are not merely tall
children. They differ from the young in many ways that influence
their learning. They have different body characteristics, different learning histories, different reaction times, different attitudes,
values, interests, motivations, and personalities. Therefore, those
who are trying to help adults learn must be aware of these differences and adjust teaching and the learning environment accordingly" (Zahn, quoted in Apps, 1979, p. 168). Some teachers of
adults, however, are either unaware of these differences or believe that they do not matter when it comes to instruction.

In a chapter on developing a teaching and learning rationale, Apps (1979, pp. 170–171) lists five criteria that would
be helpful in making decisions throughout the teaching/learn-
ing transaction. Each of these criteria reflects one's basic assumptions about teaching, learning, adult learning, and human nature. The selection of procedures should be guided by:

1.   Beliefs about the nature of human beings and the adult as
     a learner
2.   Beliefs about the purposes of continuing education
3.   Beliefs about what constitutes knowledge and curriculum
4.   A theory and definition of learning
5.   A view of where learning occurs

In summary, how strongly one believes in a particular position is manifest in the choices one makes when there are conflicting courses of action. Brockett (1988b) writes that these beliefs
are translated into one's personal value system and it is this system that lies at the heart of ethical practice. Hiemstra (1988)

has proposed a process for constructing just such a personal philosophy of education. The first stage of the process consists of articulating one's beliefs about meaning, reality, and the nature of being human. The second phase concentrates on professional practice — what one believes about the aims of education, the method, and the content. Such a statement, Hiemstra believes, can be a useful tool "for subsequent professional actions and ethical decision making" (p. 178). It is upon this foundation of personal beliefs and values that choices among alternative courses of action are made.

What Should the Goals Be? As noted above, the choices educators make among competing courses of action are guided by what one believes and values — whether or not these beliefs and values have been articulated. Determining the goals of the teaching/learning transaction is no exception. A similar question was explored in the preceding chapter on social issues. At the societal level, the question relates to the goals of the adult education enterprise. In focusing on the teaching/learning transaction, the goals of instruction relate to the individual learner. The same questions discussed in reference to the overall goals of adult education apply to the individual learning transaction: "Ethical issues in the choice of goals for intervention revolve around the question of what values are to be served by the intervention and whether these are the right values for the target population. Since answers to these questions are likely to differ for different individuals — and to differ systematically for groups with different cultural backgrounds and positions in society — the question of *what* values inevitably brings up the question of *whose* values are to be served by the intervention" (Kelman and Warwick, 1978, p. 10).

Three commonly articulated goals of the teaching/learning transaction can be used to illustrate the ethical issues involved. The transaction can be designed to meet felt needs, to remediate learner deficiencies, or to challenge learners to higher levels of development. As Kelman and Warwick point out, the ethical questions are not only what but *who* should determine learners' needs, deficiencies, or levels of development. Adult educators like to think they are responding to learner-defined needs. In reality, the learner's needs, if expressed at all, are translated into learning opportunities through the value systems of individuals, institutions, and society. To what extent should educators respond to the needs of adult learners? Suppose, for example, a group of adults asks the local continuing education program to offer a class in the operation of semiautomatic assault weapons. "If there are some needs that warrant a response by the planner and others that do not, then how is the line drawn between the two? What values are reflected by the programmer who makes these decisions? Whose ideology prevails when disagreements arise over allocating resources to meet needs?" (Sork, 1988, p. 39).

The remediation of deficiencies is a common goal of adult learning transactions. But deficiency implies there is some standard against which an adult's skills, abilities, or knowledge are measured. This standard is often socially determined and fluctuates with time. An "acceptable" level of literacy, for example, was defined much differently for our grandparents than it is for our children. And computer illiteracy, which barely existed as a concept thirty years ago, now defines "deficiency" for thousands of adult learners. When learning needs are defined by anyone other than the learner, problems for both teacher and student often result. Literacy education is a good example. Educators and society in general feel that being able to read and write, preferably with enough proficiency to achieve a high school diploma, is a desirable goal toward which many resources are channeled.

Yet only a very small percentage (less than 5 percent according to some estimates) of those in need of literacy instruction participate — and of those who do, the attrition rate is extremely high. Perhaps potential learners do not perceive themselves as deficient or have compensated for their deficiency in some way, such as being in a social exchange network (Fingeret, 1983). Perhaps, too, the specific literacy tasks identified by educators are not those that illiterates themselves consider important (Hayes and Valentine, 1989). Certainly this deficiency model presupposes certain assumptions on the part of educators. But "are there conditions under which developing such programs can be justified? Is it acceptable to engage in activities designed to 'enlighten' the learners so that they, too, acknowledge a discrepancy in their capability?" (Sork, 1988, p. 40). These are the ethical dilemmas for which there are no easy answers.

As a goal of learning, development has its own set of ethical problems. It implies movement toward some ideal that is itself considered desirable; to be a more mature person, to be more socially adept, to be a more critical thinker, is better than being less developed in these areas. Even business and industry are struggling with the extent to which personal growth should be a goal of a training program. Gordon (1989, p. 27) comments on this matter: "The grand old question has a thousand nuances, but at bottom it is this: Where is the line between legitimate job-related training and an unwarranted intrusion into employees' personal selves — their minds, their hearts, their personalities, their souls?"

Nevertheless, some training and continuing education programs are based on models of moral, ego, cognitive, and faith development in which the goal is to foster movement to higher levels. Developing critically reflective thinkers, for example, is a goal receiving much support in recent literature (Brookfield, 1986; Daloz, 1988a; Mezirow, 1989). Cunningham writes that since our personal view of reality goes largely unexamined, "the ethical role of educators [is] to provide environments that allow people to examine critically the water in which they swim" (1988, p. 135). Still one can ask, as Lasker and Moore do, 'What is wrong with being at the stage where one is? . . . Do we have the right to consciously attempt to change the stage of a learner? Is change necessary or desirable?" (1980, p. 33). Moreover, the desired direction of growth is likely to reflect the values of the instructor — and what right has the instructor to impose personal values upon learners?

In practice, the goals of an adult learning activity turn out to be some combination of addressing expressed needs, remediating deficiencies (also referred to as prescribed, or normative, needs), and facilitating development. The ethical issues inherent in determining what the goals should be are closely entwined with the question of who decides. Regardless of who

decides what, Brookfield (1986) reminds us that learning outcomes are never totally predictable. The question of outcomes —
the consequences of the learning activity — is discussed in the
final section of this chapter.

Implementing the Learning Activity

Closely related to determining the goals of a teaching/learning
transaction are the means by which they are to be achieved.
Decisions need to be made with regard to the roles of teacher
and student, the content and instructional methods, and evaluation. Many of these decisions pose ethical dilemmas for the
educator.

Learner and Teacher Roles. What should be the role of the
teacher vis-à-vis the learner? How much responsibility lies with
the teacher for facilitating learning? How much with the learner?
Soltis (1989, p. 123) observes that "the unique relationship of
teacher to student create[s] a specific moral situation where the
student place[s] his or her trust in the teacher, ha[s] a legitimate expectation of being taught a true version of the subject
matter and of not being taken advantage of or harmed in any
way, and, in general, having his or her (the student's) well being and not the teacher's as the guiding value of the enterprise."
Apps (1979, p. 148) raises several other questions: "What might
be done to help eliminate the dependency relationship that often
develops between teacher and learners? . . . How can the teacher,
who is often a specialist in a given content area, be brought
together with learners in such a way that the teacher facilitates
learning rather than imposing his or her point of view?" The
roles of teacher and learner are of course directly related to the
goals of the learning activity. If the goal is to transmit knowledge, then the teacher has a directive role in organizing and
delivering content. If meeting the learner's needs is a goal, the
teacher's role is more facilitative. This role is totally unaccept-
able, however, for those who think the teacher should challenge
learners to think critically. In just meeting expressed needs, "the
educator becomes an automaton or functionary, a technician

responding to expressed desires but with no responsibility for suggesting alternative curricula or activities. Such a view absolves the educator from ever having to make value choices or from having to prompt learners to consider the possibility of other ways of thinking, feeling, and behaving" (Brookfield, 1986, p. 222). The proactive teacher, by contrast, challenges, prompts, encourages. Daloz (1988a, p. 241) writes that "our work with adult students requires that we help them recognize both the limitations of their own insularity and the scope of their responsibility. Encouraging students to move beyond their tribal boundaries and view the world from different perspectives is a political act." The question of just how much responsibility the teacher should assume in bringing about learning-based change is not easily answered.

Content Versus Process. Equally ambiguous is the matter of determining the right amount of content versus process in the learning activity. Much of the participation literature indicates that adults are specific about what and when they want to learn. Motives for attending learning activities are pragmatic; learners want to be taught by someone who knows; they willingly become dependent on the knowledgeable teacher. Other literature suggests that adults are autonomous beings who want a part in designing, implementing, and evaluating their own learning. For them the process takes precedence over the product. By extension, the goal of a learning activity that deeply involves learners in the process is often the development of self-direction in learning.

Focusing on process rather than outcomes has its own set of ethical questions. Brockett and Hiemstra (1985) note two issues that are relevant in situations fostering self-direction in learning. One dilemma has to do with the amount of intervention appropriate for individual learners. Can too much, or the wrong kind of intervention be detrimental to the learning process? The second question pertains to quality: "Since self-directed learning implies a high degree of learner control, the facilitator has a convenient excuse for not preparing" (p. 38). But, Brockett and Hiemstra go on, some educators may misunderstand the meaning and process of self-directed learning and while a few may see the approach as a way of jumping on the latest bandwagon, the facilitator who truly understands and respects the self-directed learning process will strive to refocus, but certainly not to diminish, the nature of his or her responsibility to the learner" (pp. 38–39).

Recent research on how women learn suggests yet another dimension to ethical considerations in the delivery of learning activities. In their study of women's ways of knowing, Belenky and colleagues (1986) found that the most powerful learning experiences occurred when teachers trusted their students' thinking and worked with them in a collaborative fashion. The "banking" model of education, in which knowledge is deposited into the heads of learners, and the adversarial model, where one's thinking is challenged and doubted, were found to be "debilitating rather than energizing" for women in their study (p. 227). "Educators can help women develop their own authentic voices," the authors conclude, "if they emphasize connection over separation, understanding and acceptance over assessment, and collaboration over debate" (p. 229). These findings raise several questions with regard to the design of instruction. What is the best method for facilitating learning? Is there a "best" method for everyone? What place is there for the educator's expertise and knowledge? What instructional options should learners be presented with? To what extent should gender or age or ethnicity be taken into account in designing instruction? (See also Luttrell, 1989, for research on women's ways of knowing based on gender, race, and class.)

Evaluation and Attendance. The evaluation of a learning activity is yet another area where ethical questions are likely to arise. The nature of evaluation itself raises ethical questions because it involves judgment: Decisions have to be made as to who and what are to be judged. Most evaluations are linked to the goals of the learning activity. The first question, then, is whether the goals themselves are morally worthwhile. Brookfield (1988b) points out that "what is defined as worthwhile is, of course, culturally and historically variable. In a democratic society . . . if we train people to be exemplary concentration camp guards, perfect bigots, or highly successful exploiters of minorities, we cannot regard these as educationally worthwhile activities even though the end results are what the program organizers desired" (p. 90). Other ethical aspects of evaluation have to do with the methods used, with who is involved, and with who has access to the results of an evaluation. For example, how ethical is it to subject low-literate adult learners to a battery of written tests and measures when such an experience might produce great anxiety and frustration? Should learners themselves be the sole evaluators of their own learning? If so, what if their assessment underestimates or overestimates what the teacher perceives as having been learned? What role does professional judgment play in an evaluation? Finally, who should have access to the results: learners, administrators, funding agencies, employers?

Adult education takes pride in the fact that most adults participate in learning activities because they want to, not because they have to. The title of the first national study of participation, *Volunteers for Learning* (Johnstone and Rivera, 1965), underscores this characteristic of the adult education enterprise. In some situations attendance is compulsory, however, or at least there are strong negative consequences for not participating in certain forms of adult education. The most visible form of compulsory adult education is mandatory continuing education (MCE). Many professional groups now require their members to complete a specified number of hours in continuing education in order to retain their license to practice (Phillips, 1987). Some training programs in business and industry require attendance as part of one's job. More subtle forms include prison education programs where the chances of parole are enhanced if one has participated, welfare-mandated class attendance, and courses mandated by traffic courts.

Kelman and Warwick (1978) point out the ethical questions involved in selecting the means by which social intervention such as education occurs. The means can range from coercion to environment manipulation, from persuasion to facilitation. "Is coercion ever ethically justified in social intervention," they ask, "and, if so, under what conditions?" In adult education one might make the case that continuing education is necessary to protect patients and clients against incompetence. But if one is a firm believer in preserving the voluntary nature of adult learning, an ethical dilemma arises as to the extent one should participate in compulsory learning activities, even those that might lead to insight and change such as court-mandated alcoholic treatment programs. Sork (1988, p. 42) summarizes these ethical issues: "Putting aside the practical problem of dealing with potentially obstreperous participants, the planner is still faced with the ethical issue of whether to apply the technology of planning to the design of programs in which learners are required to participate. Does the fact that an adult is compelled to participate in a program so violate the canons of the field that planners should refuse to apply their talents in such cases? Are there types of programs for which . . . compulsory attendance can be justified? Do planners have an obligation to design effective programs regardless of the motives underlying participation or the degree of compulsion exerted on the learner?"

In summary, then, evaluation and attendance, along with instructional design and the roles of teacher and learner, are all components that may involve ethical questions. Decisions have to be made with regard to each of these components of the teaching/learning transaction. And as long as there are competing courses of action, each based on competing beliefs and assumptions, ethical dilemmas result.

Assessing the Consequences

In the movie *Educating Rita,* the protagonist enrolls in an Open University course and is introduced to a world very different from the one she has inhabited all of her life. Midway through her transformation from a working-class London hairdresser to an articulate student of great literature, Rita is invited to a party at her professor's home. In a particularly poignant scene, she stands outside the house afraid to go in. She then joins her husband and parents in a tavern where they are singing and drinking. She sits with them but remains separated from the activity.

The next day she tells her professor that she can no longer relate to her family's world, but she is not comfortable in his world
either. She is clearly in a great deal of pain. The changes that
occur as the result of actively engaging in learning activities can
be profound and disturbing to the learner. What is the educator's responsibility for the consequences of learning?

Most educators believe in the "goodness" of continued
learning—that more is better than less, that through education
both individuals and society can advance to higher levels of development. But what of the unintended outcomes of learning?
What responsibility do we have for the pain and discomfort of
our learners as well as their growth and successes? Rita for a
time finds herself between two worlds, a member of neither.
Fingeret's research (1983) with adult illiterates underscores this
concern. She found that adult illiterates are in tightly knit interpersonal networks where there is an exchange of goods and
services. In exchange for reading, for example, the illiterate
might babysit for the reader's child or employ a relative at work.
Learning to read may disrupt the network, perhaps isolating
the learner from important support. Research on reentry women
reveals the pain and disruption many of these women feel as
they become exposed to new ways of thinking and being (Lewis,
1988a).

For those who follow an empowerment model of education, the consequences of enabling adults to take control of their
own lives are fraught with ethical questions. Empowerment involves the important notion of praxis—reflection and action
(Freire, 1970b). Learners who become aware of their oppression become empowered to take action to change not only their
situation but the social structure that led to oppression in the
first place. Ewert (1982) describes his experiences working in
an African village where "linkages between oppressive social
structures and local economic problems were established beyond
reasonable doubt" (p. 33). But rather than addressing the economic problems through community development projects, the
community focused on the need for revolution. It was felt that
"the program could generate more lasting changes by distributing

guns than by talking about agriculture and health" (p. 33). This would have been a suicidal course of action. Ewert comments on the ethics involved: "Freire has been criticized by many for not coming to grips with the ethical implications of raising people's levels of consciousness through discussion of community problems. Few would now deny that defining problems in structural terms is a political process that might result in putting bullets in disadvantaged people's guns, at least within an oppressive social system. The responsibility for unleashing a process that can potentially exceed controllable limits rests with the adult educator" (p. 34).

The consequences of empowerment at the individual level are explored by Day (1988). For him, the goal of a learning activity is choice — the freedom and capacity "to choose for oneself from a set of possible alternatives" (p. 119). Developing a person's capacity to know, weigh, choose, and act, he says (p. 124), involves being aware that:

1. We are decision-making beings and are ultimately responsible for the decisions we make.
2. Our participation in a learning activity cannot be viewed in isolation from the wholeness of our lives, that is, what we learn affects what we feel and what we do.
3. The idea of increased choices and options may indeed serve as a powerful motivator for participation in learning activities.
4. The results of our learning experiences may as likely lead to discontent as to a state of well-being.
5. Generally speaking, learning produces consequences.

Learning, Day concludes, sets in motion changes that "an educator with the best of intentions has little final control over" (p. 123). What the educator can and should do is to explore with learners the potential consequences of various courses of action. The decision to proceed in a particular direction lies ultimately with the learner, not the educator. This is indeed what Daloz learned from Gladys, who "refused to grow."

Summary

Many of the ethical dilemmas found in the teaching/learning transactions are but reflections of the adult learning enterprise explored in the previous chapter. Questions about the goals of adult learning—who should decide, what these goals should be—are also asked of the field as a whole. Questions related to the implementation of a learning activity have their counterpart in policy issues related to the delivery, funding, and organization of educational opportunities. Finally, questions about the consequences of learning to the individual can be asked in reference to society as a whole. There are, of course, no simple answers to the dilemmas raised in this chapter and the preceding one. The systematic knowledge that we do have about the context of adult learning, who the adult learners are, why and how they learn—information presented earlier in this book—is only partly helpful in making ethical decisions. Social and individual values play a much larger role in shaping our practice. Competing courses of action, alternative choices, each having its own merits, means that educators, policymakers, and learners themselves must examine the beliefs and values that form the basis for choosing among alternatives. It is this kind of awareness—awareness of why we do things the way we do—that leads to responsible, ethical practice in adult learning.

Sixteen

Integrating Theory
and Practice

This book is testimony to the fact that we know quite a lot about learning in adulthood. Each chapter on the context, the learner, the process, theory building, and issues is an interpretive summary of information about some aspect of learning in adulthood. In the process of reviewing and reflecting upon all of this material, we arrived at our own understanding of learning in adulthood. We see this last chapter as an opportunity to articulate what we ourselves have learned about this phenomenon.

Most who have written on the topic of adult learning have tried to delineate principles summarizing what has been learned from research or observed in practice and axioms that can be applied to practice. Knowles's (1980) assumptions underlying andragogy discussed in Chapter Thirteen is a good example of a set of principles about adult learners that has implications for practice. Others have advanced similar lists, often with a distinctive orientation. Kidd (1973), for example, presents "concepts" regarding the life span, role changes, studentship, maturation, adult experience, self-directed learning, the significance of time, and old age that he believed could provide hypotheses for the continued investigation of adult learning. Drawing on research on adult development and learning, Knox (1977, pp. 442–443) offers six suggestions for teaching adults: Emphasize abilities, clarify structure, make learning a memorable encounter, and use personal pacing, varied resources, and feedback. Brundage and Mackeracher (1980) cite thirty-six principles and discuss how each has implications for program planning.

A somewhat different angle is taken by Brookfield (1986), who proposes six principles that underlie effective facilitation of learning. These principles address participation, mutual respect, collaboration, praxis, critical reflection, and self-direction. Smith (1982) distinguishes the learning process from the learners. He presents six observations about learning such as "learning is a personal and natural process" and "learning has its intuitive side" (p. 35) and notes four critical characteristics of adult learners: a different orientation to education and learning; an accumulation of experience; special developmental trends; and anxiety and ambivalence (pp. 38–44). Finally, in a popular version of this approach, Zemke and Zemke (1981) present "thirty things we know for sure about adult learning." Their "thirty things" are divided into subsections on adult motivation, curriculum design, and classroom practice.

We considered doing a meta-analysis of the principles, concepts, and characteristics found in these sources as well as those delineated elsewhere in this book and in some of our own work (Caffarella, 1988b; Darkenwald and Merriam 1982; Merriam, 1987). That undertaking, however, would probably have resulted in another set of principles that would not truly capture what we have come to understand about learning in adulthood. Furthermore, there is some question in our minds as to the usefulness of a set of principles for guiding either research or practice. If, as we have tried to bring out in previous chapters, learning in adulthood is embedded in its context, a single set of principles is not likely to hold true for the wide-ranging diversity of learners and learning situations.

What we have done, therefore, is to step back and think about how learning in adulthood can be distinguished from learning in childhood. Our answer, in essence a summary of the book, is that learning in adulthood can be distinguished from childhood in terms of the context, the learner, and the learning process. Furthermore, it is not just that differences can be seen in these areas. Equally important, the configuration of context, learner, and process *together* makes learning in adulthood distinctly different from learning in childhood. In this chapter we first explore these differences and then discuss how well our understanding of the phenomenon is addressed by theory and practice. Finally, we speculate on the next steps to furthering our understanding of adult learning.

The Context

An adult's life situation, the context for learning, is quite different from that of a child. A child's life situation is characterized by dependency upon others for his or her well-being. Adults, on the other hand, are adults because they have assumed responsibility for managing their own lives. As Paterson (1979) reminds us: "To say that someone is an adult is to say that he is entitled, for example, to a wide-ranging freedom of life-style and to a full participation in the making of social decisions; and it is also to say that he is obliged, among other things, to be mindful of his own deepest interests and to carry a full share of the burdens involved in conducting society and transmitting its benefits. His adulthood consists in his full employment of such rights and his full subjection to such responsibilities" (p. 10). The taking on of social roles characteristic of adulthood, roles such as worker, marriage partner, and voter, differentiates adults from children better than does chronological age.

This difference in the social position of adults and children is reflected in contextual differences in their lives and their learning. A child's life is bounded by home and school, whereas an adult's life situation is defined primarily by work and community (including family). Through home and school, children learn to be adults; going to school is a full-time job. The main purpose of both home and school is to teach young people how to function as adults. The curriculum in both settings is set primarily by others who decide what is important to know in order to become responsible members of society. Education, even undergraduate education, is basically preparatory — young people are "prepared" to be adults.

Adults, on the other hand, typically add the role of learner to other full-time occupations. The learning that adults do arises from the context of their lives, which is in turn intimately tied to the sociocultural setting in which they live. An assembly-line worker whose job is taken over by a robot will need to retrain for other employment. Likewise, a nurse will need to keep up with changes in practice and technology. Zoning and tax laws, waste disposal management, and so on that affect citizens' lives in communities lead to new learning. Thus learning in adulthood is characterized by its usefulness for immediate application to the duties and responsibilities inherent in the adult roles of worker, spouse, parent, citizen, and so on.

The differences in context between children's and adults' lives and how these differences influence learning are highlighted in an article by Resnick (1987) contrasting learning in school and outside school. She writes that "school is a special place and time for people—discontinuous in some important ways with daily life and work" (p. 13). There are four ways that school learning differs from other (mostly adult) learning. First, in school individual cognition is primarily rewarded whereas outside school shared cognition is the norm: "For the most part, a student succeeds or fails at a task independently of what other students do. . . . In contrast, much activity outside school is socially shared. Work, personal life, and recreation take place within social systems, and each person's ability to function successfully depends on what others do and how several individuals' mental and physical performances mesh" (p. 13). Second, school values pure mentation as opposed to the tool manipulation that is valued outside. That is, "school is an institution that values thought that proceeds independently, without aid of physical and cognitive tools," at least in testing situations (p. 13). In the real world, people use all sorts of tools such as books, notes, calculators, and computers to solve problems and function more effectively. Resnick points out that it is the use of tools that allows "people of limited education to participate in cognitively complex activity systems" and cites Brazilian black market bookies' use of prepared probability tables for functioning in a demanding mathematical system (p. 14). In our own society, personnel in fast-food restaurants ring up our order on a computer where the food items are keyed by picture and word.

The third and fourth distinctions between learning inside school and outside are closely related. She notes that symbol manipulation is valued in school whereas outside one's "actions are intimately connected with objects and events . . . without necessarily using symbols to represent them" (p. 14). Too often school learning is decontextualized, resulting in little transfer between school and real-world reasoning. Resnick's fourth observation is that generalized learning occurs in school, but situation-specific competencies are needed out of school: "Schools aim to teach general, widely usable skills and theoretical principles. . . . Yet to be truly skillful outside school, people must develop situation-specific forms of competence" (p. 15). What people in all settings (including, Resnick points out, adult technical training, management, and continuing professional education) need to learn is "to be good *adaptive learners,* so that they can perform effectively when situations are unpredictable and task demands change" (p. 18). Resnick's analysis underscores the contextual differences between learning in childhood and in adulthood.

In delineating differences between children and adults regarding the concept of context, we note that these differences have ramifications with regard to social and ethical issues. Since children's education is preparatory, for example, they are expected to learn certain social and moral values as well as certain bodies of knowledge. As discussed in Chapter Fourteen, adult education struggles with issues of provision and access to learning opportunities, perhaps because adult education is primarily a voluntary activity whereas schooling for children is compulsory. Likewise, the ethical issues involved in adult learning differ somewhat in that an adult's learning is intimately tied to his or her life situation and status as an independent adult. Questions thus arise regarding agency and responsibility in the learning activity, as well as the outcomes of that interaction.

In summary, then, the context in which adult learning takes place generally differs from the context of most childhood learning. Moreover, every adult learning situation differs from every other situation, whether the learning is done in a formal setting or on one's own. As we pointed out in Chapter Two, three major factors affect learning in formal settings: people, structure, and culture. Students, teachers, administrators, indeed, everyone involved in the learning process, interacts to "shape the form and process of the resultant program" (Brookfield, 1986, p. 277). So do the structural factors of the institution itself, such as facilities, the organization's mission, and its operating procedures. Finally, every organization has a culture — a system of shared beliefs and values — that interacts with people and structure and produces different learning contexts even for the same type of provider, such as higher education.

And certainly informal learning contexts vary from individual to individual. The learning that adults do on their own has been shown, in fact, to be a function of the circumstances of each person's life (Spear and Mocker, 1984). In a provocative article titled "Meaning in Context: Is There Any Other Kind?" Mishler (1979, p. 2) writes that "human action and experience are context dependent and can only be understood within their contexts. . . . As theorists and researchers, we tend to behave as if context were the enemy of understanding rather than the resource for understanding which it is in our everyday lives." It is our view that adult learning is best understood when the context is considered with the same attention as the teaching and learning interactions occurring within it.

The Learner

There are marked differences between adults and children that help distinguish learning in adulthood from learning in childhood. The nature of experience differs; adults are dealing with different developmental issues than children; and there are differences in what motivates adults to participate in learning activities.

The comparatively richer life experiences of the adult have been cited by nearly all writers as a key factor in differentiating adult learning from child learning. Kidd (1973) notes that "adults have *more* experiences, adults have different *kinds* of experiences, and adult experiences are *organized differently*" (p. 46). He goes on to observe that "these points seem self-evident. An adult's sexual or social experiences are of a kind that mark him off from the world of children. The same can be said of his experiences of a job, or politics, or war" (p. 46). If accumulated life experiences differentiate children from adults, they also differentiate one adult from another. A group of sixty-year-olds will have less in common than a group of twenty-year-olds.

Experience is a major assumption "that can arguably lay claim to be viewed as a 'given' in the literature of adult learning" (Brookfield, 1986, p. 98). Knowles (1980) conceives of it in terms of a "growing reservoir of experience" that functions as "a rich resource for learning" (p. 44). It also establishes a person's self-identity: "Adults derive their self-identity from their experience. They define who they are in terms of the accumulation of their unique sets of experiences." And "because adults define themselves largely by their experience, they have a deep investment in its value" (p. 50).

Life experience functions in several ways that are idiosyncratic to adult learning. First, as Knowles observes, adult learners themselves become important resources for learning. Adults can call upon their past experiences in the formulation of learning activities, as well as serve as one another's resources in a learning event. Second, the need to make sense out of one's life experiences is often an incentive for engaging in a learning activity in the first place. Third, the actual engagement of past experiences with learning is different for adults than children. Smith, quoting Brundage, writes that "the adult's fund of past experience brings about a learning process that 'focuses on modifying, transferring, and reintegrating meanings, values, strategies, and skills, rather than forming and accumulating as in childhood'" (1982, p. 41). Finally, it should be noted that an adult's past experiences can become obstacles to new learning. Some may have to unlearn negative attitudes toward learning, old ways of doing things, prejudicial views, and so on.

The arena of development is another way in which adults are differentiated from children. While it is true that both adults and children are involved in developmental processes, the *nature* of the processes is qualitatively different. This difference can be clearly illustrated with Havighurst's developmental tasks for different life stages (1972). For infancy through adolescence the tasks reflect physical maturation (learning to walk, getting ready to read) or preparatory activities needed for future adult roles.

Beginning with the tasks of young adulthood, there is a shift to functioning well as an adult—bringing up young children, managing a home, achieving adult civic and social responsibilities, and so on. Erikson's life stages also reflect a shift from childhood dependence to adult-oriented dilemmas. In the first five stages of infancy through adolescence, the child deals with establishing trust, autonomy, initiative, industry, and identity. Adults struggle with intimacy, generativity, and integrity, characteristics manifested in adult roles of spouse, parent, worker, and citizen. In at least one developmental theory the notions of adult experience and development converge. Part of Kohlberg's (1973) theory of moral development stipulates that one cannot attain the higher stages of development until one has experienced irrevocable moral decision making. Fowler (1981), whose stages of faith build on Kohlberg's idea, also maintains that later stages cannot be attained until adult life.

In addition to a stage or task-specific view of development, two other frameworks discussed in Chapter Six—life events and transitions—differentiate adult learning from child learning. Many of the life events and transitions adults face are peculiar to adulthood and require adjustments—adjustments often made through systematic learning activity. It is these transitions and life events that result in significant, meaningful learning (Merriam and Clark, forthcoming) and in motivations for learning that differ from children's motivations. Aslanian and Brickell (1980), for example, found that 83 percent of adult learners in their study were involved in learning to cope with a transition. The transitions were primarily career-related (56 percent), followed by family life transitions (35 percent). "To know an adult's life schedule," they concluded, "is to know an adult's learning schedule" (pp. 60–61).

As noted in Chapter Five, there is a strong link between the motivation to participate in a learning activity and an adult's life experiences and developmental issues. Several theories of adult learning acknowledge this link. Knox's proficiency theory, for example, is based on the premise that adults experience a gap between their current level of proficiency and a desired level (1985). The proficiencies are related to major adult roles such as spouse or worker. Mezirow's process of perspec-

tive transformation is precipitated by a "disorienting dilemma" —
that is, one's familiar patterns of coping with life events prove
ineffective (1981, p. 8). Daloz talks about two major "crossings"
in the journey of human development: One is moving from
childhood into adulthood; the second is attempted when the beliefs, behavior, or mores of one's "tribe" come into question. In
both cases there is a "gap between old givens and new discoveries" (1988a, p. 238). Finally, Jarvis relates context to adult life
experiences in order to explain the motivation of adults to participate in learning: "The reason for participation does not always lie within the learner but in the dynamic tension that exists
between the learner and his socio-cultural world" (1983, p. 67).

Being an adult is thus a crucial factor in distinguishing
between learning in adulthood and learning in childhood. The
accumulation of experience, the nature of that experience, the
developmental issues adults deal with, how the notions of experience and development relate to motivation to participate — all
further differentiate adult learners from children.

The Learning Process

Of the three areas of context, learner, and process, there are
fewer dramatic differences between adults and children in the
learning process than in the other two areas. Houle, one of the
field's most respected adult educators, maintains that the process
of learning is fundamentally the same for adults as for children
(1972). Research in the last twenty years, however, has uncov-
ered some differences — differences that when linked together
with context and learner help distinguish adult learning from
child learning. This section draws from Chapters Six through
Ten to highlight some of the learning process differences between adults and children.

The separation of cognitive factors inherent in learning
ability from noncognitive factors that *affect* learning ability has
led to a better understanding of adult learning. Three noncognitive factors in particular — pacing, meaningfulness, and motivation — have been shown to affect adult learning. Pacing refers
to the time a person has to examine a problem or respond

to a situation. An adult's ability to respond slows with age, and time limits and pressures have a negative effect on learning performance. Perhaps because an adult's learning is so closely tied to his or her life situation, adults are not inclined to engage in learning unless it is meaningful. Adults are thus likely to do poorly on recall of nonsense syllables, for example, compared with younger learners who are more conditioned by school experiences to learn material that may not be immediately relevant. Linked to the meaningfulness of material is the noncognitive variable of motivation. Kidd (1973) explains that "one of the reasons that adults continue to learn well . . . is that they concentrate their learning in the areas of experience in which their interests also lie. Thus their motivation is substantial and, as everyone knows, wanting to learn is the greatest aid to learning. During childhood, varied learning is common; in maturity, active learning is usually practiced in areas defined in terms of interest" (p. 91).

There are other age-related factors that may affect learning in adulthood. Adults are likely to have more health problems than children. Fatigue, medication, disuse of abilities, interference from previous learning, environmental conditions, and so on certainly affect new learning. Acquisition of information for short-term memory may become impaired as all five senses deteriorate with age. These and other factors have been covered in depth elsewhere in the book. The point to be made here is that the nature of the learning process in adulthood is likely to be different from a child's because of the greater incidence of these occurrences and the greater impact of these factors on older learners.

By linking an adult's greater experiential base to learning, a case can be made that cognitive functioning in adulthood is qualitatively different from childhood. Ausubel, for example, maintains that the prior accumulation of knowledge is crucial to the integration of new learning (1968). By extension, then, "adults who have accumulated more knowlege than children are in a better position to learn new things, and, barring physiological impairments, learning potential increases with age" (Darkenwald and Merriam, 1982, p. 104). Others focus not so much on the accumulation of knowledge as on the *transformation* of experience as a characteristic of adult learning. (See Boyd and Myers, 1988; Daloz, 1986; Mezirow, 1981, 1985, 1990.)

Finally, it should be noted that those who posit stages of cognitive development in adulthood different from those unfolding in childhood contribute to our understanding of how the learning process may be different for adults. Arlin (1975), Flavell (1970), Riegel (1973), and others "introduce the hypothesis that mature adult thought, or the type of thought which adults have the potential to develop, is qualitatively different from the thought of adolescents or very young adults" (Allman, 1983, p. 112). Arlin, for example, proposes a fifth stage (after Piaget's four stages) of cognitive development occurring in adulthood called problem finding (1975). Riegel proposes a dialectical state "to explain the more complex and adaptive forms of thinking that adults have the potential to develop as they interact with adult life experiences, and the complex problems which arise from those experiences" (Allman, 1983, p. 111). Effective adult thinking, according to Riegel, "is not that which provides immediate answers but that which first discovers the important questions and exposes the important problems" (p. 111).

The Configuration of Context, Learner, and Process

As stated at the beginning of this chapter, we believe that learning in adulthood can be distinguished from childhood learning by the way in which context, learner, and learning process blend in adulthood. Quite simply, the configuration looks different than it does in childhood. In our discussion of each component we noted how the context of adult learning is different from the context of child learning, how adults are different from children, and how certain features of the learning process are unique to adults. Although we have attempted to discuss these components separately, our discussion reflects their natural interaction. An adult's life experiences, for example, are a function of the sociocultural environment and the learner's personality. Knox (1977) writes about this interaction with regard to an adult's work experiences: "Social change, as reflected in a rapidly changing occupational structure, contributes to more widespread shifts from one type of job to another during the occupational life cycle. Self-concept affects career selection, which in turn helps establish one's self-concept as well as one's level of living and prestige. Career development is also influenced by such attitudes as assertiveness and willingness to accept new responsibilities" (p. 559).

How an adult processes information from the sociocultural context, and even what an adult attends to in the environment, is wrapped up with the developmental concerns of the moment. A parent of teenagers, for example, is much more likely to notice and perhaps attend a workshop on teenagers and drugs than someone not involved with that age group. Likewise, the state of the economy is likely to be of great interest to someone nearing retirement who might then design a learning project on the topic. In both examples, the sociocultural context, the accumulated life experiences, developmental concerns, and presumably the nature of ensuing learning experiences converge to make learning in adulthood qualitatively different from learning in childhood.

In presenting this summary of learning in adulthood, we also asked ourselves to what extent theory and practice might reflect this holistic perspective of adult learning. The work on self-directed learning reviewed in Chapter Eleven and the models of participation reviewed in Chapter Twelve, by definition, focus on a particular aspect of the phenomenon. The self-directed learning frameworks emphasize the process and, to a lesser extent, the context and the learner. Likewise, the participation models do not deal with the learning process per se — the context and the learner are the most important variables.

Chapter Thirteen presents theory-building efforts that purport to explain learning in adulthood. The theories were organized for discussion according to those that focus on adult characteristics, those that emphasize an adult's life situation, and those that center on changes in consciousness. These three categories can be loosely equated with the adult, the context, and the learning process. Knowles's popular notion of andragogy is almost entirely focused on how the adult learner is different from a preadult learner. So too is Cross's model, although she does bring in contextual variables. McClusky, Knox, and Jarvis all attend to the adult's life situation and social context from which the need or interest in learning arises. Of the three, Jarvis devotes the most attention to the learning process in addition to the context. He has not yet explained, however, how it might be a uniquely *adult* model.

For the last two theorists reviewed, Mezirow and Freire, learning in adulthood is a transformative rather than an additive process. It requires the ability to reflect critically upon one's thoughts and assumptions — a particularly "adult" skill. Both theories also account for adult characteristics, in particular life experiences and developmental concerns unique to adulthood. And in both theories the sociocultural context is a critical component. It is in the sociocultural context that adults have experiences that must be processed. The two differ, however, in the notion of being emancipated through this learning process. For Freire, being emancipated from false consciousness requires political action aimed at changing society. Mezirow, while not outlawing social change as an outcome of perspective transformation, emphasizes personal psychological change (1989). While Mezirow's theory of perspective transformation comes closest to taking into account our notions of context, learner, and process, there are still some questions as to just how comprehensive his theory is. Is the process he outlines unique to adulthood? What about adults who do not reflect critically? Are they therefore not learning? His theory seems most appropriate for nonformal, self-directed learning situations. What about learning in adulthood that is additive, that takes place in formal, institutionally based settings? Perhaps a wedding of Jarvis's model, which does account for all types of learning, with aspects of Mezirow's theory would best reflect our understanding of learning in adulthood.

How well does practice account for the uniqueness of adult learning? This question is difficult to answer without looking at a specific learning situation. Furthermore, it is basically a question about the relationship between theory and practice. To what extent is the knowledge that we have accumulated about adult learning, knowledge reviewed in this book, reflective of what actually happens in practice? Moreover, to what extent is the knowledge that we do have derived from practice, and to what extent does it inform our practice? Cervero (1991) has delineated four positions relative to the interaction between knowledge and practice, each of which can be applied to adult learning. A review of these positions allows us to see how the knowledge presented in this book and practice are related.

The first position is that the practice of adult learning has been carried out without reference to what is known about how adults learn. This in fact characterizes much of adult learning, since only a small percentage of teachers, administrators, program developers, and others have had any formal training in adult education. From this position, those working with adult learners rely on common sense and intuition—less formal but certainly no less valuable sources of guidance for practice.

The second position is that a systematically collected knowledge base illuminates practice. It is thought that if this knowledge is disseminated through professional preparation, in-service staff development, and so on, practice will be enhanced. Lists of principles and guidelines, for example, such as those reviewed at the beginning of the chapter, are often disseminated through workshops and in-house publications, ostensibly to improve one's practice in adult learning. There are also numerous publications that attempt to show how knowledge about context, learner, and process could be put into practice. *Andragogy in Action* (Knowles, 1984), for example, presents thirty-six case studies of how characteristics of adult learners can be incorporated into the planning of learning activities in settings ranging from business and government to universities and volunteer organizations. In another publication, *Improving Higher Education Environments for Adults,* Schlossberg, Lynch, and Chickering (1989) show how adult life experiences and adult developmental theory can form the basis for programs and support services for learners in higher education. Finally, Mezirow's *Fostering Critical Reflection in Adulthood* reviews exemplary programs and suggests methods "for precipitating and fostering transformative learning in the context of the classroom, in special workshops, in informal group settings, in collective social action, in counseling sessions, and in the workplace" (1990, p. xv).

The third position on the relationship between knowledge and practice is that educators operate intuitively with an understanding of adult learning whether or not that knowledge is articulated. This theory-in-practice position holds that "practitioners actually do operate on the basis of theories and knowledge" and that "theory can be derived from practice by systematically articulating the subjective meaning structures that influence the ways that typical individuals act in concrete situations" (Cervero, 1991, chap. 2). This notion has been investigated with regard to professional practice (Schön, 1983, 1987) and is just beginning to be developed in adult education. With regard to the learning situation and other aspects of adult education, the central task of this approach is to "describe educational practice and help practitioners become more reflective about their own individual actions" (Cervero, 1991, chap. 2). The orientation of our book—in particular our attending to context and exploring social and ethical issues—models the critical stance toward practice inherent in this position.

The fourth position on theory and practice is that they are indivisible. Here the focus is on "what counts as knowledge and how, where, and by whom this knowledge is produced" (Cervero, 1991, chap. 2). Understanding the production of knowledge is emancipating. This perspective is best illustrated by Freire's and to some extent Mezirow's views on learning. More than the first three positions, this perspective—that theory and practice are indivisible—takes into account the sociocultural context in which learning occurs. Examples of adult education practice from this perspective are community-based literacy programs (Fingeret, 1984), popular education programs (Hamilton and Cunningham, 1989), and participatory research activities (Merriam, 1991). Participatory research "has faith in people's ability to produce their own knowledge through collective investigation of problems and issues, collective analysis of the problems, and collective action to change the conditions that gave rise to the problems in the first place" (Gaventa, 1988, p. 19). This method of producing knowledge "represents an effort to recover alternative knowledge systems that have been excluded from the 'official' body of knowledge in adult education" (Cervero, 1991, chap. 2).

For the most part, the material presented in this book is representative of "official" knowledge. More certainly could be done through collaborative research efforts with learners themselves to illuminate learning in adulthood.

Some Concluding Thoughts

In this final chapter, we have articulated our understanding of learning in adulthood and assessed how well context, learner, and process as a unique configuration in adulthood are reflected in theory and in practice. We conclude with some observations and suggestions. First of all, we think the field has developed a significant knowledge base about learning in adulthood, much of it of fairly recent origin. We are optimistic that learning in adulthood will continue to interest researchers and educators and that we will know quite a bit more within the decade. Second, the nature of contributions in this area is changing: Adult educators are moving from description to theory building; we are considering the sociocultural context in which learning takes place, thus shifting from a primarily psychological orientation to a broader psychosocial view; we are more cognizant of the social issues and ethical dilemmas involved in the provision and practice of adult learning; and we are examining notions about how knowledge about adult learning is produced and legitimized.

A potential result of this last development is that learners themselves will be a major source of our understanding of learning in adulthood. We would in fact suggest that future research in adult learning be collaboratively designed with adults who are learning on their own or in informal ways, as well as with participants in formal learning activities. We also suggest that research which takes into account the sociocultural and political context of adult learning might well advance our understanding of the problems of access and opportunity that continue to trouble the field. Finally, much of what we know about learning itself is derived from nonadults or select adult populations such as college students and the elderly. We suggest that there is still much to be learned about learning that takes place in adulthood.

References

Aagaard, L., and Langenbach, M. "A Factor Analytic Study of an Adult Classroom Environment Scale." Paper presented at the annual meeting of the Adult and Continuing Education Association, Miami, Florida, 1986.

Abeles, R. P., and Riley, M. W. "Longevity, Social Structure, and Cognitive Aging." In C. Schooler and K. Schaie (eds.), *Cognitive Functioning and Social Culture Over the Life Course.* Norwood, N.J.: Ablex, 1987.

Allerton, T. D. "Selected Characteristics of the Learning Projects Pursued by Parish Ministers in the Louisville Metropolitan Area." Doctoral dissertation, University of Georgia, 1974.

Allman, P. "The Nature and Process of Adult Development." In M. Tight (ed.), *Adult Learning and Education.* London: Croom Helm, 1983.

Alpaugh, K. P., Parham, I. A., Cole, K. D., and Birren, J. E. "Creativity in Adulthood and Old Age: An Exploratory Study." *Educational Gerontology,* 1982, *8,* 101–116.

Anderson, J. R. "Acquisition of Cognitive Skill." *Psychological Review,* 1982, *89,* 369–406.

Anderson, J. R. *The Architecture of Cognition.* Cambridge, Mass.: Harvard University Press, 1983.

Anderson, R. A., and Darkenwald, G. G. *Participation and Persistence in American Adult Education.* New York: College Entrance Examination Board, 1979.

Apps, J. W. *Toward a Working Philosophy of Adult Education.* Syracuse, N.Y.: Syracuse University Publications in Continuing Education, 1973.

Apps, J. W. *Problems in Continuing Education.* New York: McGraw-Hill, 1979.

Apps, J. W. *Improving Practice in Continuing Education: Modern Approaches for Understanding the Field and Determining Priorities.* San Francisco: Jossey-Bass, 1985.

Apps, J. W. "Adult Education and the Learning Society." *Educational Considerations,* 1987, *14* (2-3), 14-18.

Apps, J. W. *Higher Education in a Learning Society.* San Francisco: Jossey-Bass, 1988.

Apps, J. W. "Providers of Adult and Continuing Education: A Framework." In S. B. Merriam and P. M. Cunningham (eds.), *Handbook of Adult and Continuing Education.* San Francisco: Jossey-Bass, 1989.

Arlin, P. K. "Cognitive Development in Adulthood: A Fifth Stage?" *Developmental Psychology,* 1975, *11,* 602-606.

Arlin, P. K. "Adolescent and Adult Thought: A Structural Interpretation." In M. L. Commons, F. A. Richards, and C. Armon (eds.), *Beyond Formal Operations: Late Adolescent and Adult Cognitive Development.* New York: Praeger, 1984.

Arlin, P. K. "Wisdom: The Art of Problem Finding." In R. J. Sternberg (ed.), *Wisdom: Its Nature, Origins, and Development.* Cambridge: Cambridge University Press, 1990.

Aslanian, C. B., and Brickell, H. M. *Americans in Transition: Life Changes as Reasons for Adult Learning.* New York: College Entrance Examination Board, 1980.

Ausubel, D. P. "A Cognitive Structure Theory of School Learning." In L. Siegel (ed.), *Instruction: Some Contemporary Viewpoints.* San Francisco: Chandler, 1967.

Ausubel, D. P. *Educational Psychology: A Cognitive View.* New York: Holt, Rinehart & Winston, 1968.

Axinn, J. "Women and Aging: Issues of Adequacy and Equity." In J. D. Garner and S. O. Mercer (eds.), *Women as They Age: Challenge, Opportunity, and Triumph.* New York: Haworth Press, 1989.

Bagnall, R. C. "Researching Participation in Adult Education: A Case of Quantified Distortion." *International Journal of Lifelong Education,* 1989, *8* (3), 251-260.

Bagnall, R. C. "Education Beyond Macro-level Needs: A Critique of Boshier's Model for the Future." *International Journal of Lifelong Education,* 1990, *9* (4), 317–330.

Baltes, P. B. "Life-Span Development Psychology: Some Conveying Observations on History and Theory." In K. W. Schaie and J. Geiwitz (eds.), *Readings in Adult Development and Aging.* Boston: Little Brown, 1982.

Baltes, P. B., Dittmann-Kohli, F., and Dixon, R. "New Perspectives on the Development of Intelligence in Adulthood: Toward a Dual Process Conception and a Model of Selective Optimization with Compensation." In P. B. Baltes and O. G. Brim (eds.), *Life-Span Development and Behavior.* Vol. 6. Orlando, Fla.: Academic Press, 1984.

Baltes, P. B., Reese, H. W., and Nesselroade, J. R. *Life-Span Developmental Psychology: Introduction to Research Methods.* Monterey, Calif.: Brooks/Cole, 1977.

Baltes, P. B., and Smith, J. "Toward a Psychology of Wisdom and Its Ontogenesis." In R. J. Sternberg (ed.), *Wisdom: Its Nature, Origins, and Development.* Cambridge, Cambridge University Press, 1990.

Baltes, P. B., and Willis, S. L. "Plasticity and Enhancement of Intellectual Functioning: Penn State's Adult Development and Enrichment Project (ADEPT)." In M. Craig and S. Trehub (eds.), *Aging and Cognitive Processes.* New York: Plenum, 1982.

Bandura, A. "Modeling Theory." In W. S. Sahakian (ed.), *Learning: Systems, Models, and Theories.* (2nd ed.) Chicago: Rand McNally, 1976.

Bandura, A. *Social Learning Theory.* Englewood Cliffs, N.J.: Prentice-Hall, 1977.

Bandura, A. *Social Foundations of Thought and Action: A Social Cognitive Theory.* Englewood Cliffs, N.J.: Prentice-Hall, 1986.

Bard, R. "Foreword." In M. S. Knowles and Associates (eds.), *Andragogy in Action.* San Francisco: Jossey-Bass, 1984.

Baruch, G. K., Barnett, R. C., and Rivers, C. *Lifeprints.* New York: McGraw-Hill, 1983.

Basseches, M. *Dialectical Thinking and Adult Development.* Norwood, N.J.: Ablex, 1984.

Baum, J. "Testing the Theory of Margin Using a Population

of Widows." *Proceedings of the Adult Education Research Conference,* no. 21. Vancouver: University of British Columbia, 1980.

Bayha, R. A. "Self-Directed Learning of Northwest Missouri Farmers as Related to Learning Resource Choice and Valuing." Doctoral dissertation, Kansas State University, 1983.

Beder, H. "Dominant Paradigms, Adult Education, and Social Justice." *Adult Education Quarterly,* 1987, *37* (2), 105–113.

Beder, H. "The Purposes and Philosophies of Adult Education." In S. B. Merriam and P. M. Cunningham (eds.), *Handbook of Adult and Continuing Education.* San Francisco: Jossey-Bass, 1989.

Beder, H. "Reasons for Nonparticipation in Adult Basic Education." *Adult Education Quarterly,* 1990, *40* (4), 207–218.

Beder, H., and Carrea, N. "The Effects of Andragogical Teacher Training on Adult Students' Attendance and Evaluation of Their Teachers." *Adult Education Quarterly,* 1988, *38* (2), 75–87.

Beder, H., and Darkenwald, G. "Differences Between Teaching Adults and Pre-Adults: Some Propositions and Findings." *Adult Education,* 1982, *32* (3), 142–155.

Beder, H., Darkenwald, G., and Valentine, T. "Self-Planned Professional Learning Among Public School Adult Education Directors: A Social Network Analysis." *Proceedings of the Adult Education Research Conference,* no. 24. Montreal: Université de Montréal, 1983.

Beder, H., and Valentine, T. "Motivational Profiles of Adult Basic Education Students." *Adult Education Quarterly,* 1990, *40* (2), 78–94.

Bee, H. L. *The Journey of Adulthood.* New York: Macmillan, 1987.

Beer, C. T., and Darkenwald, G. G. "Gender Differences in Adult Student Perceptions of College Classroom Social Environments." *Adult Education Quarterly,* 1989, *40* (1), 33–42.

Bejot, D. D. "The Degree of Self-Directedness and the Choices of Learning Methods as Related to a Cooperative Extension Program." Doctoral dissertation, Iowa State University, 1981.

Belenky, M. F., Clinchy, B. M., Goldberger, N. R., and Tarule, J. *Women's Ways of Knowing: The Development of Self, Voice, and Mind.* New York: Basic Books, 1986.

Benack, S., and Basseches, M. A. "Dialectical Thinking and Relativistic Epistemology: Their Relation in Adult Development." In M. L. Commons, J. D. Sinnott, F. A. Richards, and C. Armon (eds.), *Adult Development.* New York: Praeger, 1989.

Berger, N. "A Qualitative Study of the Process of Self-Directed Learning." Doctoral dissertation, Division of Educational Studies, Virginia Commonwealth University, 1990.

Birren, J. E., and Fisher, L. M. "The Elements of Wisdom: Overview and Integration." In R. J. Sternberg (ed.), *Wisdom: Its Nature, Origins, and Development.* Cambridge: Cambridge University Press, 1990.

Bischof, L. J. *Adult Psychology.* New York: Harper & Row, 1969.

Bode, H. B. *Conflicting Psychologies of Learning.* New York: Heath, 1929.

Bonham, L. A. "Theoretical and Practical Differences and Similarities Among Selected Cognitive and Learning Styles of Adults: An Analysis of the Literature, Vol. I and II." Doctoral dissertation, Department of Adult Education, University of Georgia, 1987.

Bonham, L. A. "Learning Style Use: In Need of Perspective." *Lifelong Learning,* 1988, *11* (5), 14–17.

Bonham, L. A. "Self-Directed Orientation Toward Learning: A Learning Style." In H. B. Long and Associates (eds.), *Self-Directed Learning: Emerging Theory and Practice.* Norman: Oklahoma Research Center for Continuing Professional and Higher Education, University of Oklahoma, 1989.

Boone, E. J., Shearon, R. W., White, E. E., and Associates. *Serving Personal and Community Needs Through Adult Education.* San Francisco: Jossey-Bass, 1980.

Boshier, R. "Motivational Orientations of Adult Education Participants: A Factor Analytic Exploration of Houle's Typology." *Adult Education,* 1971, *21* (2), 3–26.

Boshier, R. "Educational Participation and Dropout: A Theoretical Model." *Adult Education,* 1973, *23,* 255–282.

Boshier, R. "Motivational Orientation Re-visited: Life-Space Motives and the Education Participation Scale." *Adult Education,* 1977, *27* (2), 89–115.

Boshier, R. "Adult Learning Projects Research: An Alchemist's Fantasy." Invited address to American Educational Research Association, Montreal, April 1983.

Boshier, R. "Proaction for a Change: Some Guidelines for the Future." *International Journal of Lifelong Education*, 1986, *5* (1), 15–31.

Boshier, R., and Collins, J. B. "The Houle Typology After Twenty-Two Years: A Large-Scale Empirical Test." *Adult Education Quarterly*, 1985, *35* (3), 113–130.

Botwinick, J. "Intellectual Abilities." In J. E. Birren and K. W. Schaie (eds.), *Handbook of the Psychology of Aging*. New York: Van Nostrand Reinhold, 1977.

Boucouvalas, M. "Learning Throughout Life: The Information-Knowledge-Wisdom Framework." *Educational Considerations, Comparisons and Applications of Developmental Models*, 1987, *14* (2–3), 32–38.

Boucouvalas, M. "An Analysis and Critique of the Concept of Self in Self-Directed Learning: Toward a More Robust Construct for Research and Practice." *Proceedings of SCRUTREA* (Leeds, England), 1988a, 55–61.

Boucouvalas, M. "Research and Development in the Neurosciences: Relevance for Adult Education." *Proceedings of the Adult Education Research Conference*, no. 29. Calgary: University of Calgary, 1988b.

Boyd, E. M., and Fales, A. W. "Reflective Learning: Key to Learning from Experience." *Journal of Humanistic Psychology*, 1983, *23* (2), 99–117.

Boyd, R. D., and Myers, J. G. "Transformative Education." *International Journal of Lifelong Education*, 1988, *7* (4), 261–284.

Brandenburg, D. C. "Training Evaluation: What's the Current Status?" *Training and Development Journal*, 1982, *36* (5), 14–19.

Bray, D. W., and Howard, A. "The AT&T Longitudinal Studies of Managers." In K. W. Schaie (ed.), *Longitudinal Studies of Adult Development*. New York: Guilford, 1983.

Bridges, W. *Transitions*. Reading, Mass.: Addison-Wesley, 1980.

Brim, O. G. "Adult Socialization and Society." In J. Clausen (ed.), *Socialization and Society*. Boston: Little, Brown, 1968.

Brim, O. G., and Ryff, C. D. "On the Properties of Life Events."

In R. Baltes and O. Brim (eds.), *Life-Span Development and Behavior.* Vol. 3. New York: Academic Press, 1980.

Briscoe, D. B., and Ross, J. M. "Racial and Ethnic Minorities and Adult Education." In S. B. Merriam and P. M. Cunningham (eds.), *Handbook of Adult and Continuing Education.* San Francisco: Jossey-Bass, 1989.

Brockett, R. G. "Methodological and Substantive Issues in the Measurement of Self-Directed Learning Readiness." *Adult Education Quarterly,* 1985a, *36* (1), 15-24.

Brockett, R. G. "The Relationship Between Self-Directed Learning Readiness and Life Satisfaction Among Older Adults." *Adult Education Quarterly,* 1985b, *35* (4), 210-219.

Brockett, R. G. "A Response to Brookfield's Critical Paradigm of Self-Directed Adult Learning." *Adult Education Quarterly,* 1985c, *36* (1), 55-59.

Brockett, R. G. (ed.). *Ethical Issues in Adult Education.* New York: Teachers College Press, 1988a.

Brockett, R. G. "Ethics and the Adult Educator." In R. G. Brockett (ed.), *Ethical Issues in Adult Education.* New York: Teachers College Press, 1988b.

Brockett, R. G., and Hiemstra, R. "Bridging the Theory-Practice Gap in Self-Directed Learning." In S. Brookfield (ed.), *Self-Directed Learning: From Theory to Practice.* New Directions for Continuing Education, no. 25. San Francisco: Jossey-Bass, 1985.

Brockett, R. G., and Hiemstra, R. *Self-Direction in Adult Learning: Perspectives on Theory, Research, and Practice.* London and New York: Routledge & Kegan Paul, 1991.

Bronfenbrenner, U. *The Ecology of Human Development.* Cambridge, Mass.: Harvard University Press, 1979.

Brookfield, S. "Independent Adult Learning." *Studies in Adult Education,* 1981, *13* (1), 15-27.

Brookfield, S. "Self-Directed Adult Learning: A Critical Paradigm." *Adult Education Quarterly,* 1984, *35* (2), 59-71.

Brookfield, S. "Analyzing a Critical Paradigm of Self-Directed Learning: A Response." *Adult Education Quarterly,* 1985, *36* (1), 60-64.

Brookfield, S. *Understanding and Facilitating Adult Learning.* San Francisco: Jossey-Bass, 1986.

Brookfield, S. *Developing Critical Thinkers.* San Francisco: Jossey-Bass, 1987.

Brookfield, S. "Conceptual, Methodological and Practical Ambiguities in Self-Directed Learning." In H. B. Long and Associates (eds.), *Self-Directed Learning: Application and Theory.* Athens: Adult Education Department of the University of Georgia, 1988a.

Brookfield, S. "Ethical Dilemmas in Evaluating Adult Education Programs." In R. G. Brockett (ed.), *Ethical Issues in Adult Education.* New York: Teachers College Press, 1988b.

Brundage, D. H., and Mackeracher, D. *Adult Learning Principles and Their Application to Program Planning.* Toronto: Ministry of Education, Ontario, 1980.

Bruner, J. "In Defense of Verbal Learning." In R. C. Anderson and D. P. Ausubel (eds.), *Readings in the Psychology of Cognition.* New York: Holt, Rinehart & Winston, 1965.

Bryant, J. "Normal Adult Development: But What About the Rest of Us?" Unpublished paper, Virginia Commonwealth University, 1989.

Bühler, C. "The Developmental Structure of Goal Setting in Group and Individual Studies." In C. Bühler and F. Massarik (eds.), *The Course of Human Life.* New York: Springer, 1968.

Burgess, P. "Reasons for Adult Participation in Group Educational Activities." *Adult Education,* 1971, *22,* 3–29.

Caffarella, R. S. "Ethical Dilemmas in the Teaching of Adults." In R. G. Brockett (ed.), *Ethical Issues in Adult Education.* New York: Teachers College Press, 1988a.

Caffarella, R. S. *Program Development and Evaluation Resource Book for Trainers.* New York: Wiley, 1988b.

Caffarella, R. S., and Caffarella, E. P. "Self-Directedness and Learning Contracts in Adult Education." *Adult Education Quarterly,* 1986, *36,* 226–234.

Caffarella, R. S., Loehr, L., and Hosick, J. "Cognition in Adulthood: Current Research Trends." *Proceedings of the Adult Education Research Conference,* no. 30. Madison: University of Wisconsin–Madison, 1989.

Caffarella, R. S., and O'Donnell, J. M. "The Culture of Adult

Education Institutions." *Life-Long Learning: An Omnibus of Practice and Research,* 1987a, *11,* 4–6.

Caffarella, R. S., and O'Donnell, J. M. "Self-Directed Adult Learning: A Critical Paradigm Revisited." *Adult Education Quarterly,* 1987b, *37,* 199–211.

Caffarella, R. S., and O'Donnell, J. M. "Research in Self-Directed Learning: Past, Present, and Future Trends." In H. B. Long and Associates (eds.), *Self-Directed Learning: Application and Theory.* Athens: Adult Education Department, University of Georgia, 1988a.

Caffarella, R. S., and O'Donnell, J. M. "Self-Directed Learning: The Quality Dimension." *Proceedings of the Adult Education Research Conference,* no. 29. Calgary: University of Calgary, 1988b.

Caffarella, R. S., and O'Donnell, J. M. *Self-Directed Learning.* Nottingham, England: Department of Adult Education, University of Nottingham, 1989.

Caffarella, R. S., and O'Donnell, J. M. "Judging the Quality of Work Related, Self-Directed Learning." *Adult Education Quarterly,* in press.

Caffarella, R. S., and Olson, S. K. "The Psychosocial Development of Women: A Critical Review of the Literature." *Proceedings of the Adult Education Research Conference,* no. 27. Syracuse, N.Y.: Syracuse University, 1986.

Cameron, S. W. "The Perry Scheme: A New Perspective on Adult Learners." *Proceedings of the Adult Education Research Conference,* no. 24. Montreal: Université de Montreal, 1983.

Candy, P. C. "Evolution, Revolution or Devolution: Increasing Learner Control in the Instructional Setting." In D. Boud and V. Griffin (eds.), *Appreciating Adults Learning: From the Learner's Perspective.* London: Kogan Page, 1987a.

Candy, P. C. "Reframing Research into 'Self-Direction' in Adult Education: A Constructivist Perspective." Doctoral dissertation, Department of Adult and Higher Education, University of British Columbia, 1987b.

Candy, P. C. "Constructivism and the Study of Self-Direction in Adult Learning." *Studies in the Education of Adults,* 1989a, *21* (2), 95–116.

Candy, P. C. "The Transition from Learner-Control to Auto-didaxy: More Than Meets the Eye." Paper presented at the 3rd North American Symposium on Adult Self-Directed Learning, University of Oklahoma Center for Continuing Education, Norman, February 1989b.

Carnevale, A. P. "The Learning Enterprise." *Training and Development Journal,* 1989, *43* (2), 26–33.

Carnevale, A. P., and Gainer, L. J. *The Learning Enterprise.* Alexandria, Va.: American Society for Training and Development; Washington, D.C.: U.S. Department of Labor Employment and Training Administration, 1989.

Carp, A., Peterson, R., and Roelfs, P. "Adult Learning Interests and Experiences." In K. P. Cross, J. R. Valley, and Associates (eds.), *Planning Nontraditional Programs: An Analysis of the Issues for Postsecondary Education.* San Francisco: Jossey-Bass, 1974.

Cattell, R. B. "Theory of Fluid and Crystallized Intelligence: A Critical Approach." *Journal of Educational Psychology, 1963, 54* (1), 1–22.

Cattell, R. B. *Intelligence: Its Structure, Growth and Action.* Amsterdam: North-Holland, 1987.

Center for Education Statistics. *Digest of Education Statistics — 1987.* Washington, D.C.: Office of Educational Research and Improvement, U.S. Department of Education, 1987.

Cervero, R. M. "Professionalization as an Issue for Continuing Education." In R. G. Brockett (ed.), *Continuing Education in the Year 2000.* New Directions for Continuing Education, no. 36. San Francisco: Jossey-Bass, 1987.

Cervero, R. M. *Effective Continuing Education for Professionals.* San Francisco: Jossey-Bass, 1988.

Cervero, R. M. "A Framework for Effective Practice in Adult Education." *Proceedings of the Adult Education Research Conference,* no. 30. Madison: University of Wisconsin, 1989.

Cervero, R. M. "Relationships Between Theory and Practice." In J. Peters and P. Jarvis (eds.), *Adult Education as a Field of Study: Its Evolution, Achievements, and Future* (tentative title). San Francisco: Jossey-Bass, 1991.

Cervero, R. M., and Kirkpatrick, T. E. "Determinants of Participation in Adult Education." Paper presented at the 1989 annual conference of the American Educational Research Association, San Francisco, March 29, 1989.

Cervero, R. M., and Kirkpatrick, T. E. "The Enduring Effects of Pre-Adult Factors on Participation in Adult Education." *American Journal of Education*, 1990, *99*, 77–94.

Cetron, M. J., Soriano, B., and Gayle, B. *Schools of the Future: How American Business and Education Can Cooperate to Save Our Schools*. New York: McGraw-Hill, 1985.

Chapman, M. "Contextuality and Directionality of Cognitive Development." *Human Development*, 1988, *31*, 92–106.

Charner, I., and Rolzinski, C. A. "New Directions for Responding to a Changing Economy: Integrating Education and Work." In I. Charner and C. A. Rolzinski (eds.), *Responding to the Educational Needs of Today's Workplace*. New Directions for Continuing Education, no. 33. San Francisco: Jossey-Bass, 1987.

Chene, A. "The Concept of Autonomy: A Philosophical Discussion." *Adult Education Quarterly*, 1983, *34*, 38–47.

Chi, M.T.H., Glaser, R., and Farr, M. J. (eds.). *The Nature of Expertise*. Hillsdale, N.J.: Erlbaum, 1988.

Chickering, A. W., and Associates. *The Modern American College*. San Francisco: Jossey-Bass, 1981.

Chimene, D. "Beyond 1984: Future Participants in Adult Education." *Proceedings of the Adult Education Research Conference*, no. 24. Montreal: Concordia University/University of Montreal, 1983.

Clark, M. C. "Structuring and Restructuring of Meaning: An Analysis of the Impact of Context on Transformational Learning." Dissertation prospectus, Department of Adult Education, University of Georgia, 1990.

Clark, M. C., and Wilson, A. L. "Through the Paradigm: An Analysis of Mezirow's Theory of Adult Learning." *Adult Education Quarterly*, 1991, *41* (2), 75–91.

Claxton, C. S., and Murrell, P. H. *Learning Styles: Implications for Improving Educational Practices*. ASHE-ERIC Higher Education Reports, no. 4. Washington, D.C.: Association for the Study of Higher Education, 1987.

Clayton, V. "A Multi-dimensional Scaling Analysis of the Concept of Wisdom." Doctoral dissertation, University of Southern California, 1976.

Clayton, V. "Wisdom and Intelligence: The Nature and Function of Knowledge in the Later Years." *International Journal of Aging and Human Development,* 1982, *15,* 315–323.

Clayton, V., and Birren, J. E. "The Development of Wisdom Across the Life Span: A Reexamination of an Ancient Topic." In R. Baltes and O. Brim (eds.), *Life-Span Development and Behavior.* Vol. 3. New York: Academic Press, 1980.

Cochrane, M. J. "The Meanings That Some Adults Derive from Their Personal Withdrawal Experiences: A Dialogical Inquiry." *Dissertation Abstracts International,* 1981, *42,* 10A.

Coles, R., and Coles, J. H. *Women of Crises.* New York: Dell, 1978.

Coles, R., and Coles, J. H. *Women of Crises II.* New York: Dell, 1980.

Collard, S., and Law, M. "The Limits of Perspective Transformation: A Critique of Mezirow's Theory." *Adult Education Quarterly,* 1989, *39* (2), 99–107.

Collins, M. "Self-Directed Learning or an Emancipatory Practice of Adult Education: Re-thinking the Role of the Adult Educator." *Proceedings of the Adult Education Research Conference,* no. 29. Calgary: University of Calgary, 1988.

Commons, M. L., Richards, F. A., and Armon, C. (eds.). *Beyond Formal Operations: Late Adolescent and Adult Cognitive Development.* New York: Praeger, 1984.

Cookson, P. S. "A Framework for Theory and Research on Adult Education Participation." *Adult Education Quarterly,* 1986, *36* (3), 130–141.

Cookson, P. S. "The Interdisciplinary, Sequential Specificity, Time Allocation, Lifespan Model of Social Participation: A Report of Two Applications in Adult Education." *Proceedings of the 1987 Lifelong Learning Research Conference.* College Park: University of Maryland, 1987a.

Cookson, P. S. "The Nature of the Knowledge Base of Adult Education: The Example of Adult Education Participation." *Educational Considerations,* 1987b, *14* (2–3), 24–28.

Coolican, P. M. "The Learning Styles of Mothers of Young Children." Doctoral dissertation, Syracuse University, 1973.

Coolican, P. M. *Self-Planned Learning: Implications for the Future of Adult Education.* Technical Report 74-507. Syracuse: Syracuse University, 1974. (ED 095 254)

Coombs, P. H., Prosser, R. C., and Ahmed, M. *New Paths to Learning for Rural Children and Youth.* New York: International Council for Educational Development, 1973.

Courtney, S. "Visible Learning: Adult Education and the Question of Participation." Doctoral dissertation, Department of Adult Education, Northern Illinois University, 1984.

Courtney, S. "Visible Learning: Adult Education and the Question of Participation." *Proceedings of the Adult Education Research Conference,* no. 26. Tempe: Arizona State University, 1985.

Courtney, S. *Why Adults Learn: Toward a Theory of Participation in Adult Education.* New York: Routledge, Chapman & Hall, 1991.

Craig, R. L. (ed.). *The Training and Development Handbook.* (3rd ed.) New York: McGraw-Hill, 1987.

Craik, F.I.M. "Age Differences in Human Memory." In J. E. Birren and K. W. Schaie (eds.), *Handbook of Psychology and Aging.* New York: Van Nostrand Reinhold, 1977.

Craik, F.I.M., and Rabinowitz, J. C. "Age Differences in the Acquisition and Use of Verbal Information." In H. Bouma and D. G. Bouwhuis (eds.), *Attention and Performance and Control of Language Processes.* Hillsdale, N.J.: Erlbaum, 1984.

Cross, K. P. "Adult Learners: Characteristics, Needs, and Interests." In R. E. Peterson and Associates (eds.), *Lifelong Learning in America: An Overview of Current Practices, Available Resources, and Future Prospects.* San Francisco: Jossey-Bass, 1979.

Cross, K. P. *Adults as Learners: Increasing Participation and Facilitating Learning.* San Francisco: Jossey-Bass, 1981.

Cross, K. P., and McCartan, A. *Adult Learning: State Policies and Institutional Practices.* ASHE-ERIC Higher Education Research Reports, no. 1. Washington, D.C.: Association for the Study of Higher Education, 1984.

Cross, K. P., Valley, J. R., and Associates. *Planning Nontradi-*

tional Programs: An Analysis of the Issues for Postsecondary Education. San Francisco: Jossey-Bass, 1974.

Culter, R. G. "Life-Span Extension." In J. L. McGaugh and S. B. Klesler (eds.), *Aging, Biology and Behavior.* New York: Academic Press, 1981.

Cunningham, P. M. "The Adult Educator and Social Responsibility." In R. G. Brockett (ed.), *Ethical Issues in Adult Education.* New York: Teachers College Press, 1988.

Daloz, L. A. *Effective Teaching and Mentoring: Realizing the Transformational Power of Adult Learning Experiences.* San Francisco: Jossey-Bass, 1986.

Daloz, L. A. "Beyond Tribalism: Renaming the Good, the True, and the Beautiful." *Adult Education Quarterly,* 1988a, *38* (4), 234–241.

Daloz, L. A. "The Story of Gladys Who Refused to Grow: A Morality Tale for Mentors." *Lifelong Learning: An Omnibus of Practice and Research,* 1988b, *11* (4), 4–7.

Danis, C., and Tremblay, N. A. "Propositions Regarding Autodidactic Learning and Their Implications for Teaching." *Lifelong Learning: An Omnibus of Practice and Research,* 1987, *10* (7), 4–7.

Danis, C., and Tremblay, N. A. "Autodidactic Learning Experiences: Questioning Established Adult Learning Principles." In H. B. Long and Associates (eds.), *Self-Directed Learning: Application and Theory.* Athens: Adult Education Department, University of Georgia, 1988.

Dannefer, D. "Adult Development and Social Theory: A Paradigmatic Reappraisal." *American Sociological Review,* 1984, *49,* 100–116.

Dannefer, D., and Perlmutter, M. "Development as a Multidimensional Process: Individual and Social Constituents." *Human Development,* 1990, *33,* 108–137.

Darkenwald, G. G. "Assessing the Social Environment of Adult Classes." *Studies in the Education of Adults,* 1987, *19* (2), 127–136.

Darkenwald, G. G. "Comparison of Deterrents to Adult Education Participation in Britain and the United States." *Papers from the Transatlantic Dialogue* (University of Leeds), 1988, 126–130.

Darkenwald, G. G. "Enhancing the Adult Classroom Environment." In E. Hayes (ed.), *Effective Teaching Styles*. New Directions for Continuing Education, no. 43. San Francisco: Jossey-Bass, 1989.

Darkenwald, G. G., and Gavin, W. J. "Dropout as a Function of Discrepancies Between Expectations and Actual Experiences of the Classroom Social Environment." *Adult Education Quarterly*, 1987, *37*, 152–163.

Darkenwald, G. G., and Merriam, S. B. *Adult Education: Foundations of Practice*. New York: Harper & Row, 1982.

Darkenwald, G. G., and Valentine, T. "Factor Structure of Deterrents to Public Participation in Adult Education." *Adult Education Quarterly*, 1985, *35* (4), 177–193.

Darkenwald, G. G., and Valentine, T. "Measuring the Social Environment of Adult Education Classrooms." *Proceedings of the Adult Education Research Conference*, no. 27. Syracuse, N.Y.: Syracuse University, 1986.

Datan, N., Rodeheaver, D., and Hughes, F. "Adult Development and Aging." *Annual Review of Psychology*, 1987, *38*, 153–180.

Davenport, J., and Davenport, J. "A Chronology and Analysis of the Andragogy Debate." *Adult Education Quarterly*, 1985, *35* (3), 152–159.

Day, M. "Educational Advising and Brokering: The Ethics of Choice." In R. G. Brockett (ed.), *Ethical Issues in Adult Education*. New York: Teachers College Press, 1988.

Deal, T. E., and Kennedy, A. A. *Corporate Cultures*. Reading, Mass.: Addison-Wesley, 1982.

Denney, N. W. "Aging and Cognitive Changes." In B. B. Wolman (ed.), *Handbook of Developmental Psychology*. Englewood Cliffs, N.J.: Prentice-Hall, 1982.

Derber, C. "Worker Education for a Changing Economy: New Labor-Academic Partnerships." In I. Charner and C. A. Rolzinski (eds.), *Responding to the Educational Needs of Today's Workplace*. New Directions for Continuing Education, no. 33. San Francisco: Jossey-Bass, 1987.

Deroos, K.K.B. "Persistence of Adults in Independent Study." Doctoral dissertation, University of Minnesota, 1982.

Deshler, D. "Metaphor Analysis: Exorcising Social Ghosts." In J. Mezirow and Associates (eds.), *Fostering Critical Reflection in Adulthood.* San Francisco: Jossey-Bass, 1990.

Dimmock, K. H. "Models of Adult Participation in Informal Science Education." *Proceedings of the Adult Education Research Conference,* no. 27. Syracuse: Syracuse University, 1986.

Di Vesta, F. J. "The Cognitive Movement and Education." In J. Glover and R. Ronning (eds.), *Historical Foundations of Education.* New York: Plenum, 1987.

Dychtwald, K., and Flower, J. "The Third Age." *New Age Journal,* 1989, *6* (1), 50–59.

Ekpenyong, L. E. "Studying Adult Learning Through the History of Knowledge." *International Journal of Lifelong Education,* 1990, *9* (3), 161–178.

Ellsworth, E. "Why Doesn't This Feel Empowering? Working Through the Repressive Myths of Critical Pedagogy." *Harvard Educational Review,* 1989, *59* (3), 297–324.

"Employee Training in America." *Training and Development Journal,* 1986, *40* (7), 34–37.

Ennis, C. D., and others. "Educational Climate in Elective Adult Education: Shared Decision Making and Communication Patterns." *Adult Education Quarterly,* 1989, *39,* 76–88.

Erikson, E. H. *Childhood and Society.* (2nd ed., rev.) New York: Norton, 1963.

Erikson, E. H. *Adulthood.* New York: Norton, 1978.

Erikson, E. H. *The Life Cycle Completed: A Review.* New York: Norton, 1982.

Erikson, E. H., Erikson, J. M., and Kivnick, H. O. *Vital Involvement in Old Age.* New York: Norton, 1986.

Ernest, R. C. "Corporate Cultures and Effective Planning." *Personnel Administrator,* 1985, *30,* 49–60.

Eurich, N. *Corporate Classrooms: The Learning Business.* Princeton, N.J.: Carnegie Foundation for the Advancement of Teaching, 1985.

Ewert, D. M. "Involving Adult Learners in Program Planning." In S. B. Merriam (ed.), *Linking Philosophy and Practice.* New Directions for Continuing Education, no. 15. San Francisco: Jossey-Bass, 1982.

Farley, F. "Biology and Adult Cognition." In R. A. Fellenz (ed.),

Cognition and the Adult Learner. Bozeman: Center for Adult Learning Research, Montana State University, 1988.

Fay, C. H., McCune, J. T., and Begin, J. P. "The Setting for Continuing Education in the Year 2000." In R. G. Brockett (ed.), *Continuing Education in the Year 2000.* New Directions for Continuing Education, no. 36. San Francisco: Jossey-Bass, 1987.

Featherman, D. L., and Lerner, R. M. "Ontogenesis and Sociogenesis: Problematics for Theory and Research About Development and Socialization Across the Lifespan." *American Sociological Review,* 1985, *50,* 659–676.

Field, D., Schaie, K. W., and Leino, V. E. "Continuity in Intellectual Functioning: The Role of Self-Reported Health." *Psychology and Aging,* 1988, *3* (4), 385–392.

Field, L. "An Investigation into the Structure, Validity, and Reliability of Guglielmino's Self-Directed Learning Readiness Scale." *Adult Education Quarterly,* 1989, *39* (4), 235–245.

Field, L. "Guglielmino's Self-Directed Learning Readiness Scale: Should It Continue to Be Used?" *Adult Education Quarterly,* 1991, *41* (2), 100–103.

Finger, M. "Hermeneutics, Critical Theory and the Biographical Method as an Alternative in Adult Education Research." *Proceedings of SCRUTREA* (Leeds, England), 1988, *1,* 166–171.

Fingeret, A. "Social Network: A New Perspective on Independence and Illiterate Adults." *Adult Education Quarterly,* 1983, *33* (3), 133–146.

Fingeret, A. *Adult Literacy Education: Current and Future Directions.* Information Series no. 284. Columbus, Ohio: ERIC Clearinghouse on Adult, Career, and Vocational Education, 1984.

Finkel, C. "Where Learning Happens." *Training and Development Journal,* 1984, *38* (4), 32–36.

Finkel, C. "Pick a Place, But Not Any Place." *Training and Development Journal,* 1986, *40* (2), 51–53.

Flavell, J. H. "Cognitive Changes in Adulthood." In L. R. Goulet and P. B. Baltes (eds.), *Life-span Developmental Psychology: Research and Theory.* New York: Academic Press, 1970.

Flavell, J. H. *Cognitive Development.* Englewood Cliffs, N.J.: Prentice-Hall, 1985.

Fowler, J. *Stages of Faith: The Psychology of Human Development and the Quest for Meaning.* New York: Harper & Row, 1981.

Fox, R. D., and West, R. F. "Personality Traits and Perceived Benefits Associated with Different Approaches of Medical Students to Self-Directed Learning Projects." *Proceedings of the Adult Education Research Conference,* no. 24. Montreal: Université de Montréal, 1983.

Frenkel-Brunswick, E. "Adjustments and Reorientation in the Course of the Life Span." In R. G. Kuklen and G. T. Thompson (eds.), *Psychological Studies of Human Development.* East Norwalk, Conn.: Appleton-Century-Crofts, 1963.

Freire, P. *Cultural Action for Freedom. Harvard Educational Review,* Monograph Series No. 1. Cambridge, Mass.: Center for the Study of Development and Social Change, 1970a.

Freire, P. *Pedagogy of the Oppressed.* New York: Seabury Press, 1970b.

Gagne, R. M. *Instructional Technology: Foundations.* Hillsdale, N.J.: Erlbaum, 1987.

Gagne, R. M., and Briggs, L. J. *Principles of Instructional Design.* (2nd ed.) New York: Holt, Rinehart & Winston, 1979.

Gardner, H. *Frames of Mind.* New York: Basic Books, 1983.

Gardner, H. "Art and Intelligence: A Personal Perspective." Keynote address presented at The Human Spirit: The Arts in Education, Greeley, Colo., Sept., 1990.

Gardner, H., and Hatch, T. "Multiple Intelligences Go to School." *Educational Researcher,* 1989, *18* (8), 4–10.

Garrison, D. R. "Predicting Dropout in Adult Basic Education Using Interaction Effects Among School and Nonschool Variables." *Adult Education Quarterly,* 1985, *36,* 25–38.

Garrison, D. R. "Dropout Prediction Within a Broad Psychosocial Context: An Analysis of Boshier's Congruence Model." *Adult Education Quarterly,* 1987a, *37* (4), 212–222.

Garrison, D. R. "Self-Directed and Distance Learning: Facilitating Self-Directed Learning Beyond the Institutional Setting." *International Journal of Lifelong Education,* 1987b, *6* (4), 309–318.

Garrison, D. R. "Facilitating Self-Directed Learning: Not a Contradiction in Terms." In H. B. Long and Associates (eds.), *Self-Directed Learning: Emerging Theory and Practice.* Norman:

Oklahoma Research Center for Continuing Professional and Higher Education, University of Oklahoma, 1989.

Gaventa, J. "Participatory Research in North America." *Convergence,* 1988, *21* (2-3), 19-28.

Geisler, K. K. "Learning Efforts of Adults Undertaken for Matriculating into a Community College." Doctoral dissertation, Texas A&M University, 1984.

Gerstner, L. "On the Theme and Variations of Self-Directed Learning: An Exploration of the Literature." Doctoral dissertation, Teachers College, Columbia University, 1987.

Gibbons, M., and Phillips, G. "Self-Education: The Process of Life-Long Learning." *Canadian Journal of Education,* 1982, *7* (4), 67-86.

Gibbons, M., and others. "Toward a Theory of Self-Directed Learning: A Study of Experts Without Formal Training." *Journal of Humanistic Psychology,* 1980, *20* (2), 41-56.

Gilligan, C. *In a Different Voice: Psychological Theory and Women's Development.* Cambridge, Mass.: Harvard University Press, 1982.

Giroux, H. A. *Theory and Resistance in Education.* South Hadley, Mass.: Bergin & Garvey, 1983.

Giroux, H. A. "Literacy and the Pedagogy of Voice and Political Empowerment." *Educational Theory,* 1988, *38,* 61-75.

Glaser, R. "Education and Thinking: The Role of Knowledge." *American Psychologist,* 1984, *39* (2), 93-104.

Glaser, R. "All's Well That Begins and Ends with Both Knowledge and Process: A Reply to Sternberg." *American Psychologist,* 1985, *40,* 573-574.

Glaser, R. "Thoughts on Expertise." In C. Schooler and K. Schaie (eds.), *Cognitive Functioning and Social Structure Over the Life Course.* Norwood, N.J.: Ablex, 1987.

Glaser, R., and Chi, M.T.H. "Overview." In M.T.H. Chi, R. Glaser, and M. J. Farr (eds.), *The Nature of Expertise.* Hillsdale, N.J.: Erlbaum, 1988.

Glenn, L. L. "Learning Plan to Get Test Here: City to Become Education Base." *Battle Creek Enquirer,* Jan. 17, 1989, *3A,* 1.

Goldin, C., and Thomas J. "Adult Education in Correctional Settings: Symbol or Substance." *Adult Education Quarterly,* 1984, *34,* 123-134.

Goodnow, J. J. "Using Sociology to Extend Psychological Accounts of Cognitive Development." *Human Development,* 1990, *33,* 81–107.

Gordon, J. "Where's the Line Between Training and Intrusion?" *Training,* 1989, *26* (3), 27–39.

Gorham, J. "Differences Between Teaching Adults and Pre-Adults: A Closer Look." *Adult Education Quarterly,* 1985, *35* (4), 194–209.

Gould, R. *Transformations: Growth and Change in Adult Life.* New York: Simon & Schuster, 1978.

Greeno, J. G. "Psychology of Learning, 1960–1980." *American Psychologist,* 1980, *35* (8), 713–728.

Griffin, C. *Adult Education as Social Policy.* London: Croom Helm, 1987.

Griffith, W. S., and Fujita-Starck, P. J. "Public Policy and Financing of Adult and Continuing Education." In S. B. Merriam and P. M. Cunningham (eds.), *Handbook of Adult and Continuing Education.* San Francisco: Jossey-Bass, 1989.

Grippin, P., and Peters, S. *Learning Theory and Learning Outcomes.* New York: University Press of America, 1984.

Gross, R. *The Lifelong Learner.* New York: Simon & Schuster, 1977.

Grow, G. "Teaching Learners to be Self-Directed: A Stage Approach." *Adult Education Quarterly,* 1991, *41* (3).

Gruber, H. E. "Courage and Cognitive Growth in Children and Scientists." In M. Schwebel and J. Raph (eds.), *Piaget in the Classroom.* New York: Basic Books, 1973.

Guglielmino, L. M. "Development of the Self-Directed Learning Readiness Scale." Doctoral dissertation, University of Georgia, 1977.

Guglielmino, L. M., and Guglielmino, P. "Self-Directed Learning in Business and Industry: An Information Age Imperative." In H. B. Long and Associates (eds.), *Self-Directed Learning: Applications and Theory.* Athens: Adult Education Department, University of Georgia, 1988.

Guglielmino, L. M., Long, H. B., and McCune, S. K. "Reactions to Field's Investigation into the SDLRS." *Adult Education Quarterly,* 1989, *39* (4), 235–245.

Guilford, J. P. *The Nature of Human Intelligence.* New York: McGraw-Hill, 1967.

Gur, R. C. "Imaging the Activity of the Brain." *National Forum,* 1987, *68* (2), 13–16.

Gutmann, D. "The Cross Cultural Perspective: Notes Toward a Comparative." In K. W. Schaie and J. Geiwitz (eds.), *Readings in Adult Development and Aging.* Boston: Little, Brown, 1982.

Haan, N., and Day, D. "A Longitudinal Study of Change and Sameness in Personality Development: Adolescence to Later Adulthood." *International Journal of Aging and Development,* 1974, *5,* 11–39.

Habermas, J. *Knowledge and Human Interests.* Boston: Beacon Press, 1970.

Hamilton, E., and Cunningham, P. M. "Community-Based Adult Education." In S. B. Merriam and P. M. Cunningham (eds.), *Handbook of Adult and Continuing Education.* San Francisco: Jossey-Bass, 1989.

Hannay, H. J., and Levin, H. S. "Celebration About the Brain." *National Forum,* 1987, *67* (2), 1–3.

Hart, G. "Investing in People for the Information Age." *Futurist,* 1983, *17* (1), 10–14.

Hart, M. "Critical Theory and Beyond: Future Perspectives on Emancipatory Education and Social Action." *Adult Education Quarterly,* 1990, *40* (3), 125–138.

Hartree, A. "Malcolm Knowles' Theory of Andragogy: A Critique." *International Journal of Lifelong Education,* 1984, *3* (3), 203–210.

Hassan, A. M. "An Investigation of the Learning Projects Among Adults of High and Low Readiness for Self-Direction in Learning." Doctoral dissertation, Iowa State University, 1981.

Havighurst, R. J. *Human Development and Education.* New York: Longmans, Green, 1953.

Havighurst, R. J. *Developmental Tasks and Education.* (3rd ed.) New York: McKay, 1972. (Originally published 1952.)

Hawk, T. "Determinants of Part-Time Adult Student Participation in Education." Paper presented at the meeting of the American Educational Research Association, New Orleans, April 5–9, 1988. (ED 292 524)

Hayes, E. "A Typology of Low-Literate Adults Based on Perceptions of Deterrents to Participation in Adult Basic Education." *Adult Education Quarterly,* 1988, *39* (1), 1–10.

Hayes, E., and Darkenwald, G. G. "Participation in Basic Education: Deterrents for Low-Literate Adults." *Studies in the Education of Adults* (U.K.), 1988, *20* (1), 16–28.

Hayes, E., and Snow, B. R. "The Ends and Means of Adult Literacy Education." *Lifelong Learning: An Omnibus of Practice and Research,* 1989, *12* (8), 12–15.

Hayes, E., and Valentine, T. "The Functional Literacy Needs of Low-Literate Adult Basic Education Students." *Adult Education Quarterly,* 1989, *40* (1), 1–14.

Hayslip, B., and Panek, P. *Adult Development and Aging.* New York: Harper & Row, 1989.

Heckhausen, J., Dixon, R. A., and Baltes, P. B. "Gains and Losses in Development Throughout Adulthood as Perceived by Different Adult Age Groups." *Developmental Psychology,* 1989, *25* (1), 109–121.

Heise, D. R. "Sociocultural Determination of Mental Aging." In C. Schooler and K. Schaie (eds.), *Cognitive Functioning and Social Culture Over the Life Course.* Norwood, N.J.: Ablex, 1987.

Henry, W. A. "Beyond the Melting Pot." *Time,* April 9, 1990, pp. 28–31.

Hentges, K. "The Holistic Life Cycle Curriculum in Adult Education: A Proposal." *Lifelong Learning: An Omnibus of Practice and Research,* 1983, *7* (2), 16–17.

Hergenhahn, B. R. *An Introduction to Theories of Learning.* (3rd ed.) Englewood Cliffs, N.J.: Prentice-Hall, 1988.

Hiemstra, R. "The Older Adult's Learning Projects." *Educational Gerontology: An International Quarterly,* 1976, *1,* 331–341.

Hiemstra, R. *Policy Recommendations Related to Self-Directed Learning.* Occasional Paper no. 1. Syracuse, N.Y. Syracuse University, 1980.

Hiemstra, R. "Creating the Future." In R. G. Brockett (ed.), *Continuing Education in the Year 2000.* New Directions for Continuing Education, no. 36. San Francisco: Jossey-Bass, 1987.

Hiemstra, R. "Self-Directed Learning: Individualizing Instruction." In H. B. Long and Associates (eds.), *Self-Directed Learning: Application and Theory.* Athens: University of Georgia, 1988a.

Hiemstra, R. "Translating Personal Values and Philosophy into Practical Action." In R. G. Brockett (ed.), *Ethical Issues in Adult Education*. New York: Teachers College Press, 1988b.

Hiemstra, R., and Sisco, B. *Individualizing Instruction: Making Learning Personal, Empowering, and Successful*. San Francisco: Jossey-Bass, 1990.

Hilgard, E. R., and Bower, G. H. *Theories of Learning*. New York: Appleton-Century-Crofts, 1966.

Hill, R. N., and Mattessich, P. "Family Development Theory and Life-Span Development." In P. B. Baltes and O. G. Brim (eds.), *Life-Span Development and Behavior*. Vol. 2. New York: Academic Press, 1979.

Hill, S. T. *Trends in Adult Education: 1969-1984*. Washington, D.C.: Center for Educational Statistics, Office of Educational Research and Improvement, U.S. Department of Education, n.d.

Hill, W. F. *Learning: A Survey of Psychological Interpretations*. (3rd ed.) New York: Crowell, 1977.

Holliday, S. G., and Chandler, M. J. *Wisdom: Explorations in Adult Competence: Contributions to Human Development*. Vol. 17. Basel: Karger, 1986.

Horn, J. L. "The Theory of Fluid and Crystallized Intelligence in Relation to Concepts of Cognitive Psychology and Aging in Adulthood." In F.I.M. Craik and S. Trenub (eds.), *Advances in the Study of Communication Affect*. New York: Plenum Press, 1982.

Horn, J. L., and Donaldson, G. "On the Myth of Intellectual Decline in Adulthood." *American Psychologist*, 1976, *31*, 701-719.

Houle, C. O. *The Inquiring Mind*. Madison: University of Wisconsin Press, 1961.

Houle, C. O. *The Design of Education*. San Francisco: Jossey-Bass, 1972.

Houle, C. O. *Continuing Learning in the Professions*. San Francisco: Jossey-Bass, 1980.

Houle, C. O. *Patterns of Learning: New Perspectives on Life-Span Education*. San Francisco: Jossey-Bass, 1984.

Houle, C. O. "A Twenty-five Year Retrospective Look at Self-Directed Learning." Paper presented at the annual conference of the Commission of Professors of Adult Education, Milwaukee, November 1985.

Houle, C. O. *The Inquiring Mind.* (2nd ed.) Madison: University of Wisconsin Press; Norman: Oklahoma Research Center for Continuing Professional and Higher Education, 1988.

Hughes, D. C., Blazer, D. G., and George, L. K. "Age Differences in Life Events: A Multivariate Controlled Analysis." *International Journal of Aging and Human Development,* 1988, *27* (3), 207–219.

Hultsch, D. F., and Dixon, R. "Memory for Text Materials in Adulthood." In P. Baltes and O. G. Brim (eds.), *Life Span Development and Behavior.* Vol. 6. New York: Academic Press, 1984.

Hultsch, D. F., and Plemons, J. K. "Life Events and Life Span Development." In P. B. Baltes and O. G. Brim (eds.), *Life-Span Development and Behavior.* Vol. 2. New York: Academic Press, 1979.

Hunter, E. K. "Perspective Transformation in Health Practices: A Study in Adult Learning and Fundamental Life Change." Doctoral dissertation, University of California, Los Angeles, 1980.

Huyck, M. H., and Hoyer, W. J. *Adult Development and Aging.* Belmont, Calif.: Wadsworth, 1982.

James, D. "Educational Gerontology and the Biomedical Approach to Aging." *Educational Gerontology,* 1989, *15,* 151–160.

Jarvis, P. *Adult and Continuing Education: Theory and Practice.* London: Croom Helm, 1983.

Jarvis, P. *The Sociology of Adult and Continuing Education.* London: Croom Helm, 1985.

Jarvis, P. *Sociological Perspectives on Lifelong Education and Lifelong Learning.* Athens: Adult Education Department, University of Georgia, 1986.

Jarvis, P. *Adult Learning in the Social Context.* London: Croom Helm, 1987a.

Jarvis, P. "Meaningful and Meaningless Experiences: Towards an Analysis of Learning from Life." *Adult Education Quarterly,* 1987b, *37* (2), 164–172.

Jarvis, P. "Learning as the Transformation of Meaning: A Discussion with Jack Mezirow." Paper presented at the American Association of Adult and Continuing Education Annual Conference, Atlantic City, October 1989.

John-Steiner, V. *Notebooks of the Mind: Explorations of Thinking.* Albuquerque: N. Mex., 1985.

Johns, J.W.E. "Selected Characteristics of the Learning Projects Pursued by Practicing Pharmacists." Doctoral dissertation, University of Georgia, 1973.

Johnstone, J.W.C., and Rivera, R. J. *Volunteers for Learning: A Study of the Educational Pursuits of Adults.* Hawthorne, N.Y.: Aldine, 1965.

Jones, E. V., and Cooper, C. M. "Adult Education Programming and Memory Research." *Lifelong Learning,* 1982, *6* (3), 22–23.

Jones, H. E., and Conrad, H. S. "The Growth and Decline of Intelligence." *Genetic Psychology Monographs,* 1933, *13,* 223–298.

Kalleberg, A., and Loscocco, K. A. "Age, Values, and Rewards: Explaining Age Differences in Job Satisfaction." *American Sociological Review,* 1983, *48,* 78–90.

Kasworm, C. E. "An Examination of Self-Directed Contract Learning as an Instructional Strategy." *Innovative Higher Education,* 1983a, *8* (1), 45–54.

Kasworm, C. E. "Toward a Paradigm of Developmental Levels of Self-Directed Learning." Paper presented at the American Educational Research Association, Montreal, 1983b. (ED 230 705)

Kathrein, M. A. "A Study of Self-Directed Continuing Professional Learning of Members of the Illinois Nurses' Association: Content and Process." Doctoral dissertation, Northern Illinois University, 1981.

Kazemek, F. E. "Adult Literacy Education: An Ethical Endeavor." Cheney: Department of Education, Eastern Washington University, 1984. (ED 239 043)

Keating, D. P., and MacLean, D. J. "Reconstruction in Cognitive Development: A Post-Structuralist Agenda." In P. B. Baltes, D. L. Featherstone, and R. M. Lerner (eds.), *Life Span Development and Behavior.* Vol. 8. Hillsdale, N.J.: Erlbaum, 1988.

Keddie, N. "Adult Education: An Ideology of Individualism."
In J. L. Thompson (ed.), *Adult Education for a Change*. London: Hutchinson, 1980.

Kegan, R. *The Evolving Self: Problem and Processes in Human Development*. Cambridge, Mass.: Harvard University Press,
1982.

Kelman, H. C., and Warwick, D. P. "The Ethics of Social Intervention: Goals, Means, and Consequences." In G. Ber-
mant, H. C. Kelman, and D. P. Warwick (eds.), *The Ethics
of Social Intervention*. Washington: Hemisphere, 1978.

Kemp, J. E. *The Instructional Design Process*. New York: Harper
& Row, 1985.

Kidd, J. R. *How Adults Learn*. (rev. ed.) New York: Association Press, 1973.

Kimmel, D. C. *Adulthood and Aging*. (3rd ed.) New York: Wiley,
1990.

King, P. M., and others. "The Justification of Beliefs in Young
Adults: A Longitudinal Study." *Human Development*, 1983, *26*,
106–116.

Kirby, P. *Cognitive Style, Learning Style and Transfer Skill Acquisition*. Columbus: Ohio State University National Center for
Research in Vocational Education, 1979.

Kirkpatrick, D. L. "Evaluation." In R. L. Craig (ed.), *Training
and Development Handbook*. (3rd ed.) New York: McGraw-Hill,
1987.

Kitchener, K. S., and King, P. M. "Reflective Judgement: Concepts of Justification and Their Relationship to Age and Education." *Journal of Applied Development Psychology*, 1981, *2*, 89–
116.

Knowles, M. S. *Self-Directed Learning*. New York: Association
Press, 1975.

Knowles, M. S. *The Modern Practice of Adult Education: From Pedagogy to Andragogy*. (2nd ed.) New York: Cambridge Books,
1980.

Knowles, M. S. *The Adult Learner: A Neglected Species*. (3rd ed.)
Houston: Gulf, 1984.

Knowles, M. S. "Adult Learning." In R. L. Craig (ed.), *Train-

ing and Development Handbook. (3rd ed.) New York: McGraw-Hill, 1987.

Knowles, M. S., and Associates. *Andragogy in Action: Applying Modern Principles of Adult Learning.* San Francisco: Jossey-Bass, 1984.

Knox, A. B. *Adult Development and Learning.* San Francisco: Jossey-Bass, 1977.

Knox, A. B. "Proficiency Theory of Adult Learning." *Contemporary Educational Psychology,* 1980, *5,* 378–404.

Knox, A. B. "Adult Learning and Proficiency." In D. Kleiber and M. Maehr (eds.), *Advances in Motivation and Achievement.* Vol. 4: *Motivation in Adulthood.* Greenwood, Conn.: JAI Press, 1985.

Knox, A. B. *Helping Adults Learn.* San Francisco: Jossey-Bass, 1986.

Knox, A. B., Grotelueschen, A., and Sjogren, D. D. "Adult Intelligence and Learning Ability." *Adult Education Journal,* 1968, *18* (3), 188–196.

Knox, A. B., and Sjogren, D. D. "Achievement and Withdrawal in University Adult Education Classes." *Adult Education,* 1965, *15* (2), 74–88.

Kohlberg, L. "Continuities in Childhood and Adult Moral Development." In P. Baltes and K. Schaie (eds.), *Life-span Developmental Psychology: Personality and Socialization.* New York: Academic Press, 1973.

Kolb, D. *Experiential Learning: Experience as the Source of Learning and Development.* Englewood Cliffs, N.J.: Prentice-Hall, 1984.

Kramer, D. A. "Post-Formal Operations? A Need for Further Conceptualization." *Human Development,* 1983, *26,* 91–105.

Kramer, D. A. "Development of an Awareness of Contradiction Across the Life Span and the Question of Postformal Operations." In M. L. Commons, J. D. Sinnot, F. A. Richards, and C. Armon (eds.), *Adult Development: Comparisons and Applications of Developmental Models.* New York: Praeger, 1989.

Kramer, D. A., and Woodruff, D. S. "Relativistic and Dialectical Thought in Three Adult Age Groups." *Human Development,* 1986, *29,* 280–290.

Kratz, R. J. "The Effects of Programs Which Foster Self-Directed Learning on the Dropout Rate, the Length of Stay, and the Preferences for Self-Directed Learning of Adult Basic Education Students." Doctoral dissertation, State University of New York, 1978.

Kulich, J. "An Historical Overview of the Adult Self-Learner." *International Congress of University Adult Education*, 1970, *9*, 22–32.

Labouvie-Vief, G. "Beyond Formal Operations: Uses and Limits of Pure Logic in Life-Span Development." *Human Development*, 1980, *23*, 141–161.

Labouvie-Vief, G. "Logic and Self-Regulation From Youth to Maturity: A Model." In M. L. Commons, F. A. Richards, and C. Armon (eds.), *Beyond Formal Operations: Late Adolescent and Adult Cognitive Development*. New York: Praeger, 1984.

Labouvie-Vief, G. "Models of Cognitive Functioning in the Older Adult: Research Needs in Educational Gerontology." In R. H. Sherron and D. B. Lumsden (eds.), *Introduction to Gerontology*. (3rd ed.) New York: Hemisphere, 1990.

Laird, D. *Approaches to Training and Development*. (2nd ed.) Reading, Mass.: Addison-Wesley, 1985.

Lamont, M., and Lareau, A. "Cultural Capital: Allusions, Gaps, and Glissandos in Recent Theoretical Developments." *Sociological Theory*, 1988, *6*, 153–168.

Langenbach, M., and Aagaard, L. "A Factor Analytic Study of the Adult Classroom Environment Scale." *Adult Education Quarterly*, 1990, *40*, 95–102.

Lasker, H., and Moore, J. "Current Studies of Adult Development: Implications for Education." *Adult Development and Approaches to Learning*. Washington, D.C.: National Institute of Education, U.S. Department of Education, 1980.

Lave, J., Murtaugh, M., and de la Roche, O. "The Dialectic of Arithmetic in Grocery Shopping." In B. Rogoff and J. Lave (eds.), *Everyday Cognition: Its Development and Social Context*. Cambridge, Mass.: Harvard University Press, 1984.

Lefrancois, G. R. *Psychological Theories and Human Learning*. (2nd ed.) Monterey, Calif.: Brooks/Cole, 1982.

Levine, A. "Getting Smarter About I.Q." *U.S. News and World Report*, November 23, 1987, pp. 53–55.

Levinson, D. J. "A Conception of Adult Development." *American Psychologist,* 1986, *41* (1), 3–13.

Levinson, D. J., and others. *The Seasons of a Man's Life.* New York: Knopf, 1978.

Levy, J. "Research Synthesis on Right and Left Hemispheres: We Think with Both Sides of the Brain." *Educational Leadership,* 1983, *40,* 66–71.

Lewin, K. "Frontiers in Group Dynamics: Concept, Method, and Reality in Social Science." *Human Relations,* 1947, *1,* 5–41.

Lewis, L. (ed.). *Addressing the Needs of Returning Women.* New Directions in Continuing Education, no. 39. San Francisco: Jossey-Bass, 1988a.

Lewis, L. "Adults and Computer Anxiety: Fact or Fiction?" *Lifelong Learning,* 1988b, *11* (8), 5–8.

Lewis, L. "New Technologies and the Future." In S. B. Merriam and P. M. Cunningham (eds.), *Handbook of Adult and Continuing Education.* San Francisco: Jossey-Bass, 1989.

Little, D. "Adult Learning and Education: A Concept Analysis." In P. Cunningham (ed.), *Yearbook of Adult and Continuing Education, 1979–1980.* Chicago: Marquis Academic Media, 1979.

Lloyd, A. S. "Freire, Conscientization, and Adult Education." *Adult Education,* 1972, *23* (1), 3–20.

Loevinger, J. *Ego Development: Conceptions and Theories.* San Francisco: Jossey-Bass, 1976.

Long, H. B. *Adult Learning: Research and Practice.* New York: Cambridge, 1983.

Long, H. B. "Self-Directed Learning: Emerging Theory and Practice." In H. B. Long and Associates (eds.), *Self-Directed Learning: Emerging Theory and Practice.* Norman: Oklahoma Research Center for Continuing Professional and Higher Education, University of Oklahoma, 1989.

Long, H. B., McCrary, K., and Ackerman, S. "Adult Cognition: Piagetian Based Research Findings." *Adult Education,* 1979, *30* (1), 3–18.

Lorge, I. "Intellectual Changes During Maturity and Old Age." *Review of Educational Research,* 1944, *14* (4), 438–443.

Lorge, I. "Intellectual Change During Maturity and Old Age." *Review of Educational Research,* 1947, *17* (5), 326–330.

Lovell, R. B. *Adult Learning.* London: Croom Helm, 1980.

Luttrell, W. "Working-Class Women's Ways of Knowing: Effects of Gender, Race, and Class." *Sociology of Education,* 1989, *62,* 33–46.

McClusky, H. Y. "The Course of the Adult Life Span." In W. C. Hallenbeck (ed.), *Psychology of Adults.* Washington, D.C.: Adult Education Association, 1963.

McClusky, H. Y. "An Approach to a Differential Psychology of the Adult Potential." In S. M. Grabowski (ed.), *Adult Learning and Instruction.* Syracuse, N.Y.: ERIC Clearinghouse on Adult Education, 1970.

McClusky, H. Y. *Education: Background.* Report prepared for the 1971 White House Conference on Aging. Washington, D.C.: White House Conference on Aging, 1971.

McCune, S. N. "A Meta-Analytic Study of Adult Self-Direction in Learning: A Review of Research from 1977 to 1987." Doctoral dissertation, Department of Interdisciplinary Studies, Texas A&M University, 1988.

McKeachie, W. J. "Psychology and Adult Cognition." In R. A. Fellenz (ed.), *Cognition and the Adult Learner.* Bozeman, Mont.: Center for Adult Learning Research, 1988.

Main, K. "The Power-Load-Margin Formula of Howard Y. McClusky as the Basis for a Model of Teaching." *Adult Education,* 1979, *30* (1), 19–33.

Maples, M. F., and Webster, J. M. "Thorndike's Connectionism." In G. M. Gazda and R. J. Corsini (eds.), *Theories of Learning.* Itasca, Ill.: Peacock, 1980.

Marcus, E. E., and Havighurst, R. J. "Education for the Aging." In E. J. Boone, R. W. Shearon, E. E. White, and Associates (eds.), *Serving Personal and Community Needs Through Adult Education.* San Francisco: Jossey-Bass, 1980.

Marien, M. "Some Questions for the Information Society." *World Future Society Bulletin,* 1983, *17* (5), 17–23.

Marsick, V. J. *Learning in the Workplace.* London, England: Croom Helm, 1987.

Marsick, V. J. "Learning in the Workplace: The Case for Reflectivity and Critical Reflectivity." *Adult Education Quarterly,* 1988, *38,* 187–198.

Marsick, V. J. "Altering the Paradigm for Theory Building and Research in Human Resource Development." *Human Resource Development Quarterly,* 1990, *1,* 5–24.

Martindale, C. J., and Drake, J. B. "Factor Structure of Deterrents to Participation in Off-Duty Adult Education Programs." *Adult Education Quarterly,* 1989, *39* (2), 63–75.

Maslow, A. H. *Motivation and Personality.* New York: Harper & Row, 1954.

Maslow, A. H. *Motivation and Personality.* (2nd ed.) New York: Harper & Row, 1970.

Mehan, H. "Institutional Decision-Making." In B. Rogoff and J. Lave (eds.), *Everyday Cognition: Its Development and Social Context.* Cambridge, Mass.: Harvard University Press, 1984.

Mercer, S. O., and Garner, J. D. "An International Overview of Aged Women." In J. D. Garner and O. Mercer (eds.), *Women as They Age: Challenge, Opportunity, and Triumph.* New York: Haworth Press, 1989.

Merriam, S. B. *Themes of Adulthood Through Literature.* New York: Teachers College Press, 1983.

Merriam, S. B. *Adult Development: Implications for Adult Education.* Columbus, Ohio: ERIC Clearinghouse on Adult, Career, and Vocational Education, 1984.

Merriam, S. B. "Adult Learning and Theory Building: A Review." *Adult Education Quarterly,* 1987, *37,* 187–198.

Merriam, S. B. "How Research Contributes to the Knowledge Base of Adult Education." In P. Jarvis and J. Peters (eds.), *Adult Education as a Field of Study: Its Evolution, Achievements and Future* (tentative title). San Francisco: Jossey-Bass, 1991.

Merriam, S. B., and Clark, M. C. *Work, Love, and Learning in Adult Life* (tentative title), San Francisco: Jossey-Bass, forthcoming.

Merriam, S. B., and Cunningham, P. M. *Handbook of Adult and Continuing Education.* San Francisco: Jossey-Bass, 1989.

Messick, S. "Personality Consistencies in Cognition and Creativity." In S. Messick and Associates, *Individuality in Learning: Implications of Cognitive Styles and Creativity in Human Development.* San Francisco: Jossey-Bass, 1976.

Messick, S. "The Nature of Cognitive Styles: Problems and Promise in Educational Practice." *Educational Psychologist,* 1984, *19* (2), 59–74.

Mezirow, J. "A Critical Theory of Adult Learning and Education." *Adult Education,* 1981, *32* (1), 3–27.

Mezirow, J. "Concept and Action in Adult Education." *Adult Education Quarterly,* 1985, *35* (3), 142–151.

Mezirow, J. "Transformation Theory and Social Action: A Response to Collard and Law." *Adult Education Quarterly,* 1989, *39* (2), 170–176.

Mezirow, J. "Conclusion: Toward Transformative Learning and Emancipatory Education." In J. Mezirow and Associates (eds.), *Fostering Critical Reflection in Adulthood: A Guide to Transformative and Emancipatory Education.* San Francisco: Jossey-Bass, 1990.

Mezirow, J., and Associates. *Fostering Critical Reflection in Adulthood: A Guide to Transformative and Emancipatory Education.* San Francisco: Jossey-Bass, 1990.

Miles, C. C., and Miles, W. R. "The Correlation of Intelligence Scores and Chronological Age from Early to Late Maturity." *American Journal of Psychology,* 1932, *44,* 44–78.

Miller, H. L. *Participation of Adults in Education: A Force-Field Analysis.* Boston: Center for the Study of Liberal Education for Adults, Boston University, 1967.

Mills, H., and Dejoy, J. K. "Applications of Educational Technology in a Self-Directed Learning Program for Adults." *Lifelong Learning: An Omnibus of Practice and Research,* 1988, *12* (3), 22–24.

Mincer, J. "Human Capital and the Labor Market: A Review of Current Research." *Educational Researcher,* 1989, *18* (4), 27–34.

Mishler, E. G. "Meaning in Context: Is There Any Other Kind?" *Harvard Educational Review,* 1979, *49* (1), 1–19.

Mocker, D., and Spear, G. *Lifelong Learning: Formal, Informal, and Self-Directed Learning.* Kansas City: Center for Resource Development Education, University of Missouri–Kansas City, 1982. (ED 220 723)

Moebius, B. H. "Educating Small Business for an International

Marketplace." In I. Charner and C. A. Rolzinski (eds.), *Responding to the Educational Needs of Today's Workplace.* New Directions for Continuing Education, no. 33. San Francisco: Jossey-Bass, 1987.

Morris, J. F. "The Planning Behavior and Conceptual Complexity of Selected Clergymen in Self-Directed Learning Projects Related to Their Continued Professional Education." Doctoral dissertation, University of Toronto, 1977.

Morstain, B. R., and Smart, J. C. "Reasons for Participation in Adult Education Courses: A Multivariate Analysis of Group Differences." *Adult Education,* 1974, *24* (2), 83–98.

Munson, L. S. *How to Conduct Training Sessions.* New York: McGraw-Hill, 1984.

Naisbitt, J. *The Year Ahead, 1986.* New York: Warner Books, 1985.

Naisbitt, J., and Aburdene, P. *Megatrends 2000: Ten New Directions for the 1990s.* New York: Morrow, 1990.

National Center for Education Statistics (NCES). *Participation in Adult Education: Final Report, 1969.* Washington, D.C.: Government Printing Office, 1974.

National Center for Education Statistics (NCES). *Participation in Adult Education: Final Report, 1975.* Washington, D.C.: Government Printing Office, 1978.

National Center for Education Statistics (NCES). *Participation in Adult Education: 1978 Preliminary Report.* Washington, D.C.: Department of Education, 1980a.

National Center for Education Statistics (NCES). *Preliminary Data: Participation in Adult Education, 1978.* Washington, D.C.: Office of Education, Department of Health, Education and Welfare, 1980b.

National Center for Education Statistics (NCES). *Participation in Adult Education, 1981.* Washington, D.C.: Government Printing Office, 1982.

Nef, J. "Concepts from Political Studies." In D. J. Blackburn (ed.), *Foundations and Changing Practices in Extension.* Guelph, Ontario: University of Guelph, 1989.

Neugarten, B. "Adaptation and the Life Cycle." *Counseling Psychologist,* 1976, *6,* 16–20.

Neugarten, B. "Time, Age, and the Life Cycle." *American Journal of Psychiatry,* 1979, *136,* 887–893.

Neugarten, B., and Datan, N. "Sociological Perspectives on the Life Cycle." In P. Baltes and K. W. Schaie (eds.), *Life-Span Developmental Psychology: Personality and Socialization.* New York: Academic Press, 1973.

Neugarten, B., and Associates. *Personality in Middle and Late Life: Empirical Studies.* New York: Atherton Press, 1964.

Nordhaug, O. "Structured Determinants of Publicly Subsidized Adult Education." *Adult Education Quarterly,* 1990, *40* (4), 197–206.

Nowlen, P. M. *A New Approach to Continuing Education for Business and the Professions.* New York: Macmillan, 1988.

Oddi, L. F. "Development of an Instrument to Measure Self-Directed Continuing Learning." Doctoral dissertation, Northern Illinois University, 1984.

Oddi, L. F. "Development and Validation of an Instrument to Identify Self-Directed Continuing Learners." *Adult Education Quarterly,* 1986, *36,* 97–107.

O'Keefe, M. *The Adult, Education, and Public Policy.* Cambridge, Mass.: Aspen Institute for Humanistic Studies, 1977.

Oliver, L. P. *Study Circles.* Washington, D.C.: Seven Locks Press, 1987.

Orwoll, L., and Perlmutter, M. "The Study of Wise Persons: Integrating a Personality Perspective." In R. J. Sternberg (ed.), *Wisdom: Its Nature, Origins, and Development.* Cambridge: Cambridge University Press, 1990.

Ozanne, J. *Regional Surveys of Adult Education.* New York: American Association for Adult Education, 1934.

Palmore, E. "The Social Factors in Aging." In E. W. Busse and D. G. Blazer (eds.), *Handbook of Geriatric Psychiatry.* New York: Van Nostrand, 1980.

Papalia, D. E., and Bielby, D.D.V. "Cognitive Functioning in Middle and Old Age Adults." *Human Development,* 1974, *17,* 424–443.

Pascual-Leone, J. "Growing into Maturity: Towards a Metasubjective Theory of Adulthood Stages." In P. B. Baltes and O. G. Brim, Jr. (eds.), *Life Span Development and Behavior.* Vol. 5. New York: Academic Press, 1983.

Paterson, K. W. *Values, Education, and the Adult.* London: Routledge & Kegan Paul, 1979.

Peck, T. A. "Women's Self-Definition in Adulthood: From a Different Model." *Psychology of Women Quarterly,* 1986, *10,* 274–284.

Penland, P. R. *Self-Planned Learning in America.* Final Report of Project 475AH COO58, Office of Libraries and Learning Resources, U.S. Department of Health, Education, and Welfare. Pittsburgh: Graduate School of Library and Information Science, University of Pittsburgh, 1977. (ED 184 589)

Penland, P. R. "Self-Initiated Learning." *Adult Education,* 1979, *29,* 170–179.

Penland, P. R. *Towards Self-Directed Theory.* Washington, D.C.: National Institute of Education, 1981. (ED 209 475)

Perlmutter, M., and Hall, E. *Adult Development and Aging.* New York: Wiley, 1985.

Perry, W. *Forms of Intellectual and Ethical Development in the College Years.* New York: Holt, Rinehart & Winston, 1970.

Perry, W. "Cognitive and Ethical Growth: The Making of Meaning." In A. W. Chickering and Associates, *The Modern American College.* San Francisco: Jossey-Bass, 1981.

Peters, J. M. "Toward a New Procedure for Learning Project Research." *Proceedings of SCRUTREA* (Leeds, England), 1988, *1,* 340–345.

Peters, J. M. "Programming Through the Client's Lifespan." In D. J. Blackburn (ed.), *Foundations and Changing Practices in Extension.* Guelph, Ontario: University of Guelph, 1989a.

Peters, J. M. "Self-Direction and Problem Solving: Theory and Method." Paper presented at the 3rd North American Symposium on Adult Self-Directed Learning, Norman, Oklahoma, February 1989b.

Peters, J. M., and Gordon, S. R. *Adult Learning Projects: A Study of Adult Learning in Urban and Rural Tennessee.* Knoxville: University of Tennessee, 1974. (ED 102 431)

Peters, J. M., and Lazzara, P. J. "A Knowledge Acquisition Model for Building Expert Systems: Studying Adult Reasoning and Thinking." *Proceedings of the Adult Education Research Conference,* no. 29. Calgary: University of Calgary, 1988.

Peters, T. J., and Waterman, H. R. *In Search of Excellence.* New York: Harper & Row, 1982.

Petska, D. E. "Adult Education for the Year 2000." *Lifelong Learning: The Adult Years,* 1982, *5* (5), 21–23.

Phares, E. J. "Rotter's Social Learning Theory." In G. M. Gazda and R. J. Corsini (eds.), *Theories of Learning.* Itasca, Ill.: Peacock, 1980.

Phillips, L. E. "Is Mandatory Continuing Education Working?" *Mobius,* 1987, *7,* 57–64.

Piaget, J. *The Origins of Intelligence in Children.* New York: International Universities, 1952.

Piaget, J. *Psychology of Intelligence.* Totowa, N.J.: Littlefield, Adams, 1966.

Piaget, J. "Intellectual Evolution from Adolescent to Adulthood." *Human Development,* 1972, *16,* 346–370.

Poon, L. "Differences in Human Memory with Aging: Nature, Causes, and Clinical Implications." In J. E. Birren and K. W. Schaie (eds.), *Handbook of the Psychology of Aging.* (2nd ed.) New York: Van Nostrand Reinhold, 1985.

Poon, L., Walsh-Sweeney, L., and Fozard, J. "Memory Skill Training for the Elderly: Salient Issues on the Use of Imagery Mnemonics." In L. Poon and others (eds.), *New Directions in Memory and Aging: Proceedings of the George A. Talland Memorial Conference.* Hillsdale, N.J.: Erlbaum, 1980.

Poon, L., and others (eds.). *New Directions in Memory and Aging.* Hillsdale, N.J.: Erlbaum, 1980.

Pratt, D. D. "Andragogical Assumptions: Some Counter-Intuitive Logic." *Proceedings of the Adult Education Research Conference,* no. 25. Raleigh: North Carolina State University, 1984.

Pratt, D. D. "Andragogy as a Relational Construct." *Adult Education Quarterly,* 1988, *38* (3), 160–181.

Price, G. E. "Diagnosing Learning Style." In R. M. Smith (ed.), *Helping Adults Learn How to Learn.* New Directions for Continuing Education, no. 19. San Francisco: Jossey-Bass, 1983.

Quigley, B. A. "Influencing Social Policy." In B. A. Quigley (ed.), *Fulfilling the Promise of Adult and Continuing Education.* New Directions for Continuing Education, no. 44. San Francisco: Jossey-Bass, 1989a.

Quigley, B. A. "Social Policy and Adult Education: Research Framework and Taxonomy for the Future." *Proceedings of the Adult Education Research Conference,* no. 30. Madison: University of Wisconsin, 1989b.

Quigley, B. A. "Hidden Logic: Reproduction and Resistance in Adult Literacy and Adult Basic Education." *Adult Education Quarterly,* 1990, *40* (2), 103–115.

Rachal, J. R. "Assessing Adult Education Research Questions: Some Preliminary Criteria." *Adult Education Quarterly,* 1986, *36* (3), 157–159.

Rachal, J. R. "The Social Setting of Adult and Continuing Education." In S. B. Merriam and P. M. Cunningham (eds.), *Handbook of Adult and Continuing Education.* San Francisco: Jossey-Bass, 1989.

Reese, H. W., and Overton, W. F. "Models of Development and Theories of Development." In L. R. Goulet and P. B. Baltes (eds.), *Life-Span Developmental Psychology: Interventions.* New York: Academic Press, 1970.

Reese, H. W., and Smyer, M. A. "The Dimensionalization of Life Events." In E. J. Callahan and K. A. McCluskey (eds.), *Life-Span Developmental Psychology: Nonnormative Events.* New York: Academic Press, 1983.

Resnick, L. "Learning In School and Out." *Educational Researcher,* 1987, *16* (9), 13–20.

Richards, R. K. "Physicians' Self-Directed Learning." *Mobius,* 1986, *6* (4), 1–13.

Richardson, P. L. "The Lifelong Learning Project Revisited: Institutionalizing the Vision." *Educational Considerations,* 1987, *14* (2–3), 2–4.

Riegel, K. F. "Dialectic Operations: The Final Period of Cognitive Development." *Human Development,* 1973, *16,* 346–370.

Riegel, K. F. "Adult Life Crises: A Dialectical Interpretation of Development. In N. Datan and L. H. Ginsberg (eds.), *Life-Span Developmental Psychology: Normative Life Crises.* Orlando, Fla.: Academic Press, 1975.

Riegel, K. F. "The Dialectics of Human Development." *American Psychologist,* 1976, *31,* 689–700.

Robinson, D. N. "Wisdom Through the Ages." In R. J. Sternberg (ed.), *Wisdom: Its Nature, Origins, and Development.* Cambridge: Cambridge University Press, 1990.

Robinson, R. D. *An Introduction to Helping Adults Learn to Change.* Milwaukee: Omni Books, 1979.

Rockhill, K. "Researching Participation in Adult Education: The Potential of the Qualitative Perspective." *Adult Education,* 1982, *33* (1), 3-19.

Rogers, C. R. *Freedom to Learn for the 80's.* Columbus: Merrill, 1983.

Rogoff, B., and Lave, J. (eds.). *Everyday Cognition: Its Development in Social Context.* Cambridge, Mass.: Harvard University Press, 1984.

Rose, A. "Beyond Classroom Walls: The Carnegie Corporation and the Founding of the Field of Adult Education." *Adult Education Quarterly,* 1989, *39* (3), 140-151.

Rosenblum, S., and Darkenwald, G. "Effects of Adult Learner Participation in Course Planning on Achievement." *Adult Education Quarterly,* 1983, *33* (3), 147-160.

Rossman, I. "Bodily Changes with Aging." In E. W. Busse and D. G. Blazer (eds.), *Handbook of Geriatric Psychiatry.* New York: Van Nostrand Reinhold, 1980.

Rotter, J. B. *Social Learning and Clinical Psychology.* Englewood Cliffs, N.J.: Prentice-Hall, 1954.

Rubenson, K. "Participation in Recurrent Education: A Research Review." Paper presented at a meeting of national delegates on Developments in Recurrent Education. Paris: Organization for Economic Cooperation and Development, 1977.

Rubenson, K. "Background and Theoretical Context." In R. Hoghielm and K. Rubenson (eds.), *Adult Education for Social Change.* Lund, Sweden: Liber, 1980.

Rubenson, K. "Adult Education Research: In Quest of a Map of the Territory." *Adult Education,* 1982, *32* (2), 57-74.

Rubenson, K. "Sociology of Adult Education." In S. B. Merriam and P. M. Cunningham (eds.), *Handbook of Adult and Continuing Education.* San Francisco: Jossey-Bass, 1989.

Rumelhart, D. E. "Schemata: The Building Blocks of Cognition." In R. J. Spiro (ed.), *Theoretical Issues in Reading Comprehension.* Hillsdale, N.J.: Erlbaum, 1980.

Rumelhart, D. E., and Norman, D. A. "Accretion, Tuning, and Restructuring: Three Models of Learning." In J. W. Cotton and R. L. Klatzky (eds.), *Semantic Factors in Cognition*. Hillsdale, N.J.: Erlbaum, 1978.

Rybash, J. M., Hoyer, W. J., and Roodin, P. A. *Adult Cognition and Aging*. New York: Pergamon, 1986.

Sahakian, W. S. *Introduction to the Psychology of Learning*. (2nd ed.) Itasca, Ill.: Peacock, 1984.

Salthouse, T. A. *Adult Cognition*. New York: Springer-Verlag, 1982.

Salthouse, T. A. *A Theory of Cognitive Aging*. Amsterdam: North Holland, 1985.

Salthouse, T. A. "Initiating the Formalization of Theories of Cognitive Aging." *Psychology and Aging,* 1988, *3,* 3–16.

Savićević, D. M. "Self-Directed Education for Lifelong Learning. *International Journal of Lifelong Education,* 1985, *4* (4), 285–294.

Scanlan, C., and Darkenwald, G. "Identifying Deterrents to Participation in Continuing Education." *Adult Education Quarterly,* 1984, *34* (3), 155–166.

Schaie, K. W. "The Primary Mental Abilities in Adulthood: An Exploration in the Development of Psychometric Intelligence." In P. B. Baltes and O. G. Brim (eds.), *Life-Span Development and Behavior.* Vol. 2. New York: Academic Press, 1979.

Schaie, K. W. (ed.). *Longitudinal Studies of Adult Development.* New York: Guilford, 1983.

Schaie, K. W. *Manual for the Schaie-Thurston Adult Mental Abilities Test (STAMAT).* Palo Alto, Calif.: Consulting Psychologist Press, 1985.

Schaie, K. W. "Applications of Psychometric Intelligence to the Prediction of Everyday Competence in the Elderly." In C. Schooler and K. Schaie (eds.), *Cognitive Functioning and Social Culture Over the Life Course.* Norwood, N.J.: Ablex, 1987.

Schaie, K. W., and Hertzog, C. "Fourteen-Year Cohort-Sequential Analyses of Adult Intellectual Development." *Developmental Psychology,* 1983, *19* (4), 531–543.

Schaie, K. W., and Labouvie-Vief, G. "Generational Versus

Ontogenetic Components of Change in Adult Cognitive Behavior: A Fourteen Year Cross Sectional Study." *Developmental
Psychologist,* 1974, *10* (3), 305–320.

Schaie, K. W., and Parham, I. A. "Cohort-Sequential Analysis of Adult Intellectual Development." *Developmental Psychology,* 1977, *13* (6), 649–653.

Schaie, K. W., and Willis, S. L. *Adult Development and Aging.*
(2nd ed.) Boston: Little, Brown, 1986.

Schlossberg, N. K. *Counseling Adults in Transition.* New York:
Springer, 1984.

Schlossberg, N. K. "Taking the Mystery Out of Change." *Psychology Today,* 1987, *21* (5), 74–75.

Schlossberg, N. K., Lynch, A. Q., and Chickering, A. W. *Improving Higher Education Environments for Adults.* San Francisco:
Jossey-Bass, 1989.

Schön, D. A. *The Reflective Practitioner.* New York: Basic Books,
1983.

Schön, D. A. *Educating the Reflective Practitioner.* San Francisco:
Jossey-Bass, 1987.

Schulz, R., and Ewen, R. B. *Adult Development and Aging.* New
York: Macmillan, 1988.

Scribner, S. "Studying Working Intelligence." In B. Rogoff and
J. Lave (eds.), *Everyday Cognition: Its Development in Social Context.* Cambridge, Mass.: Harvard University Press, 1984.

Sheehy, G. *Passages.* New York: Dutton, 1976.

Sheffield, S. B. "The Orientations of Adult Continuing Learners." In D. Solomon (ed.), *The Continuing Learner.* Chicago:
Center for the Study of Liberal Education for Adults, 1964.

Shor, I., and Freire, P. *A Pedagogy for Liberation.* South Hadley,
Mass.: Bergin & Garvey, 1987.

Shuell, T. J. "Cognitive Conceptions of Learning." *Review of
Educational Research,* 1986, *56,* 411–436.

Simpson, E. L., and Supapidhayakul, S. "The Influence of Cognitive Style upon Adult Nursing Student Performance, Attitude Toward Learning and Preferences for Learning Environments." *Proceedings of the Adult Education Research Conference,* no.
27. Syracuse, N.Y.: Syracuse University, 1986.

Sinnott, J. D. "Postformal Reasoning: The Relativistic Stage."
In M. L. Commons, F. A. Richards, and C. Armon (eds.),

Beyond Formal Operations: Late Adolescent and Adult Cognitive Development. New York: Praeger, 1984.

Sisco, B. R. "An Analysis of the Cognitive Profiles of Selected University Adults." *Proceedings of the Adult Education Research Conference,* no. 28. Laramie: University of Wyoming, 1987.

Sisco, B. R. "The Relevance of Robert Sternberg's Triarchic Theory of Human Intelligence to Adult Education." *Proceedings of the Adult Education Research Conference,* no. 30. Madison: University of Wisconsin, 1989.

Six, J. E. "The Generality of the Underlying Dimensions of the Oddi Continuing Learning Inventory." *Adult Education Quarterly,* 1989, *40* (1), 43–51.

Skaggs, B. J. "The Relationship Between Involvement of Professional Nurses in Self-Directed Learning Activities, Loci of Control, and Readiness for Self-Directed Learning Measures." Doctoral dissertation, University of Texas at Austin, 1981.

Skinner, B. F. *Beyond Freedom and Dignity.* New York: Knopf, 1971.

Skinner, B. F. *About Behaviorism.* New York: Knopf, 1974.

Smith, D. H. "Determinants of Individuals' Discretionary Use of Time." In D. H. Smith, J. Macaulay, and Associates (eds.), *Participation in Social and Political Activities.* San Francisco: Jossey-Bass, 1980.

Smith, J., Dixon, R. A., and Baltes, P. B. "Expertise in Life Planning: A New Research Approach to Investigating Aspects of Wisdom." In M. L. Commons, J. D. Sinnott, F. A. Richards, and C. Armour (eds.), *Adult Development Comparisons and Applications of Development.* New York: Praeger, 1989.

Smith, R. M. *Learning How to Learn: Applied Learning Theory for Adults.* Chicago: Follett, 1982.

Smith, R. M. (ed.). *Theory Building for Learning How to Learn.* Chicago: Educational Studies Press, 1987.

Smith, R., Kidd, J. R., and Aker, G. (eds.). *Handbook of Adult Education in the United States.* New York: Macmillan, 1970.

Soltis, J. F. "The Ethics of Qualitative Research." *Qualitative Studies in Education,* 1989, *2* (2), 123–130.

Sork, T. J. "Ethical Issues in Program Planning." In R. G. Brockett (ed.), *Ethical Issues in Adult Education.* New York: Teachers College Press, 1988.

Sork, T. J., and Caffarella, R. S. "Planning Programs for Adults." In S. B. Merriam and P. M. Cunningham (eds.), *Handbook of Adult and Continuing Education.* San Francisco: Jossey-Bass, 1989.

Spear, G. E. "Beyond the Organizing Circumstance: A Search for Methodology for the Study of Self-Directed Learning." In H. B. Long and Associates (eds.), *Self-Directed Learning: Application and Theory.* Athens: Department of Adult Education, University of Georgia, 1988.

Spear, G. E., and Mocker, D. W. "The Organizing Circumstance: Environmental Determinants in Self-Directed Learning." *Adult Education Quarterly,* 1984, *35* (1), 1–10.

Spear, G. E., and Mocker, D. W. "The Future of Adult Education." In S. B. Merriam and P. M. Cunningham (eds.), *Handbook of Adult and Continuing Education.* San Francisco: Jossey-Bass, 1989.

Springer, S. P. "Educating the Left and Right Sides of the Brain." *National Forum,* 1987, *67* (2), 25–28.

Staddon, J.E.R. "Social Learning Theory and the Dynamics of Interaction." *Psychological Review,* 1984, *91* (4), 502–507.

Sternberg, R. J. *Beyond I.Q.: A Triarchic Theory of Human Intelligence.* Cambridge: Cambridge University Press, 1985.

Sternberg, R. J. *Intelligence Applied: Understanding and Increasing Your Intellectual Skills.* San Diego: Harcourt Brace Jovanovich, 1986a.

Sternberg, R. J. "Intelligence, Wisdom, and Creativity: Three Is Better Than One." *Educational Psychologist,* 1986b, *21* (3), 175–190.

Sternberg, R. J. *The Triarchic Mind: A New Theory of Human Intelligence.* New York: Viking Press, 1988.

Sternberg, R. J. "Real Life vs. Academic Life Problems." In R. A. Fellenz and G. J. Conti (eds.), *Intelligence and Adult Learning.* Bozeman, Mont.: Center for Adult Learning, 1990a.

Sternberg, R. J. "Thinking Styles: Keys to Understanding Student Performance." *Phi Delta Kappan,* 1990b, *31,* 92–106.

Sternberg, R. J. "Understanding Adult Intelligence." In R. A. Fellenz and G. J. Conti (eds.), *Intelligence and Adult Learning.* Bozeman, Mont.: Center for Adult Learning, 1990c.

Sternberg, R. J. "Wisdom and Its Relations to Intelligence and Creativity." In R. J. Sternberg (ed.), *Wisdom: Its Nature, Origins, and Development.* Cambridge: Cambridge University Press, 1990d.

Sternberg, R. J. (ed.), *Wisdom: Its Nature, Origins, and Development.* Cambridge: Cambridge University Press, 1990e.

Sternberg, R. J., and Berg, C. A. "What Are Theories of Adult Intellectual Development Theories Of?" In C. Schooler and K. Schaie (eds.), *Cognitive Functioning and Social Culture Over the Life Course.* Norwood, N.J.: Ablex, 1987.

Sternberg, R. J., and Wagner, R. K. (eds.). *Practical Intelligence.* Cambridge: Cambridge University Press, 1986.

Stevenson, J. J. "Load, Power and Margin in Older Adults." *Geriatric Nursing,* 1980, *1* (2), 50–55.

Stillings, N. A., and others. *Cognitive Science.* Cambridge, Mass.: MIT Press, 1987.

Sugarman, L. *Life-Span Development: Concepts, Theories and Interventions.* New York: Methuen, 1986.

Super, D. E. "Coming of Age in Middletown: Careers in the Making." *American Psychologist,* 1985, *40* (4), 405–414.

Suttle, B. B. "Adult Education: No Need for Theories?" *Adult Education,* 1982, *32* (2), 104–107.

Swedish National Board of Education. *Adult Learning, Work and Citizenship: Impressions and Reflections from the New Sweden '88 Adult Education Seminars in the USA and Canada, October–November 1988.* Stockholm: Division of Adult Education/Swedish Institute, 1988.

Takeda, S., and Matsuzawa, T. "Age-Related Brain Atrophy: A Study with Computer Tomography." *Journal of Gerontology,* 1985, *40* (2), 159–163.

Taranto, M. A. "Wisdom and Logic." *Proceedings of the 17th Annual Symposium of the Jean Piaget Society.* Philadelphia: n.p., 1987. (ED 282 099)

Tennant, M. *Psychology and Adult Learning.* London: Routledge, 1988.

Tennant, M. "Life-Span Developmental Psychology and Adult Development: Implications for Adult Learning." *International Journal of Lifelong Education,* 1990, *9* (3), 223–236.

Theil, J. P. "Successful Self-Directed Learning Styles." *Proceedings of the Adult Education Research Conference*, no. 25. Raleigh: North Carolina State University, 1984.

Thompson, R. A. "Early Development in Life-Span Perspective." In P. B. Baltes, D. L. Featherman, and P. M. Lerner (eds.), *Life-Span Development and Behavior*. Vol. 9. Hillsdale, N.J.: Erlbaum, 1988.

Thorndike, E. L., Bregman, E. O., Tilton, J. W., and Woodyard, E. *Adult Learning*. New York: Macmillan, 1928.

Thurstone, L. L., and Thurstone, T. G. *Factorial Studies of Intelligence*. Psychometric Monographs, no. 2. Chicago: University of Chicago Press, 1941.

Tootle, A. E. "An Analysis of the Relationship Between Cognitive Style (Field Dependence–Independence) and Levels of Learning." *Proceedings of the Adult Education Research Conference*, no. 26. Tempe: Arizona State University, 1985.

Torrance, E. P., and Mourad, S. "Some Creativity and Style of Learning and Thinking Correlates of Guglielmino's Self-Directed Learning Readiness Scale." *Psychological Reports*, 1978, *43*, 1167–1171.

Tough, A. "The Assistance Obtained by Adult Self-Teachers." *Adult Education U.S.*, 1966, *17* (1), 31–37.

Tough, A. *Learning Without a Teacher*. Educational Research Series, no. 3. Toronto: Ontario Institute for Studies in Education, 1967.

Tough, A. *The Adult's Learning Projects: A Fresh Approach to Theory and Practice in Adult Learning*. Toronto: Ontario Institute for Studies in Education, 1971.

Tough, A. "Major Learning Efforts: Recent Research and Future Directions." *Adult Education*, 1978, *28* (4), 250–263.

Tough, A. *The Adult's Learning Projects: A Fresh Approach to Theory and Practice in Adult Learning*. (2nd ed.) Toronto: Ontario Institute for Studies in Education, 1979.

Troll, L. E. *Continuations: Adult Development and Aging*. Monterey, Calif.: Brooks/Cole, 1982.

Turnbull, C. M. *The Human Life Cycle*. New York: Simon & Schuster, 1983.

Turner, T. C. "An Overview of Computers in Adult Literacy Programs." *Lifelong Learning*, 1988, *11* (8), 9–13.

U.S. Department of Education, Office of Educational Research and Improvement, Center for Statistics. *Bulletin*. Washington, D.C.: Department of Education, 1986.

U.S. Department of Education, Office of Educational Research and Improvement, Center for Education Statistics. *Digest of Education Statistics — 1987*. Washington, D.C.: Department of Education, 1987.

U.S. Office of the Secretary of Education. *Lifelong Learning: A Policy Perspective on Learning, Opportunity, and Access*. Washington, D.C.: Department of Health, Education, and Welfare, 1978.

Vaillant, G. *Adaptation to Life*. Boston: Little, Brown, 1977.

Valentine, T., and Darkenwald, G. G. "Deterrents to Participation in Adult Education: Profiles of Potential Learners." *Adult Education Quarterly*, 1990, *41* (1), 29–42.

Valentine, T., and Ehringhaus, C. "The Measurement of Cognitive Ability in Adult Basic Education." *Proceedings of the Adult Education Research Conference*, no. 30. Madison: University of Wisconsin, 1989.

Verner, C. "Definition of Terms." In G. Jensen, A. A. Liveright, and W. Hallenbeck (eds.), *Adult Education: Outlines of an Emerging Field of University Study*. Washington, D.C.: Adult Education Association, 1964.

Watkins, K. "Business and Industry." In S. B. Merriam and P. M. Cunningham (eds.), *Handbook of Adult and Continuing Education*. San Francisco: Jossey-Bass, 1989.

Wechsler, D. *The Measure and Appraisal of Adult Intelligence*. (4th ed.) Baltimore: Williams & Wilkins, 1958.

Welford, A. T. "Psychomotor Performance." In C. Eisdorfer (ed.), *Annual Review of Gerontology and Geriatrics*. New York: Springer, 1984.

Westwood, S. "Adult Education and the Sociology of Education: An Exploration." In J. L. Thompson (ed.), *Adult Education for a Change*. London: Hutchinson, 1980.

Whitbourne, S., and Weinstock, C. *Adult Development*. New York: Holt, Rinehart & Winston, 1979.

Willen, B. *Self-Directed Learning and Distance Education: Can Distance Education Be a Good Alternative for the Self-Directed Learners?* Sweden: Uppsala University, 1984. (ED 257 430)

Williams, G. H. "Perspective Transformation as an Adult Learning Theory to Explain and Facilitate Change in Male Spouse Abusers." *Dissertation Abstracts International,* 1985, *47,* 01A.

Williams, H. Y., and Willie, R. "Research on Adult Development: Implications for Adult Education." *International Journal of Lifelong Education,* 1990, *9* (3), 237–243.

Willis, P. E. *Learning to Labour: How Working Class Kids Get Working Class Jobs.* Farnborough, England: Saxon House, 1977.

Willis, S. L., and Schaie, K. W. "Practical Intelligence in Later Adulthood." In R. J. Sternberg and R. K. Wagner (eds.), *Intelligence in the Everyday World.* New York: Cambridge University Press, 1985.

Witelson, S. F., and Swallow, J. A. "Individual Differences in Human Brain Function." *National Forum,* 1987, *67* (2), 17–23.

Yesavage, J. A. "Imagery Pretraining and Memory Training in the Elderly." *Gerontology,* 1983, *29,* 271–275.

Young, J. "An Examination of Cognitive Restructuring in an Adult Continuing Education Workshop." Doctoral dissertation, Department of Adult Education, Northern Illinois University, 1986.

Zemke, R., and Zemke, S. "30 Things We Know for Sure About Adult Learning." *Training,* 1981, *18,* 45–49.

Name Index

A

Aagaard, L., 32–33
Abeles, R. P., 178
Aburdene, P., 10, 11, 18
Ackerman, S., 183
Ahmed, M., 19
Allerton, T. D., 210
Allman, P., 259, 311
Alpaugh, K. P., 145
Anderson, J. R., 75, 170
Apps, J. W., 12, 15, 20, 30, 34, 282, 289, 293
Aristotle, 123
Arlin, P. K., 183, 187–188, 198, 311
Aslanian, C. B., 58, 69, 70, 71, 72, 73, 78, 82, 96, 108, 109, 237, 238, 244, 308
Ausubel, D. P., 130, 138, 310
Axinn, J., 13

B

Bagnall, R. C., 74, 233, 243
Baltes, P. B., 96, 116, 144, 148, 149, 151, 152, 153, 155, 156–157, 198, 200
Bandura, A., 135, 138, 211
Bard, R., 250
Barnett, R. C., 117
Baruch, G. K., 117
Basseches, M. A., 122, 184, 186
Baum, J., 254
Bayha, R. A., 43, 51, 209
Beder, H., 18–19, 21, 51, 90, 251, 273

Bee, H. L., 98, 99, 100, 101, 102, 104, 110, 112,. 162, 163, 164, 183, 197
Beer, C. T., 31, 32
Begin, J. P., 9, 13, 16
Bejot, D. D., 209, 215
Belenky, M. F., 183, 190, 192–194, 295
Benack, S., 186
Berg, C. A., 153
Berger, P., 189
Berger, N., 44, 46, 48, 49, 50, 52, 210, 211–212, 219
Bielby, D.D.V., 183
Binet, A., 141
Birren, J. E., 145, 197, 198
Bischof, L. J., 158
Blazer, D. G., 107
Bode, H. B., 128
Bonham, L. A., 175, 176, 177, 208
Boone, E. J., 23
Boshier, R., 36–37, 84, 85–86, 95, 204, 207, 210, 225, 230–233, 234, 237, 243, 245, 246
Botwinick, J., 152, 154–155
Boucouvalas, M., 15, 101, 167, 197, 215, 218
Bower, G. H., 125
Boyd, E. M., 262
Boyd, R. D., 311
Brandenburg, D. C., 24
Bray, D. W., 112
Brenda, 41–42, 50–51
Brickell, H. M., 58, 69, 70, 71, 72, 73, 768, 82, 96, 108, 109, 237, 238, 244, 308

363

Subject Index

371